THE ROARING SILENCE

THE ROARING SILENCE
John Cage: A Life

DAVID REVILL

Arcade Publishing ● New York

First U.S. edition

PICTURE SOURCES

Artservices: pages 1, 2 *top left & right*, 3, 6 *top &*
bottom right, 7 *top*, 10 *bottom left*, 12 *bottom*
John Cage: page 8 *bottom*
Crown Point Press: pages 13, 14
Harvard University Archives: page 9
Henmar Press, Inc., reproduced by permission of Peters
Edition Limited: pages 8 *top & middle*, 9 *top*, 11 *bottom*
15 *top*
James Klosty: pages 5 *top*, 10 *bottom right*, 11 *top*, 12 *top*
Manfred Leve: page 7 *bottom*
Los Angeles Public Library: page 2 *bottom*
Beatriz Schiller: page 15 *bottom*
Virginia Tech Media Services: page 16 *bottom left & right*
Nancy Walz: page 16 *top*
Hans Wild: page 10 *top*
Yasuhiro Yoshioka: page 9 *bottom*

Library of Congress Cataloging-in-Publication Data

Revill, David, 1965–
The roaring silence: John Cage: a life/David Revill.—
1st U.S. ed.
p.   cm.
Includes bibliographical references and index.
ISBN 1-55970-166-8
1. Cage, John. 2. Composer—United States—Biography.
I. Title.
ML410.C24R5   1992
780'.92—dc20
[B]   92-5917

Published by Arcade Publishing, Inc., New York
Distributed by Little, Brown and Company
10 9 8 7 6 5 4 3 2 1

MV-NY   ˌ

Printed in the United States of America

TO WHOM THE BOOK CONCERNS

CONTENTS

ACKNOWLEDGMENTS

My thanks to John Cage for his interest in my work (all of it), for his cooperation, his time and his example. There are many other people whose help I would like to acknowledge. The guiding theme of my book crystallized in the first place largely due to the intervention of Norman O. Brown and a few cuppas with Gordon Mumma. I am much indebted to Earle Brown and Jasper Johns for rewarding and enjoyable conversations, and to the hospitality and advice of Margaret Leng Tan, Kathan Brown, Tom Marioni, Margarete Roeder, Mimi Johnson, James Pritchett, Richard Swift, Debbie Campana and Rita Bottoms; Stanley Lunetta, Paul Hillier, Robert Black and Richard Bernas; concerning Ernö Goldfinger, Peter Goldfinger and James Dunnett; at WGBH in Boston, Joel Gordon, Ellen Kushner and Michelle Sweet; and the long-distance interventions of Ray Kass, Lilah Toland, Francine Seders and my detective at the J. Walter Thompson Company, Laura Cheshire, and to the JWT archivist at Duke, Ellen Gartrell. Invaluable help came from Victoria Pope and Fiona Flower of Peters Edition, London, and from Don Gillespie in New York.

A note of thanks to my publishers on both sides of the Atlantic, in the first place to J. Nigel Newton at Bloomsbury Publishing, and to my editor David Reynolds, and then to Jeannette and Richard Seaver at Arcade. Others whose assistance I recall with gratitude and pleasure include, at Columbia, Alice Rwabazaire, Hollee Haswell, Ken Lohf and Corinne Rieder, and, for inside information on Suzuki's classes, Theodore de Bary, Miwa Kai and Philip Yampolsky; at Harvard, Millard Irion and the staff of the archive; at WGBH, Frank Lane; Jasper John's assistant, Sarah Taggart; at the Crown Point Press, Constance Lewellen and Karin Victoria; at KNX, Ed Pyle: at the University of California, Davis, Jerome Rosen, Una McDaniel, D.A. Rohde, John Skarstad and Don Kunitz, the librarian who knew everything; Robert Worby; Maria Sansalone for

1

translations from Italian; at Les Ateliers UPIC, Massy, Gerard Pape; at Universal Edition, London, Eric Forder. Thanks to mine hosts Alex Madonik and Eve Sweetser, and, for their hospitality, Narrye Caldwell and the highly cybersonic Gordon Mumma. For comments on the draft, Laurie Taylor, Brian Morton and in particular Mark Doran. Two other people deserve mention, without whom and so on: Dr. Aaron Esterson and my mother, Anne Revill.

PREFACE

I

One day while I was bathing, the telephone rang. A man's voice said, "Is David Revill there?" My mother had answered, and she thought from his unusual voice that this was one of my friends fooling around. She said, "No. Can I take a message?" The man's voice said, "Well, it's not important. Just tell him John Cage rang."

An open-minded browse through a percussion textbook had taught me that there was more to music than just Beethoven; there was an innovative and thoughtful American composer named John Cage. As I heard and played his music and read his books (I was still a teenager), I was entranced. When I learned he was performing in London, I had written to ask if we could meet. Now here I was, dripping water on to the carpet as we set up our appointment. I spent half of the following Tuesday with John Cage in his friend Bonnie Bird's London flat and at the East–West Centre on Old Street, talking about Georges Méliès, anarchism and macrobiotic food, and sampling mekkabu soup. Cage told me, "You chew very well."

That first meeting intensified my interest. He seemed a man of joyous integrity, with a rare continuity between life, work and ideas. As I heard, read and played more of Cage's work, and we met again, the idea of this book emerged. Despite the extent of his fame and influence in twentieth-century culture, and the existence of articles, numerous interviews and several anthologies, there has been no general book-length account of his life, work and thought. Whatever the value of Cage's work and ideas, they are baffling to many people – even to many sympathetic to modern arts. My aim in this book is to further the understanding and appreciation of Cage's work and thought, and to give an account of his life.

3

My first step was to approach Cage for his blessing, and this book has benefited enormously from that "blessing" (a word of mine which he slipped into quotation marks when writing back), and from the hours he generously gave to interviews and conversations.

II

Whether one agrees with his ideas or appreciates his art, anyone interested in the culture of the twentieth century, its philosophy, sociology and history, needs to know about John Cage.

One can gauge Cage's importance from the company he has kept. At first musicians such as Henry Cowell and Arnold Schoenberg were his mentors. Then his circle was one of peers, for instance, those who knew him in his percussion work in the forties, such as Lou Harrison, and those with whom he worked closely in the fifties – Morton Feldman, Christian Wolff and Earle Brown in particular, and David Tudor. In Europe, Cage met Pierre Boulez and Karlheinz Stockhausen, and with them he had first cordial and subsequently somewhat hostile relations; he also came to know, less closely, composers such as Luciano Berio and Luigi Nono.

Then he himself began to adjust to the role of mentor. In the sixties, his company included composers such as Ben Johnston, Alvin Lucier, Gordon Mumma and Robert Ashley, Lejaren Hiller and Nam June Paik, all of whom record his significance. Minimalist musician Philip Glass said that Cage's book *Silence* "changed my life and the way I think." Among rock musicians, John Cale, Brian Eno and David Byrne have spoken of the influence of Cage, and he was not only a friend but also a neighbor of John Lennon and Yoko Ono.

A similar change of role occurs too in his associations with non-musicians. As a college dropout he worked with the architect Ernö Goldfinger; he became a friend of the novelist John Steinbeck, worked for choreographer Martha Graham, and came to know Max Ernst and Peggy Guggenheim. In the fifties his circle included not only Brown, Feldman and Wolff, but also Robert Rauschenberg and, subsequently, Jasper Johns. In the following decade he became close to Marcel Duchamp. But the relationship with the deepest importance for Cage is with the dancer and choreographer Merce Cunningham; they have for decades been partners both in their art and in their private lives.

All the foregoing is simple sociology – noting Cage's pivotal place in twentieth-century culture and, especially, in the rarefied society of the avant-garde. His influence is a different issue. Cage is one of the seminal figures of twentieth-century arts and letters; to speak of the extent of his influence encompasses its depth, and its ramifications not only in music but also in manifold cultural forms, over a protracted period. Yet these are difficult phenomena to treat; the more influential a person becomes, the harder it is to specify and the easier it is to oversimplify the nature of their influence. As with all seminal figures, Cage's ideas have been so assimilated, refracted and often denatured that they define the cultural climate, at a level where they are everywhere and nameless.

Cage is not only important in the sociology of modern arts and their changing ideas and strands of influence, but also for the philosophical and aesthetic questions his activities still raise. What is music? Why do we make music? What is music analysis about? What is beauty? However, I do not consider Cage as "primarily" of interest as a thinker. One lesson of his ideas is that each thing is at once itself and in a relationship to every other thing. He produces work, has ideas, and lives his daily life. As he does so, his ideas do not subordinate his work; they form a dimension of a whole, which in his case is most important.

A fourth remarkable facet of Cage is the exemplary value of his activities. Whether one appreciates his art or agrees with his ideas, his life is a rare lesson in commitment, discipline and integrity. The following pages tell the uncommon true story of a man utterly dedicated to the task he has uncovered, who through it has found a path in life. His mistakes and compromises are incidental to, not the stuff of, his direction – his path is always clearer than his diversions. Cage nurtured his strengths and, just as importantly, made the most of his weaknesses: part of his success comes from his poise in failing. The least appreciated of Cage's qualities is his understanding of the spiritual dimensions of life, which conditions his whole being but is especially obvious in his seriousness of endeavor.

Exemplary, too, are his enormous productivity and the range of his work. When Frederic Lieberman told Cage he planned to lecture on his musical style, Cage replied, "You have a problem – there are so many." This difficulty has been compounded as Cage has become a prolific writer and visual artist. "What is to be said of a figure like John Cage," ask Appleton and Perera, "who is known to some as a composer, to others as a mycologist, a poet, or a graphic artist, or to still others as an influential writer on social and economic issues?" These days, after centuries of increasing specialization that has now become destructive, to live as a Renaissance polymath meets a pressing historical need.

Cage's life as one of the greats of modern art keeps him deluged with work, attention and demands on his time, but in this big world of plural narrowness his is a very small field indeed. To be in industry, in government, in the armed forces, agriculture or the European aristocracy – to be alive today in one's specific social location – may be to have a full life but not usually one which directly touches a range of others. Avant-garde artists know one another, but the baker across the street has never heard of even the most famous of them. With this in mind I consider that the most important reason for paying attention to Cage is the quality of his whole life, not because he developed indeterminate notations or knew Marcel Duchamp.

III

At first ignored or ridiculed, Cage is now in an even harder position – adored or ridiculed. It is a paradox, shared with many a seminal figure, that his vilification and even the attribution of his huge importance have usually been founded on a failure to understand his work and ideas. One side of the coin is laziness, especially on the part of critics; the other is his refusal to compromise on the degree of complexity and experimentation in his work. Cage developed an art which, by exemplifying rather than expressing (as I shall explain below), was beyond the reach of customary approaches and generated work not immediately attractive to many people and incomprehensible to most. I have written this book in the hope of helping more people decide there is something rewarding for them about Cage and his work; of grounding evaluation in adequate understanding; and also with the possibility in mind of prompting work which picks up from where Cage, and not our misunderstanding of him, leaves off.

I have not primarily written a sociological biography, a history of art or a study of cultural context, though these have a place (the agenda of modernism, for instance, the climate of atheism, the American character, the flowering of Eastern thought in the West). It is neither a sceptical biography, in the sense of setting out to disprove Cage's claims about himself, nor a sensationalist one. My main concern – it increasingly seemed the most interesting and useful focus as I wrote and rewrote the book – is to describe how Cage made himself who he is, because his direction is extraordinary and exemplary, and is the foundation for understanding the individual details of his life, work and thought. Developing that unifying thread has produced a book of this length and, as Cage frequently said to critics of his work, do not complain you wanted a pork chop when you are offered steak.

At first I was daunted and not a little bemused by the challenge of making an account of this vast range of difficult work. Mere chronology did not seem enough, although it forms the backbone of this book, augmented by more lateral discussions when particular events raise general points. As I wrote, however, what came through with unexpected force was the way the life, work and thought of John Cage form not an assembly of facts but a story with a unifying theme: Cage making himself through ever more adequate ways of transforming internal tendencies into external actions, which clarify the internal in turn. He develops through his activities a self-clarifying line which is almost exclusively ascetic and, emotionally but not epistemologically, transcendental.

What is involved here is the universal necessity, especially pronounced for artists, of finding a place to conduct and direct one's life between the poles of light and dark, unity and dispersion, calm and passion; poles expressed in mythology by figures such as Apollo and Dionysos, Bodhidharma and Hotei. I was surprised by how much light this shed on Cage. Insofar as greatness involves an enriching handling of such universals, it reveals Cage, for all his reluctance to make a masterpiece, as a great artist. Cage is a modern artist, but at its most valuable the "modern" in modern art implies a historical period, a style, perhaps local concerns or problematics; there can be a basic continuity of subject. As Cage once observed, "I'm afraid I'm more traditional than all those traditionalists."

Cage's achievements, in other words, in all their range and scale, are best understood in the light of his inner development, in the way his life, work, ideas and temperamental inclinations have clarified, refined and reinforced one another: the way he made himself who he is.

IV

To conclude this preface, I should like to say a little about how my work on this book has refined my understanding of understanding itself, because this may help explain the approach to Cage I have taken. I have been struck most forcefully by the laziness of our perception and the laxness of our categories, whether in woolly notions of common sense or the wasted complexities of philosophy. Words like "influence" or "greatness" are in general parlance ill-defined, even if it is not necessary for them to remain so. This is more destructively true as regards comprehension – words such as "understanding," "motive," "why" and to some extent "how" – and volition ("will" is a term mentioned below). We seek to answer questions with the limits of the question undefined, making thought inefficient.

Cage, a master at asking questions, is instructive here: one seeks, he often says, the kind of question which will produce good answers. The better-defined the query, the more productive will be our response, because it will be more attuned to the reality about which one is inquiring.

Understanding, meaning and will are much nearer the facts than is usually realized. When one asks "How is it that John Cage wrote *4'33"*?", the question most usefully concerns the way rather than the why – "how is it that" taken as "in what fashion did." Understanding the life, work and thought of Cage cannot mean causal explication. It means uncovering information, making forgivable juxtapositions, suggesting an overall shape by highlighting themes.

I have tried to make this book as light as possible, building from contiguities and not connections, providing information but few instructions. An incidental effect, I feel, of this approach is that it can give a sense of the buoyant amusement which Cage often presents at his own observations. My only recurring exception has been to describe as "interesting" points which I feel to be revealing, often in multifaceted ways.

The key to understanding is to look. In examining Cage's development, certain inclinations constantly surface, are realized and thus clarified in changing ways – inclinations toward asceticism, austerity, the transcendental, quiescence; a sense of marvel and wonder; a yearning for the spiritual. In working these tendencies through, Cage reinforces and deepens them, like canalizing water, as he finds ways of living and working which suit him better. I think here in terms of *existential placement*, the particular ways in which a person realizes his or her inclinations. As we act we clarify what we are about, and our existential placement is the matching of being and doing, which we try on for size and change as it suits us.

It is sometimes hard for explanations to be adequate, especially concerning tastes and emotions rather than facts. When Cage discusses his dislike for Beethoven, or his fondness for Mozart or Grieg, this is an account, but it smacks of rationalization. Likes and dislikes are subjective: something personal and something irrational. Rarely – except in the case of phobias and erethisms whose origin can be remembered – is there an answer to the "why" and "how" of taste.

Although, as Cage says, "everything we come across is to the point," we only do one thing next; and we can never be exhaustive, or we would fill time like the map described by Borges, drawn to such accuracy that it exactly covered the country it charted. As Cage is aware, any account is a fabulation.

> I once asked Aragon, the historian, how history was written. He said, "You have to invent it." When I wish, as now, to tell of critical incidents, persons and events which have influenced my life and work, the true answer is – all of the incidents were critical. All of the people influenced me. Everything that happened and that is still happening influences me.

Though the following pages tell a story, I am not writing fiction.

When I began this book I had a vague but strong conviction that psychoanalysis was inapplicable to biography. As I worked, I realized that certain psychoanalytic orientations, freed from doctrinal narrowness, are invaluable, provided one is realistic about their range. When one lives a certain way, with certain inclinations, one retains traces of irrelevant secondary features. If one is ascetic and transcendental, as in the case of Cage, the passions do not go away. If such secondary features are not integrated into the main stream of a person's life, they continue to exist as an incidental, contradictory stream; they reveal themselves not as complements, which temper the main stream, but as little fissures which alert us to something missing, like the tics of a scratched recording.

Fissures of this kind can be found in Cage's life: the puzzling attitude he develops toward jazz, or his predilection for quantitative complexity. Interestingly, Cage's giveaways often appear at first to be telling the whole story (his description of his courtship and marriage, for instance, or his single encounter with and dismissal of psychotherapy); then, when one examines the information, one realizes he has said next to nothing, just thrown up a brief, fairytale *trompe l'oeil*. Wherever I make such a point, it is an observation and not a criticism; a fissure is not a deficiency in a pejorative sense. Cage is in all significant respects uncommonly successful; achieving wholeness is, after all, a tall order. Rather than constituting criticism, an account of a person's shortcomings makes him or her more fully appreciated; heroes are cut out of the murkiness of reality, not cardboard.

9

While writing, I recalled Cage's response when once I told him I was wary of churning out material: "I think you have to do a bit of churning." Studying a figure like Cage could easily become an interminable task; for this reason I am fortunate to have had the external lure of completing *The Roaring Silence* in time to celebrate his eightieth birthday.

PRELUDE

On Friday, August 29, 1952, beginning at a quarter past eight, a benefit concert for the Artists' Welfare Fund was given at the Maverick Concert Hall in Woodstock, New York, by John Cage, composer, and David Tudor, pianist. Composers featured on the program included Pierre Boulez, Earle Brown, Henry Cowell, Morton Feldman and Christian Wolff. There were two pieces by Cage. The first, taking its title on this occasion from the date of performance, was a somewhat theatrical piece the composer had finished earlier in the year, which we know as *Water Music*. The other, the penultimate item of the evening, was scheduled innocuously, and inaccurately, as *Four Pieces*. After everything that had gone before, the listeners might have been forgiven for expecting, whether with relish or reluctance, more effusive experimental fireworks.

David Tudor set off a stopwatch, just as he had for the *Water Music*. He sat down and closed the piano lid. He timed three movements. Nothing for thirty seconds. Then for two minutes twenty-three seconds; then one minute forty seconds. Tudor raised the piano lid and stood up. *4'33"*, of silence.

The aftershocks of that night in Woodstock are still being felt today. Why did a man just turning forty write a piece of music with no sounds in it? Is he a composer? A musician? A mystic? Is he a Dadaist? A Zen Buddhist? Is he making fun, pulling off a stunt? How is it that John Cage wrote *4'33"*?

Forty years later, John Cage lives in the middle of Manhattan with his companion and colleague, the choreographer Merce Cunningham, on one generous floor in a building that formerly housed the Altman department store. The apartment is bathed in light from seven large windows and a skylight twenty feet square. A large stone crock of soup is in a permanent position on the stove. By now Cage has around two hundred plants – clivias, begonias, Norfolk pines and orchids.

11

He is a tall man, though old age has stooped him a little; he is more slender now than before, due both to stringent diet and advancing age. His face is habitually taken up by a vast Cheshire-cat smile, which would be a fixed grin if it did not appear so easily. He talks in a thin, singy, slightly androgynous voice which always seems about to vanish into silence except that laughter bubbles up frequently – laughter that forms the stock-in-trade of Cage interview transcriptions: an uncomplicated joy that slides into a silent, open-mouthed chuckle. Although once somewhat dandy, Cage's choice of clothes, no longer needed to make a statement, follows the principle of the Model T Ford: he will wear anything so long as it is his blue jeans, his one denim shirt, and a loose blouson jacket.

He has cultivated a native simplicity. I once discussed with Cage a performance the previous night of one of Morton Feldman's later pieces; he found its repetitiveness uninteresting. "So, you fell asleep," I said, with a laugh. "Well," Cage replied, "I just, simply didn't stay awake." The simplicity shades into humor. Cage once asked, partway through a conversation, "And how are you, David?" Caught unawares, I asked back, "In what way?" "In any way you like," he said: laughter.

Leonard Mayer, recalling his contact with Cage at Wesleyan in 1961, said, "I was naive, pretending to be sophisticated. He was sophisticated, seeming to be naive." Cage's humorous simplicity makes him vulnerable to not being taken seriously – especially as, for most people, his work is baffling; we tend to expect our artists to say great things, for which we pay the price of swallowing ponderous, vacuous things. "I have a horror of appearing an idiot," Cage said some years ago. "I'm a serious person."

His work is his life: the reverse is equally true. "I spend most of the day working," Cage explains. "I don't have any leisure." He never goes to the movies; he reads newspapers only over people's shoulders, hears the radio if he passes one by, and attends concerts only when in residency at festivals and the like. "It's not that I have my nose to the grindstone. I enjoy my work. Nothing entertains me more than to do it. That's why I do it. So I have no need for entertainment. And my work is not really fatiguing, so that I don't need to relax."

Wherever Cage goes, he takes the most pressing work that he can carry. "If I, for instance, have a doctor's appointment I take it with me and use the time in the doctor's office," he explains, "so I'm prepared to work at the drop of a hat. I've made that a habit through the years; otherwise, I wouldn't have gotten all the things done that I have done."

Cage begins a day with exercises for his back, then waters the plants. Most days he shops for food. In the evening, he unwinds with a game of chess – his concession to leisure? "Chess is not the place where I'm going to give all my attention," he says, "but a place where I'm going to enjoy myself – or rather the chess." Sometimes he dines out, for instance at David Waltuck's Chanterelle on Harrison Street. When he is within easy reach of the countryside, he will forage for wild mushrooms. The rest is work.

His predilection is for doing rather than thinking. "I like it better," he said, "when something is being done than when something is being said." He is insistent that everything he has produced can be put to use in the way he designed it. Even his talks about music are themselves music.

This is American pragmatism, doing what it does best. In Cage's case it runs deeper than a culturally specific style, and he uses it effectively. Cage's pragmatism, like, arguably, all disciplines for self-realization (whether psychological or spiritual), emphasizes vision and action rather than reflection and emotion: look at what is the case and at what can tangibly be done.

Cage's dogged devotion to originality is striking. A journalist from Illinois once asked him to put his philosophy in a nutshell. The reply did not concern our integration into daily life, or optimism about it (two likely contenders, one might think), but was a reflexive pun: "Get out of whatever cage you find yourself in." The implication is thus of escaping from oneself as well as external constraints, and, as advice for others, has the added flavor of "if you meet the Buddha on the road, kill him."

> I'm devoted to the principle of originality. Not originality in the egoistic sense, but . . . in the sense of doing something which it is necessary to do. Now, obviously, the things it is necessary to do are not the things that have been done, but the ones that have not yet been done.

One of the pointers, for Cage, is the assimilation of his work. "If my work is accepted, I must move on to the point where it isn't."

While integrity has become a risky, unfashionable word to use, it is fundamental to his argument. Integrity is the congruence of one's actions with one's principles, deliberately followed. Cage could not do cynically the things "that have not yet been done," since cynicism requires direction oriented toward other people's expectations, or a response to or manipulation of existing style (if only by reacting against it). Cage is proposing – or noting – that each person does their own work, for since at least his college days he has been convinced "we get more done by not doing what someone else is doing." A school is out of the question: "Two people making same kind of music is one music too many."

The dedication to originality colors Cage's attitude to his work. He does not sit on his laurels but does what comes next, and his compositional development, at least since these ideas crystallized, is founded not on a self-consuming formal principle, but, as it were, a self-annulling one, one whose terms point beyond itself, whose progress hinges on the unexpected. This will become clear when we come to look at the approach to composition developed by Cage in the fifties. Apart from a special fondness for *4'33"*, he insists that the piece of his which he prefers is the one he has not yet written.

"My favorite music is the music I haven't yet heard," says Cage. "I don't hear the music I write. I write, in order to hear the music I haven't yet heard. That's my tendency – to be interested most in what I haven't yet done. But," he adds, "if I have to be interested in what I *have* done – to be interested in the most recent."

His quest for originality is not smudged into a desire for fame. "I am not interested in success," he notes, "but simply in music" – action, again, rather than ideas. "I am not a genius," he told a reviewer at the start of the fifties. "I have no message and I don't write masterpieces."

His lack of interest in fame relates to his general simplicity. It contrasts with the self-consciousness of many artists. He remembers, for example, a comment made by William de Kooning. Cage took round a beautifully rendered copy of the *Seven Haiku* of which de Kooning was a dedicatee (which would place the incident around 1952). Twenty-five years later Cage recalled, "He had what has never appealed to me, and he explained that he had it, which was the desire to be a great artist. I remember that he didn't turn the light on, and it was getting dark outside, and he said, 'You and I are very different. I want to be a great artist.'"

Alongside the deftness of his action is an unusually simple and positive approach to life. The world, for Cage, has a tendency toward good, and there is no reason why he cannot be completely happy, at least no reason in the world. "I have the feeling that optimism is a natural state of the human *attitude*. And that there's only fatigue that makes one . . . pessimistic, even if the situation is very difficult."

Cage is the quintessential optimist, redeemed by the gift, he said, of a sunny disposition. He issues surprisingly obvious reasons to be cheerful: "supreme good fortune: we're both alive!" Asked at a concert in Greenwich Village if he had enjoyed the piece by Kurt Schwitters, he replied, "I enjoy everything."

14

PRELUDE

For many years Cage has found the ten ox-herding pictures, a classic Buddhist parable of spiritual progress, especially inspiring. There are two possible endings after the experience of nothingness which constitutes enlightenment. One is withdrawal from the world and attainment, in traditional Buddhist terms, of Nirvana as something above and beyond the world. The other option available to the enlightened monk is to return to the village bearing gifts, the fruits of revelation. Cage, then, is a tall, thin man with a big smile on his face, who returns to the global village bearing an inexhaustible bag of gifts. His work shows us how "excellent" and "productive of joy" is the world in which we live. "The question is," Cage asks, "how immediately are we going to say Yes?"

ONE

I'm an Englishman. I have a little French blood and a little Scottish blood. I would love to have some Irish blood, but I don't. Maybe if I were ill and had to have a transfusion in Dublin, I could have some Irish blood.

Cage to Stephen Montague (1985)

In Virginia, around 1740, an English colonel called William Cage was named a trustee in the will of Lady Fairfax, thereby becoming embroiled in the dispute over her local estate. Into the next generation was born a John Cage who, as an adult, was to help George Washington survey the state and, in the Revolutionary War, fought in the Eighth Virginia Regiment on the Continental Line.

The story of the Cages we seek begins with a man of the same generation in the same state, William Cage, born in 1745. He met and married Elizabeth Douglass, third child of Colonel Edward Douglass and Sarah George of Farquier County. William and Elizabeth had ten children; William was to marry again later in life and produce, with Ann Morgan, another six, one of whom was to marry Jack Hays, the Texas Ranger. At the age of forty, William moved his family to Sumner County, Tennessee; his home became known as Cage's Bend. His in-laws moved too, settling at Station Camp Creek, just north of Gallatin.

William Cage fought in the war, with the rank of major. When the Territorial Government was set up in 1790, Governor Blount made Cage county sheriff. He served in that post for six years, to be succeeded by his son Reuben and then, from 1800, another son James; he died at Cage's Bend on March 12, 1811.

Wilson Cage, the second child of William and Elizabeth, married a local girl, Polly Dillard, and she gave birth to a dozen. Their penultimate child, Adolphus (1819–1905), farmed in west Tennessee for many years, and preached at the Methodist Episcopal Church at Wouth – to both white and black, he was proud to say, despite, as one could expect, owning some of the latter. Shortly before the outbreak of the Civil War, at the age of fifty-three, he set off west with two of his brothers. One then moved south and was never heard of again; the other, Wilson junior, settled in Dent County, Missouri, where he died in 1876 at the age of seventy-two, leaving a profusion of offspring. Adolphus moved on to Colorado, becoming an early settler of the Greeley colony, preaching for the church and investing thousands in developing irrigation for the district.

Adolphus married a Miss Boyd and, short-changed at two children, Charlotte Anna Green (1825–91). The third of their five children, Gustavus Adolphus Williamson Cage, would be the grandfather of John Cage. Gustavus was in the first graduating class at the State University at Boulder, then took a postgraduate course at Denver University. Making a profession of his father's devotions, he became an itinerant preacher for the Methodist Episcopalian Church. In 1882 Gustavus married Mary Lou Newsom, who came from Nashville, Tennessee. The couple spent some time in California, and began their family: Mary Lou and Willis Green. In Los Angeles in 1886, Mary Lou senior gave birth to John Milton Cage. They were to have one other child, Rebecca, who died in infancy.

The course of Gustavus's career can be followed in the conference yearbooks of the church. After preaching ineffectually against Mormonism in Utah, he came in 1890 to Denver, where his grandson has stated in interviews he established the church, although it appears to have already existed. He was sent that year as a missionary to Rawlins, Wyoming, and was ordained as an Elder by Isaac Joyce at Laramie on June 18. At the Church's conference in 1894 Gustavus was one of four assistant treasurers and was an Elder at Erie in Greeley District, which had ninety full members at the time. That year he married again – Fannie Davis, who came from Weldon, Iowa. They were to have three children – Amasa Adolphus, who died in infancy, Arthur Edgar and Lucile Elizabeth.

The following year Gustavus endorsed the activities of the Woman's Foreign Missionary Society. A tantalizing yearbook note records that his "case" was referred to the presiding Elder for investigation. In 1896 he worked at Bald Mountain, Greeley; that year the minutes state: "The case of G A W Cage, in view of rumors affecting his character, was referred to the Committee on Conference Relations." The next day the Committee resolved that, "We find nothing in the new evidence submitted to change the verdict formerly rendered in his case."

John Cage remembers Gustavus as "a man of extraordinary puritanical righteousness," who "would get very angry with people who didn't agree with him." He was wary of music, considering the violin an instrument of the devil. His son, John Milton Cage, grew up in Colorado, due to his father's missionary work, and was considered the black sheep of the family, running away from home whenever he got the chance.

The pianist at the First Methodist Episcopalian Church was Lucretia Harvey. A year older than John Milton, Lucretia – Crete to friends and family – became his wife. She had been born at Des Moines, Iowa, in 1885, daughter of James Carey and Minnie Harvey. She had one brother and four sisters, Sadie, Josie, Phoebe and Marge. It was a family suspicious of learning; only Shakespeare and the Bible were allowed at home, though Crete concealed some other books in her room.

She had already been married twice. John Cage did not know this of his mother until adulthood when his Aunt Marge told him at least part of the story. Then, after John Milton's death, he was filling out forms to increase his mother's social security. "There's something I've never told you," Crete said. "I know," Cage interrupted. "Aunt Marge told me you were married before marrying Dad." "That's not all," she returned. "I was married twice before that."

"What was your first husband's name?" asked Cage. "You know? I've tried and tried," Crete answered, "but I've never been able to remember."

The attempts of John Milton and Crete to produce children initially met with little success. Their first child, Gustavus Adolphus Williamson III, was stillborn. Gustavus Adolphus Williamson IV, their second son, was born deformed, with a head larger than his body, and died at two weeks. Then in Los Angeles' Good Samaritan Hospital, at five o'clock in the morning of September 5, 1912, John Milton Cage junior was born.

TWO

I

On Friday the 13th in the year his son was born, John Milton Cage sent a crew of thirteen underwater in a "submarine boat" of his design. After thirteen hours, the vessel resurfaced and the crew scrambled from the conning tower, gasping for breath.

Gustavus Cage had been something of an inventor – in 1909, he patented a touch-key finder for typewriters. For John Cage senior, however, inventing was a life's work, and over the course of his career his innovations were wide-ranging. After building the submarine, he was involved with related technology for some time. From 1916 to 1921 he worked with Hugh Keller, a professor at the University of Michigan, on adapting the gasoline engine for use in submarines; he patented a steering and propulsion system in 1918; during the First World War he devised a hydrophone, for submarine detection, which he demonstrated in London – it was used in the English Channel against U-boats. From 1919 until the end of the twenties, he designed improvements to the internal combustion engine, producing a six-stroke three-phase engine in 1921 and a sleeve-valve engine five years later.

In Massachusetts in the forties, John senior worked on tire vulcanizing processes. He invented the first radio powered by alternating current, so that it could be plugged into the electric light system, and devised an inhaler for treating colds, mixing menthol and thymol in an alcohol suspension; Henry Cowell, Cage's future teacher, called it his favorite drink.

John senior was not only practical, but visionary. Later in life, in his laboratory, he made pith-balls swirl in an electrostatic field in a way that mimicked planetary orbit. The scientists of Cal Tech at Pasadena granted that it worked, but could not understand why. John senior inferred a general "electrostatic field theory" to explain the workings of the cosmos. Gravity he related to electrostatics, associating gravitational attraction, so it seems, with mass. He took the accepted relation between the two and made it, to characterize Cage's account, both simpler and grander in scope. As Cage explains, "We don't fall off the earth because of our electrical contact with the earth; but if there were a sphere of an optimum size, we would have to hold it down to keep it here." This led John senior – although he was to die three years before the first lunar landing – to speculate on space travel without fuel. If a sphere was made at that optimum size, "it would assume a charge opposite to the earth, and it would automatically move away." The problem then to be solved was how to cause the sphere to be attracted by another planet's gravity.

Cage has often spoken of his father, generally as an inventor. John senior taught him the pioneer urgency of innovation. "My father told me," Cage relates, "that if someone says 'can't,' that shows you what to do." Two of the comments Cage most often recounts about himself concern invention. He discovered years after studying with Arnold Schoenberg that Schoenberg had viewed him as "an inventor – of genius"; and to John senior, his son was his best invention.

John senior reaped little reward for all his creativity. Sometimes his designs failed; in 1918 he built an airplane engine which, too powerful for the quality of alloys and precision of engineering available, shook to pieces before it left the ground. More often the problem was that he did not think sufficiently of commercial considerations. The patent for his submarine was granted on January 26, 1915. Others were working on similar technology; for example, Isaac Rice of the Electric Boat Company patented an underwater vessel around the same time, which Krupps tried to patent for Germany after the First World War began. John senior had devised a highly theatrical launch for his submarine – it held the world underwater endurance record – but the key advantage of underwater travel had eluded him: his engine blew bubbles, making its presence obvious to everyone on the surface. To John senior, the submarine was well designed; if an accident occurred, the bubbles would let rescuers know where the craft lay. To the Navy, it was useless. Cage's father went bankrupt; henceforth the family property had to be held in the name of his wife.

Crete was very active in women's clubs. She was a founder member of the Lincoln Study Club in Detroit, then later in Los Angeles, holding various secretarial positions. The Los Angeles district of the Californian Federated Women's Clubs made her Press Chairman, and she joined the executive board of the Long Beach Ebell Club. By the time her son was a youth, she was writing for the *Los Angeles Times*, which in the mid-twenties had the largest circulation of any newspaper in the world. First she was a court reporter, then club editor.

"She was never happy," Cage recalls. On Sunday drives there would always be someone or other she rued not bringing with them. Every so often she would leave the house, saying she was never coming back, and each time John senior would console his frightened son, assuring him that before long she would return. On one occasion when Cage became embroiled in an argument with his mother, he turned to his father for support. "Son John," his father replied, "your mother is always right. Even when she is wrong." Since John senior invented at home, he was, as Cage puts it, "kept busy running errands" for his wife. Their marriage was a "good one between bad people."

John senior's work ensured that their address changed almost as quickly as their financial fortunes. As a baby Cage lived at 605 Cedar Avenue, Long Beach; between the ages of two and four, at 1707 East Broadway. Then his father began work with Keller in Michigan and the family moved first to Ann Arbor, then to Detroit.

Crete kept a scrapbook in which she preserved some battered note-paper from the Stevenson Hotel on Davenport Avenue, Detroit. Some stars and stripes stickers, with which Cage would have played, have been stuck down on it, and a five-year-old Cage has written, "I see a boy it is a good boy, his name is John."

His teachers appreciated his imagination and willingness to learn. Within the first year or two of his schooling, one of them commented, "He hasn't any conceit has he? He sits and makes up these 'stories' as he calls them. Is learning rapidly and is a dandy youngster." In Michigan and later back in Los Angeles he received "A" grades in all subjects.

With his peers, however, he fared less well. "I was what is called a sissy," Cage remembers rather dispassionately, "so that I was continually under attack from other children. They would lie in ambush to make my going home or coming to school physically painful and would laugh at me every time I answered a question in school." His parents arranged for him to travel to another school where he would not suffer to the same extent. "I was one of the first examples of bussing," Cage observes.

After a spell in Canada (Ford City, Ontario), the family returned to the Los Angeles area by the time Cage was eight, first back in Long Beach and, by 1921, Santa Monica.

Of all the New World, California was the newest, the paradisical land beyond the mountains where anything was possible. From the gold rushes to the movie rushes, its uncharted newness was the climate for innovators and adventurers, from the most opportunist to the most dedicated.

The layout of streets in Los Angeles encodes the city's history; the nuclear cluster of the old town was laid out so the wind would clear the litter and the dust, then later, roads were set with unthinking rationality on a sprawling north–south grid. In Cage's part of town, "the place was full of vacant lots; there was a sense of country in the city, particularly with the orange and white poppies and the lupine." The boy sought adventure, exploring the canyons and marshes of the inland countryside, spying one day on a gypsy encampment.

The family moved across town to Ocean Park. Cage was sent down to the beach each morning, and he would spend the day building courses in the sand, rolling a small hard rubber ball in front of him down meandering tracks with inclines and tunnels. Summer temperatures in southern California routinely soar into the nineties; Cage recalled that the pavement would stick to his feet when he stepped off the streetcar and he would have to run to avoid blisters. He grew accustomed to going blind at noon, when the heat made him faint; he would fumble his way to a hamburger stand, order something to eat, and sit in the shade while he revived. Only much later did it occur to him to protect himself against the heat.

Around 1923 or 1924 the family moved to 2708 Moss Avenue, Little Rock, between the Rock and Glendale. The extended family would convene for outdoor picnic suppers of salads and desserts, in one of the city parks, on the beach, or in Sycamore Grove.

II

From an early age Cage was drawn to music. "I remember loving sound before I ever took a music lesson," he reports. "So we make our lives by what we love." When he was five years old his mother took the risk of bringing him along to a symphony orchestra concert, only to find that, for the entire two hours, he stood in the aisle utterly absorbed. He also enjoyed the music he heard in church.

It was specifically music that attracted him at this time. Ambient sounds did not arrest his attention. "I don't remember the sounds," he reflects. "The character of sounds is that they are ephemeral and the sounds that one hears now are more important than those that one heard as a child, which are gone." He did not aspire to be a composer; his background and education did not present that as an option open to him.

Cage does not see his family as particularly musical, although his mother, two of her sisters and a brother made music at various times in their lives. Though, as noted earlier, Crete had played the piano in Gustavus Cage's church, she neither practiced nor performed by the time Cage was a boy. Aunt Marge had a beautiful contralto voice; as a child, Cage loved to hear her sing at church every Sunday. Sometimes she sang at home on weekdays. Uncle Walter, however, had insisted when they married that she give up any hope of a career, and later forbade her to sing at home. She accepted this, although it is perhaps significant that when Cage visited her one laundry day, she told him, "You know? I love this machine much more than I do your Uncle Walter." Young Cage thought it obvious that she should be permitted to sing, but he never said so to Walter.

Cage's parents tried at first to dissuade him from becoming a musician. "The general feeling," he recalls, "was that it wasn't a good thing to be." Moreover, the precarious finances of his father meant that both parents wanted to instill in him a feeling for the importance of money. "They knew from previous family experience that music was not a profession, that it was insufficient for making a living." Persistence paid off. Cage studied the violin briefly, then was bought a baby grand piano which he recalls playing on while the removal men were carrying it into the house. He was virtually its sole user.

"I remember loving the idea of taking music lessons," Cage recollects. While in the fourth grade he passed a notice for a teacher living nearby. "When I saw a sign saying 'piano lessons,' I begged my mother and father to let me have them," he remembers. They acquiesced. Cage began with five-finger exercises, "but I became more interested in sight-reading than in running up and down the scales. Being a virtuoso didn't interest me at all."

His next teacher was his aunt, Phoebe James. She was devoted to late nineteenth-century music and expected her charge to feel the same way. Bach, even Beethoven, could not possibly interest him; she never once mentioned Mozart, who was, it is true, going through a phase of relative unfashionability. Cage was introduced instead to the work of Moritz Moszkowski (1854–1925), who wrote mainly for piano, and he studied other composers through a tutor entitled *Music the Whole World Loves to Play*. From this book and from Aunt Phoebe's enthusiasm, Cage became entranced by the work of Grieg ("all those fifths"): "For a while

I played nothing else. I even imagined," he remembered, "devoting my life to the performance of his works alone, for they did not seem to me to be too difficult, and I loved them." He would make innumerable visits to the Los Angeles Public Library, exploring their shelves of music.

Phoebe was an imaginative teacher. She used pianologues with her students, pieces to be played on the piano while reading aloud a short story, often on a Spanish theme. "You would do it as a recital in costume," Cage recalls. "Aunt Phoebe gave a recital with all of her students, doing a series of pianologues." Cage does not recall his own role. After Cage, as a young man, left for Seattle, she taught at UCLA elementary school: "Her colleagues ... testified to her supremely imaginative and resourceful improvisations that on a moment's notice could imitate any sound from the creaking of covered wagons crossing the plains to the exultant shouts of Vikings as they approached land." Some sounds, however, were forbidden; the principal and the director told her not to play "keyboard imitations of warlike Indians' whoops while scalping their enemies nor was she allowed to imitate sounds connected with any other 'antisocial behavior.'"

III

At the age of twelve Cage cycled from his home on Moss Avenue into Hollywood and up to the studios of KFWB Radio. These were still the pioneering days of wireless. Only a few years earlier Frank Conrad, a Westinghouse engineer, had set up 8XK from his garage and, by playing records on the air, assured himself a claim to fame as the first disc jockey in the world. Radio programs came from a wide range of sources. Child performers were a frequent feature; for instance, in the January of Cage's visit in 1925, KHJ had presented Jane Adele Ridley, reader, aged five, and Craig Fulsem, piano, aged eight. There was farm information, weather reports, and church services – especially, in Los Angeles in the mid-twenties, Aimee Semple McPherson's fire and brimstone sermons. KDKA began physical education classes by wireless in 1924.

Despite East Coast radio having the higher profile, the Los Angeles area had a large number of stations of its own: Express, Anthony, Kierhoff and Ravenscroft, the K.M. Turner Corporation, the Island Station, Angelus Temple and the Bible Institute. The early stations often broadcast in fits and starts; a family might put out a few features an hour or so after supper.

As often happens with innovations, irrelevant aspects of associated fields carried over; actors would stand behind the microphone in full costume (in England announcers wore full evening dress). Years later there would be a spate of shows featuring ventriloquists. Inversely, the exigencies of radio had their own spillover effects. Crooning, the singing style pioneered by Vaughn de Leath, became the vocal style of the thirties on radio, stage and disc, but it developed as a response to soprano high notes causing transmitter tubes to blow.

Innovations also tend to be bought up by existing interests, keen both to exploit and control their potential. Radio was big business, with phenomenal demand for receivers through the twenties; in 1924 alone, fifty million dollars worth of radio equipment was sold, and the trade was open to stock market speculation. The *Los Angeles Times* ran their own station, KHJ. The main commercial interest in southern California radio, however, was from the Hollywood movie studios, which were also one of the area's main employers. The Dream Factory bought into radio – Warner Brothers had their own station – and used it for publicity. Their stars, however, did not tend to appear on radio, because they might lose their mystery and, as the talkies would soon demonstrate, many of them would never be famous for their voices.

Twelve-year-old Cage was a Tenderfoot in the Boy Scouts, and had thought up a Boy Scout radio program, to be presented and performed by members. "Did the Boy Scouts send you?" asked the staff at KFWB. He replied that he had simply had the idea and come over. They told him to run along.

Their refusal did not deter the boy; he rode his bike over to the next station, KNX, which had only just opened but was well on the way to being one of the top ten stations. Owned by the *Los Angeles Evening Express* and Paramount Pictures, it stood on the Paramount lot and, under the direction of an innovative Briton named Naylor Rogers, was pioneering daylight programs and outside broadcasts. The turns at KNX included Bert Butterworth and his Optomistic Do-Nuts, Salinas' Mexican Serenaders, Tom Brenaman and his mule Hercules, and Billy Van, the "modern Paul Revere." Unusually, KNX broadcast Hollywood stars such as Clara Bow, Bill Hart, Lillian Roth and, subsequently, Gary Cooper featuring on a Sunday night two-hour "Paramount Picture Hour" that publicized current Paramount releases.

The staff at the station were enthusiastic about the idea of a Boy Scout program. The only thing they asked was that Cage secure the permission of the Scouts. He contacted them and explained that KNX had said he could give an hour's show every week. They gave him permission, but would not help him in any way; he asked many times if the Boy Scout band could appear, but he was refused.

Undeterred, Cage began his radio career. In the course of the week he would arrange for as many Scouts as possible to appear. Every Friday after leaving school he would cycle up to the station for his show late in the afternoon. His guest Scouts would sing, play trumpet, trombone, violin or piano solos, or speak of their experiences building fires and tying knots. If guests were in short supply, Cage would play solos from *Music the Whole World Loves to Play*. Ten minutes were given over to an inspirational talk by a guest from a local synagogue or church. As soon as the show began, fan mail arrived and increased every month; Cage would read some of the letters over the air.

THREE

I

Since 1923 Cage had been attending the Los Angeles high school, in the park-like campus at Olympic and West Boulevard to which it had moved in 1916. Among the six members of the music faculty was Fannie Charles Dillon, who became his next piano teacher.

Dillon was born in Denver in 1881. She spent from 1900 to 1906 in Berlin, studying composition with Hugo Kaun and piano with Leopold Godowsky. Returning to America, she taught privately in Los Angeles; in 1910 she began giving classes at Pomona College in Claremont, northeast of downtown Los Angeles, and from the end of the First World War until she retired in 1941, she taught at the high school.

Her opus list runs to 118 pieces, for piano, organ, voice, chorus, saxophone and piano, violin and piano, piano trio, string quartet, band, and orchestra, as well as three scores for local outdoor pageants. One compositional inspiration to which she returned a number of times was transcription of bird-song, for instance in her four piano pieces *Little Bird Stories*. *Birds at Dawn*, opus 20 number 2, written in the year Cage was born, was inspired by calls she heard in the Sierra Madre mountains. Dillon was a composer with an experimental streak, and a firmly independent mind, critical of the way American music was constantly judged against European standards.

Cage was a sensitive player. "I had what was called a beautiful touch, which means that you have a sense of continuity." A fellow-pupil at the high school, Kimmis Hendrick, recalled that as a teenager Cage played Chopin "charmingly and there was all the flexibility he wanted in the waltzes." He disliked scales and other technical exercises.

His musical confidence was, however, badly shaken by Verna Blythe, who ran the high school Glee Club. While he was in the sixth grade it occurred to Cage that he would enjoy singing in the Club. He dropped in on an evening meeting and announced he would like to join. Blythe told him it was not enough to want to join; he would have to pass a voice test. Cage did not pass: she told him, as he has recounted many times, that he did not have a voice.

To the traditional canons of music and music education, Cage has long evinced a mixture of responses. One which has come through over the years is incomprehension. One of his few memories of music classes in school "was teachers putting needles down on the records and then taking them off and asking us who wrote the music." He could not see what purpose this could serve. Tonal theory seemed equally fruitless. This is how he understood leading tones in the fifties: "Progress in such a way as to imply the presence of a tone not actually present; then fool everyone by not landing on it. Land somewhere else. What is being fooled? Not the ear but the mind."

Another response, especially when he was young, emerges from what Hans Keller referred to as Cage's feelings of musical inferiority. Cage loved music, but had not developed the unshakable confidence he would display as an adult. "I believed that what they said was true," he recalled. "When the people would sing in church, I just didn't. Because I didn't have a voice there was no sense in doing it." This insecurity applied to his piano playing, where he already had some competence. "I remember having a kind of sinking feeling every time Aunt Phoebe or Miss Dillon played for me," he recalled, "because the music they played was fantastically difficult and I knew I would never be able to play that well."

As he grew older, Cage gained confidence and began to construe any shortcomings in his abilities as defining the nature of his success rather than making it impossible. "I didn't have the desire to overcome these absences in my faculties," he said. "I rather used them to the advantage of invention." He offered a comparison with the great ancient Greek orator Demosthenes, who at the outset was plagued by a stutter, so taught himself his craft by addressing the roaring sea with a mouth full of stones.

From the fifties onwards – and often when he tells the Glee Club story – Cage celebrates his avowed ineptness at traditional musical skills. "I can't keep a tune," he proclaims in his book *A Year from Monday*. "In fact, I have no talent for music." To William Duckworth he testified that he cannot recall melodies; there comes a point, even in the tunes he has heard most often, at which he can no longer remember what happens next. "The whole pitch aspect of music eludes me," Cage told Alan Gillmor. "Whether a sound is high or low is a matter of little consequence to me."

Cage tends to play down his musical abilities across the board, but his disclaimers seem a little ingenuous. Possibly he did not have a conventionally excellent singing voice; perhaps, as we shall hear from one of his later teachers, he had no feeling for harmony as a structural resource; maybe his native response to the idea of a leading tone is one of incomprehension. There is, however, a great deal of evidence in his music of an acutely musical ear – for timbral combinations, for instance; for a precision in preparation, and for interpretive sensitivity.

II

The Boy Scout show at KNX remained hugely popular into 1926. It had been playing for two hours a week for some time when Boy Scout headquarters telephoned the station and said they had never authorized the program. Cage suggests they were jealous. Now the show was prestigious, they insisted they should take it over. KNX felt compelled to comply. "They accepted the real Boy Scouts, because I was only second class," is how Cage remembers it. "I was not even a first-class scout. They accepted the real ones, and the real ones used it in a quite different way." The Boy Scout band, which had been denied Cage, played. The "real Boy Scouts," said Cage, "were very ostentatious and pushy." After a couple of broadcasts, KNX closed the show.

The KNX story is interesting, not only as a cautionary tale of institutional stupidity, but also as an incident Cage remembers vividly, and retells in the way he does. It is a parable: KFWB and the Boy Scouts have foolishly closed minds; KNX wins because it does not, but finally opts out and lets the little guy down. The tone of Cage's account recalls that which he uses to describe his rejection by the Glee Club.

While his contact with the Glee Club and the Boy Scouts led to rejection, Cage was very successful at school. In the Latin class of Dr. Walker Edwards, his translations from book five of Virgil's *Aeneid* were especially praised. He was also studying literature, botany and geometry, though he never studied calculus. Cage met with great success as an orator. He won second place in the City World Friendship oratorical finals in Los Angeles, with an address on international patriotism, and in 1927 he won first place for his school in the Southern California Oratorical Contest with his speech, *Other People Think*, which he declaimed at the

Hollywood Bowl. In it Cage asserted that the American people, their industry and government, should not be thinking in parochial terms, but of the Americas as a whole. He suggested, interestingly, that the United States could properly lead the world by "Appreciating, Respecting and Sympathizing with others," that "we should be hushed and silent," and that at the heart of that undisturbed calm "would be the hour most conducive to the birth of a Pan-American conscience."

It was a subtly perceptive address, which displayed awareness both of the limited validity and the shortcomings of oppositional thinking. It was utopian, but riven with facts which Cage manipulated persuasively and, it has turned out, prophetically. One may infer that Cage still feels some fondness for the speech; he allowed it to be reprinted, mentions it in his later writings, and delivered it again in Los Angeles on September 9, 1987 during his seventy-fifth birthday celebrations.

As his high school days drew to a close, the vocational plans of Cage were, following in his grandfather's footsteps, to become a minister in the Methodist Episcopalian Church. He seems to have been suffused, temperamentally, by a far-reaching religious outlook. "As a child," he recalls, "I was very much impressed by the notion of turning the other cheek. You know, if someone struck me on one cheek, I actually *did* turn the other cheek. I took that seriously." Into most of his adult life Cage carried a feeling of a beneficent security. In an interview Jeff Goldberg asked Cage if he had ever felt he was going mad. "The feeling is not familiar to me," Cage replied, and went on to observe, "I used to have a feeling, which was that I had, so to speak, a guardian angel."

To further his vocation Cage began to study Greek – the classics as well as the New Testament. In his young teens he also agreed to spend a summer vacation learning Hebrew with the local rabbi. His scholarly seriousness met with opposition, not, this time, from elementary school bullies, but from his family. Crete's sister Josie urged Crete to deter her son from studying with the rabbi. "She said that I should instead have spent the summer picking apricots," Cage remembers. "That would make a man out of me." Crete agreed, and he spent the summer garnering fruit rather than tasting from the tree of knowledge.

During his last year at high school Cage heard of the recently established Liberal Catholic Church. St. Alban's, their place of worship, stood in exotic surroundings on Argyle Avenue, up in the Hollywood Hills near Franklin Avenue. Built in 1921, it was a lavish four-hundred seater in the Spanish style, with a splendid organ loft. The Liberal Catholic observance was a kaleidoscope of the most theatrical elements of the principal Occidental and Oriental rituals.

Cage was, he said, "fascinated." "There were clouds of incense, candles galore, processions in and around the church," he recalled. He decided to join the church, then become an acolyte in the Mass. John senior and Crete objected strenuously, and eventually told him he had to decide between them and the church. Cage recalled the invitation of Jesus to "leave your father and mother and follow me." He went to the Liberal Catholic priest, the Reverend Tettemer, described the ultimatum, and announced that he had decided in favor of the church. Tettemer told Cage to go home and not be a fool. "There are many religions," he chided. "You have only one mother and father."

That year Cage was contributing editor of *Le Flambeau*, the French-language newspaper which pupils produced monthly. He became class valedictorian, and the faculty voted him an "Ephebian" on the basis of his "merit in scholarship, leadership, and character." Among a class of 408 seniors, his older contemporary Kimmis Hendrick recalled, "he was notably among the brilliant and promising," and graduated with the highest scholastic average in the history of the school. These facts and reflections are, like his early interest in music, worth recording, but should not be overloaded with significance in retrospect, since much the same is true of peers who have never been heard of since.

Cage prepared a graduation talk on eating flowers. "Neither of us knew anything about mushrooms in those days," recalls Kimmis Hendrick, "but we liked to think we were exotic." Cage was much amused when he imagined everyone taking his speech seriously. "Everybody will think I mean more than I do!" he laughed.

III

Shortly before his seventeenth birthday Cage enrolled at Pomona College in Claremont, northeast of Los Angeles. His parents were delighted; neither of them had had a college education. Pomona, founded in 1888, was intended to be somewhat exclusive, admitting only 750 students each year (Vladimir Ussachevsky, another future composer, also attended); the tuition fees, at three hundred dollars, were on a par with those of the New England private colleges on which it was modelled.

The student listed in the records as Jonathan Cage took lodgings at 347 West 6th Street, Claremont. His adolescent photographs present him as vital, confident and, in common with most teenagers, rather narcissistic. No records exist of him taking part in any musical events or organizations. However, he came to know Tamio Abe, a Japanese tennis player who was resting due to injury and was taking a few classes to put his convalescence to good use. Abe was devoted to the Beethoven string quartets and owned a large record collection, which he played to his young friend. Cage also worked with Don Sample to set up an exhibition of "modern paintings."

Despite his earnest hiccup with the Liberal Catholics, Cage sustained his intention to enter the ministry throughout his first year at Pomona. In the course of his second year he lost this direction, and decided he would become a writer. He won second prize in the Jennings English contest, and was writing both poetry and prose; he had begun to read the work of Gertrude Stein. His college daily, *The Student Life*, described him as a "prominent campus writer," and the college literary magazine, *Manuscript*, published a short story by Jonathan Cage in its issue of January 10, 1930. *The Immaculate Medawering* is most interesting in hindsight for the accommodating aesthetic of its female lead.

> Verlaine Medawering hates dirt of any kind with a passion. Although strongly attracted to beauteous Dorothy, he refuses to share with her a sandwich on which flies have crawled. He recoils from her young brother because chocolate has dirtied the boy's sticky fingers. She urges him to see beauty even in books with soiled covers and grimy pages.

Writing, Cage said later, was his response to an unfocused urge to create. It had still not occurred to him that he could write music. "When you feel the inclination to make something," he explained, "writing is one of the ways you can create without any other training."

Along with the change in direction came a change in application. In the second semester of the year Professor Raymond Brooks gave Cage a B grade in religious orientation; his other grades dropped to B or C level. Entries in his Pomona file reveal a new rebelliousness. As a freshman he had listed his recreational interests as swimming, tennis and riding, and recorded that he had spent the summer of 1928 down at the beach, with a camping trip in July. Now his recreational interests were stealing, sleeping and talking, and over the summer of 1929 "I merely proved that I possess neither character, will power, nor backbone."

"I was in the predicament so many young people are in," Cage explained. "In our education, we are given a taste of so many things and never encouraged to study in any one direction. In fact, if a student does show an inclination to concentrate on one thing, he is usually discouraged." He had also become thoroughly disenchanted – even disgusted – by what seemed to him inefficient, regimented teaching methods. The turning point came when the history professor gave the whole class an assignment to read a certain number of pages of a book. Cage was shocked to see (though it cannot have been for the first time) a hundred of his classmates in the library reading copies of the same book. It seemed so obviously mistaken; to paraphrase his observation of later years, a hundred students could read a hundred books and pool the information. Not only did it seem foolish but, interestingly, it "revolted" him; "we could all sit there like criminals," as he described it, "reading the same thing."

Instead of following the herd, Cage went into the library stacks and read the first book written by an author whose name began with Z, and, in an interesting hint of a system he would apply years later, he read other materials at random, preparing by that means for his examinations in due course. He was given an A. "That convinced me that the institution was not being run correctly," Cage recounts. "If I could do something so perverse and get away with it, the whole system must be wrong."

Cage decided to pay the system no more attention from then on. He took to writing answers to examinations in the style of Stein. "I got an A on the first and failed the second," he recollects. "After that I just lost interest in the whole thing." His report for June 1930 reads, "Does not plan to return. Going to travel in Europe." To his parents he made the case that academic conformity was irrelevant when he wanted to be a writer. "I told mother and dad I should travel to Europe and have experiences, rather than continue in school," he remembers. They agreed to give him a small allowance for the duration of his trip. He hitched to Galveston, Texas, and booked a passage on a boat bound for France.

FOUR

I

Paris was the first port of call for Cage. His immediate preoccupation was not with writing but with architecture. "I was struck first of all by the Gothic," he remembers. "I preferred the flamboyant style of the fifteenth century." The enthusiasm Cage feels for complexity is an interesting feature of his work and an element in his appreciation of phenomena as diverse as modern life, the music of Mozart and, here, the High Gothic style. Cage was particularly attracted to stone balustrades. He began to study them exhaustively at the Bibliothèque Mazarin. For between six weeks and a few months – his accounts vary – he waited by the door for opening time and left only when the library closed.

At one of the Paris railroad stations, Cage met Jose Pijoan, one of his former professors at Pomona. Pijoan asked him what he was doing; when Cage told him he received, literally, a furious kick in the pants. Pijoan said he was a fool and that he should be working on modern architecture. It is indeed surprising that Cage's mind had tied itself up exclusively with the Middle Ages, when already his taste in literature had taken in Stein alongside Aeschylus. "Go tomorrow to Goldfinger," Pijoan barked. "I'll arrange for you to work with him. He's a modern architect."

Ernö Goldfinger was not much older than Cage – he had been born in Budapest in 1902 – and had studied in Switzerland and at the Ecole Nationale et Supérieure des Beaux-Arts in Paris. Architectural education was based on attendance at workshops by established practitioners. Goldfinger had been a founder-member of the Atelier August Perret, a pariah of the Beaux-Arts, and in 1924 had set up his own practice. A formidable and dominating man (one apprentice years later was said to have lasted only one morning: he had his coat sent on), Goldfinger was part of the varied and innovative artistic world of twenties Paris, numbering among his friends some of the leading Surrealists, the Dadaist Marcel Duchamp, and Helena Rubinstein.

It is not clear whether, when Cage arrived, Goldfinger had moved to his new studio on the rue de la Cité Universitaire, or whether he was still designing it from his studio on Boulevard August Blanquin. Goldfinger set his charge to work, "measuring the dimensions of rooms which he was to modernize, answering the telephone, and drawing Greek columns." They were tasks which could be performed by a student who knew nothing; sketching the Greek orders was also a useful preparatory exercise for a would-be architect, though an interestingly conservative exercise to be set by a modernist such as Goldfinger.

During his time in Paris Cage became interested in painting; he studied German art, expressionism and abstract art, and tried a little himself. Then another associate from Pomona introduced him to one of the most influential women of the Paris musical world, the Baronne d'Estournelles. Cage was asked one evening to play a Beethoven piano sonata for her. He felt his technique to be insufficient to tackle the opening movement, but offered to play the andante with pleasure. The Baronne protested at his modesty but told him to play on and, when he finished, praised his touch. She introduced him to Lazare Levy, the leading piano teacher at the Conservatoire. Cage was accepted as a pupil, but took only one or two lessons. "I could see that his teaching would lead to technical accomplishment," Cage noted but, as before, this was not of interest to him. What Levy did provide, however, was an introduction to the music of the classical period, by arranging for him to attend a Bach festival. "I was completely stunned by it," as he recalled. "It was just plain beautiful."

On his own initiative, Cage went to a concert of modern piano music given by John Kirkpatrick, which included pieces by Stravinsky and Scriabin. He later called on Kirkpatrick. In the music shops he bought a collection of modern music, *Das neue Klavierbuch*, as well as the *Preludes* of Scriabin and the Bach *Inventions*, and practiced hard.

After a month working for Goldfinger, Cage overheard him talking to "some girlfriends." He was saying that to be an architect required devoting one's life solely to architecture. His buildings are a direct reflection of his temperament. To Goldfinger, the creator of architecture had to be an artist capable of grasping the technical potentialities of the time and wedding them with its social requirements. To do so required complete commitment. Cage felt strong attractions to other things – poetry, painting and music – so did not feel he could dedicate his life to a single discipline, and he earnestly said so to Goldfinger. He left the company soon afterwards.

Homesickness began to trouble him; he tried to assuage it by reading *The Leaves of Grass* by Walt Whitman. He wrote to his parents, telling them he was coming home. "Don't be a fool," Crete wrote back. "Stay in Europe as long as possible. Soak up as much beauty as you can. You'll probably never get there again."

After six months Cage left Paris – not for home but, on a whim, for Capri – and ended 1931 wandering rather aimlessly: Biskra, Madrid, Berlin, Italy and North Africa. He painted and wrote poetry. In Seville, "I found myself at an intersection and I felt a sudden joy upon realizing that I could hear different musics at the same time." During a sojourn in Majorca, or perhaps Mallorca, he had access to a piano, and he tried for the first time to compose music: very brief pieces written to a complex mathematical system whose inspiration is unclear and which he saw as emulating the structural order of Bach. Cage now felt that he could not only write but also paint, compose, even dance, without any technical training. Contact with modern art had given him the feeling "that if other people could do things like that I myself could." "The trouble was," Cage recalls, "the music I wrote sounded extremely displeasing to my own ear when I played it." He dumped his first scores to lighten his luggage.

II

In the fall of 1931, after eighteen months in Europe, Cage returned to the United States. He drove across country in a Model T Ford and moved into his parents' home on the Pacific Palisades to the northwest of Los Angeles. Proceeding with his writing and painting, he worked through a new compositional method, improvising in relation to texts. He set to music experimental writings from *transition* magazine, texts by Gertrude Stein, and choruses from the *Persians* by Aeschylus. He also wrote an *Allemande*, and in 1932, despite renouncing his religious vocation, songs from Ecclesiastes, which were lost until the late eighties. "These compositions were improvised at the piano," Cage explains, and quickly notated before they were forgotten. "The style of the songs are, so to speak, transcriptions in repetitive language put to a repetitive music."

Cage was becoming increasingly interested in the work of Arnold Schoenberg. Born in Vienna in 1874, Schoenberg had been largely self-taught as a musician. His reluctant revolution grew out of developments made by the previous generation. The tonal system, the basis for the intelligibility of Western music since the seventeenth century, had been so thoroughly assimilated that composers, notably Brahms and Wagner, had written music of which the harmonic and formal innovations were in danger of not making sense.

Schoenberg's integrity pushed him to carry this direction still further in spite of his temperamental conservatism. "So you are this famous Schoenberg, then," snapped his army officer in the Great War. "Yes, sir," he replied. "No one else wanted the job, so I had to take it on." He subsequently wrote, "If you choose to listen to the wave, you must accept what the wave brings. I am following an inner compulsion that is stronger than education, stronger than my artistic training." Schoenberg saw that the frontiers of musical language had expanded so far in every direction that tonality could no longer guarantee the possibility of communication. His work both compounded the problem and attempted a solution.

In his first decade he developed stylistically at a pace greater than many composers achieve in a life. His rich studies in senescent romanticism gave way to music which incorporated fluctuating or suspended tonality for increasing spans of time. Tonal implications arise but are not consistently satisfied. By, say, 1908, "emancipation of the dissonance," which to Schoenberg meant that dissonance was as *comprehensible* as consonance to modern musicality, had banished the tonal system from the surface of his music.

Schoenberg began to systematize this practice from the dawn of the twenties in serial or twelve-tone music. He would take a basic figure – usually a melodic inspiration – and abstract from it a "series" or "row" which included all twelve notes of a chromatic octave. This was not intended as a hegemonic style, but an attempt to replace the threatened functions of tonal harmony. The pattern of interval relations embodied in the series substituted for tonality as the foundation for the work's basic unity, even when subjected to traditional contrapuntal operations – inverted, played backwards and fragmented. Schoenberg maintained that he was writing as he had in his earliest works; people did not yet recognize the fact. He was writing "twelve-note *compositions*, not *twelve-note* compositions."

Schoenberg was still in Europe, moving around because of both ill-health and, as a Jew, growing Nazism; but in the course of his researches Cage had come upon the name of Richard Buhlig, who had presented the United States premiere of the *Three Pieces for Piano*, opus 11, the first piece by Schoenberg consistently to abjure tonality. Without rational grounds, Cage decided Buhlig lived in Los Angeles and, looking in the telephone directory, found that he did. Cage called and asked if he could come over and hear Buhlig play opus 11. Buhlig brusquely refused and hung up.

The family fortunes, meanwhile, continued to go up and down. The year before, John senior had patented a system for protection against lightning He also worked on a dehydrator for oil and water emulsions which he was to develop in patents in 1932 and 1938. As his son described it years later, the dehydrator consisted of "a contained electrostatic field, one electrode down the center, the other the container's inner wall. Principal problem was finding a dielectric to separate the two. Refuse oil poured in came out as oil of highest grade, dry chemicals and drinking water." The Petroleum Rectifying Company, to whom the patent was assigned, never used it.

Faced with financial difficulties, the Cages gave up their house in the Palisades and moved into an apartment in Los Angeles. The Depression was at its height. Since the black days of 1929 the bottom had fallen out of the stock market. The price per share of U.S. Steel, for instance, fell from $262 in 1929 to $22 in 1932. In the course of 1931, 2298 banks crashed. The only rising statistic was for unemployment, with end-of-year figures rising from a million and a half in 1929 to five million in 1930, nine million in 1931 and eleven million in 1932.

Cage could not afford to attend concerts. He became a gardener at an auto-court in Santa Monica, working in return for an apartment and a large room over the garage, and also hired himself out to cook exotic meals. He decided to make a little money from his enthusiasm for modern painting and music. He canvassed door-to-door, asking Santa Monica housewives if they would be interested in a series of lectures on modern art, ten for $2.50. "I didn't want to be a professor, I just wanted to get by," Cage remembered. "I explained to the housewives that I didn't know anything about either subject but that I was enthusiastic about both of them. I promised to learn faithfully enough about each subject so as to be able to give a talk an hour long each week." Thanks to the lectures, he met the Arensbergs, who had a large collection of works by Duchamp.

The classes were held in the large room above the garage. Despite the economic climate, more than twenty – possibly up to forty – housewives attended, making it his most profitable enterprise thus far. Each week he researched exhaustively in the Los Angeles Public Library. He found the deadlines provided a marvelous incentive for learning. "In this way," Cage recalled, "I taught myself what was going on in these two fields."

It also gave him the intuition "that music was not merely felt, but that it was constructed."

"I came out of these lectures," he stated, "with a devotion to the painting of Mondrian, on the one hand, and the music of Schoenberg on the other." What Cage found so thrilling about the notion of twelve-tone music "was that those twelve tones were all equally important, that one of them was not more important than another. It gave a principle that one could relate over into one's life and accept, whereas the notion of neo-classicism one could not accept and put over into one's life."

When Cage decided to talk about Schoenberg, he could not find any recordings and, except for the minuet of the *Suite for Piano*, opus 25, the music was too difficult for him to play. Richard Buhlig sprang to mind; Cage decided to approach him again for help, this time in person. He hitched into Los Angeles as quickly as he could.

When he knocked on Buhlig's door around noon, there was no reply. Pulling a small bough from a tree, Cage stripped the leaves off one by one, divining alternately "He'll come home, he won't come home." Always the answer came back that Buhlig would return, and Cage continued to wait. It was around midnight when Buhlig showed up, and when Cage explained how he had waited for twelve hours, Buhlig invited the young man indoors. His response to the suggestion that he illustrate the lecture on Schoenberg was to tell Cage, in polite middle-class American, to scram. However, they arranged to meet the following week, for he expressed an interest in Cage's compositions.

Cage somehow blundered through the lecture. He set off for his meeting with Buhlig, again hitchhiking into Los Angeles, and the vagaries of his mode of transport meant he arrived early. He rang the bell. Buhlig opened the door and told him, "You're half an hour early. Come back at the correct time." In his bag were books which had to be returned to the library, so Cage decided he would squeeze the visit into the intervening time. By the time he returned to Buhlig's house, he was half an hour late and his teacher was furious. He took Cage inside and, refusing to look at his work, lectured him for two hours on the "absolutely fundamental character of time," especially in music and for anyone who proposed to devote their life to it.

In *Silence*, Cage implies that this lecture occurred on his first lesson with Buhlig, although he implies otherwise in *For the Birds*. But neither account mentions any emotional reaction to this tirade, nor its wider ramifications for punctuality and work discipline (at which Cage now excels). It is instead described in rather safe and narrow relation to music. "Since then," he recalled, "I have always considered time as the essential dimension of all music."

Buhlig cautioned Cage that he taught piano rather than composition, but that he would do his best to help. His first suggestion after examining the music was that Cage needed to learn something about structure. The pieces were not really composed, he proposed, because they lacked a firm structural framework. Buhlig advised Cage to read Ebenezer Prout's textbooks *Harmony* and *Musical Form*. He also introduced Cage to one of his other pupils, Grete Sultan, who had already studied with Edwin Fischer and Claudio Arrau; Cage and Sultan would collaborate much later, first in 1956 and, in a major way, from the middle of the seventies onwards. "Buhlig was a wonderful, cultivated man," Cage recalls, "and he taught me a great deal."

In the course of 1933 Cage made what little money he could by carrying out research assignments. "I either did library research for my father," he remembers, "or other people – people who were running for governor, who wanted this data or whatever." Crete had opened a non-profit arts and crafts shop, to give artists the opportunity to sell their goods; sometimes Cage would work behind the counter, at quiet times writing music at the rear of the shop.

One day a young woman walked in, tall, thin, with striking aquiline features. "It was love at first sight on my part, not on hers," Cage recollected. "The moment I saw her I was convinced that we were going to be married." He went up to her and asked if he could be of assistance. She said she needed "no help whatsoever," as Cage recalls. He retired to his desk and his music; the young woman looked around for a little longer and quite soon departed. He was convinced she would return.

By the time that she did, a few weeks later, Cage had carefully prepared what he was going to say to her; he asked her to have dinner with him that night. Her name, it turned out, was Xenia. Xenia Andreevna Kashevaroff came from Juneau, Alaska, one of six mercurial daughters of Andrew Petrovitch Kashevaroff (1863–1940), a Russian Orthodox priest. He was librarian of the Alaska Territorial Library, curator for the museum, and a noted writer on local subjects. When Xenia was a child, she and her friends had a club with only one rule: no silliness. Now she was an art student at Reed College.

Pursuing his first impression, Cage took the opportunity provided by dinner to ask for her hand in marriage. "She was put off a little bit," recalls Cage. "She said she'd have to think about it."

Between March and May of 1933 Cage worked on a *Sonata for Clarinet*.

Buhlig suggested that he send the work to *New Music Quarterly*, to enquire about the chances of publication. Its editor was Henry Cowell, a man Buhlig much respected, an adventurous composer and a rich source of contacts in modern music. His *New Musical Resources* had been published by Knopf in 1930; his best-known piece is *Banshee*, the first known composition to use the sounds of the piano strings directly strummed and plucked. He had played at Pomona in December 1929, though there is no evidence that Cage attended.

Cowell did not offer to publish the *Sonata*, but he arranged for it to be played at one of his concerts in San Francisco. Cage hitchhiked, arriving on the afternoon of the performance day. He discovered that the clarinettist had not looked at the score until that day and, having glanced at it, decided it was too difficult to play. Cage presented it himself, on a piano. The piece suffered another affront when Cage showed it to the principal clarinet player of the Los Angeles Philharmonic. "This is not the way to write music," the principal said, suggesting instead that Cage might imitate Mozart.

In the months that followed Cage developed a means of composition using two ranges of two chromatic octaves; he put it to use in the *Sonata for Two Voices* written in Santa Monica in November and dedicated to Buhlig. The instrumentation is not important provided that the specifications of range are satisfied; it may be varied if desired at any set of double bars. The upper octave of the lowest voice is the same as the lowest octave of the other. Cage established the rule that no single pitch in the shared octave was to be repeated until at least eleven other pitches had intervened; no pitch in either of the unique octaves could be played again until all twenty-five notes of its respective two-octave chromatic range had appeared.

The technique bears some resemblance to the serialism of Schoenberg, but this is largely a superficial similarity, and might well have borne much more relation to Cage's attempts at mathematical composition in Majorca. It is possible, providing one is wary of over-simplification, to see Schoenberg's development of twelve-tone writing as emerging from protracted engagement with atonal composition, giving it a structural handle. Schoenberg may be one of only a handful of composers of whom it can justifiably be said that they could think, could intuit, serial music.

The method employed in the *Sonata for Two Voices* is more cerebral. Cage came up with something raw, unrooted; it is a puzzle to solve. This is not to suggest that the cerebral is completely separate from the intuitive, but that particular activities such as, here, musical compositions can be situated at different points along a continuum from cerebral to intuitive. If this phase in the music of Cage, for instance, can be described as cerebral, that is a shorthand way of saying that it is appreciably more cerebral than intuitive. Nor is it to suggest that cerebral work must be uninspired and cold; all methods emerge from investigation and, often, out of the best efforts of their originator. A final observation prompted by the twenty-five-note method is that, although it is common for composers to seek a rational basis for their work, this attempt at a cool, guiding structure is interesting in the light of Cage's subsequent development.

The *Sonata for Clarinet* is to some extent closer to the approach of Schoenberg. While the first and last movements constitute a less rigorous essay in the twenty-five-note technique, the pitches of one consisting of the retrograde of the other, the short middle movement employs a twelve-note set which is presented, inverted, played backwards; the retrograde form is repeated with slight alterations, followed by a barely related twelve-tone row and a retrograde inversion.

At the beginning of 1934 Cage moved to Carmel, on the Monterey Peninsula. Originally a missionary settlement, Carmel had from the early years of the twentieth century been colonized by the unconventional – poets and writers such as Upton Sinclair, Mary Austin, Robinson Jeffers, Jack London and Sinclair Lewis, and left-wing activists such as Mabel Dodge Louhan and Lincoln Steffens.

Short of money as usual, Cage foraged for wild strawberries but could only find mushrooms. He satisfied himself that they were edible by checking them in the public library, then made them his staple diet. When, after a few days, he set off for a friend's wedding, he found he could scarcely walk. Though edible and filling, mushrooms are not notably nutritious.

Cage made a meager living washing dishes and scrubbing vegetables at the Blue Bird Tearooms on Ocean Avenue. He was paid a dollar for a twelve-hour day. "I washed all the dishes and pots and pans," Cage recalled, "scrubbed the floor, washed the vegetables, crates of spinach for instance; and if the owner came along and found me resting, she sent me out the back yard to chop wood." The one boon was that he could eat steak for free a couple of times a day.

On one occasion a famous concert pianist was to give a recital at the Sunset Auditorium and Cage discharged his duties as quickly as possible so that he would not miss the performance. As chance would have it, he found himself seated next to the lady who owned the tearooms, who had come along with her daughter. Cage bade them good evening. "She looked the other way, whispered to her daughter," Cage remembered. "They both got up and left the hall." It was not the first time he had encountered such social divisiveness; he remembers being dismissed from a post as lawyer's clerk for inviting his superior to join him for a concert.

His activities mirrored the content of his earlier classes for the housewives. He wrote a great deal of music; while in Carmel he finished, on March 7, 1934, *Solo with Obbligato Accompaniment*, and, on April 5, the *Six Short Inventions* which accompany it. Then he moved to Ojai, northwest of Los Angeles, where he wrote the *Composition for Three Voices*. The *Solo* employs a variety of rhythmic canons; the *Composition* extends the twenty-five-note technique of the *Sonata for Two Voices*, with thirteen pitches, from d to d', held in common by all three parts. The voices run through their respective groups of twenty-five pitches with only occasional anticipations and cross-fertilizations; Cage attempts to avoid the possible bunching together of the shared pitches by distributing them, with a rather square evenness, over the measures. Certain lines are used as motifs with transpositions and minor rhythmic shifts.

As well as writing music, Cage was enthusiastically painting what he characterized later as "squintings at the landscape" – landscapes which suggested the influence of Van Gogh. He then became preoccupied with depicting the reflections on curved surfaces such as car headlights – painting simple forms, for instance the mirror-image of buildings, stretched in complex ways by optical distortion. Next Cage experimented with abstract shapes. "What was interesting to me then," Cage remembers, "was to make a very thin application of the oil on canvas, and to make it by using, not a brush, but steel wool, so that I was rubbing the paint on to the surface." He could not decide between painting and music, though he saw the need to do so; Gounod and, indeed, Schoenberg painted, but first and foremost they were composers.

Cage showed his work to people he respected, presenting his painting to Galka Scheyer – the artist and collector who had brought the Blue Four (Lionel Feininger, Alexej Jawlensky, Vassily Kandinsky and Paul Klee) from Munich to the States – and to Walter Arensberg, who held a great collection assembled by the Dadaist, Marcel Duchamp.

Those who heard the music of Cage were more encouraging than those who examined his visual work. However abortive the performance of the *Clarinet Sonata*, the score had sufficiently interested Henry Cowell for him to propose that Cage become his student for a semester. Buhlig had meanwhile decided that he could no longer be of much help to

Cage. "When I first met John Cage about 1932," Cowell wrote later in his brusque manner, "he was writing strange little piano pieces with an unusual sense of the sound-interest created by odd tonal combinations. He studied dissonant counterpoint and composition with me in California." This interest from Cowell was another strong incentive for Cage to conclude that it was music, rather than architecture or art, to which he would dedicate his life.

"Henry Cowell looked at my work," Cage remembered, "and told me that of all the living masters, the best one for me would be Schoenberg." Many composers impressed Cage; Grieg in his youth, and now Cowell, and subsequently Varèse, Satie, Ives and, for a while, Boulez. At this time, however, Cage saw the basic choice of his generation as between Schoenberg and Stravinsky. "In the thirties we didn't take Bartok seriously," Cage stated. "We took Stravinsky and Schoenberg as the two directions that one could legitimately take." Cowell's suggestion confirmed an inclination which Cage had felt strongly for some time. Since there were gaps in his musical training, Cowell proposed he first study in New York with Adolf Weiss. As the spring of 1934 drew to a close, Cage hitched his way across country on an eastbound freight train.

III

Despite his Teutonic name, Adolf Weiss had been born in Baltimore in 1891 and, from 1924 to 1927, he had become the first native-born American to study with Arnold Schoenberg. He was one of the pioneer explorers of the formal or numerical dimensions of serialism, whose experiments included the writing of music in columns of figures which he transcribed into notes.

Whereas Schoenberg saw to it that whatever he had written was performed, very little of Weiss's music was ever played. "He was such a bitter, ugly-tempered man as a result," Cage recalls. "I knew I didn't want to become that way." This was a major influence on Cage's later dictum that one should never consider one's compositions finished until one has heard them performed. When as the years passed and Cage's work attracted attention, "Weiss got very angry at me simply because I became famous. He was sure I was, in some way, being dishonest because he had been honest all his life and he'd never become famous."

Henry Cowell was in New York, too, teaching non-Western, folk and contemporary music at the New School for Social Research on West

12th Street. Cage became his assistant, which exempted him from fees for classes by Cowell in rhythm and modern harmony.

Cage rented a string of cheap furnished rooms and took "a rather important job washing walls at the Brooklyn YWCA." He found that the number of tasks had to be plodded out to fill the set time; the other wall-washer was an experienced hand, and directed Cage in how many walls to wash each day. "In this way," Cage remembers, "he checked my original enthusiasm, with the result that I spent a great deal of time simply reading the old newspapers which I used to protect the floors." The ludicrousness of this employment was heightened by the fact that the wall-washers always had to appear busy, so they had to be ready at any moment to start scrubbing energetically should the housekeeper come by.

While working at the YWCA, Cage was accused of being a Peeping Tom. The cleaners would look in the keyhole before entering a room: if the key of the occupant was not on the inside, they would assume the room to be empty and enter. Cage was called in to the manager and told that one of the long-term residents had said he had been spying on her. He vigorously protested his innocence. The manager then told him not to worry, for every year the woman made the same accusation against whoever was washing the walls.

In the evenings Cage would play bridge with Mr. and Mrs. Weiss, sometimes with Cowell, too, other times with the American symphonist Wallingford Riegger. They would stop about midnight. However late he went to bed, Cage rose at four, and until eight o'clock would prepare his work for the day's lesson with Weiss. At the last possible moment he would rush to the subway to ride to Brooklyn. "I saw the same people every morning in the same car," he recollects. "*They* all went there at the last possible moment; they didn't like their jobs any more than I liked mine." Back in Manhattan, he would eat, study his harmony and composition with Weiss, and then play bridge again until midnight. Cage spent just over a year in New York, then moved back to the West Coast, and to Schoenberg.

FIVE

I

Schoenberg lived in a dark, Spanish-looking house on North Rocking-ham. Recalling his impressions, Cage said, "He wasn't tall and he had very poor taste in clothes. He was almost bald and he looked as though he was haunted." He had no grand piano in his home, just an upright; his tennis partners included George Gershwin and the Marx brothers.

Having decided on Schoenberg as his master – a puzzling choice, as will become increasingly clear – study with him became hugely important to Cage. In a revealing observation made to William Duckworth, Cage noted a pattern in his life of devotion to masters: "I didn't study music with just anybody; I studied with Schoenberg.... I've always gone, insofar as I could, to the president of the company."

When they first met, Schoenberg told Cage, "You probably can't afford my price." Cage told him there was no question of affording his price as he had absolutely no money. Schoenberg asked him if he would devote his life to music. Cage, who had been unable to promise to dedicate his life to architecture, said yes. It is a promise which has never been far from his mind since. "In that case," Schoenberg concluded, "I will teach you free of charge."

The timing of Cage's studies with Schoenberg is not clear. It certainly was not 1933, as Cage once claimed. Nor is it likely that Cage approached Schoenberg in the fall of 1934, as Calvin Tomkins suggests. David Nicholls has pointed out that Schoenberg arrived in America on October 31, 1934, but did not move from Boston to Hollywood until eleven months later. He suggests Cage returned to California in May 1935 and took Schoenberg's course at the University of Southern California in June or July.

The nature and extent of their contact is not formally documented.

47

Hans Keller, the British musician and critic of Austrian birth, went so far as acerbically to dismiss Cage's "public fantasies about his lessons with Schoenberg." "So long as Schoenberg was alive, we didn't hear about Cage's studies with him," wrote Keller, "Schoenberg would have denied them. Whatever he did with Schoenberg, he never came to 'study' with him." David Nicholls vouches for Cage's attendance at the six-week USC course; the biography of Schoenberg by Stuckenschmidt only mentions Cage taking the summer course. That Schoenberg taught Cage is not necessarily remarkable; as the former recognized, whereas in Vienna he had taught the most promising students, in the United States – especially in California, to which he moved principally for his health – he could not pick and choose, and often had to instruct beginners. Cage's own account is that "I studied counterpoint at his home and attended all his courses at USC and later at UCLA when he moved there. I also took his course in harmony." One of the classes, according to Cage, had only three or four students.

"Schoenberg was a magnificent teacher, who always gave the impression that he was putting us in touch with musical principles," Cage recalls. "I saw in him an extraordinary musical mind, one that was greater and more perceptive than the others." For Cage, "he was not an ordinary human being," but "superior to other people." Time and again he records, "I literally worshipped him," "like a god."

"Studying with him meant believing what he had to say," as Cage defined it. "It didn't mean having an opportunity to argue with him, as so many college students do with their teachers, whom they may not have elected to study with. . . . The only reason I went to study with Schoenberg was because I believed in what he had to say."

So great was the partisanship of Cage for Schoenberg that when a Los Angeles concert of music by Stravinsky was billed as "music of the world's greatest living composer," Cage marched indignantly into the promoter's office and told him to think twice before making such claims in the very city in which Schoenberg was living.

Cage recalls an occasion when Schoenberg sent his harmony students to the blackboard with a problem in counterpoint using their customary *cantus firmus*, C D F E D C. As each student turned around with a solution, he would check it and ask for another. After Cage had presented about nine solutions, he told Schoenberg, not quite sure of himself, that there were no more solutions. "That's also right," his teacher answered, and then asked, "What is the principle underlying all of the solutions?" Cage was taken aback and was unable to answer. The question remained and the answer eluded him for decades. It made him consider Schoenberg even more highly than he had before; "he simply ascended," Cage remembered.

The teaching methods of Schoenberg were autocratic and quite ruthless. As Cage described it, "he kept his students in a constant state of failure." He once instructed a student to play a piece on the piano. She demurred, saying it was too difficult. He asked if she was a pianist and she said yes. "Then go to the piano," barked Schoenberg. As she did so, she said she would play it slowly to avoid making mistakes. "Play at the proper tempo and do not make mistakes," he commanded. She began. Presently he stopped her, pointing out that she was making mistakes. She resumed. "You're not going fast enough," Schoenberg observed. She tried several more times and on each occasion was interrupted. The girl burst into tears, and explained between sobs that she had had a tooth pulled that morning. Schoenberg said, "Do you have to go to the dentist in order to make mistakes?"

Schoenberg complained incessantly that none of his pupils did enough good work. When a student followed the rules, he would ask why they did not take a little more liberty; when a student stretched the rules he would ask why they did not follow them. Once he asked Gerard Strang, who was in the small group, why he had broken the rules, to which Strang replied, "I wanted to see what you would say." Schoenberg rejoined, "Why don't you follow the rules and see what I say?" On another occasion he became exasperated at the low productivity of a female student, and asked the group to decide whether she should be excluded from the class. He sent her out ahead of him and, as he left, wheeled around and said with a charming smile, "Of course we'll keep her."

Schoenberg would never look at Cage's compositions. When he once presented a long fugue subject, the only comment Schoenberg made was to tell him to save it for his first symphony. Any comments Cage made on the work of his fellow students, Schoenberg would ridicule. When Cage tried to enquire about twelve-tone composition, which Schoenberg made a point of never teaching, he said, "That's none of your business." It was not until years later that Cage was to hear a good word from Schoenberg. Peter Yates told Cage that he had once asked Schoenberg if any of his pupils in America had been interesting. In a letter, he had named Lou Harrison among others, but not Cage. To Yates, Schoenberg's immediate reply was that there were none, but then he had smiled and mentioned Cage, saying, "Of course he's not a composer, but an inventor – of genius."

II

While Cage had been in New York, Xenia had considered the merits of his proposal of marriage, and had decided in its favor. In Yuma, just over the border into Arizona, near the desert, they married at five o'clock on the sunny morning of June 7, 1935. That same day Crete published an article headlined "Tenth District P.–T.A. Speaker Urges 'Lessons in Manners' at Conventions." At first the Cages lived with his parents at 1207 Miramar. By 1937 they had a place of their own at 1916 Walcott Way in East Hollywood. The marriage was to last ten years.

In the months leading up to their marriage Cage had been as productive as usual, composing the *Three Pieces for Flute Duet*, the piano solo *Quest* and *Two Pieces* for piano. The *Two Pieces* resembles the work he produced before his time in New York, insofar as he uses only flats as accidentals and omits markings for phrasing and dynamics. They are, however, constructed in a different way, using the twelve-note row as the source for a narrow repertoire of small motifs. These are presented at the very beginning and are not transposed or rhythmically modified, which suggests either a deliberate interest in self-limitation, external organization rather than freedom, and austerity, or a failure to create organically. The repetition, and sometimes *ostinati*, produce work which, as Paul Griffiths observes, "has absolutely nothing in common with other serial music being composed in the 1930s."

Most significantly, Cage wrote a twenty-minute *Quartet* for unspecified percussion instruments. After its first performance Crete said, "I enjoyed it, but where are you going to put it?" It was the dawn of a prolonged involvement with percussion. What prompted Cage to write the *Quartet* is not clear; the work is far from the spirit of the teacher he worshipped, and has more in common with the works of a number of less well-known artists. In the decade from 1910 to 1920 the Futurists had celebrated the dynamism of mechanical processes in their writings, paintings and music. Philippo Marinetti, the leader of the group (principally because he wrote the obligatory manifesto, *Foundation and Manifesto of Futurism*), was a playwright and poet who made experimental use of sound. Luigi Russolo created an "art of noises" with noise-making machines of his own invention. Cage may have come across the works of these or other Futurists when in Europe, although he never suggested any special debt to or knowledge of them. Then there was George Antheil, whom Cage would shortly meet and whose *Ballet mécanique* incorporates a range of industrial noises. Edgard Varèse was on his way to America in 1935, bearing his powerful *Ionisation* (1931) for thirteen percussion players. Other composers quite unconnected to European music had begun independently to explore percussion writing, for example, Amadeo Roldan and, in pieces such as *Toccata*, Carlos Chavez. Cowell's neo-primitivism also tended in this direction.

Another possible influence is the research into the use of percussion instruments in other cultures: the music of the Caribbean; the gamelan, which he may have heard in Cowell's classes; and Balinese music, the subject of research by Colin McPhee published in *Modern Music* in 1935.

Whereas in the past a composer's influences came from his or her saturation in the music of their own continent, Cage was a member of the first generation whose artistic influences could come from across the world, though necessarily neither with as deep an understanding nor with as much cultural cohesion as the previous, narrower world had made possible. Cage's interest in percussion typifies this perfectly. Such a background of diverse uprooted influences is an ideal context within which inventiveness can operate.

With his first exploration of percussion music and the range of inputs this implies, we see the first clear evidence of Cage's devotion to originality, as well as at this time uncertainty about whether he could be true to it. "I'd read Cowell's *New Musical Resources* and . . . *The Theory of Rhythm*. I had also read Chavez's *Towards a New Music*," recollected Cage. "Both works gave me the feeling that everything that was possible in music had already happened. So I thought I could never compose socially important music. Only if I could *invent* something new, then would I be useful to society. But that seemed unlikely then."

Galka Scheyer, whom Cage had consulted concerning his visual work before leaving for New York, found the *Quartet* interesting, and on the strength of it she introduced him to Oscar, sometimes Oskar, Fischinger. These were still the early days of the talkies and Fischinger made abstract films to follow music; until meeting Cage, he had been using popular classics such as the *Hungarian Dances* by Brahms. Scheyer thought it would be mutually beneficial for the two men to work together. Fischinger commissioned Cage to write for one of his films, and to acquaint Cage with the way they were made, he enrolled him as his assistant. "I was moving bits of colored cardboard hung on wires. I had a long pole with a chicken feather, and I would move it and then have to still it," Cage recorded. "When I got perfectly still – he was sitting in an armchair at the camera – he would click it and take another frame. In the end it was a beautiful film in which these squares, triangles and circles and other things moved and changed color."

One day, in the midst of this work, Fischinger suggested to Cage, "Everything in the world has its own spirit, and this spirit becomes audible by setting it into vibration." "That set me on fire," Cage recalls. "He started me on a path of exploration of the world around me which has never stopped – of hitting and stretching and scraping and rubbing everything." This enthusiasm of Cage for what someone else might have dismissed as a rather quaint and inconsequential claim is perhaps not only confirmation of his predilection for experiment, but also a first glimpse of an appreciation of the spiritual dimensions of music – one which is intrinsically connected with sensual attraction to the everyday. "I was not inclined towards spiritualism," Cage said, "but I began to tap everything I saw."

Inspired by Fischinger, Cage prepared a new percussion piece. The *Trio* calls for a rather narrow timbral palette, especially in comparison with early percussion works by other composers, and this can be related to the austere leanings of his earlier work: pieces of wood of gradated length, tom-toms, bass drum, and bamboo sticks tapped against one another like claves. Performance benefits, Cage suggests, from spatial separation of the woodblocks of the different players; it is not clear whether this, later characteristic suggestion dates from the time of composition or closer to the time of publication years later.

Xenia's interest in crafts had led her to become an apprentice to Hazel Dreis, a bookbinder ("I mean a real bookbinder – not a casemaker," Cage once specified emphatically) who had studied with Lawrence de Coverley in London, and Cage began to learn how to design covers. Dreis had a large house which she shared with her apprentices; the Cages moved in. The apprentices became musicians in the evenings, playing Cage's percussion pieces as he wrote them. Working with these untrained musicians seemed to Cage preferable to working with musicians like the clarinettist who, assigned his *Sonata*, had first neglected and then rejected it out of hand.

Cage asserts that it was not only experimentation but poverty which made him work with sound-sources from the junkyard. "Everyone," he said of the Dreis household, "was as poor as a church mouse." To raise extra money he once again carried out research work, this time for local lawyers, which brought home fifty dollars a month, making him the only person in the house apart from Dreis with anything like an external income. Any fruit trees overhanging the Santa Monica alleyways were treated as common property and summarily stripped. Cage toured the local wrecking shops, buying brake drums, hubcaps and spring coils for use as percussion instruments; he also employed kitchen utensils, and the woodblocks which formed part of Dreis's bookbinding equipment.

He was deriving diminishing benefit from his studies with Schoenberg. It is curious and in some respects revealing that a quintessential American experimental composer, with a modern range and depth of influence, had subscribed to the rigorous tutelage of this most European of European masters (had, moreover, worshipped him), when there were others with whom he could collaborate or study who worked in a way nearer to his own, and would appreciate his work. One area, however, in which Cage and Schoenberg agreed was clarity and seriousness of endeavor, which transcended differences in the way they chose to pursue their work. "I stand by my work, always, unfalteringly," wrote Schoenberg. "With these four notes," he would say, demonstrating, "Bach did this, Beethoven this, Brahms this, and Schoenberg," using the third person, "did this." Cage feels he has inherited this attitude, in that however many changes his compositional approach has undergone, they are made only when they seem absolutely necessary.

In other respects Cage and Schoenberg were far apart. When Cage was heartened to find outsiders beginning to attend and enjoy the percussion concerts, he asked Schoenberg to come along to hear the bookbinders in action. "Ah, so?" replied Schoenberg inscrutably, "I'm not free that night." Cage offered to arrange a concert for the following week. "No," his teacher responded, "I will not be free at any time."

Their pedagogical relationship faced difficulties more practical than Schoenberg's lack of interest in the work of his pupil. The traditional musical skills of Cage were, as we have seen, of varied quality; he had a "beautiful touch" but "no voice." Cage recounts years later, "When I last saw her, Aunt Phoebe said, 'You're in the wrong field.'" One shortcoming in particular drove a wedge between Schoenberg and Cage. "It became clear to both of us," the latter recalls, "that I had no feeling for harmony." To Schoenberg, skill in harmony was the prerequisite of a composer, because, as he understood it, it functioned not merely as coloristic chord-building, but as the central structural resource of a musical work. Without a feeling for harmony, he warned, Cage would always be thwarted in his efforts to write music, as if he would come to a wall through which he could not pass. Recalling hs promise to devote his life to music, Cage responded, "In that case I will devote my life to beating my head against that wall."

"Maybe", he wondered in retrospect, "this is what I've been doing ever since. A decade after their exchange Cage wrote that he felt Schoenberg's warning "was like my grandmother saying I should be born again. It may have been true and it may not have been, but it didn't have anything to do with what I was doing." Deaf or blind to harmony, in Schoenberg's sense, over the years he developed structural means with a different basis and thus a different focus, and in due course circumvented the traditional meanings and function of structure altogether, turning a probable serious shortcoming for a Western composer to his advantage.

"I had studied harmony with Weiss without liking it or feeling any natural inclination to use it," Cage noted in about 1940. "The reason that I couldn't be interested," furthermore, "was that harmony didn't have anything to say about noise." Cage "saw the *New Music* publication of Percussion Music, heard Schoenberg call it nonsense, doubted whether it was nonsense."

The final straw came when, in front of a large class at the University of Southern California, Schoenberg proclaimed, "My purpose in teaching you is to make it impossible for you to write music." The other students took his words as helpful rather than devastating because they thought so highly of him; Cage, for the first time, felt himself revolt, against Schoenberg's words rather than his person, though he did not protest out loud. He readdressed himself to his promise made at the outset, to devote his life to music; quite soon it was to be without his teacher.

III

As Cage was already beginning to be aware, the lack of commonality with Schoenberg was only the tip of an iceberg of dismissive incomprehension from those who called themselves musicians. He increasingly felt that music was the most sluggish and reactionary of the arts. Ironically, now he had committed himself to music rather than visual art, it was painters, and dancers, who were for years in the vanguard as champions of his work.

From the fall semester of 1937 Cage was an assistant in the UCLA elementary school; as an accompanist he played Bartok, Copland, Hindemith and Scriabin. He also presented classes in percussion at UCLA and became a member of the Training School faculty at Westwood. A major inspiration for the dancers he met was Martha Graham. Her influence meant that the dancers were interested in new music and, moreover, were keen to commission it for their performances. Cage improvised at the piano for the technique classes of a modern dance group, and shortly began to compose percussion pieces for their dances.

Cage was asked to write for the annual water ballet of the UCLA swimming team. He found the swimmers could not hear music under-water. In order to mark time, it occurred to him that he could dip a vibrating gong in the water. When he tried it out he found that submersion progressively shortened the resonating area and the sound scooped low in pitch. The effect so delighted Cage that he used it in many subsequent compositions, quite unconnected with the aquatic ballet.

In the spring semester of 1938 Cage joined with Aunt Phoebe in offering a UCLA extension course on "Musical Accompaniments for Rhythmic Expression" that met at Van Nuys elementary school, January 25 to May 10 from four until six in the afternoon; fifteen Tuesdays for twelve dollars. They encouraged the students to experiment with all kinds of sound-sources – balloons squeezed with wet fingers, filled with rice and shaken, or radiators struck with tires. Cage removed the cover of the upright piano and tied the strings with various objects.

Cage had a teaching post for the summer thanks to a referral by Cowell, who had suggested that Cage go to San Francisco to visit Lou Harrison. Harrison was teaching at nearby Mills College, and pulled strings to have Cage appointed to the faculty for the same program. Backed up by his UCLA experience, he composed music for choreographer Marian van Tuyl. It was an exciting and productive summer, for three of the best-respected contemporary dance groups and some of the leading lights of the Chicago School of Design, among them Gyorgy Kepes and Laszlo Moholy-Nagy, were present. The President of the College, Aurelia Henry Reinhardt, was a devotee of Gertrude Stein. In July Cage met the wife of George Antheil, which opened up the possibility of correspondence.

One day Cage travelled to San Francisco and found four jobs in one day. Of the four, Cage opted to work for Bonnie Bird, formerly of the Graham troupe and now teaching at the Cornish School in Seattle.

SIX

I

Nellie Centennial Cornish (1876–1956) had founded the Cornish School of Music in Seattle in 1914; seven years later the school had moved to a new building at Harvard Avenue South and East Roy Street, with an annex which held the radio station and now accommodates a pottery workshop. Cage particularly appreciated Cornish's insistence that students should not specialize but study every subject offered.

Bonnie Bird was born the year the school opened, daughter of Mr. and Mrs. Scott E. Bird, who came from Seattle. A few months before Cage arrived, on May 19, 1938, she had married Ralph Gundlach, an associate professor of psychology at the University of Washington. Cage became her composer-accompanist, and set about organizing a percussion orchestra.

Among the others Cage met at the Cornish School were Doris Dennison, who was teaching Dalcroze Eurhythmics, and an extraordinary black dancer, Syvilla Fort. Fort was a local woman who had already graduated from the Cornish School but was continuing to take the classes offered by Bird, earning part of her tuition expenses by modelling fashions for Seattle department stores.

It was a meeting with another dancer which was to have the widest ramifications for Cage's life. Mercier Cunningham had been born at Centralia, Washington, on April 16, 1919, the son of Clifford and Marion Cunningham; they had an elder son, Jack. Clifford enjoyed gardening; Marion had the same amusingly acerbic domination over men which Crete possessed. Young Mercier took his first dance lessons locally at the age of ten, though he had danced a sailors' hornpipe in public two years earlier. By the time he was twelve he was studying tap and ballroom dancing with Maude Leon Barrett, touring the West Coast in the mid-thirties with her and her daughter Marjorie. Mrs. Barrett used to say she had one foot in the grave and jiggled the other to stay out. After graduating from high school, he studied for a year at George Washington University in Washington, D.C., then returned to Washington state and enrolled at the Cornish School, first as a drama student, then, after taking up the classes of Bonnie Bird, in the dance department, where he prepared his first choreography.

In his dance composition classes, Cage was encouraging students to write music for their own dances. He was also setting up a percussion orchestra, which Dennison and Cunningham as well as Xenia joined; his first Seattle percussion concert was booked for December 9.

II

Among those who saw the poster for the concert was Morris Graves. Later Graves was to move flamboyantly in royal circles, befriending among others the Duke and Duchess of Windsor, but at this time he was one of many artists in the Seattle area, unknown but thriving on extravagant, decisive, stylized gestures. He made up his mind very quickly. Graves decided to attend Cage's concert the better to mock it, and arrived with a large bag of peanuts, a lorgnette with doll's eyes in place of the glass, and a number of acolytes. Everyone prepared themselves for trouble. Eyeing Graves' towering frame, a certain Mrs. Beck ordered, "if he does anything upsetting, throw him out."

Despite his worst intentions, Graves found himself enjoying the music. At the end of the third movement of Cage's *Quartet*, he cried enthusiastically, "Jesus in the everywhere!" Taking this as their expected cue, the men around him lifted him bodily and bustled him down the aisle as if he were on a stretcher. Graves beheld the large bosom of Mrs. Beck looming ahead. Her silhouette spoke. "I am Mrs. Beck." Graves replied, "Good evening, Mrs. Beck." Mrs. Beck had the men throw him out on the patio. Free, and with the fast drumming of the *Quartet*'s final movement under way, Graves began immediately to move. "His dance," Mrs. Beck later reported, "was very sinuous."

The next day Graves met Cage and asked to play in the orchestra. As one piece called for a human wail, he became the wailer. Later, Graves, Cage and Xenia were to live on the same floor of a tenement building. The couple had three rooms – a kitchen and living room halfway down the hall, and, at its end, a bedroom, with the bathroom opposite. Graves lived in the front room down the corridor. Cage had recently bought a copy of Joyce's newly published *Finnegans Wake* from one of the department stores and would read "the Ondt and the Gracehopper" out loud to entertain his friends.

As they grew to know one another, Cage saw more of his new friend's extravagant nature. "Six feet four, mind a whirlwind," Cage would later say. Graves owned an old Ford, from which he had removed all the seats, replacing them with a table and chairs so that the car became a small furnished room with books, a vase of flowers, and so on. "One day he drew up to a luncheonette," recalls Cage in *A Year From Monday*, "parked, opened the door on the street side, unrolled a red carpet across the sidewalk." Graves walked along the carpet, into the luncheonette and ordered some food – variously a hamburger or a lettuce sandwich, according to Cage. "A crowd gathered, expecting something strange to happen. However, all Graves did was eat the hamburger, pay his bill, get back in the car, roll up the carpet, and drive off."

Another time, Cage recalls, "he filled a baby carriage with rocks and, with strings, made a trailer for it of toothbrushes. He pushed it downtown to the Olympic Hotel, through its halls to the main dining room. After placing a rock at each chair but one, he then sat down and ordered dinner."

While in Seattle Cage and Xenia availed themselves of their training with Dreis, arranging an exhibition of hand-bound books at the school. They also acted as hosts for an exhibition of paintings by Alexej Jawlensky – first introduced to America by Galka Scheyer. After seeing Graves' series *The Purification of Cardinal Pacelli*, the couple arranged for its display at the school.

Another painter Cage came to know was Mark Tobey (d. 1976). They had close contact for a much shorter time than Cage and Graves, but when they were both living in Seattle they met frequently. Tobey, said Cage, "had a great effect on my way of seeing." Cage admired the complexity of Tobey's work and the diffuse attention it requires. His influence, however, was most important on Cage's involvement with everyday life. Cage has frequently recalled a walk he took at this time with Tobey and some other friends, from the Cornish School to the Japanese restaurant at which they planned to eat. Normally a forty-five-minute walk, it took several hours because of Tobey's insistent attention to visual detail. "He would continually stop to notice something surprising everywhere – on the side of a shack or in a space ... which we normally didn't notice when we were walking, and his gaze would immediately turn them into a work of art. He was attentive to the slightest detail. For him, everything was alive. He had an extraordinary sense of the presence of things." Cage was delighted and surprised. "It was the first time that someone else had given me a lesson in looking without prejudice, someone who didn't compare what he was seeing with something before."

A few years later, after he had moved to New York, Cage visited an exhibition at the Willard Gallery – one of the early promoters of the work of Tobey and Graves. Waiting for the bus at a corner of Madison Avenue, Cage noticed that looking at the pavement beneath his feet was as enriching an experience as viewing the white Tobey paintings he had just seen. It was an attitude of attention which in later years would be very important in Cage's aesthetic. Waiting for the bus

i happened to look at the paveMent
I wAs standing on;
noticed no diffeRence between
looKing at art or away from it

III

The extant work of Cage up to the end of the thirties becomes sufficiently delineated stylistically for a few comments to be made concerning the significance of his writing in the history of rhythmic complexity, his attempts to generate a structural means to substitute for harmony, and the corollaries of these attempts.

The first decade of Cage's music forms a qualitatively important sample of the history of rhythmic complexity. It was produced at a time when Western music was moving out of a lengthy phase of neglecting rhythm. Informed reconstruction suggests that late medieval music featured highly complex rhythms, not, incidentally, because all medieval musicians were virtuosi, but because the understanding of rhythm was based on additive rather than divisional measurement. The avant-garde of the mid-twentieth century produced music whose rhythms strained the limits of notation and technique, and arguably of perceptibility, made all the more difficult by a change in the way performers understood it. The piano pieces of Karlheinz Stockhausen and Pierre Boulez are prime examples, and left a challenging legacy carried on, for instance, in the eighties in England by the "new complexity" of composers such as Brian Ferneyhough and Richard Barrett. Between, say, 1500 and 1950 lay a long fallow period of unchallenging rhythmic writing, broken in

Europe by the diverse, barbarous rhythms of Stravinsky and in America by composers such as Ives. Gardner Read suggests that the first notation of quintuplets appeared around 1870, at about the same time as the first use of the $\frac{5}{4}$ time signature.

In such a context, the rhythmic complexity of Cage's early music is adventurous without being remarkable. His rhythmic innovations were still to come, and as we shall see, such pieces as the *Music of Changes* and *Water Music* are as challenging to the idea of rhythm and notation as they are to the performer.

Where Cage was much more remarkable in the thirties was as a champion of music for percussion. For as long as there had been classical music, the percussionist had tended to be seen as the poor relation of the orchestra, whose role was merely of punctuation and whose principal talent was counting interminable stretches of bars' rest. Cage was one of the first to write for an ensemble of nothing but percussionists, and it is noteworthy that neither in Santa Monica nor in Seattle were his performers trained musicians.

The intervention of Fischinger edged Cage toward an almost mystical respect for all sounds. Always on the side of the innocent underdog, Cage argued – let's not say he reasoned – that since noises were excluded by the rules of music what was needed was a music of noise. "All sounds are useful in music," Cage told a reporter, "if they occur in music." He felt composers should be "directing their search towards those fields in sound which hitherto have not been considered musical."

This predilection, and polemic for noise rather than pitch, fitted well with his lack of skill and harmony. It necessitated a different basis for structure, and Cage successively experimented with three such bases through the thirties. In the *Trio*, for instance, he employed motifs or silences of equal length, arranged in his compositional materials in a circle. The piece progressed by the particular part moving a step forward or backward in the cycle of motifs. Timbrally, structurally and motivically, the pieces written in this way are extremely basic. The motifs are simple, and the structure permits neither complexity nor leeway for deviation; it is either followed or it is not. Whether he could see a way of developing this technique or not, Cage dropped it almost as soon as he had devised it.

In his presentation of 1937, *Credo*, Cage suggested that another structuring factor might be that "whereas, in the past, the point of disagreement has been between dissonance and consonance, it will be in the immediate future between noise and so-called musical sounds."

While interestingly traditional as a variation of the tension and release theme, the practical ramifications of this idea never became very clear.

Cage's third idea flowered into the structural basis for his next decade of music. The obvious foundation for structuring percussion music was duration. Cage devised a system which he called "micro-macrocosmic rhythmic structure," in which the small units of the composition stood in the same proportion of time-lengths to the large parts as the parts to the whole. "The large parts of the composition," as he once put it, "had the same proportion as the phrases of a single unit. Thus, an entire piece had that number of measures that had a square root." Cage described how "One could . . . emphasize the structure at the beginning and move into far-reaching variations."

Paul Griffiths has suggested various antecedents of Cage's approach: ironically, the work of Stravinsky in pieces such as *Les Noces* and *Le Sacre du printemps*, and Antheil's *Ballet mécanique*, which employs a "time–space principle" by which, Griffiths suggests, "musical structure is geared to lengths of time as a building to its girders." Colin McPhee's numerical transcription of *ostinato* pitches in Balinese music may have suggested to Cage an analogous process in rhythm, just as he would later read lists of numbers by Satie as evidence that the latter made use of rhythmic structure. Cage relates his approach to his work with dancers, since time–length was the common denominator between sound and movement; his new structural means facilitated his writing for dance.

As Cage develops it, the system does not provide a regular, metrical pulse that functions as the foreground in which sounds are based. Instead it serves as a measure of duration he increasingly treats with so little accentuation that it comes to seem less a measure of time than of space. There is little variety of time-signature, but for no more convoluted reason than to simplify the proportional mathematics. Cage said at the time, "There's none of this *boom*, boom, boom, business in my music . . . a measure is taken as a strict measure of time – not a *one* two three four – which I fill with various sounds." Later he explained, "It's not the rhythmic structure that I was concerned with, it was the phraseology and the relation of the parts."

What is also noteworthy is that this type of formal structure was inimical to any kind of self-expression through music. If self-expression had been paramount among Cage's aims in writing music, it is unlikely that he would have developed along the lines he did. Whereas for the inventor of serialism the technique had "no other aim than comprehensibility," an attempt to provide a basis for communication by ensuring basic unity, for Cage the degree of formalism it made possible was attractive precisely insofar as it precluded musical communication. Communication of course takes place but with music not so much the medium as the object; not through music but with it. This putative direction could be seen not only in his dalliance with serialism but also in his restricted timbral palette; it was anticipated in his work with dance, which, as Calvin Tomkins has observed, led him to compose according to the external structure provided by the movements, which had already been choreographed and timed.

Since Cage's structural means were based on time rather than on harmony, they could be articulated by any sounds, whether pitch or noise, which thus had equal status within the system. Not only did all sounds have a potential structural function, but the structure could also be articulated by silence. This was possible too when structure was actualized in time, because silence is the thinnest element of music; sounds last a certain time, have a spatial location, a certain dynamic, tone color, and a register if not a definable pitch, whereas silence can be specified only as a duration.

Composers generally have used silence as they have percussion: for its emphatic or dramatic function. It supports the sounds (for instance, in Beethoven's work, silence usually supports the sounds it follows). However, most work falls back unquestioningly on to the received ideas of the age. Western thinking is riddled with fear, if not denial, of nothingness, and this can be seen in the impoverished use of silence as a mere comma to the downbeat. "Curiously enough," Cage would say in 1958, "the twelve-tone system has no zero in it." What was new was to *highlight* silence, and by so doing invest it with an independent value, as well as using it to complement sound. Anton Webern has long been seen as moving in this direction in his instrumental music from 1908 onwards. Marinetti, the Futurist, was a champion of silence, incorporating in *I Silenzi Parlano fra di Loro* and *Battaglio di Ritmi* silences of respectively, between eight and forty seconds, and up to three minutes.

In New York, prior to developing his rhythmic structure, Cage tended to treat sound and silence identically, which led Weiss to complain that "no sooner had I started a piece, than I brought it to an end." In pieces such as the *Duet for Two Flutes*, Cage said, "I'm always introducing silence right near the beginning when any composer in his right mind would be making things thicker ... I was getting thinner and thinner." The nearest precedent to Cage's integration of silence was not in music but, as Calvin Tomkins convincingly suggested, in sculpture, with the use of "negative space," open space, as an integral compositional element.

The attention to silence, and the provision of a structural function for it, represents, like the valorization of noises, Cage's enthusiasm for giving a place to the excluded and forbidden. Having now not only become preoccupied with percussion, noise and silence, but also having formalized their place by the structural means he developed, Cage was outside the orbit of Schoenberg in practical terms. He felt people were so protective of the term "music" that it might be better to find another word. Toward the end of the thirties he frequently stated, with Futurist overtones, that he preferred the term "art of noise" or "organization of sound" to "percussion music." The expression "experimental music" troubled him for different reasons, in that it implied a certain ignorance and arbitrariness on the part of composers that could mean their works were not taken seriously.

Cage was not only interested in the noise provided by existing instruments, however exotic, or by found objects; he also gravitated toward the sound-sources which modern technology could provide. By the end of the thirties America was firmly in the electrical age. All but very poor households had electricity wired in, and most – many more than in his days at KNX – owned a radio. Although widespread, electrical technology was still novel (the talkie was scarcely a decade old). Experiments had already been made in the application of electronics to music – by Milhaud, Toch and Hindemith, for example – but Cage had reservations. In the case of the Theremin, for instance, he was concerned that players tried to make it imitate traditional instruments. Marinetti had used sound effects on disc in concert: a baby's cries, the coos of a girl, the sounds of a boxing match. His 1933 manifesto, *Futurist Radiophonic Theater*, discusses the amplification of sounds which would otherwise not be audible – what Cage would later call "small sounds."

During his researches for his father, Cage had become interested in the possible uses of recorded sound in music, and read up on the most recent developments in recording on wire. Talking to a newspaper reporter, he predicted an "electrical music in which new notes will be heard and photoelectrical devices which measure time by fractional seconds and create strange qualities." In a manuscript from around 1940 he envisaged how with "the acquisition of a library of templates i.e. a film library, the most practical exploration of sound may be made. . . . I believe that film will make noise available for musical purposes and that electrical means will make tones available for musical purposes." With this in mind, he set John senior to work designing equipment "which should give rich possibilities in the overtone structure of a tone." Concerts could one day take place, he predicted in 1941, "in the midst of a fantastic assemblage of wires and electrical connections."

Cage presented his formalization of these hopes in his *Credo*, a talk given to the Seattle Arts Society in 1937. "I believe that the use of noise to make music will continue and increase until we reach a music produced through the aid of electrical instruments which will make available to composers any and all sounds that can be heard." He continued: "Photoelectric, film and mechanical mediums for the synthetic production of music will be explored." In the manuscript he added, "Insist on music made out of twentieth-century materials."

A lecture which he presented to the Seattle Pro Musica on October 8 of the following year, "Some Aspects of Modern Music," features the same preoccupations with percussion and noise, rhythm as a structural resource, and electrical instruments. "If you think modern music, with its use of very close intervals, is terrible," he warned, "shudder to consider what the music of the future will be, when instruments are perfected to meet the demands of composers."

As over the years Cage put into words his motives for making music, one reason for this remorseless experimentation remains constant, with only changes in emphasis. This is the notion that music, based in this case on noise, can be used by people to help them integrate their experiences of daily life – which they often feel are unpleasant – rather than being used to nurture an aesthetically superior realm apart from the world. "Through organization," Cage writes in a 1942 press release, city sounds "lose their nerve-racking character, and become the materials for a highly dramatic and expressive art form." It is not clear when or how Cage began to think this way. His view echoes that of Maxim Gorky, for whom "aesthetics is the ethics of the future"; as Terry Measham put it, "Art shows us how to adapt our traditions energetically to ever-changing conditions. That is how art enhances life."

"People may leave my concerts thinking they have heard 'noise'," Cage explained in 1943, "but will then hear unsuspected beauty in their everyday life. This music has a therapeutic value for city dwellers." These ideas were expanded in a program note written in 1940. Listening to music by percussion composers, Cage claims, "is quite different from listening to the music, say, of Beethoven. In the latter case we are temporarily protected or transported from the noises of everyday life. In the case of percussion music, however, we find that we have mastered or subjugated noise. We become triumphant over it and our ears become sensitive to its beauties."

William Carlos Williams provided a model, but rare, response in his note for the premiere of Cage's *First Construction* in 1939:

> I felt that noise, the unrelated noise of life, such as this in the subway, had not been battened out as would have been the case with Beethoven still warm in the mind, but it had actually been mastered, subjugated. The composer has taken this hated thing, life, and rigged himself into power over it by his music. The offense had not been held, cooled, varnished over, but annihilated, and life itself made thereby triumphant. This is an important difference. By hearing such music, seemingly so much noise, when I actually came upon noise in reality, I found I had gone up over it.

IV

The staff of the Cornish School radio station were willing to help Cage investigate the application of electrical technology to music. He experimented with small-sound amplification, and was delighted to discover in the studio variable-speed turntables, for "test purposes," equipped with a clutch to shift between speeds. Cage thought of using records on the turntables as instruments, producing different frequencies and siren-like *glissandi*.

Early in 1939 he was asked to write music for a Seattle performance of *Marriage at the Eiffel Tower* by Jean Cocteau; he made this the occasion to try out his ideas in a composition. Cage wrote a six-minute piece for muted piano, cymbal and two of the variable-speed turntables. The first of these played a Victor frequency record, 84522B, and a constant-note record, No. 24; on the second was Victor frequency record 84522A. Intended as a radio broadcast (like Marinetti's *Radiophonic Theater*), the piece was performed by Cage, Xenia, Doris Dennison and Margaret Jansen in two separate studios, mixed in the control room, and beamed the few steps' distance to the theater. The *Imaginary Landscape No. 1* was premiered as accompaniment to the Cocteau piece on March 24, 1939, and was later used at Mills College for Marion van Tuyl's dance *Horror Dream*; it has a convincing claim to being the first electroacoustic composition.

It was also in the *Imaginary Landscape* that Cage first employed his system of rhythmic structure. The simple figures that constitute the piece fit into a scheme of four sections consisting of three times five measures which are separated by interludes which increase in length additively from one to three measures; the piece ends with a four-measure code.

Cage had attempted to stir up interest in percussion writing after the December 1938 concert by sending a mailing to numerous composers, telling them of the resources available and inviting them to submit compositions. Lou Harrison was one enthusiastic respondent. By October 1939, having known of the piece for some time, Cage acquired his own copy of *Ionisation*, Varèse's work for thirteen percussionists. In the next few years, in good part thanks to Cage's efforts, the number of compositions for percussion grew, until by 1942 there were over a hundred known to him.

For once, the most immediate response to the concert had been financial. Morris Graves paid for a pair of Puerto Rican maracas; Nicolas Slonimsky gave ten dollars to buy a pair of bongos and a guero. George Mantor – a keen iris gardener, as every reader of *Silence* will know – put in two dollars for eight anvils. By the middle of 1940 the inventory of the Cage Percussion Players was impressive, including a Noh drum, ten tom-toms, bongos, quijadas and claves; temple-blocks, a tortoise-shell, sistrum, finger cymbals, a Zildjian cymbal and tambourine; three peedle pipes, one tolling bell, a conch shell and nine chopsticks; a bass drum pedal (quite an early instance); a lion's roar, a slap-stick, a washtub, six curtains and a dinner-bell.

In January 1939, the Players had performed at the University of Idaho. Tobey, the novelist John Steinbeck and his wife (who were then living in Los Gatos), and Cage's Seattle colleague Nancy Wilson Ross financed a concert to be held in Seattle at the end of the year. Unfortunately, by the date of the performance Cage had to replace one of his performers: at the Bennington College Summer School of the Dance, Mercier Cunningham had been asked by Martha Graham to join her company in New York. Graham (1894–1991) had made an early start in vaudeville and made her solo debut in Manhattan in 1926. She was more than a choreographer; she was the originator of a dance method focused on a unity of body and mind, and supreme physical control put to dramatic use. Her early interest in native American society and its mysticism yielded to a reinterpretation of myths and the lives of historical characters, in second-generation Freudian fashion.

Cunningham moved to New York in September and danced his first role in December; Cage was not to see him again for any appreciable length of time for another four years.

With the forthcoming concert in mind, Cage spent November composing *First Construction (In Metal)*, for six percussion players, plus an assistant, playing, as the title suggests, metal instruments that included a string piano and thundersheets; Cage also made his first concert use of the water gong he had devised for the swimmers at UCLA. Both the work's title and subtitle are suggestive of sculpture, and the formalist approach of constructivism. Paul Griffiths has suggested that the choice of metal sound-sources may be a reference to the sonorities of Balinese music which, as we have seen, was a possible influence in the conception of rhythmic structure.

The *First Construction* is one of Cage's most convincing and perennial early pieces. His use of rhythmic structure is far in advance of the *Imaginary Landscape* of nine months earlier, and Cage employs it with almost textbook clarity. The palindromic structure of the piece is 4/3/2/3/4, a total of sixteen units, each unit a measure of $^4_4$ time. These proportional divisions are obvious from even a cursory glance at the opening measures of the score.

The sixteen-measure structure is employed sixteen times. The first four occasions constitute what might loosely be called the "exposition" of the work, furnishing a variety of motifs set off by contrasting rhythmic patterns and instrumentation that are then developed in the sections which follow, grouped correspondingly into three sections, two, three and four. The piece ends with nine measures which are exempt from the proportional rule, so that the whole piece lasts for 256 measures. The *Construction* was premiered in the Cornish Theater on December 9 alongside, among others, an early example of microtonal competition, *Dirge* by Mildred Couper, for two pianos tuned a quarter-tone apart.

In the new year Cage wrote the *Second Construction* for percussion quartet. It has a sixteen by sixteen measure structure like the first, divided 4/3/4/5, which is made very clear in the opening measure but ignored in the final six sections in favor of a development of the opening sleigh bells' solo in a fugue-like fashion that Cage later dismissed as uninteresting. His enthusiasm for electrical technology had been fired by the realization of the *Imaginary Landscape*, but he knew that to pursue it in depth would entail considerable expense which would require institutional support. He therefore began to canvas businesses and institutions for funding, his main aim being to set up a studio to carry out the necessary work. In a letter to George Antheil, he records:

I am doing everything I can to establish a "center of experimental music." The purpose of this center will be to do research, composition and performance in the field of sounds and rhythms not used in the symphony orchestra: the ultimate purpose will be the use of electrical instruments which will make available the entire desirable field of sound.

Both Aurelia Henry Reinhardt at Mills and Laszlo Moholy-Nagy at the Chicago School of Design were keen to house the "center" but did not have the resources to fund it themselves. As Cage continued to try to make his dream reality over the years, he heard the same story again and again.

SEVEN

I

Syvilla Fort was booked to dance in the Cornish Theater one Friday in March 1940, yet by the beginning of the week she had no music for her energetic solo, *Bacchanale*. On Tuesday she asked Cage to help her out; he was the only composer available.

Cage brought along a metronome and chronometer, and asked Fort for the measurements of the dance. He planned, as was his custom, to follow its structure, and relate it to some form of rhythmic structure he was still developing. The instrumentation, however, proved difficult. The Cornish Theater had a small performance space, with neither wings nor pit. Cage could not write for percussion orchestra because there would not be room for Fort to dance. The only available resource was a small grand piano at the front, to the left of the audience. A piano piece suggested to Cage the type of pitch organization he had developed during his studies with Buhlig, Weiss and Schoenberg, but he could not find an African pitch set. "I knew that wouldn't work for *Bacchanale*," recalled Cage, "which was rather primitive, almost barbaric."

He finally resolved that, since he only had a piano, he would change it. "I decided that what was wrong was the piano, not my efforts," Cage recorded, adding typically, "because I was conscientious." He remembered the way Henry Cowell had played inside the piano, strumming, striking or plucking the strings, muting them and running their length with darning needles. "He used a darning egg," related Cage, "moving it lengthwise along the strings while trilling, as I recall, on the keyboard; this produced a glissando of harmonics." Cage particularly enjoyed *The Banshee* (1925). "He got an idea," wrote Cowell, "by knowing my own things for the strings and piano very well, first learning them. I gave them up about 1930. . . . When I gave up this sort of writing for piano in order

69

to write more symphonic music, John was very annoyed. I said, 'Why don't you do it?', so he did do it, and he took it up and prepared the strings, which I had never done." Similar experiments, of which Cage shows no awareness, were going on in popular music, such as pressing tacks into piano hammers to imitate the harpsichord, and jazz musicians tying paper into their strings.

With the performance deadline looming, Cage tried placing objects in the piano, running in rapid succession through newspapers, magazines, ashtrays, books and a pie plate, and playing a few keys to hear the result. The piano sound was modified along the lines Cage sought – making it buzz or thud, not ring – but each object he tried bounced, so that the keys whose sound was modified changed constantly. He wondered if the solution was to insert objects which could be fixed in place, so the type of modification could be depended upon. Cage pressed a nail between the strings, but it slipped and fell into the piano. Then it occurred to him that the thread of a wood-screw, wound between two strings of a single note, would ensure it stayed in place; bolts, too, were threaded, and could be fastened with a nut. After experimentation, he wrote the *Bacchanale* for a piano treated with a small bolt, a screw with nuts, and some fibrous weather-stripping. "I was delighted to notice that by means of a single preparation two different sounds could be produced," Cage recounted. "One was resonant and open, the other was quiet and muted. The quiet one was heard whenever the soft pedal was used."

The instrument possessed the dynamic range of the harpsichord. Rather than producing a scalar succession of pitches, different registers of the keyboard yielded varied timbres. The relation of musical notation to what one would hear was not predictable in the direct manner for which Western notation had developed; if an E♭ was specified, striking the E♭ key could produce a ring or a plink or a thud, pedalling would change the sound again, and playing E♭ in a different octave would have a quite different result. Only memory specific to the piece in hand could tell a person reading the score what to expect. "Notation became a way to produce something," Cage explained. "The performer no longer had the impression that he would be able to hear the piece immediately on the first reading, the way it was going to sound."

He dubbed his invention the "prepared" – sometimes in early statements the "altered" – piano. Cage was able to install a percussion orchestra in the Cornish Theater – inside the piano, under the fingers of a single player. "I invited Mark Tobey and Morris Graves over to listen to it," he recalls. "They were delighted. So was Syvilla, and so was I,

70

and so was Xenia. We were all so happy, happy as could be. When Lou Harrison heard it, he said 'Oh dammit! I wish I'd thought of that!'"

In the above I have followed Cage's account, which is likely to be correct as to what went on at the time but plays down the length of the gestation period for the notion of extended techniques on the piano. Teaching with Aunt Phoebe at UCLA in 1938, Cage had tied the strings with various objects; he called for the piano strings to be played directly in the *First Construction*. The piano part of the *Second Construction* features hand muting and the application of a steel slide to the strings; it also requires the insertion of a screw and, between A and E♭, in the treble clef, muting with a piece of cardboard.

The prepared piano became Cage's principal resource through the next decade. It stood in relation to timbre as micro-macrocosmic rhythm was to structure, an innovation he could explore and which thereby set limits to his wider musical peregrinations. He wrote for it into the late fifties and, as we shall see, it would affect the way he wrote for other instruments. Forty years after his hurried invention Cage dedicated a few lines to Syvilla Fort:

> had there been two compoSers
> You
> might haVe asked the other one
> to wrIte your music.
> i'm gLad
> i was the onLy one
> Around.

The Cages were preparing to leave Seattle for San Francisco. As usual, money was short; Cage made copies of useful articles by typing them up. When Cowell had shown him the manuscript of his book on rhythm, which was not commercially available, Cage wrote it out by hand in its entirety. The January inventory of the couple included outlay for food, hotels, travel and personal expenses; Cage blew a dime on the slot machines and won a wristwatch.

They were still in Seattle in May. Cage performed music he had written for *America was Promises* and *Spiritual*, on the 7th, and Fort revived *Bacchanale*, and *Spiritual*, on June 5. By September the Cages were living at 228 Seventeenth Avenue in Richmond, San Francisco, and John Cage was working for the Works Progress Administration.

71

II

The Works Progress Administration was a pragmatically Keynesian response to the Depression. In his inaugural speech as president on March 4, 1933, Roosevelt proposed a New Deal: "Our greatest primary task is to put people to work. . . . It can be accomplished in part by direct recruiting by the government itself, treating the task as we would treat the emergency of war, but at the same time, through this employment, accomplish greatly needed projects."

In the length of its existence, the WPA employed eight and a half million individuals at a cost of around eleven billion dollars, paying a rather low average monthly wage of $54.33 per person. It accomplished tasks which, if not viable in a free market, were highly useful. Between 1935 and 1938 the WPA was the vehicle of the building or improvement of over 2,500 hospitals, 5,900 schools and 13,000 playgrounds; 78,000 bridges; 651,000 miles of road; and it reforested 20,000 acres. Hot lunches were given to poor children, day care provided for the children of working mothers, and literacy and naturalization classes run for immigrants. Funds were provided for federal theater, artists and writers; more than two and a half thousand public murals were painted, and guide books were written.

At the end of the thirties the administration faced growing charges of mismanagement and of complacency in the face of workers abusing the program. Support for the arts came under particular attack and was in time discontinued. From 1938 onward, the agency was reoriented for military purposes, making machine tools and constructing barracks, airfields and standby factories. When war came it brought full employment: on June 30, 1943, the WPA was terminated.

Cage applied to work on the WPA Music Project, but those in charge did not accept he was a musician. The Music Project was confined to performers on more traditional instruments, who were sent out to establish glee clubs and the like. Instead it was proposed that he join the recreation project, which generally organized classes in embroidery, weaving, woodworking, pottery, basket-weaving, first aid or swimming; the aim was "employment of semi-skilled, skilled and professional workers to provide leadership in leisure-time pursuits for children and adults as amateur participants." Cage was a fairly typical recruit; only about one percent of staff could be classed as professional recreationists, but nearly eighty-five percent were high-school educated, and more than forty percent had spent a year or more at college.

Cage worked in hospitals and community centers. His first assignment was to entertain the children of visitors to a hospital in San Francisco. That may have first suggested *4'33"*, he claims. "I was not allowed to make any sound ... for fear that it would disturb the patients. So I thought up games involving movement around the rooms and counting ... dealing with some kind of rhythm in space."

He worked with black and Italian children. In a Catholic school after hours he taught Chinese children in a class at which attendance was voluntary. "I got along best with the Chinese because I'm very permissive and the Chinese are highly organized," as Cage recalled the paradox. He set up sound-sources such as flowerpots and invited the children to improvise. They all made the same gesture, as if they were choking themselves; they did not know how to enjoy this freedom. Cage wondered if they would act differently without him, so he went to the other end of the room – it was long – and feigned attention to the blinds. "Before I knew it, I was hearing music," he remembers, "and gradually they were playing beautiful things."

The class folded because, as his young charges told him, Cage was not teaching them anything about counterpoint. What happened, and the way Cage recounts it, are both typical of the first half of his career. Cage reflected years later, "I think the teachers in the real school had thought that my work with them was not in the right direction."

Cage wrote the *Living Room Music* while in San Francisco in 1940, for four performers who played any household objects, furniture, or parts of the architecture. The pitch range gradually drops from the first to the fourth player: the first three use the three middle fingers of both hands, the fourth uses fists. The piece is written in four movements, "To Begin," "Story," "Melody" and "End." The text of the "Story" comes from Gertrude Stein – "once upon a time the world was round and you could go on it around and around" – set to busy sixteenth note rhythms in a structure of seven by seven measures. The "Melody," written with sharps only as accidentals (he had tended to use flats), may be played on any suitable instrument. The simplicity of the piece evokes the music he wrote for the bookbinders; it parallels the *Furniture Music* of Satie, though it is not clear whether Cage knew of it at this time.

Beginning on January 29, 1941, Cage taught an extension course in percussion at Mills College: fifteen meetings for twelve dollars, every Wednesday from four to five. The course, the prospectus notes, involved "systematic examination of new sound materials," with "particular emphasis on sound in relation to the modern dance."

III

The work of Cage at this time has often been seen as aligned with that of a West Coast Group or Californian Percussion School alongside Cowell, Harrison, William Russell, the early investigator of microtonal scales Harry Partch, and later Alan Hovhaness. Early in 1941 Cage and Harrison together organized a concert at the California Club in San Francisco, and decided jointly to write a percussion piece, using Cage's rhythmic structure as the unifying feature. They agreed on a six-minute duration and divided it into specific numbers of eighth notes, grouped in measures of $^4_4$ for convenience, at a given metronome mark; and they opted for metal instruments including a water gong and Japanese temple gongs, which can be played by friction on the edge, rather like playing a wine glass. Recognizing that the emergence of the sound is rather unpredictable, they suggest "the tone may begin earlier than notated." Instruments may be substituted provided – as Cage ruled for *Living Room Music* – the high-to-low stepping of the four parts remains clear. Cage wrote parts for the first and third voices, Harrison for the others; Harrison's parts were composed in groups of nine-and-a-half measures, and those of Cage were set against his scheme, with the third voice written in sections of seven and fourteen measures, and the first voice a freely written solo.

The score is dated April. It was the first time Cage had collaborated on composition, normally the provenance of the solitary artist – notwithstanding most of the arrangements being made by telephone – and, as he said years later, "I have always been fond of working in a team." He added, anachronistically with regard to *Double Music*, "the more egos you have, the better chance you have of eliminating the ego altogether." Between March and April 1941 Cage also worked on the *Third Construction*, dedicated to Xenia for their wedding anniversary.

Cage and Harrison also cooperated on a recording of the latter's *Third Symphony*, having chosen the work by audience poll at their public concerts. They advertised it as the first recording of music of organized sound; Cage had recently found the term in an article by Varèse in *Commonweal* and used it in preference to his own "organization of sound" simply for its conciseness. When they sent an advance copy of the disc to Varèse, he responded with a telegram asking them not to use his phrase. Cage and Harrison could only apologize, since the recording was already released.

From May 18, until June 1, Cage was again enrolled on the Recreation

Project, teaching for the University of California Extension Division at the Pomo Trail Camp for Recreation Counsellors in Mendocino County. In July he returned to Mills, where he met Virgil Thomson; it was their first encounter, although Thomson, living in Paris at the time, had received one of the letters sent out by Cage in search of new percussion music after his first Seattle concert.

Cage also became reacquainted with Moholy-Nagy, setting up a course in collaboration with him. He invited Cage to teach a class in experimental music at the Chicago School of Design. It seemed to offer, if not much of a salary, new opportunities – there was at least a whiff of Cage's plan for a center for experimental music – and the Cages moved to Chicago over the summer of 1941, renting an apartment at 323 West Cermak near Chinatown.

The School was very much a transplanted Bauhaus. The rise of Hitler had driven not only musicians such as Schoenberg into the arms of America, but visual artists too. As well as Moholy-Nagy, the faculty included Mies van der Rohe, and Josef Albers, who taught color and design; Albers' wife gave classes in weaving. Guest artists from across America visited; in Cage's first year there, Harry Partch passed through, presenting a "tone declamation" of his *Chinese Poem*, and the *Hitch-hikers' Ballad*, which use his forty-three-tone scale, and Mark Tobey came from Seattle to teach, and criticize, painting.

Cage's course profile promises "exploration and use of new sound materials; investigation of manual, vocal, mechanical, electrical and film means for the production of sound; sound in the theater, dance, drama, and the film; group improvisation; creative musical expression; rehearsal and performance of experimental music; the orchestra." The class presented its first group improvisation, conducted by Cage, on November 18. The amount of noise created by his classes led to a number of complaints.

Cage also worked at the University of Chicago as accompanist to dance classes by Katherine Manning, and wrote music for dances by Gertrude Lippincott. Since the *Third Construction* and *Double Music*, Cage had shown a proclivity for found and invented instruments. Wishing to experiment with the sound of metal pipes, he went to the nearest junkyard. After burrowing around for a while, the junkman asked him why he wanted the pipes. He replied that he was going to use them for music. As if stating the obvious, the junkman rejoined, "In that case, I suggest you go to a plumbing shop."

At one of the Chicago radio stations Cage prepared a second and third *Imaginary Landscape*. There is also mention in 1942 of a fourth *Construction*, which may never have been finished. *Imaginary Landscape No. 2* uses tin cans, as did the *Third Construction*, and a coil of wire amplified via a gramophone cartridge. The third calls for a much more ambitious range of electrical resources: a battery-powered buzzer, a radio coil attached to a cartridge, an audio-frequency oscillator, and three variable-speed turntables of the type he had used in Seattle, playing in this case constant frequency recordings on two of them and a recording of a generator whine on another, plus a marimbula fitted with a primitive contact microphone. Cage asks that the loudspeakers be placed so that the orchestral sound is localized (he would seek the opposite effect in later years). The increased use of electrical instruments further showed the limits of traditional notation, already suggested by the Japanese temple gongs of *Double Music,* since it was difficult to mark the start, progress and finish of the sound.

Imaginary Landscape No. 3 was premiered at the Chicago Arts Club on March 3, 1942, with the new percussion orchestra consisting of Xenia, Manning, Brabazon Lindsey, Marjorie Parkin and Stuart Lloyd.

The work of Cage up to this time attracted both criticism and praise. One line taken by detractors was that performance of the music needed no skill, the implication being that it was thereby invalidated. "It doesn't take much skill to smash a beer bottle with a mighty heave," said the reporter from the *San Francisco Chronicle* back in 1939, referring to the Cage Players' performance of a William Russell piece. "It does take a lot of skill to play the timpani, which were not in evidence." Other critics suggested that it had all been done before and was thus not interesting. "I can only say," said Cecil Smith of the *Chicago Daily Tribune*, "that we went thru all this once before in this (sic) 1920s, when George Antheil and Edgar (sic) Varèse were at work, and I suppose we can go thru it again."

Interest in the work of Cage mostly came from artistically literate members of the public. He began to receive letters asking for advice on setting up percussion bands, some of which were followed up. Positive comments in the media mostly took the form of recognition of this attention. The *Chicago Sun* called percussion concerts the "newest rage among the musical intelligentsia," and after the Arts Club concert, the *American Magazine* contacted Cage and featured him in their "Interesting People" column.

Cage continued to spend many hours preparing letters seeking support for a center for experimental music. On the back of his inventory of percussion instruments he scribbled one night, "Composers interested in electrical: Jacob Weinberg, Henry Brant, Paul Bowles, William Schumann (sic)." He wrote to movie studios, universities, foundations, laboratories and assorted tycoons. Carl Seashore at the University of Iowa – who was conducting path-breaking work in the psychology of music – expressed a great interest but, like Moholy-Nagy and Reinhardt, he could only offer the center a home, not financial support.

IV

During the preparation of the Arts Club concert Cage had met numerous influential locals, and he liaised with Urban Johnson of CBS Radio, whose offices were in the same building as the Club, for the loan of electrical equipment. This encouraged Cage to approach Davidson Taylor at CBS in New York to ask if he might write music for one of their Columbia Workshop radio plays. His own hope, he explained, was to explore the raising of sound effects to the level of music.

Taylor was interested and asked Cage if he had a scriptwriter in mind. The name which sprang casually to mind was Henry Miller, an interesting choice, so Cage was authorized to offer him the commission. Miller suggested adapting one of his books and recommended that Cage read them; since they were classified as pornographic, he had to write a letter of introduction to enable Cage to extract them from the stacks of the New York Public Library. Cage did not feel any of them would furnish good material for radio, and asked Miller to write something especially for the program. When Miller refused, Cage contacted his second choice, Kenneth Patchen, whose *Journal of Albion Moonlight* he had read with relish. Patchen accepted, producing *The City Wears a Slouch Hat*, a not quite naturalistic, meandering chronicle of "The Voice," a mysterious, Messianic male figure who drifts across an unnamed city encountering different people and situations.

With a deadline finalized for the recording, Cage wanted to work out the most efficient way of composing. As a first step, he asked the CBS sound effects engineer which sounds he could use for the piece, and was told that anything was possible. Cage spent hours cruising downtown on the El, closing his eyes, listening, dreaming up textures, which he wrote down using words and sometimes musical notation. "I wanted to produce a musical continuity," he explained later, "which would also be directly linked to the subject of the text by means of the naturalistic character of the sounds used."

He returned to the studio with a 250-page schema for an hour's music, for which he had allowed just under a week for recording. The effects engineer told him that while the score was technically feasible it was practically impossible, because of the expense. Cage then had four days in which to write a new hour of music; he stayed up day and night, with only the occasional nap. He resorted to the percussion and electrical instruments to which he was accustomed. Xenia copied as he wrote, and the players stood by to begin rehearsals section by section. *The City Wears a Slouch Hat* went out nationally according to schedule.

After the broadcast, Cage received a large number of enthusiastic letters from the West and Middle-West. He and Xenia had recently met Max Ernst when Ernst visited Chicago; he had only arrived in the United States in 1941, where he would remain until 1953. Ernst had been born in 1891 at Bruhl, near Cologne. He rejected the traditional view of art exemplified by his father, a leisure-time painter who once left a tree out of a representational image because it disturbed the painting, and then chopped down the tree so the painting was accurate. Ernst began to paint hallucinatory images which came to his mind from close attention to tiny details of existing visual fields such as floorboards (he later described his favorite occupation as "looking"). Ernst's painting from the end of 1922, *Le Rendezvous des Amis*, shows his company at that time: Jean Arp, Paul Eluard, Luis Aragon, André Breton and Giorgio de Chirico. His brand of surrealism, with frequent religious undertones, was widely lauded (Ernö Goldfinger bought one of his works in the mid-thirties).

Ernst issued an open invitation to the Cages to stay in New York in the apartment he shared with Peggy Guggenheim. Guggenheim was planning to open her gallery, Art of this Century, on West 57th Street, and proposed that Cage direct a concert of percussion music to celebrate the opening; in return she would pay the fees for the transportation of the instruments from Chicago. Xenia had recently inherited a small amount of money and so, says Cage, retrospectively invoking his *naïveté*, the couple decided, "We would come to New York and make our fortune."

V

They left Chicago in the spring of 1942 with just enough money to pay the bus fare, arriving in New York with only twenty-five cents between them. Cage used a nickel to call Max Ernst who, upon answering, failed to recognize Cage's voice. At last he asked if Cage was thirsty and, hearing that he was, suggested that he come round for cocktails, and promptly hung up. Cage returned to Xenia and recounted the exchange. She sent him back with another nickel, pointing out that they had everything to gain and nothing to lose. "Oh, it's you," exclaimed Ernst. "We've been waiting for you for weeks. Your room's ready. Come right over."

Cage found New York extremely stimulating – not just the general bustle of the city but, at this time, the people he was able to meet. It was one of the principal places of refuge for artists fleeing the Nazis, making it suddenly as "brilliant" as Paris had been. In a handful of evenings at Guggenheim's apartment overlooking the East River, Cage remembers, "You met an entire world of both American and European artists." Cage has been described as an inveterate name-dropper, and whether it implies a concern with self-validation or simply pleasure at a certain quality of company – a fine division in any case – his list for 1942 was impressive; apart from Virgil Thomson, with whom he was already acquainted, Cage met André Breton, Piet Mondrian and Gypsy Rose Lee. Guggenheim was already interested in Jackson Pollock, and Joseph Cornell was a frequent visitor; later Cage would be introduced to Gorky, and Matta, whom he considered brilliant. That other pioneer of abstract expressionism, Robert Motherwell (1915–91), exhibited at Art of this Century in 1943. "I was just flabbergasted by the whole situation," Cage recalled. "Somebody famous was dropping in every two minutes, it seemed."

Cage's attempts to establish his center had increased his ambition; his performances drew ever more substantial audiences. That, together with the concert planned for Art of this Century, and the richness of his company, all encouraged him to think "I might become an artist after all." His pleasure was heightened when he succeeded in arranging a percussion concert for the Museum of Modern Art as part of the twentieth birthday celebrations of the League of Composers.

Then his luck changed. Soon after their arrival in New York the Cages called on Varèse and his wife Louise. It was, Cage recorded in a telling choice of words, "the first duty I felt . . . because it was his work that had preceded mine." The ladies sat at one end of the room and the gentlemen at the other, talking separately. After only a short while Xenia came over and told Cage that they must leave. As he described his thoughts later, in an interesting juxtaposition, "I knew that if she said that, we should. My father told me, 'Your mother is always right, even when she's wrong!'"

When Cage and Xenia reached the street she explained that her conversation with Louise Varèse had come round to the telegram

Varèse had sent to Harrison and Cage objecting to their use of the term "organized sound" on their record of Harrison's *Third Symphony*. "The reason we sent that telegram," Louise Varèse had said – Cage then surmised the decision had been hers – "was because we didn't want your husband's work confused with my husband's work, any more than you'd want some . . . any artist's work confused with that of a cartoonist." (When asked later how he took such a remark, Cage replied with telling evasiveness, "Well, Xenia took it as an insult.")

Martha Graham had written a letter which had given him the impression that he might become an accompanist for dance classes in her school and perhaps write music. When Cage visited her, he remembered, "It was a late afternoon, it was quite dark. She didn't turn any lights on. She seemed very mysterious and very powerful, and I was already put off." As they talked, "It turned out that she hadn't meant anything, that she didn't want me to work for her at all." Cage left unimpressed and unemployed, "somewhat liberated, I remember . . . from her kind of power."

It also emerged that fan mail for *The City Wears a Slouch Hat* had, indeed, come from the West and Midwest; the East Coast reaction turned out to be largely dismissive.

When Guggenheim learned that Cage had arranged a concert at the Museum of Modern Art, she was furious, cancelled his performance at her gallery, declined to pay for transportation of the percussion instruments, and made clear what until then had not been, that he and Xenia could only stay with her temporarily. Hearing all this, Cage burst into tears.

In the adjoining room to the rear of the apartment sat a man in a rocking chair, smoking a cigar. It was Marcel Duchamp. He asked Cage why he was crying and Cage explained. Duchamp said little in reply, "but his presence was such that I felt calmer . . . he had calmness in the face of disaster."

The Cages were penniless, with no work and no place to stay. Over the summer of 1942 they stayed with the dancer Jean Erdman and her husband, the mythologist Joseph Campbell, in their apartment in Waverley Place. Erdman was planning a program for the Bennington Summer School in collaboration with Merce Cunningham, who since his days in Seattle had studied enough dance to elide his forename. She suggested that Cage reciprocate in agreeable kind for his lodgings by writing music. He wrote *Forever and Sunsmell* for voice and percussion duo for one of her dances and, for a duo choreographed by Cunningham,

Credo in US, scored for percussion quartet with piano and record player or radio. This is the first use of sound material intentionally created by persons other than Cage incorporated into his work, and, here, dislocated in Procrustean fashion by rhythmic structure. He suggested Dvorak, Beethoven, Sibelius or Shostakovitch for the discs – especially popular classical composers of the time. The option to use radio is extremely interesting, since it supplies whatever happens to be on the air at the time; Cage would use radio a great deal in the fifties.

The arrangement with Erdman solved the accommodation problem, but the couple still had no money. "It was the first time I'd actually been at the point of not having anything, not even a nickel," Cage recalled. This is the earliest instance on record of Cage displaying a characteristic buoyancy in the face of an insuperable problem; he felt relieved, he says, and describes the strictures as if they were something positive. "I simply took the attitude that people should give me money," he said. He wrote to friends, in Chicago and elsewhere, and received around fifty dollars. John Steinbeck, whom Cage knew from California, came visiting and took the couple to the 21 Club on 52nd Street. The club was renowned and expensive; Cage was horrified to discover that at this time when he did not even have a nickel in his pocket, Steinbeck had treated them to one lunch which cost more than a hundred dollars.

By the end of the summer Cage had clawed together a handful of deals for dance music, at the rate of five dollars per minute of music. His parents were now living on Grove Street in Upper Montclair, New Jersey, and Cage took on some library work for his father. John senior was working again on submarine detection, devising the "sonobuoy," and experimenting with vision systems for airplanes in fog which led to work with radar detection and to a patent in 1946 for an "invisible ray vision system."

The involvement of Cage in the project was timely, and not only as a way to pay for the groceries. On December 7, 1941 two young soldiers in Hawaii had been practicing on a temporary radar station and detected a sky full of planes approaching from the north; Edgar Rice Burroughs, creator of Tarzan, was taking a breather outside his house in Honolulu and noticed that an extraordinarily realistic attack drill had just started down at Pearl Harbor. Within days the United States had entered the Second World War.

Since John senior's work contributed to the war effort, Cage's involvement allowed him to avoid the draft. "Had I been drafted, I would not have refused," he once stated. His central concern, typically, was with sustaining his work; he continued, "there are so many examples of people who were able to continue their work in the Army. . . . In other words," Cage explained, in one of his occasional Methodist comparisons, "I believe in the principle of Daniel in the Lion's Den, so I would not want to keep myself out of it, if I were obliged to go into it." "On the other hand," he adds, "I am glad not to have gone into it, as I have never in my life shot a gun."

Cage could thus proceed in his work with only the customary practical hindrances. In November 1942 the vocalist Janet Fairbanks asked him for a song. Three years earlier he had bought a copy of *Finnegans Wake*, but had never made time to read it in its entirety. Now he browsed its pages looking for a lyrical passage which he might set, and found the lines beginning "night by silentsailing night." In the resulting piece, *The Wonderful Widow of Eighteen Springs*, Cage eschewed all precompositional organization, including rhythmic structure. "The music," he reports, "resulted from the impression received from the text." As in *Forever and Sunsmell*, the voice part is to be sung without vibrato, and any transposition may be made to set the part comfortably low in the range. It consists, with further wilful paucity of means, of permutations of three notes, notated as A, B and E, and is accompanied by sounds of the closed piano: the body of the piano struck in four different places by fingers or knuckles.

Contrasting with the lullaby quality of the *Widow* is Cage's next work for prepared piano, *In the Name of the Holocaust*, completed on Boxing Day 1942 for a dance by Merce Cunningham. Cage's appreciation of the chaos of war, and a belief in personal relationships as its antidote, were uppermost in his mind as he wrote; there is disillusionment, if not a slight bitterness, expressed in the punning title, invoking as it does not only the holocaust but a receding Holy Ghost. *Imaginary Landscape No.3* had been intended to suggest war and devastation, and *Credo in US* had also been a wartime piece (a note concerning the use of the radio recommends that the player "avoid news programs during national or international emergencies"), "a kind of satire on America"; the "US" of *Credo* concerns not just the first person plural but also the United States, the tendency to think in nationalist terms or in terms of any external crutch. Into the New Year, Cage wrote the rather more gentle *Four Dances* for piano, percussion and wordless voice.

VI

Cage's concert at the Museum of Modern Art, 11 West 53rd Street, began at 8.45 p.m. on February 7, 1943. The players included Xenia and Cunningham. The event was highly publicized and widely reviewed, including a feature in *Life* which appeared on March 15. Naively ambitious as he was, Cage was again flushed with the feeling that his fortune would be made. "I discovered," he said in retrospect, "that no matter how well-known you are, it doesn't mean anything in terms of employment or willingness to further your work or do anything."

In the program was the *First Construction* and the *Imaginary Landscape No.1*. The sound-effects department at CBS lent electronic equipment. A new piece was included, *Amores*, consisting of two solos for prepared piano and two trios for percussion; one of the latter recycles the waltz finale of the *Trio* of 1936. The piano preparation is not elaborate, but the directions are more specific than before. Cage requires the pianist to perform without sensing he or she is playing a prepared piano, or even a piano. As he puts it, "An instrument having convincingly its own characteristics, not even suggesting those of a piano, must be the result."

Its Latin title gives no hint that *Amores* is the first piece by Cage to embody an interest in Eastern thought. He told a reporter from *Time*, "*Amores* is intended to arouse, shall we say, the feelings of love." The piece is an attempt to express the combination of the erotic and the tranquil, two of the permanent emotions of traditional Indian wisdom. If one considers the instrumentation at all allegorical, it is interesting to consider that Cage was inventor of the prepared piano and champion of percussion. *Amores* is the first piece in a line of development one might draw from 1943 to 1951, which makes Lou Harrison's review from the year after the premiere all the more fitting, as will become clear. "*Amores*," he wrote, "strikes perhaps the last note in the romantic era; it reaches a maximum of personalization in every one of its elements."

EIGHT

I

Cage could attempt to combine the erotic and the tranquil in his music and could posit intimate relationships as the repository of beauty in a world at war, but both moves were wishful thinking, divorced from the fact that Cage, exempted as he was from military service, was more at war in his own apartment.

The imminent breakup with Xenia was not only the loss of one relationship, an important one, but of a sexual orientation and an identity. The catalyst can be seen, with hindsight, as Merce Cunningham; he and Cage would become partners in the personal as well as artistic sense. Exactly what happened is not clear and not important. It is not clear because the protagonists have kept the matter private (indeed, one young speaker at a conference at Stanford University in 1992 was censured by the chairman for mentioning Cage's homosexuality "because" Cage does not). The details are not important given the aims of this book; all that is important is that a crisis of a marriage and a sexual orientation occurred, and Cage's life-decisions, work and thought need to be placed within that context.

It is possible to read in the titles of Cage's music of 1944 an allegory of this pivotal moment in his development: *The Perilous Night, Root of an Unfocus, Spontaneous Earth, The Unavailable Memory Of, Prelude for Meditation, Four Walls*. He was writing increasingly for prepared piano and no longer for percussion orchestra because in the bustle of New York "everyone was so busy with his own schedule . . . it was easier to work alone at the prepared piano than it was to organize a group of people to play percussion instruments." Cage wrote *A Valentine Out of Season* for Xenia to play on prepared piano, but the title was symbolic. In 1945 Cage and his "love at first sight" separated. By December he

84

was living on the top, sixth floor of 550 Hudson, with views of East River Drive and Grand Street; in the course of the following year he moved to chic Sutton Place, again overlooking the river. Presently the couple divorced. Xenia stayed in New York and became a museum curator.

As all this ran its course, Cage poured his confusion and his sadness into a six-movement suite for prepared piano, *The Perilous Night*, written in the winter of 1943–44. The piano is prepared, Cage said, with more than wood: "my mother had the idea that the effects would be better if I put natural things in the piano." It is a lost, sad, and rather desperate piece. The title derives from an Irish folktale he remembered from a volume of myths collected by Joseph Campbell, concerning a perilous bed which rested on a floor of polished jasper. The music tells the story of the dangers of the erotic life, the misery of "something that was together that is split apart," the "loneliness and terror that comes to one when love becomes unhappy." Lou Harrison described it at the time as "a set of whispers about some unknown plot in some other-worldly bedchamber."

The Perilous Night has proved a compelling piece, the subject of a series of paintings by Jasper Johns. The interest of Cage owes more to its emotional than its compositional investments. He remembers it much more clearly than *Four Walls*, written only months later, which lasts more than four times as long. One colleague recalls Cage talking for longer about *The Perilous Night* than he had ever heard Cage discuss a single piece of his, yet when asked about *Four Walls* Cage could remember little, saying it was "a big piano piece I wrote in the forties." After its first performance at the Perry–Mansfield workshop in Steamboat Springs, Colorado, *Four Walls* was not played (despite its only requirements being an unprepared piano and a singer), nor much mentioned, until Margaret Leng Tan revived it in 1985 and recorded it in 1990.

It is interesting not only that Cage recalls *The Perilous Night* so well but also that he remembers so little of *Four Walls*. The use of rhythmic structure and silence sets *Four Walls* in a line of technical continuity. Stylistically, and in the elusive dimension of mood, it is discontinuous; in the context of his previous and, especially, his subsequent development it is an aberration and perhaps, like Neanderthal Man, a false start, shunted into a siding and forgotten.

Four Walls uses silence as a structural resource on such a scale – up to forty-four measures of rest – that it seems fit to break its moorings and become autonomous. In rhythm and pitch the piece is simpler than anything he had written up to then; its nearest equivalent at the time was the aptly titled *Prelude for Meditation* for prepared piano, with its tiny range of sounds and rhythmic simplicity. In place of the plentiful, complex abstraction of percussion instruments and the prepared piano, and Cage's customary way of writing for them, we have the static translucence of diatonic pitches and chords in simple rhythms, sometimes reminiscent of Erik Satie, and which would feature somewhat in Cage's music later in the forties such as *Suite for Toy Piano* (1948).

From this point onward Cage sought a balance of his emotions, exercised largely in his work and thought. While from the beginning of the fifties he would seek balance in the tranquility of emptiness, in *Four Walls* he takes a parallel route, which makes it a case study of existential placement – the way what can be inferred as the same leanings can be made concrete in different ways: he seeks balance in the suspended stillness of contemplative rapture.

The piece – which has some thirteen scenes – is widely held to be, like its contemporaries, another investigation of disturbances of the mind. Insofar as this is true, the disturbance is approached differently, with an anticipatory detachment. Again, from the beginning of the fifties Cage would seek detachment through quiescence and emptiness, thus moving to transcend his emotions and inclinations, his human fire; the detachment of *Four Walls* is rapt, in that the fire has fibrillated to stillness, and so in a rather pure way is integrated. It is thus a quite different register of detachment from that developed later by Cage. It looks down as well as up.

Merce Cunningham's text for the vocal interlude of scene seven reads:

> Sweet love sweet love my throat is gurgling
> the mystic mouth leads me so defted
> my throat is gurgling the mystic mouth leads me so defted
> and the deep black nightingale turned willowy
> and the deep black nightingale turned willowy
> by love's tossed treatment berefted

Phrases are repeated as if the speaker were dazed or in a trance. The action is observed passively as it arises. "My throat is gurgling," wordless, like someone left to die; "the mystic mouth leads me so defted" – deft is not generally used as a verb, though it has an ancillary meaning of "quiet"; the nightingale, traditional romantic symbol of separation at dawn, singer, according to legend, of a plaint for the loss of its mate, is deep and black like a raven and has "turned willowy" – resembling, the dictionary tells us, "a willow in its flexibility and drooping gracefulness." It is lifeless but not sad, "berefted" – forcibly deprived (of what?) – by the casual "tossed" treatment of love. No blame: "sweet love" is the addressee.

II

Cage became so disturbed that several friends advised him strongly to undergo psychoanalysis. He went to a Jungian analyst for a preliminary consultation – why the approach of Jung attracts artists is an intriguing question. Cage described what happened as follows: "It must have been around 1945. I was disturbed . . . some friends advised me to see an analyst. All the psychoanalyst was able to tell me was that thanks to him I was going to be able to produce more music, tons of music! I never went back." Or, as he recounted the story earlier:

I was never psychoanalyzed. I'll tell you how it happened . . . When I went to the analyst for a kind of preliminary meeting, he said, "I'll be able to fix you so that you'll write much more music than you do now." I said, "Good heavens! I already write too much, it seems to me." That promise of his put me off.

It is impossible to tell from the available information whether this analyst was a crass one, concerned only with "adjustment" in the narrow sense of greater career productivity and "success"; but while it is true that Cage is immensely productive, he also comes across in all other situations as wanting to be maximally so. It seems unlikely that the possibility of completing more work would stop him returning.

"I always had a chip on my shoulder about psychoanalysis," Cage says in *Silence*. "I knew the remark of Rilke to a friend of his who wanted him to be psychoanalyzed. Rilke said, 'I'm sure they would remove my devils, but I fear they would offend my angels.'" In 1972 Cage would allude to "the things we know about Freud, which brought about the inability eventually to act at all. Guilt, shame, conscience."

The object of these reservations is Cage himself rather than psycho-analysis. If psychoanalysis works, which may unavoidably be a personal judgment, it does so by clarifying to the analysand the structures and routines which they have accumulated, and which may help or hinder the way they relate to and operate in the world. The desired result is that the self becomes lighter, freer, better able to act. It requires reflexive confrontation with oneself in the form of intense introspection. Cage declined to engage in such confrontation, perhaps because his pragmatic temperament sat uneasily with introspection, or because he did not want to confront himself for negative reasons; a "chip on my shoulder" generally refers to the quarrelsomeness which emerges from feelings of fear and inferiority. Perhaps the things he knew about himself would bring about the inability to act at all, would bring down guilt, shame and conscience, would offend his angels.

The account of this episode is of broader interest in that Cage seems to be open about everything, yet what is said does not directly let us understand what happened. We know Cage divorced and that he visited an analyst, but when Cage says "I'll tell you how it happened," he does not; in the anecdote quoted above from *Silence*, he does not mention any reason whatsoever for his abortive encounter, nor why he declined to pursue it further, and only the words which follow, "and then in the nick of time," admit any sense of crisis.

A person's shortcomings can be seen in the fissures of their account, the incongruities, irrationalities and lapses of clarity. Only the viewer's shortcomings lead to an interpretation of "shortcomings" as an evaluative rather than descriptive term. Indeed, as Cage implies elsewhere, life is a unity, so the shortcomings are part of the person; they may be a handicap, but they can define the way to success, as we shall see in the case of Cage, and if integrated can contribute positively to it.

The confusion Cage felt was not confined to his emotional life, but spread to his art. "I was disturbed," he recalls, "both in my private life and in my public life as a composer." More than at any time before or since, the works written in Chicago and New York – the pieces preoccupied with the promises of personal relationships and the horrors of a society at war, *Imaginary Landscape No.3, Credo in US, In the Name of the Holocaust* – had been intended to express and communicate his feelings and ideas. Yet expression, as he explains, was apt to be misunderstood. "I noticed that when I conscientiously wrote something sad, people and critics were often apt to laugh," he remembers. "I could not accept the academic idea that the purpose of music was communication."

At the end of this line of development came *The Perilous Night*, loaded with Cage's deepest grief and fear; but dismissed by a critic as sounding like "a woodpecker in a church belfry." "I had poured a great deal of emotion into the piece, and obviously I wasn't communicating this at all," Cage recorded. "Or else, I thought, if I *were* communicating, then all artists must be speaking a different language, and thus speaking only for themselves. The whole musical situation struck me more and more as a Tower of Babel." He says, "I determined to give up composition unless I could find a better reason for doing it than communication."

Cage was not primarily rejecting communication because of bad reviews; incomprehension by audiences and critics is an occupational hazard of art with something new to say, one which Cage became generally adept at brushing off. Impersonalism, like asceticism, was already latent in his approach to music. The avoidance of expression within this also cut a mooring from engagement with the passions.

He needed a new reason to be and to do, one which would give his life clarity and direction, answer the difficulties he had come upon in his private and professional life, and accommodate them. As with many breakthroughs in people's lives, the ingredients had already been tasted – they only needed a new relevance, an awakening, to be built on. What "performed for me the function that psychoanalysis might have performed" was spiritual thought, not in the Christian tradition of his inheritance, nor European myth such as he had found in Joseph Campbell (and which, distilled, is the world of *Four Walls*), but from Eastern thought, first visited in *Amores*.

III

Gita Sarabhai was a young woman from a wealthy Indian family who, concerned about the invidious influence of Western music on the music of her native land, had come to New York for six months to study the enemy at first hand. She met Cage, and they agreed that he would teach her contemporary music and counterpoint, and in exchange she would teach him about Indian music and the ideas and traditions behind it. Cage had a general interest in ethnic music; he had taken Cowell's courses, and in the thirties had been attracted by the rhythmic complexities of Nbudi music. "We were together almost every day," Cage recollects, "often with Lou Harrison." What struck Cage first was the similarity of his rhythmic structure to the *tala* which organizes rhythm in Indian music, although he had retained "the Western character of a beginning and an ending."

"The solution of rhythmic structure traditional to the Orient is arrived at with us just at the time that we profoundly sense our need for that other tradition of the Orient," said Cage with uncharacteristic use of the first person plural: "peace of mind, self-knowledge." He received his first intimation of the content of that other tradition when he asked Sarabhai one day what her teacher had considered to be the function of music.

He had said, she told Cage, that "the purpose of music is to sober and quiet the mind, thus making it susceptible to divine influences."

"And I believe it is true," concludes Cage. "I was tremendously struck by this. I decided then and there that this *was* the proper purpose of music."

By coincidence, fortuity, or synchronicity, Lou Harrison had been researching early English music and had stumbled on a statement by Thomas Mace, in the seventeenth century, expressing the same idea in almost identical terms. The link between art and the divine forms a slender but luminous thread throughout history, from Gregorian chant to Gospel choirs, from Dante's "art is to God like a nephew" to Tolstoy's "art arouses religious emotion." "This is the traditional reason for making music," wrote Cage, "which, since I came to know it, I have always accepted." It provided Cage with a new clarity and purpose. He made of it a reinforcement of his native reservations about expressive music. "All art before the Renaissance, both Oriental and Western, has shared this same basis, that Oriental art had continued to do so right along," and, said Cage, moving perhaps a little quickly, "the Renaissance idea of self-expressive art was more heretical."

Most importantly the notion that music has a spiritual function gave a reference point and a clarity to his compositional activities, and impetus, importance and a new agenda to his devotion. A few years later Cage opened his article "Forerunners of Modern Music" with a paragraph on the purpose of music: "Music is edifying, for from time to time it sets the soul in operation." His discovery of Eastern philosophy meant that he could refresh his intuition of spiritual experience as a spur to action, whereas Christianity had become a deadening religious institution. Sarabhai's words suggested to him that music, and later discipline in general, could function as the place in which he could work out his spiritual longings.

As with many revelations, the immediate intuitive conviction felt by Cage then had to coexist with the exploration of what the formula meant and what it leads one to do. What is a "sober" and "quiet" mind? What are "divine influences"? Over the years Cage came to believe that a sober mind is one which is equable in noisy as well as quiet environments, "as close to zero as possible," and divine influences are "all the things that happen in creation. There's nothing that isn't."

Cage's personal distress had returned him both to music and to the spiritual, and had tied the two together. His spiritual thirst led him to read widely. At about the same time as he worked with Sarabhai, he was studying the writings of Ananda Coomaraswamy, who was on the staff of the Museum of Fine Arts in Boston and author of a number of books and articles including *Am I My Brother's Keeper?* and *Spiritual Authority and Temporal Power in the Indian Government.* He gave lectures for a time at the Brooklyn Academy of Music; Cage attended them, noting a statement by Coomaraswamy that the responsibility of the artist is to imitate nature in her manner of operation.

As with Sarabhai's notion, Cage might have come to the same conclusion by some route or other earlier, but now he was receptive; likewise, while immediately convincing, the idea would take time to clarify. What is nature's "manner of operation"? Our understanding of what this means, Cage would say in 1963, changes according to advances in science. Is the word "imitation" significant, or is it nature's "manner" which is to be imitated – and her manner, not of appearance, nor of creation, but of operation?

Cage was devouring the works of the fourteenth-century mystic Meister Eckhardt. Sarabhai gave him a copy of the *Gospel* of Sri Ramakrishna. Born in a small Bengali village in the early nineteenth century, Ramakrishna moved to Calcutta at the age of sixteen. He was repulsed by its materialism. In 1855 he became a priest at Dakeshineswar Temple, where he remained for the rest of his life. Widely recognized as a holy man, he was visited by people of many faiths and backgrounds, and after his death a Ramakrishna Mission was established. Max Muller published *Ramakrishna – His Life and Sayings* in 1898; a five-volume *Gospel* of Sri Ramakrishna appeared in Bengali, consisting of sayings recorded by one of his disciples. Selections appeared in translation in 1907; a different, full translation was made in 1942, which Sarabhai gave to Cage. For Ramakrishna, religion was like a lake, to which people who are thirsty come from different directions, calling its water by different names.

IV

The study by Cage of the work of Coomaraswamy deepened his knowledge of the nine permanent emotions of Indian aesthetics. Four were white: the heroic, the erotic, the mirthful and the wondrous. Four were black: fear, anger, sorrow and disgust or "the odious." At the center, without color, was tranquility, to which the others tended. Coomeraswamy suggested that these emotions could be found codified in both East and West.

Cage sought to explore their musical correlatives, making the emotions more central and deeper than in *Amores*. The central emotion, tranquility, became his lodestar, and the way to make himself susceptible to "divine influences." "My first reaction was to express this idea as far as I could in discourse," he relates.

Cage's study of Eastern philosophy was most evident in his more ambitious compositions of the latter half of the forties. In February 1946 he began his magnum opus for prepared piano, the *Sonatas and Interludes*; he was to work on it for over two years, distressed, from time to time, by friends who wanted to hear what well-known tunes – "God Save the King" for instance – would sound like played on the prepared piano. A year later Lincoln Kirstein commissioned a ballet score from Cage, which was to be his first work for orchestra, an expression of the Indian view of the seasons: spring as creation, summer as preservation, fall as destruction and winter as quiescence. *The Seasons* is dated February 1947, and consists of a movement for every season with a prelude before each, beginning with winter and ending with fall and a recapitulation, without the repeats, of the first prelude (the only differences are attributable to copying errors). The premiere of the full ballet, with sets by Isamu Noguchi, took place on May 18.

The Seasons is a work which seriously qualifies Cage's claim that he has no feeling for harmony; while it may be strictly true that he does not use it structurally, nor in relation to a system of rules for harmonic combination, his local use – its coloristic function – is striking. "On this evidence," proposed one commentator, perhaps a little narrowly, "Cage could have been one of the supreme orchestral colourists of the mid-twentieth century." Contemporary reviewers compared the writing to Schoenberg, Ravel and Stravinsky.

The piece also serves as a landmark in Cage's inner itinerary. With a view of the purpose of music, he strove to live up to it; Eastern philosophy seemed the key. The *Sonatas and Interludes* involves both a psychological classification and a higher end. "Activity involving in a single process the many," Cage said in 1949, "turning them, even though some seem to be opposites, towards oneness contributes to a good way of life." In *The Seasons* Cage tries for size an intuition of order which arises from cyclical processes, and attempts to find a programmatic musical correlative. The result manifests much the same existential placement as *Four Walls* – impersonal but of the world – only better understood and more organized.

As we shall see, the quest for the colorless tranquility at the center would continue to be pursued by Cage through impersonal means, but not through circles or cycles. He would opt instead for a transcendental route, and would attempt to relate his thought to his work in ways quite different from the programmatic. However, the cycle of the seasons continued to interest him; the Indian interpretation would inform his *String Quartet* in 1948–49, and he considered collaborating with Allen Ginsberg on a seasons project in the fifties. From then onward, for a number of years, he had it in mind to relate the Indian theory to four of his close friends. David Tudor would be creation, spring; Jasper Johns would be preservation, summer; Merce Cunningham would be destruction, fall; Robert Rauschenberg would be quiescence, winter.

The other works by Cage through 1947 were less strenuously connected with his investigation of Eastern thought. The *Music for Marcel Duchamp* was written as accompaniment for the color animation sequence in the movie by Hans Richter, *Dreams that Money Can Buy*, using a rhythmic structure of 2/1/1/3/1/2/1 measured to fill exactly the duration of the sequence. Cage gave a course in dance in relation to music at Matty Haims' studio every Thursday from September onward and was engaged on the usual round of lecture-recitals, including a presentation on modern chromatic music in Pittsburgh on May 25. There was the occasional fillip; Woody Guthrie, the folk singer, wrote to say how much he had enjoyed Maro Ajemian's new recording of *Amores* (he first heard it at the time his son was born), and on September 4 a telegram arrived: "Wish you joy serenity and an early visit to my country, love Gita."

NINE

I

Over the summer of 1948 Cunningham and Cage canvassed a number of colleges for bookings. Cage lectured to the Outliners' Club at Carnegie Tech, Oakland, in the Bay area of California; among those present was Andy Warhola, a second-year student soon to abandon his concluding vowel. Black Mountain College in North Carolina had a burgeoning reputation for adventurousness; Robert Motherwell had taught there in 1945. Cage and Cunningham were told that the college wanted them to perform, but could only offer food and accommodation, not a fee. They accepted these terms and stayed for several days (perhaps longer) in August, between engagements in Virginia and Chicago.

Cage had enough time to complete three pieces – *Experiences No.1, In a Landscape* for piano or harp, and the *Suite for Toy Piano*. In a panel discussion, he described the aim of his music in socially progressive terms. One day, he said, a new society may slowly arise from the present "schizophrenia" through the community we have wrested for ourselves; a process that begins with music and ends with a common human nature. The highest use of music is the same as that of everything produced by man, "to integrate a man's total faculties through the order of the composition."

For many years Cage had been interested in the work of Erik Satie. The leading light of *Les Six* in Paris during the twenties, Satie was an alcoholic who wore the same seven identical gray velvet suits for seven years. He loved rain and owned many umbrellas; the moment rain started, he wanted to walk outdoors. In the largely Germanic environment at Black Mountain, Satie was virtually unknown, and since Cage had few teaching commitments, he arranged a festival of Satie's music. Half-hour concerts with introductory talks were given

94

after dinner; Cage persuaded the college authorities that they would publish the lectures at the end of the summer. The main performance of the festival, on August 14, was Satie's theater piece *Le Piège de Méduse* with a future all-star cast. Cage played piano, the text was translated by Mary Caroline Richards, decor was by Willem and Elaine de Kooning. Cunningham played Jonas, "a costly mechanical donkey," and Elaine de Kooning played Frisetta, the daughter of Baron Medusa, who was played by the architect Buckminster Fuller.

That summer Fuller erected the first of the domes which would make his name. It immediately collapsed. "He was delighted," recounts Cage. His remark, "I only learn what to do when I have failures," brought John senior to mind.

Cage pursued tranquility through austerity in his music. The five movements of the *Suite for Toy Piano* used nine different pitches in the Phrygian mode. The simplicity with a modal feel of *In a Landscape* is reminiscent of Satie. Cage perhaps identified with the Frenchman. Consider, for instance, how a letter he wrote a couple of years later could apply to himself as well as to Satie: "He knew in his loneliness and in his courage where his center was: in himself and in his nature of loving music . . . he was unexceptionally the art's most serious servant." In his keynote lecture Cage propounded the idea that a then little-known programmatic orchestral piece by Satie, *Socrate*, utilized a type of rhythmic structure akin to his own; he also claimed to find it at work in the music of Schoenberg's pupil Anton Webern, which he had first heard on Lou Harrison's recommendation. Webern was in no position to argue, having been shot dead by a U.S. Military Policeman a few months after the end of the war in Europe. With his structure, Cage suggested, Satie could break with the customary grounding of structure in harmony, responsibility for which Cage laid at the door of Beethoven.

Cage's polemic teetered on the edge of universalizing his own practical and aesthetic predilections, or the exigencies of a particular phase in the development of music:

With Beethoven the parts of a composition were defined by means of harmony. With Satie and Webern they were defined by means of time-lengths. The question of structure is so basic, and it is so important to be in agreement about it, that we must now ask: Was Beethoven right, or are Webern and Satie right? I answer immediately and unequivocably, Beethoven was in error, and his influence, which has been as extensive as it is lamentable, had been deadening to the art of music.

Many members of the Black Mountain faculty were outraged, and the plan to publish the Satie lectures was dropped.

The overall reception for Cage and Cunningham at the college was excellent. There were many parties, and Cage met one of Black Mountain's painting students, Robert Rauschenberg. Born in 1925, Rauschenberg had recently returned from the Académie Julien in Paris; he was a rather naive and shy young man for whom painting was "the best way I found to get along with myself." As with many friends, Cage found that he and Rauschenberg shared the same perspective on many topics, yet for different reasons. Art for Rauschenberg was "a means to function thoroughly and passionately in a world that has a lot more in it than paint." "I do something that resembles the lack of order I see," he once said. "I feel very sorry for people who think things like soup cans or mirrors or coke bottles are ugly, because they're surrounded by things like that all day, and it must make them miserable." The only good work of art, he held, is the one which changes one's mind. If it does not, it is either not good art or it is not being looked at clearly.

Though on such points Rauschenberg and Cage would wholly concur, the former could also change Cage's mind, enabling him to enjoy representational art, for instance, which he had avoided for over a decade. "It was marvelous when I first met Rauschenberg," he recounted. "Almost immediately I had the feeling that it was hardly necessary for us to talk, we had so many points in common. To each of the works he showed me, I responded on the spot. No communication between us – we were born accomplices!" How far the agreements and similarities between people are derived from cold rationality and how far from vaguer levels such as temperament is an engrossing question (one may intensely dislike people who nevertheless agree with one completely).

Cage and Cunningham had not used their car during their stay at Black Mountain; backing away to leave, they discovered that underneath it was a welter of paintings, drawings and food which the students and staff had deposited in lieu of payment.

II

Back in New York, Dmitri Mitropulous presented the *Five Pieces for Orchestra* by Schoenberg (opus 16, 1909) on October 22 (Rauschenberg's birthday). Cage went along with Cowell and was entranced.

The *Sonatas and Interludes* had been finished in March 1948. They were not written sequentially; the sixth sonata was the last to be written. On January 11, 1949 the sixteen sonatas and four interludes were premiered by Maro Ajemian – a virtuoso, recipient of a New York Music Week gold medal at the age of six, and subsequently the youngest person ever to be admitted to the Julliard School. Among those in the audience were Conlon Nancarrow, composer of music for the player piano, who attended at the suggestion of Minna Lederman, and Burgess Meredith, who subsequently had the double honor of commissioning a dance score from Varèse and playing opposite Adam West in *Batman*. The work was published later that year in a special edition of *New Music*.

If the designation "sonata" means anything here, it is in an eighteenth-century rather than a Romantic sense. Cage wrote, "The first eight, the twelfth and the last sonatas were written in AABB rhythmic structures of varying proportions whereas the first two interludes have no structural repetitions. The difference is exchanged in the last two interludes and the sonatas nine through eleven which have respectively a prelude, interlude and postlude." Sonatas XIV and XV possess the same internal proportions, the same tempo, and a number of shared motifs. They are named as a pair, Gemini, with an added reference intended to a work by the sculptor Richard Lippold. In his show at the Willard Gallery in April and May of 1948, Lippold had dedicated his *Five Variations Within a Sphere* to Cage; his wife Louise studied with Cunningham.

The role of rhythmic structure, its relation to content, and its usefulness, were changing. The music of the early thirties actively engages and delineates the structure through *ostinati* and dynamic configurations. Later in the forties notes fill in time but do not engage and thus do not delineate the structure. Cage explores the possibility that simply to make a sound within a structure would articulate the latter. The *Sonatas and Interludes* make, as Virgil Thomson observed, "constant use of the pause as a time element in composition."

It was just beginning to occur to Cage that the way to tranquility might lie through purposefulness; as his ideas changed, his outdated tools became clumsy. The way he was using rhythmic structure made it extraneously academic; the structure was insufficiently attached to the material he wrote to be, to his way of thinking, sustainable. At times Cage seems to set up a rhythmic structure only to ignore it altogether. The *Music for Marcel Duchamp* is structured according to Cage, and according to the divisions of the score, into cycles of eleven measures. Yet it ends with seven iterations of four measures in $^5_4$ time – the four measures consist mostly of eighth notes phrased in threes which thus cross the bar – played in a slow tempo. This bears no relation, neither audibly nor visibly on the page, to the official structure.

The *Sonatas and Interludes* also marked a change in Cage's attitude to writing for the prepared piano and in the lessons he drew from it. As Paul Griffiths has suggested, Cage was very near to producing a masterpiece, a dangerously sclerozed finality from which he backed away. The elaborate preparations, of forty-five keys, required two to three hours to effect, and the instructions were more specific than ever before. Cage's concentration on the prepared piano had avoided the difficulties of organizing a percussion orchestra but had made it, if anything, harder for his music to be performed: an evening of his pieces might need half a dozen pianos if long breaks were to be obviated, and it was all too easy to prepare the instrument clumsily, so that Cage would personally prepare the piano, sometimes taking upward of ten hours, even for concerts by those such as William Masselos and Maro Ajemian who knew him and his music well.

At another level, his experience of writing for the prepared piano, and his involvement with Eastern philosophy, deepened and grew; he began to notice the fragility of his preparation instructions. Cage had developed a manner of composing for the prepared piano which he dubbed "considered improvisation," trying out preparations on his Steinway "as one chooses shells while walking along a beach." When he felt satisfied with the array of preparations he would measure them with a wooden ruler and note the result with a meticulousness which increased with the years. He kept spare screws and bolts in different envelopes which he stored in a tin box; and with a view to replicability he began to make boxed sets of preparation materials for specific pieces. Yet the more precise his instructions became, the more Cage realized that one preparation would affect no two pianos in the same way, because each is unique. The strings on different pianos are of different lengths and types, and the position of the bridge slightly differs. Even the smallest movement of a preparation will suppress and heighten quite different harmonics, and certain objects, such as screws, with their tapering diameter, produce very different sounds depending on how deeply they are inserted. As one practitioner has put it, one has to use one's ears and adjust as necessary, seeking to augment the note and color it but not to obliterate it and to retain a semblance of pitch.

III

Early in 1949 the National Institute of Arts and Letters awarded Cage a thousand dollars, which he used in the spring to travel to Paris. He rented an apartment at 31 rue Saint Louis, just east of Notre Dame on the Ile Saint Louis. In April he visited Palermo in Italy and reviewed for a New York paper a performance of Schoenberg's *Pierrot Lunaire* sung by the seventy-four-year-old Marya Freund.

Cage carried out research on Satie. He came across a three-piece suite of *Furniture Music*. He studied notebooks which contained, sprinkled among the margins, clusters of numbers, which apparently vindicated his conviction that Satie composed using rhythmic structures similar to his own. He breathlessly related this exciting discovery to the composer Darius Milhaud, who had known Satie well. "Oh no," Milhaud corrected. "Those numbers referred to shopping lists."

Henri Sauguet lent Cage a single sheet of manuscript with the title *Vexations*. The piece consists of a short theme, eleven eighth notes long, first played monodically, then with the addition of chords. Above these two systems Satie elegantly inscribed the instruction "to be played eight hundred and forty times" – after, he required, the performer had put himself into a state of "interior immobility."

Most people who heard of the piece thought it was a joke; that was how they interpreted many of Satie's other titles and directions, *Eight Pieces in the Form of a Pear*, *Seven Preludes for a Shaggy Dog*, "like a nightingale with toothache." Cage found Satie's absurdity attractive, but equally felt it contained essentially serious thought. He saw *Vexations* into print in a review entitled *Contrepoints* and kept a photostat himself with the idea of mounting a performance.

Virgil Thomson had suggested that Cage contact two young French composers, Serge Nigg and Pierre Boulez. The work of Nigg turned out to be of no interest to him, but he was enormously impressed by that of Boulez. Soon after his arrival, Cage took a short walk to 4 rue Beautreillis; he left scores and records with a covering note for Boulez, who presently appeared at Cage's door with the items in his hand. When Boulez played his *Deuxième Sonate* for piano to Cage, the latter felt himself "trembling in the face of great complexity," the kind of power he had felt in Webern's music. "I couldn't help but be stupefied by its activism," he remembers, "by the sum of the activities inherent in it." Cage played the *Sonatas and Interludes* to Boulez, and showed him some of his writings.

The circle round Boulez included the poet and dramatist Armand Gatti; Pierre Joffroy, journalist and subsequently author of a book about a "Christian" SS man; an elder contemporary, Pierre Souvchinsky; and Bernard Saby, summed up by Boulez as an "expert in Chinese culture, butterflies and moss." Boulez introduced Cage to other adventurous composers around Paris, including Pierre Schaeffer. The greatest gift to music of the Second World War had been magnetic tape as a medium for sound recording, and Schaeffer had just begun to compose using electronically modified recorded natural sounds, a technique he called *musique concrète*. Thanks to Boulez, Cage also met Messiaen, and at his invitation demonstrated the prepared piano to a class at the Conservatoire.

Cage routinely went to collect his mail from the American Express office in Paris; one day he found a letter from the Guggenheim Foundation advising him, his sins forgiven, that he had been awarded a fellowship. The short span of financial security this offered, so close on the heels of the money from the National Institute, let him feel free to begin work on a string quartet. The Guggenheim Fellowship is all the more striking, and reveals a new turn in artistic funding, when one considers that in January 1945 Schoenberg had requested a grant – with the specific aim of facilitating completion of *Die Jakobsleiter, Moses und Aron* and three textbooks – which had been refused.

In June Cunningham visited Paris to perform. He and Cage chanced to meet two members of the Ballet Society, Tanaquil le Clerq and Betty Nicholls, in a patisserie. Both wanted to dance; Cunningham added a trio, and a duet with le Clerq, to the program. They appeared, accompanied by Cage, at the studio of Jean Helion at 15 rue de l'Observatoire, in the sixth arrondissement. Alice B. Toklas, the friend of Gertrude Stein, was present, and successfully demanded a chair. The rest of the audience stood. "It was savage," she said later of the dance. The four performed again to great success at the Vieux Colombier.

In mid-June, with the collaboration of Pierre Souvchinsky and Suzanne Tezenas, Boulez arranged for Cage to play *Sonatas and Interludes* in a private performance for an invited audience of a hundred. On the night of the concert Cunningham lay resting on the floor between foyer and living room. Boulez introduced Cage with a careful lecture in which he stressed the respectable Schoenbergian credentials of his friend.

Cage, better connected than Boulez even in a foreign land, pressed Amphion and Heugel, two of the leading music publishers in France, to publish the work of his friend. In the late summer he succeeded on the eve of his return home, and a combined farewell and celebration party took place at Armand Gatti's house.

Cage returned to New York, bearing *Vexations*, the *Furniture Music*, Boulez's *Sonate*, the first pages of the *String Quartet*, and some fine Chinese paper for Lou Harrison.

While they were together in Paris, Cage and Cunningham had talked seriously of the latter founding a dance company of his own. They continued in the meantime with their collaboration, occasionally augmented by other dancers, with a repertoire based largely on the prepared piano pieces they had used for some time, such as *Root of an Unfocus, Tossed as it is Untroubled, The Unavailable Memory of, Mysterious Adventure, Spontaneous Earth, Totem Ancestor*, the *Experiences*, even *Amores* and *A Valentine Out of Season*. Their collaboration was premised on a quite different relation than Martha Graham's totalitarian domination of the music by the dance, preferring to make music, as Cage had proposed some time earlier, "identical with the dance, but not cooperative with it." Cage, *Dance* magazine had recently informed its readers, "now maintains that dance and music should complement each other and still be able to stand each by itself." It was a principle Cage and Cunningham would develop with great success in the coming decades; like many tendencies, it grew as an idea and a practice before Cage arrived at the system of thought in which he would most adequately, or eloquently, theorize it.

Cage attended a performance by the New York Philharmonic of Webern's *Symphonie*, opus 21. He was so overwhelmed by the piece that he left before the Rachmaninoff which followed. In the lobby he met a large man who had excused himself for the same reason. They introduced themselves; the man's name was Morton Feldman (1926–88) and he wrote music. Instantly they hit it off. Cage showed Feldman the Boulez *Deuxième Sonate*. Feldman strongly recommended that the first American performance be given by a bespectacled young pianist named David Tudor. Tudor had been born in Philadelphia in 1926 and had studied organ and theory with H. William Hawks, piano with Irma Wolpe Rademacher, and analysis and composition with Stefan Wolpe; he began his professional career as an organist. His technical ability was extraordinary; he did a great deal of preparation without touching the keyboard at all, since he knew his own reflexes completely. Later he became so proficient at playing indeterminate scores that he could, as the composer Roman Haubenstock-Ramati put it, "play the raisins in a slice of fruitcake."

The preparation through which Tudor would put himself was awesome. As soon as he received the Boulez score he learned the music – the nearest he had come to it was Stefan Wolpe's *Battle Piece* – and, the better to understand the piece, he learned French so that he could steep himself in the literature Boulez had been reading: René Char, Mallarmé and Antonin Artaud's *Le théâtre et son double*.

Cage had already arranged with the League of Composers that William Masselos would premiere the work. On visiting Masselos, Cage discovered he had not been able to learn it and would not be at all offended if Tudor were to take over the task. Thus it was Tudor who on December 17, 1950 presented the American premiere of the *Deuxième Sonate*.

In the meantime Tudor had learned some piano pieces by Cage, and on November 11 he accompanied Cunningham's newly inaugurated dance company. Association with Tudor was one of the practical keys to the success of Cage in the fifties in that it provided a collaborator with a sympathetic mind, dedication and virtuosity. The ways he learned to bring Cage's music to reality – such as his use of a stopwatch to pace out complex rhythms – came in turn to influence the writing. Tudor in effect became not just a pianist but an instrument in his own right for whom Cage, Feldman and many others would write.

IV

Cage's current apartment stood on the corner of Grand Street and Monroe in the shadow of the Williamsburg Bridge; its occupants named it the Bozza mansion after its landlord. His neighbors included the Lippolds and the painter Ray Johnson. The hearse which Richard Lippold drove would be pressed into service as transportation for instruments. Lippold redesigned the top floor of the tenement for Cage, hacking out a large white loft with seven high windows; it was sparsely furnished, with a grand piano, a few cushions for seating and cocoa matting underfoot. "An old shoe," in the words of Isamu Noguchi, designer for *The Seasons*, "would look beautiful in this room."

It was there that Cage presented small private concerts; his apartment became a magnet for painters, writers and young musicians, and *Harper's Bazaar* and *Vogue* sent models there to be photographed, which if nothing else helped to pay the rent. From the start Cage was presented as ringleader of the scene. "He's built up a group of young composers who hang on his word," wrote Henry Cowell.

Cage, Tudor and Feldman met in the loft almost every day; presently Feldman moved into the building. It seemed attitudes were changing daily. In the midst of a long conversation one evening Feldman left the room, returning with a composition on graph paper, notated on three levels representing high, middle and low sounds divided by a regular measurement of time, with numerals on the different levels specifying the number of sounds to be made in the specified register. Cage and Boulez were maintaining a lively correspondence, pooling their newest ideas and discoveries; Tudor and Cage together deciphered the letters as they arrived from Paris. Cowell, Virgil Thomson and Cage were also seeing one another, and between them produced the *Party Pieces*. Each took a turn at writing the music, seeing only the final measure written by his predecessor; he would continue from there for a number of measures, then pass it on to the next in the circle. Cage wrote to Boulez, "We all wish either that you were here in New York or we were all with you in Paris. It would be a marvelous life."

Cage discussed his latest aesthetic and philosophical ideas in his *Lecture on Nothing*, a text written using the rhythmic structure of his music. Many of his friends found the newest trends in his thought disturbing; one stormed out of a declamation of the *Lecture*, crying, "John, I dearly love you, but I can't stand this a minute longer." For the discussion afterwards, Cage prepared six irrelevant answers which he selected by throwing a die; in one, he alluded to the concert he had reviewed in Europe, replying, "Had you heard Marya Freund last April in Palermo singing Arnold Schoenberg's *Pierrot Lunaire*, I doubt whether you would ask that question."

He was still working on the *String Quartet* begun in Paris and in April 1950 he used the same technique to produce *Six Melodies for Violin and Keyboard*, "little scraps of ideas that were left over from the *String Quartet*." *A Flower*, for voice and closed piano, dated June, uses a double rhythmical structure, seven by seven measures of 5_4 time divided 1/3/1/2, superimposed on five by five measures of 10_4 divided $1_2/11_2/1_2/1/11_2$, a further refinement which suggests, as Paul Griffiths proposes, "that the old proportional principle had reached its period of decadence." In its audible result the piece is reminiscent of work from the forties such as *The Wonderful Widow*. Cage was also thinking of an opera, the instrumentation of which would include the prepared piano, based on the story of Mila Repa, a "Tibetan saint" who took the form of a thistle and floated over the landscape. He planned to employ the prepared piano, but the book which included the story had been borrowed from the library. By the time it was returned the idea of operatic narrative no longer interested Cage.

That summer Cage completed the *String Quartet in Four Parts*, and it was performed on August 12, 1950 at Black Mountain College. The *String Quartet* is a step further on from the *Sonatas and Interludes*, from *A Flower*, from his idea for *Mila Repa*; it is a successful still from the moment when Cage is moving without knowing to where. Its rhythmic structure is an unvarying $2^1{}_2/1^1{}_2/2/5/6/5^1{}_2/1^1{}_2$. Cage employs what he called gamut technique, which he had abstracted from his experience with the prepared piano. When a single key is depressed, some preparations would result in the production of two or more pitches. In the *String Quartet* the pitches which may accompany a given melody note are likewise kept constant. Pieces could thus be constructed from single pitches and from combinations determined by the course of the melody. As a theory it may seem a rather clumsy workshop extrapolation, taking a practice and using it to make up rules which are arbitrary because they are employed in a situation of no real similarity; but Cage produces fine aural results. On the other hand, it limits the moment by moment harmony of the piece. A fixed set of chords is established which is not to be transposed. This is evident in a piece for piano or harp written at the same time as the *Quartet*, *In a Landscape*.

The *Quartet*, on this principle, is like a monophonic melody line on a prepared piano; when more than one pitch sounds, that element of the melody line has been deemed an aggregate, as if it had a screw in it. In this way Cage treats each instrument as elements of a single instrument, so that the qualification of his title "in four parts" is not a tautology. The gamuts appear throughout in the same instrumentation and pitch level, though the melodic line can be heard moving through any of the separate pitches of the aggregate. The slow movement seems to open with the arpeggiation of a harmonized E-minor triad, but as composed was a succession of three aggregates, A to E, A♭ to G, F# to B♭ to B.

Cage employs the gamut technique in the *String Quartet* with great austerity and rhythmic simplicity. It would be difficult, accordingly, to romanticize the work in performance; it is to be played without vibrato, using the same string for any one note.

The work's simplicity is again reminiscent of Satie, and there is a further stage in the abandonment of self-expression, but what these tendencies embody was changing; increasingly for Cage, austerity was centrally concerned with the cooling out of his passions. This in turn interrelates with his study of mystical thought. *Forerunners of Modern Music*, published in March 1949, had quoted Eckhart to the effect that "a person cannot be more than single in attention," which would not be the view of Cage in later years. Like the *Sonatas and Interludes*, the *String Quartet* is "about" the Indian notion of the nine permanent emotions with tranquility at the center. Like *The Seasons*, it is "about" the Indian notion of the seasons, creation, preservation, destruction and quiescence, and likewise moves beyond the whirl of individual passions on to a global, cyclical plane while remaining of the world, in a similar existential placement to *Four Walls*.

The tempo descriptions suggest the move toward stillness. "Quietly flowing along" is followed by "Slowly rocking." The austerity is at its most crystalline in the slow third movement, marked "nearly stationary." Chords recur, on one or other of the two minim beats of each measure. The idea of oneness is expressed by a tendency toward a single central sound. The movement employs a canon for a single line; the pitches of the second half of the movement are the retrograde of the first. This was a complex exercise compositionally. Since the rhythmic structure is not a palindrome, it took some juggling to fit in the retrograde.

What Cage was attempting by the inclusion of this strict retrograde was not only economy. In an important step, he was extending his ascetic preoccupations to meet the Eastern philosophical concern with the abandonment of the will. He had joked with the idea in the blindness of the *Party Pieces* with Cowell and Thomson; now he was taking the renunciation with, perhaps rather Western, literariness. Thanks to Joseph Campbell, Cage had recently come upon an Irish folktale. As he retells it:

An Irish hero whose mother had died was required by his stepmother to set out on a journey to an island beneath the sea and to bring back some golden apples he would find there. Should he fail to return within a year, he would lose his right to the throne, relinquishing it to one of his stepbrothers. For his journey he was given a miserable shaggy nag. No sooner had he set out than the nag said, "Look in my ear. You will find a metal ball. Throw it on the path ahead of us and we will follow it wherever it goes." Unhesitatingly the prince did this, and so, proceeding by chance, they passed through many perilous situations. Finally, on the point of success, the horse said to the prince, "Now take your sword and slit my throat." The prince hesitated, but only for a moment. No sooner had he killed the horse than, lo and behold, it turned into a prince, who, except for the acquiescence of the hero, would have had to remain a miserable shabby nag.

Like *Four Walls*, much could be said about this story, and its significance will be discussed later. It is relevant here as the fable with which Cage accounted for his new music; the "nearly stationary" movement is composed by "the following willy-nilly of a ball which is rolling in front of you." In the *String Quartet*, said Cage, "the inclusion there of rigidly scored conventional harmonies is a matter of taste, from which a conscious control was absent." He later suggested, in an explanation he did not use at the time, "it's a kind of music which doesn't depend on your likes and dislikes." Cage had an intuition of where his work was going, but did not yet know the legend which would let him clarify it in thought and exploit it in action.

TEN

I

In 1869 – only sixteen years after Commodore Perry sailed up the Bay of Yedo and hustled Japan into the modern world – Daisetz Teitaro Suzuki (his first name is more accurately "Daisetsu") was born in Kanazawa, a prosperous rice-growing center two hundred miles northeast of Tokyo. His father, a doctor, died when he was six; from the age of eighteen Suzuki taught a completely inept version of English in a provincial school. With the death of his mother, he was sufficiently free of financial responsibilities to attend, with the support of an elder brother, the Imperial University in Tokyo.

His university studies were sporadic; he spent much of his time studying Zen with Shaku Soyen at Engakuji in Kamakura. At the Parliament of Religions at the Chicago World's Fair in 1893, Soyen met a publisher from nearby La Salle in need of a translator. Shaku Soyen recommended his pupil. Suzuki took up the translation job and moved to Chicago in 1897, learning Sanskrit and in his spare time rendering into English, in association with Dr. Paul Carus, the *Tao te ching* by Lao Tzu. Between 1908 and 1911 he traveled and worked in Europe, then returned to Japan, where he married Beatrice Earskine Lane, whom he had met in New York much earlier.

Over the years Suzuki came to dedicate himself to bringing Zen to ordinary people, in Japan, Europe and America. Why he wanted to do this, especially in the West, is an intriguing question. "He is neither a monk nor a practicing Zen master," as a contemporary article put it. "His position is rather that of a lay theologian." The willingness of Suzuki to relate Zen to Western thinking and religion – and the fact that he wrote books, thirty in Japanese and a score in English – made many traditional Zen practitioners suspicious. His most obvious aim was humanitarian; he

107

felt Zen would assuage the restlessness and relieve the spiritual void of modern life.

After the Second World War Suzuki came to Columbia University from the University of Chicago: the Crane Plumbing Company of Illinois donated a stipend, and Homer Friess, Ryosaku Tsunoda and William Theodore de Bary in the Department of Religion gladly accepted. Suzuki lectured at Columbia a number of times, from the late forties until at least 1957, and throughout this time he taught elsewhere – for example, a spell at the University of California at Berkeley in 1951.

When teaching at Columbia he would live in Butler Hall and then, from 1953 onward, in the second-floor apartment belonging to the family of his young assistant, Mihoku Okamura. "He loves to go to the movies," revealed a contemporary review, "having a special fondness for costume dramas like Sir Laurence Olivier's *Hamlet.*" He hoarded old clothes as dusters, and small lengths of string.

Suzuki's class was unusual, since it straddled the religion and philosophy departments, and was not for undergraduates; moreover, observers were allowed to attend. Only two or three students took the course for credit, yet the chairs were filled and the overspill stood by the door – philosophy students, painters, sculptors, scientists and psychoanalysts (among them Karen Horney). The only musician generally present was John Cage.

Exactly when Cage began to attend the Suzuki lectures is unclear. Cage often mentions that he first went along in the late forties. There were clear ramifications in his music by 1951; his first written mention was in the "Juillard lecture" of 1952, which refers to a class of the previous winter, and his attendance through 1952 has been corroborated.

At first the sessions were held in the Department of Religion, in a rather low and gloomy hall with a marbled floor and big, dark-stained wooden doors. Finally Suzuki settled on the seventh floor of Philosophy Hall, under the watchful eye of a framed photograph of the pragmatist philosopher John Dewey. The classes ran from four until seven on Fridays. There were windows on two sides of the room and in the middle a large table scattered with ashtrays; chairs surrounded the table and were set around the walls. Suzuki would enter on the arm of Mihoku Okamura, carrying his books wrapped up in a shawl; after unwrapping the books, he would discourse very quietly on the philosophy of Zen, usually from a script, with clarity and manifest certainty. Occasionally he would chalk a diagram or ideogram on the board. Otherwise he would proceed in his low voice, stroking and caressing his books as he spoke.

Most of the people in attendance would take a nap at some point. As Cage described it, "Suzuki never spoke loudly. When the weather was good, the windows were open, and the airplanes leaving La Guardia flew directly overhead from time to time, drowning out whatever he had to say. He never repeated what had been said during the passage of the airplane."

Cage recalls, "You could easily ask yourself whether you had learned anything or understood anything. Understanding came later – or not at all." He remembers three lectures in particular: "While he was giving them I couldn't for the life of me figure out what he was saying. It was a week or so later, while I was walking in the woods looking for mushrooms, that it all dawned on me." The influence of Zen on each individual is a personal matter; any relation between accumulated facts, such as the establishment of causality, is their privilege. True to the spirit of Zen, Cage juxtaposes the lecture with a revelation, but does not insist on a link.

The professors of religion who attended, among them de Bary, Yampolski, Houston Smith and Ruth Fuller, seem to agree, looking back, that the classes were not exceptional and were popularizing rather than academic, "good if you were looking for a guru," as one said. Professor de Bary comments that Cage's description "captures the flavor exactly."

Cage did not come cold to the Suzuki classes; at the Cornish School at the end of the thirties he had heard Nancy Wilson Ross lecture on Zen and Dada. He subsequently read *Zen in English Literature and Oriental Classics* by R.H. Blyth, the pioneer translator of *haiku*. Then Cage came across Alan Watts, whose *Spirit of Zen* had appeared in 1939. Cage read his work, attended his lectures, and presently socialized with him in a circle that included Joseph Campbell, Jean Erdman and Ananda Coomaraswamy's widow. In the forties Watts returned to the Christian Church, becoming a chaplain to Episcopalian students at Northwestern University, just out of Chicago, and would later express reservations about Cage's apparent use of Zen, which he withdrew after reading Cage's writings.

Cage's contemplative sensitivity and susceptibility to Eastern thought were clear and strong; his first encounters with Zen were awaiting a new relevance and a new lead. The development of his emotional and philosophical life and the power of Suzuki's teaching went hand in hand. With Suzuki, Cage devoted himself to a master, just as he had with Schoenberg: "I didn't study music with just anybody; I studied with Schoenberg." Likewise, "I didn't study Zen with just anybody; I studied with Suzuki. I've always gone, insofar as I could, to the president of the company."

The teachings of Suzuki had a startling effect on Cage. He felt that they catapulted him into conceptual and emotional adulthood; that they fulfilled for him the function of psychoanalysis. Engagement with Zen provided an existential placement which was suddenly adequate to the whole range of Cage's temperamental inclinations, allowing him to clarify them in thought and exploit them in action. It becomes of central importance to an account of his life, work and thought, and will therefore be discussed at length in the rest of this chapter.

II

Historically, Zen arose as a reaction to the rigid formality of Samurai Japan where – as Cha'an Buddhism – it originated. What Cage took to was a practical, untrammeled spiritual path, which emphasized spontaneous unmediated experience. In one formulation, Zen is direct pointing at reality.

Suzuki once went to Hawaii to attend a conference on the nature of reality. The chairman asked him if he thought the table around which they sat was real. Suzuki said yes. The chairman asked him in what sense the table was real. Suzuki said, "In every sense."

The world proceeds without our permission. It will be hot or cold, rain will fall, trees rustle in the wind; our machines will make the sounds which result from the way we use them – road drills clatter, engines wheeze and grind. Zen requires humility; Christianity took on board the idea, germinal in the Enlightenment and blooming in atheistic modernism, that humans can determine the world by their minds. A radical empiricism is the key to Zen. "Each moment presents what happens," Cage states; "everything is present in the foreground."

There is no point in judging which parts of life to attend to and which to overlook. "There is no rest of life," says Cage. "Life is one." He posits, "Whether that is right or wrong is not to the point, a 'mistake' is beside the point, for once anything happens it authentically is." Talking once with another composer, Cage said that he disagreed with his colleague's comment that there was too much pain in the world. "What?" gasped the man. "Don't you think there's enough?" Cage said, "I think there's just the right amount."

"One can go with the winds, put up a sail, and accept what happens," he proposes. "We are all heroes, if we accept what comes, our inner cheerfulness undisturbed." Or again, "What is heroic is to *accept the situation in which one finds oneself.* Yes!" The way of Zen is to avoid interposing comments, judgment and memory. Look at what is happening before you decide you know what it is. In the sixties Cage stated, "I don't think we're really interested in the validity of things. We're interested in the experience of things."

"It behooves us," Cage proposes, "to see each thing directly as it is." To kick a composer and to attack his work are two distinct activities; writing music is not the same as performing it or hearing it. When in 1958 Cage was composing *Concert for Piano and Orchestra*, he would show each page of this diversely notated score to friends as he finished it. One asked what a particular page sounded like. "You're not listening to it, you're looking at it," Cage corrected.

The central focus is the present moment. "Uniqueness," records Cage, "is extremely close to being here and now"; as René Char put it, "each moment is virgin, even the repeated one – you can't repeat anything exactly – even yourself!" An event would be a repetition only, as Cage puts it, if we thought we owned it.

Suzuki spoke of unimpededness and interpenetration. "Unimpededness," as Cage defined it, "is seeing that in all of space each thing and each human being is at the center and furthermore that each one being is at the center, is the most honored one of all." "Interpenetration means that each one of those most honored ones of all is moving out in all directions, penetrating and being penetrated by every other one no matter what the time or what the space."

The well-known emblem of Tao shows how opposites interlock in a wider circle, but also how each of them contains in its eye the germ of the whole and within this the other. It is telling that even an apparent symbol of wholeness in the West – Maurits Escher's eternal staircase – only moves around itself in one paradoxical circle. Suzuki explains:

Every individual reality, besides being itself, reflects in it something of the universal, and at the same time it is itself because of other individuals. A system of perfect relationship exists among individual existences and also between individuals and universals, between particular objects and general ideas. This perfect network of mutual relations has received the technical name of interpenetration.

Luminosity for Suzuki is the best physical analogy for universal interpenetration. He notes, "the essential nature of light is to intermingle without interfering or obstructing or destroying one another. One single light reflects in itself all other lights generally and individually." The principle may be applied to our understanding of people in relation. "You and I are inherently different and complementary," wrote Cage. "Together we average as zero, that is, as eternity."

The principle of interpenetration overrides the most extreme conceptual distinctions. Opposites are correlatives or complements. Nothingness or negation, about which the English language is extremely unsubtle, has parity with, if not priority over, being. Spiritual insight, says Suzuki, is "attainable only by transcending the dualism of being and non-being." Cage touches on this in various ways. "From the beginning of man's life, he is destroyed. Nullity is a present condition," he suggests. "Every something is an echo of nothing." Nowhere is "where we are." These are statements of fact, not an occasion for nihilism; they may subsequently be celebrated. With an elegant manipulation of the shortcomings of his language, Cage proposes, "No one loses nothing because nothing is securely possessed."

Through the principle of interpenetration, radical empiricism encourages a sensitivity to paradox, one of the best pointers to the subtleties of reality. One can recognize the discrete specificity of everything; one can recognize its connection with everything else and at one level its identity. Cage quotes Thoreau, saying, "Yes and no are lies. A true answer will not aim to establish anything, but rather to set all well afloat"; we would do well to consider yes *and* no, not either/or. Suzuki was once discussing the principle of Yu, a not-knowing which can never become a knowing. "Toward the end he laughed gently, without expressing any accomplishment," recalled Cage, "then said, 'Isn't it funny? I come all the way from Japan to explain something to you which of its nature is not to be explained?'"

William Duckworth once pointed out to Cage how contradictory it was to object to recorded music (as we shall see he does) but, because people wanted it, to record his work. "I'm not bothered by contradictions," Cage observed. "Inconsistency, we know from Emerson, is not a bad thing."

The customary Western notion of causation is inadequate. In the East, cause and effect are not stressed; the emphasis instead is on the here and now. Reality, proposed Suzuki, "is realizable only when all traces of causation are wiped off from our vision." As Cage puts it, "The truth is that everything causes everything else." And: "When one says that there is no cause and effect, what is meant is that there are an incalculable infinity of causes and effects, that in fact each and every thing in all of time and space is related to each and every other thing in all of time and space."

When one becomes concerned with causation, the ego is overreaching its remit; like taste and classification, causal thinking is an indirection of our experience. "This question of asking 'why'," proposes Cage, "is the same as asking which is the most or which is the best. They are very closely related questions that enable you to disconnect yourself from your experience, rather than to identify with it."

People say, sometimes, timidly: A vacant lot, a piece of string, or a
                                                 sunset, possessing
    neither, each acts

Similar passages appear on the same-numbered page of both *Silence* and *A Year from Monday*.

Talking about the work of Cage, Ray Kass described Zen as a "pass the potatoes level of mysticism." Cage suggests, "Progress is out of the question, a narrow-minded concept. You've got to think in terms of life's changes. When autumn becomes winter, when flowers die ... is that progress?" But, he adds, "inactivity is not what happens."

Zen works not only from radical empiricism, it works with a radical pragmatism. A woman from Oregon once wrote to Cage asking him how to recognize a work of art. He suggested that she change her mind to look at everything aesthetically, so everything is art. Then he reformulated it in a more satisfactory postscript, proposing instead that "you just start looking; in other words you start going out of yourself and looking at the world around you, and then your mind changes." There is "no need to cautiously proceed in dualistic terms of success or failure or the beautiful and the ugly or good and evil but rather simply to walk on 'not wondering,' to quote Meister Eckhardt, 'Am I right or doing something wrong.'"

What one does can be perceived with the same clarity as everything else. "What I really believe," Cage says, "is made perfectly clear by my actions." Since "a 'mistake' is beside the point," what one has done cannot be undone. "An error," Cage posited, "is simply a failure to adjust immediately from a conception to an actuality." In Zen calligraphy, it is accepted that if the line being drawn breaks, the trace of energy remains. Cage does not use an eraser; its use "means ... that an action has been made, that it has been decided that is not an action which one wishes to keep, and so it is removed." Then, intriguingly, he

113

observes an interrelationship between the spiritual value of the gesture and the financial value of the materials, without this implying the priority of either:

> Now take the way of painting that we know from the Far East, where the material upon which one is painting is of such value that one dare not make an action that requires erasure. So one prepares himself in advance before he makes a mark. He knows when he is making it that he is going to keep it. The possibility of erasing has nothing to do with that kind of activity.

III

During one lecture Suzuki sketched an egg-like shape on the board, and halfway up the left side he drew two parallel lines. "This is the structure of the Mind with a big M," he explained, "and the narrow space between these parallel lines is the ego, or mind, with a little m."

The space around the top half of the oval represented the world of relativity, and around the bottom what Suzuki referred to as the absolute, "what Eckhardt," Cage observes, "called the ground." The ego faces the world of relativity through the sense perceptions and confronts the absolute through dreams and the unconscious. It is just a sliver of a continuous line. As Suzuki explained, "The ego can cut itself off from this big Mind, which passes through it, or it can open itself up"; "whether that experience," Cage clarifies, "comes in through the day or comes to it through the night."

"Instead of cutting itself off, it can flow with its experience," Suzuki continued. "That is what Zen wants: that the flow take place. Zen would like the ego to open up to the Mind which is outside it. If you take the way of cross-legged meditation, where you go *in* through discipline, then you get free of the ego. You don't use your likes and dislikes to protect yourself in the world of relativity, but you grow with it."

Traditional arts and practices of Zen nurture the process: the tea ceremony, flower arrangement, archery, calligraphy and poetry, especially *haiku*. The excellence of what is done depends on the clear mind of the doer at the point of action. In calligraphy there is a moment of empty clarity (*konton haikai*) before and with the gesture. In archery, you stretch the bow, but it is released only when the mind is voided. With *haiku*, the poem is judged by how little thought is obvious in it, how close it comes to pure observation. The simpler a line, the more truth it contains. *Haiku* is evocative but not resonant: one does not write "April is the cruellest month"; one writes "I hear the leaking rain/Drop against a basin."

Zen is an immanent approach, confining concepts to a much narrower range of usefulness and necessity than is customary, but it is not anti-intellectual. Concept and reality are seen as two different things, and the former usually gets in the way of the latter. Cage said in 1958, "I don't want it to *mean* anything. I want it to *be*." He insists, "No thing in life requires a symbol, since it is clearly what it is." It is an unnecessary detour to go through conceptual thought on the way to living your life. "Clinging or trying to force one's life into one's own idea of it, of what it should be, is only absurd," Cage suggested. "The absurdity comes from the artificiality of it, of not living, but of having to have first an idea about how one should do it and then stumblingly trying." "Pay attention," he recommends, "but stop short of explanation."

Cage says he doesn't like it when "a particular thing is a symbol of a particular other thing. But if," he adds, alluding to the principle of interpenetration, "each thing in the world can be seen as a symbol of every other thing in the world, then I do like it." Thereby "nothing needs to be connected to anything else since they were not separated irreconcilably to begin with." Separation works to protect us from living.

The way of Zen is not a pretty idea; it is practical. If you do not require artificially clear conceptual understanding, "and are willing to put up with experience instead, then the world is far more open to you." Cage writes:

> I can accept the relationship between a diversity of elements, as we do when we look at the stars, discover a group of stars and baptize it "The Big Bear." Then I make an object out of it. I am no longer dealing with the entity itself, seen as having elements or separate parts, I have before me a fixed object which I may cause to vary precisely because I know in advance that I find it identical to itself. . . . What makes the constellation into an object is the relation I impose on its components. But I can refrain from positing that relation.

Koan and *mondo* are the question-and-answer techniques in traditional Zen which help short-circuit conceptual thought. They apply to the world of the absolute rather than that of relativity. Both are set by master to pupil; the *koan* will be pondered on, answered and answered again, whereas the *mondo* requires an immediate reply. The question posed, such as "what was your original face before your father and mother were born?", cannot be solved by reason. Even questions which seem perplexing, such as "What is Buddha?" or "Why hasn't Bodhidharma a beard?", need an answer which, even if words are used, indicates rather than constitutes the fact of one finding the solution.

Direct perception requires the giving up of likes and dislikes. All that makes one dislike one's experiences is oneself. "It is only irritating to think one would like to be somewhere else," states Cage. There is never a dull moment; "boredom takes over only if we arouse it in ourselves." We may attempt to convince ourselves that the world is how we want it to be; sometimes we act on the world to make it as we desire. No ivory tower exists, however; as Cage puts it, one day the prince will get out and become the Buddha. Sooner or later you notice the glass of the picture-frame is reflecting the spotlight; or you are immersed in a Dvorak symphony in the grandiose setting of a Gothic cathedral when the bells in the steeple chime nine o'clock, in the wrong key. That is what is actually happening, and the fact that it irritates us could be seen as stubbornness – maybe a residual infantilism – not to accept the fact.

"Each thing in the world asks us," Cage suggested, "'what makes you think I'm not something you like?'" The mind can give up the desire to improve on creation, and act as a faithful receiver of experience through concentrated attention without prejudgment. "If you ask yourself why am I turning off, rather than being pleased with turning off," Cage advised, "then you may learn something." In Zen they say that if something is boring for one minute try it for two, and if it is still boring, try it for four minutes; eventually one discovers it is interesting. Cage recommends that we "open our eyes and ears seeing life each day excellent as it is."

"To accept whatever comes, regardless of the consequences, is to be unafraid or to be full of that love which comes from a sense of at-oneness with whatever," stated Cage. "Our delight lies in not possessing anything; maintaining secure possession of nothing, there is no limit to what one may freely enjoy." Without preferences, everything we come across is to the point. "Looking for something irrelevant, I found I couldn't find it," says Cage, for, as Henri Bergson once said, disorder is merely the order you were not looking for. Some experiences provide a richer range and depth of relevance (a qualification which Cage suspends in the seventies).

Likes and dislikes lead to extreme experiences; pleasure when what we like is taking place, pain when it is not. Without such preferences, "your pleasure will be more universal," by which Cage means "both constant and more spacious."

116

Cage has retained a willingness to evaluate. He does not have favorites among his works (apart from a partiality for *4' 33"*), but he sees certain pieces, for instance *Metamorphosis*, as not good. He looks at its center, as he puts it, and finds it is not adequately what it tries to be. He uses the same approach to criticize *Imaginary Landscape No.2*, and to weed out bad ideas from good in his later visual work. Another evaluative criterion he employs is not "better" or "worse," but more or less interesting. The *Second Construction* he lambasts in the light of his ideas on the future of music. It is, he said, "a poor piece. I wasn't quite aware that/it was poor when I wrote it; I thought it was interesting. But it has carry-overs from education and theory; it's really a fugue but of a novel order. In this day and age, I think fugues are not interesting."

While it is true that Zen emphasizes spontaneous unmediated experience, and puts intellectualizing firmly in its place, discipline is never rejected; enlightened spontaneity comes only from the most thorough training and preparation. As Cage says, "to act is miracle and needs everything and every me out of the way." Discipline is a clearing exercise carried out by the will on the ego which allows this to be the case. Cage points out that discipline comes from the same root as "disciple"; one gives oneself up, administers one's life from the core of one's being so it may follow a path. "Discipline is giving yourself rather than expecting things to give themselves to you," in the formulation of Cage. "Disciplines are important as disciplines. The specific nature of the discipline is not as important as the discipline itself." He proposes, "the question is not what should I do or how to do it but how one achieves the state of being disciplined – learn true discipline to give oneself up."

"If the mind is disciplined" – Cage cites Meister Eckhardt – "the heart turns quickly from fear towards love." In the modern West, the will is widely misconstrued as primarily functioning to force the edicts of the ego on the outside world. Its foremost tenable function is to mediate between ego and reality, reconciling the former with the latter. To quote the Jewish theologian A.J. Heschel, "our will itself is obedience, an answer, a compliance." Secondarily, will is the force by which one engages with reality to achieve one's wishes. Cage plumps for the clarity of will in the former sense, as the means of accepting reality. "The mind has nothing in it," says Cage, thereby distancing himself from "everything else" that "is busy."

A Zen story tells how a man once stood on the brow of a hill. Several people walking together on the road saw him and began to speculate on why he was up there. When they reached the hilltop, they put to him their

117

suggestions. "Have you lost your pet?" asked one. The man replied he had not. "Have you not lost your friend?" asked another. The man said no. "Are you not enjoying the fresh breeze up there?" asked a third. The man said he was not.

"If you say no to all of our questions," asked one of the travelers, "why are you standing up there?"

The man said, "I just stand."

What we do, we do without purpose," Cage wrote. "The highest purpose is to have no purpose at all. This puts one in accord with nature in her manner of operation."

For the person who has learned the way of Zen, as for anyone who has made a leap in their engagement with life, whether philosophical, psychoanalytical or spiritual, the same things in life happen as happened before. One remains prone to the same errors, and above the silver lining there are higher clouds. Cage gleefully quotes the close of a book by Suzuki, a quote from a monk who records, "Now that I'm enlightened, I'm just as miserable as ever."

Before studying Zen, Suzuki told the class, men are men and mountains are mountains. While studying Zen, things become confused. After studying Zen, men are men and mountains are mountains. Someone asked what the difference is between before and after. Suzuki answered, "no difference, only the feet are a little bit off the ground."

Cage's experience of Zen is tinged by his native sunny disposition. Life, he writes, is "essentially a cause for joy." "Here we are, let us say Yes to our presence together in Chaos," he proposes. "Anything is a delight; we do not possess it and thus need not fear its loss." When all experiences are a pleasure, "as we say in the United States, 'you've got it made.' And what you've got made is the world of mind and it's become divine." On several occasions Cage quotes the Japanese, "Nichi nichi kore ko nichi" – "each day is a beautiful day."

These, then, are the main features of Zen as Cage understood it, and they constitute the key to appreciation of his mature life, work and thought. They make it possible to understand how his perspectives on art changed. Engagement with Zen brought to fruition various aspects of his aesthetic, such as impersonalism, and the belief that modern music could help reconcile listeners with modern life; it urged on the working through of his ascetic tendencies. It clarified his understanding of what constituted beauty, what constituted art, and what its function was. It gave Cage a better appreciation of those attractive but puzzling dicta of Indian thought – "to sober and quiet the mind, thus making it susceptible to

divine influences" and "to imitate nature in her manner of operation."
Most obviously, it was with Zen that a rapid change occurred in Cage's
musical world, to a way of working that suited him – and for which he
became famous.

IV

The prevailing view of beauty in the West is that it is one side of a
duality, of what is beautiful and what is not. Beauty is manifest in
nature either partially or latently, perhaps in privileged objects. In art,
it must be either constructed or nurtured. Large parts of everyday life
become rejected and unworthy of attention so that part of life may
be the opposite. "Unfortunately," Cage says elliptically, "European
thinking has brought it about that actual things that happen such as
suddenly listening or suddenly sneezing are not considered profound."
In Cage's account, "One then decides whether he enjoys it or not, and
gradually develops a set of likes and dislikes." Taste becomes codified;
it falls into social and historical regularities.

For Cage, Western art is intended either to transform or improve
reality, rather than to increase our awareness or appreciation of it.
Debates on the relation between art and life go back at least to
Aristotle. According to Schiller, the supreme function of art is the
control of form over matter. André Malraux suggests that art aims not
to imitate but to transform reality. More recently, Mario Vargas Llosa,
discussing observation in novel-writing, suggests that it becomes art
when it undergoes "scrupulous formal treatment which endows it with
exceptional character."

Such approaches, Cage implies, are founded on attachment to the
constructions of our ego. They thereby aggrandize our selves, giving
the thinking mind the illusion of being more important than it is; the
repetition and recapitulation of traditional music embody, for instance,
"the belief that one may own one's own home." Chasing after aesthetic
constructions, we miss life.

Cage said he would rather be without art which has this effect. "I can
imagine a world without art, and it would not be a bad place," he suggests.
"If there were a part of life dark enough to keep out of it a light from art,
I would want to be in that darkness, fumbling around if necessary, but
alive." He considered it difficult to listen to familiar music, observing,
"It is almost impossible to remain alive in the presence of a well-known
masterpiece."

As one may expect, music is the main focus of Cage's disparaging comments. The range of available sound is divided and structured, with some parts treated preferentially. Pitch is separated from noise. Sounds are no longer just sounds, Cage says, but are letters – A,B,C,D,E,F,G, and "if a sound is unfortunate enough not to have a letter . . . it is tossed out of the system on the grounds: it's a noise or unmusical." At this point, proposes Cage, sounds cease to be of consequence in themselves; what are important are relationships between them. Simultaneous pitched sounds are subjected to rules of harmony (or counterpoint, which Cage overlooks). "Harmony, so-called," stormed Cage, "is a forced abstract vertical relation which blots out the spontaneous transmitting nature of the sounds forced into it. It is artificial and unrealistic."

In Western music, not only are some categories of sound and certain selected relationships privileged, but some pieces, and the products of certain individuals, are valued more than others. There are great composers and masterpieces: we imagine, Cage says, that sounds are not just sounds, but are Beethoven. When certain composers have reputations as transmitters of an aesthetically, if not spiritually, superior insight into the world, all other insight can correspondingly be devalued.

"There is all the time in the world for studying music," Cage suggested, "but for living there is scarcely any time at all." "Art becomes separate from life," he proposed, "and to reach it, we must first pass through someone else's center."

The picture Cage paints is thus of a narrowing pyramid of good taste. "When a composer feels a responsibility to make, rather than accept," he posited, "he eliminates from the area of responsibility all those events which do not suggest the at that point in time vogue of profundity, for he takes himself seriously, wishes to be considered great, and he thereby diminishes his love and increases his fear and concern about what people will think."

There are degrees of abstraction; Cage mentions, for instance, what Virgil Thomson called French rhythm, based on phraseology rather than on meter, as closer to a "breathed" than a measured music. Any dualistic aesthetic, however, is very fragile. "A fugue," Cage noted, for example, "is a more complicated game, but it can be broken up by a single sound, say, from a fire engine."

Cage began to attend concerts less and less. When present at a festival, or in residence, he attends every event; "I don't avoid concerts," he explains, "but I wouldn't do it if I were at home." He ceased to derive any enjoyment from popular music. While living in Chicago in 1942 he had sat in on a jam session in Evanston, taking notes about what the four drummers present were playing. He came to dislike jazz even more than rock music, because not only was there a regular rhythm, but also what he saw as its dialogue format and cerebral quality. "Music as discourse (jazz) doesn't work," Cage wrote. "If you want a discussion, have it and use words." He says simply, "I love sounds, and I actually like them more than what we've done to them." Asked if he grew less interested in music over the years, he replies, "No, I think I've been less interested in music all along."

Cage does not argue with the premises of traditional music. He rejects them wholesale for reasons which can only be inferred from his own position. His remarks show the same kind of incomprehension he felt as a youth. "Does being musical make one automatically stupid and unable to listen?" he asked. "Which is more musical, a truck passing by a factory, or a truck passing by a music school?"

In the light of Zen, Cage's world view became consistent to an organic extent and fitted his temperament more fully than before. Along with this went a crystallization of his ideas about music. Cage started from the conviction that "our highest business is our daily life," so that art cannot be concerned with improving on reality, and if we are to experience the world directly, we must suspend our likes and dislikes. Significantly, as quickly as he identified these goals, he thought of techniques to achieve them. His most audacious innovation, still to come, both epitomized his thought and formed the foundation of his method from then onwards. The new approach also incorporated many of his earlier positions, giving them the strength of location in a system.

For years Cage had tended toward impersonalism in music. In 1944 he had suggested that "personality is a flimsy thing on which to build an art"; it has a place, for "that is what is meant by the word *style*," but not a primary one. Now impersonalism found a place in Cage's new system. "Sometimes people think of the arts as opportunities for self-expression," Cage said. "I think of it as an opportunity for self-alteration." He insisted that he does not write masterpieces (meaning he does not seek to do so) and that he has a longing to be nothing special (which by inversion suggests that he is). The notion of inspiration is also rejected. "At all costs must inspiration be avoided," Cage wrote, explaining "I would rather live in a less special situation."

Self-expression, insofar as it means anything to Cage, accords with the example of Mies van der Rohe at the Chicago School who, told by a female student that his course lacked room for self-expression, told her to sign her name, then, when she complied, responded, "There. That's what I call self-expression."

Cage was now seeking a music which does, rather than one which speaks – one concerned with the activity of the vibration of sound, rather than with the use of sound to talk about something. "There is no inner meaning in my work," he stated in 1951. "It, and the sounds I use, exist solely for their own sake unrelated to anything else." "It's very hard to give a single sound *any* meaning," Cage suggested. As he notoriously put it, "I have nothing to say and I am saying it and that is poetry as I need it."

Another of his existing perspectives which found a niche in the system was a championing of the excluded, which had already shown itself in his advocacy of percussion and other noise elements. Cage became preoccupied with ambient sounds in everyday life and how they transgress the categories of music. "Close your eyes and listen to the traffic," he suggested. "Independent of a beat, isn't it? And the sounds don't occur on the pitches of the major or minor scales, do they?"

Cage defined activity as modern – as contemporary, interestingly, rather than as successful – if it is not interrupted by the things that happen. "Music is music now if it is not interrupted by ambient sounds," he proposed. "A cough or a baby crying will not ruin a good piece of modern music."

The conviction that "our highest business is our daily life" gave a new sense of mission to his long-held belief that contemporary music could help integrate its listeners with modern living. "Art serves to the extent that it is useful in introducing a person to the life he is living," Cage proclaimed, and elsewhere, "Art and our involvement in it will somehow introduce us to the very life we are living." "What are the arts for," he asked, "except to bring about the enjoyment of life?" At times Cage describes this aim in spiritual terms, as if it will increase susceptibility to divine influences. "Make art useful to every person," he recommended, "so he will have access (in religious terms) to heaven in daily life."

"Left to itself art would have to be something very simple – it would be sufficient for it to be beautiful," Cage once elaborated. "When it's useful it should spill out of just being beautiful and move over to the other aspects of life so that when we're not with the art it has nevertheless influenced our actions or our responses to the environment." In a more specific formulation: "The function of art at the present time is to preserve us from all the logical minimizations that we are at each instant tempted to apply to the flux of events. To draw us nearer to the process which is the world we live in."

Cage was proposing "a view of the arts which does not separate them from the rest of life, but rather confuses the difference between art and life." "I wouldn't say we are interested in destroying the barrier between art and life or even blurring it," he clarified. "I would say we are interested in observing that there is no barrier between the two." Art can function "as a sort of experimental station in which one tries out living."

At times he seems to suggest he is doing people a favor. "If their ears don't get stretched by me they'll be stretched by something else later on, and it just might be more painful," he suggested. Or, inversely, if people find his music unpleasant, "they are apt to go out into daily life to find that daily life is better than what they heard in the concert hall."

Though such a stance went back over fifteen years in his development, the tenor had shifted from domination to acceptance; instead of seeking to master and subjugate noise, we need to embrace it by quiet observation.

For Cage, these were not ideas which would serve him as the skeleton for music, but were ways of living which he formulated in words to help him be true to them in his art. Sounds delight him, especially unexpected ones. "It's very beautiful," reflects Cage as he listened to traffic. "I find it more beautiful than listening to music." The word that is at the center of his appreciation of sound is *beauty*. Peter Yates recalled that when he helped friends drag a table across the room in preparation for dinner one evening, Cage rushed in from an adjacent room urgently enquiring, "What was that beautiful sound?"

He seems not only psychologically but physiologically exceptional. "I haven't heard any sounds that I don't enjoy," he observed. The volume of sound appears to make no difference. At an airport in Tokyo, a popular Japanese politician had just flown in from Europe, and the plane was brought further up the runway than usual to allow a photo-opportunity. "Most people had their fingers in their ears," Cage remembers, "whereas I left mine open to hear what there was to hear." When it is put to him that his way of experiencing needs a certain state of mind, he replies, "Well, I'm mostly that way."

The positive statements of Cage contrast with his rejection of traditional music, where he is especially prone to the hyperbole and dogmatism of the manifesto writer. According to Cage, the traditional composer "eliminates from the area of possibility all those events that do not suggest the ... vogue of profundity, for he takes himself seriously, wishes to be considered great, and he thereby diminishes his love and increases his fear and concern about what people will think." Composers, especially many of those deemed "the greatest," may be less concerned with others' opinions than Cage scathingly suggests. Above all, he does not consider how advantages might accompany the shortcomings of the traditional approach, just as with his own system there might be deficiencies as well as rewards. The best practitioners of any activity are essentially pursuing the same goals as one another, despite differences of explanatory language; ineffectual action often stems from confusing the way one talks of one's activities with the actual activities. Anyone who understands Judaism knows that its matter is just the same as that of someone who understands Buddhism; the differences are of practical emphasis of method and of descriptive system. So, too, Cage's activities can be seen as in the deepest ways identical with those of Mozart – or even Beethoven.

Cage had arrived at an aesthetic which was at root optimistic and accessible: nurturing joy in the face of everything that happens. Yet he was on the verge of some of the most baffling artistic work in history, rejected by most as incomprehensible and apparently pretentious.

The core of the problem is that Cage's position is quite different from that by which art is usually approached. To give one example, Cage's repudiation of most aspects of traditional musical organization entails the complete avoidance of the musical conventions on which expression is based. What Cage begins to do is not to *express* his ideas: he exemplifies them.

V

After one lecture by Suzuki, Cage recalls, "I saw him and expressed the view that I had made a connection between my work and his teaching. He simply said, 'I don't know anything about music.'" Cage asked what he had to say about art, and he said there was nothing he could say about that either.

"I wanted approval from him," records Cage. "When I didn't get it, I carried on regardless." The response of Suzuki, he reflected elsewhere, "may have been the Zen form of teaching without teaching. At any rate I got no help from him there and had to do my own thinking."

Cage's engagement with Zen, and the bringing of Zen in general to the West, suggest interesting questions concerning the mechanism and ramifications of social change through the meeting of cultures. Not only may the style change, but it may do so *in order to* achieve the goals it achieved in another form elsewhere. Cage asks at the start of *Silence*, "What nowadays, America mid-20th century, is Zen?" He explained, "I felt that Zen changes in different times and places, and what it is before here and now, I am not certain."

Zen has proved an expedient handle for critical and academic classification of Cage, just as he is discussed in terms of Dada or post-modernism. Developments in Dada, Ernst suggests, "are subsequently reflected in the music of John Cage," and Cage confirms, "Critics who in general link my activities with Dada are not mistaken." "I had been brought up on the twenties," he records, "I was aware of Duchamp and so forth. I liked Dada very much." ("Surrealism relates to therapy, whereas Dada relates to religion," Cage suggests elsewhere, which helps account for his preference for the one over the other.)

It would be erroneous, however, to reduce Cage's work to such categories. He was adamant that he did not want Zen to be held responsible – blamed – for what he did after coming into contact with it. The attempt to explain most things which happen to human beings in terms of a single cause is the kiss of death to the usefulness and accuracy of any theory. There are many reasons why a person does something and it is not unusual for these motivations to sit uneasily together or to conflict. Moreover, categorizing and crediting influence can easily be used so much that they become an academic disease, wasting effort which might be spent on appreciation of the experience one is having. Cage has produced his work for many reasons, which are richer and more personal than one can note through concentration on academic categories.

The most interesting work is simply itself before it is the exemplar of a category. Cage shares with much work labeled "post-modernist" an avoidance of value judgments, but for quite different reasons, and his thought includes an optimism, and even a conviction that a real world exists, which some post-modernism lacks. His inclinations, moreover – for instance the tendency to see art as capable of integrating people into daily life – exist before the terms used to categorize them, and even before studies, notably here of Zen, by which he clarified them.

ELEVEN

I

The *Sixteen Dances*, written in the spring of 1950, showed developments in Cage's musical approach which paralleled the cataclysmic changes in his thinking. Merce Cunningham had choreographed a sixteen-movement suite which reflected themes from Indian philosophy akin to those of the *Sonatas and Interludes* by Cage. Cunningham correspondingly "wanted a music which would express emotions."

In the course of their correspondence, Cage had learned that Boulez had been using diagrams resembling the magic square as part of his precompositional tools, putting in numbers to make more rigorous serialization possible. Cage thought he could adapt the idea to his own purposes. "I was wondering how to achieve a clear graphic view of the rhythmic structures I wanted to use," he explained. "I arrived at the idea of using charts. Instead of numbers, I put sounds, groups of sounds, into the sequence." Cage recorded in *Silence*, "The elements of the gamuts were arranged unsystematically in charts and the method of composition involved moves on these charts analogous to those used in constructing a magic square."

The breakthrough came out of this experiment. "While notating the sounds and aggregates of sounds on those diagrams, I realized that by thus inscribing them, they were sufficient in themselves"; rather than using the chart materials to clarify his conscious structuring of the piece, he could use the chart to avoid it. "I reached the conclusion," Cage remembered, "that I could compose according to moves on these charts instead of according to my own taste."

Zen had clarified Cage's understanding of beauty, of art and of its function, and in the light of it he developed a world view which incorporated and synergetically reinforced many of his earlier tendencies.

126

Here, however, came the most striking leap: not only to move away from expression, but also to reject the very foundation of the personal work of art – aesthetic choice. With the *Sixteen Dances*, Cage took a remarkable bold first step into composition by chance operations. Henceforth, he would develop more and more thorough ways to determine the artistic material without him choosing it. Composition by chance would permit the exclusion from his music of the likes, dislikes, tastes and memory which he sought in general to avoid. Just like the man on the hill who just stands, Cage decided, "I do not deal in purposes: I deal in sounds."

Cage had first attempted to circumvent his likes and dislikes as early as the *String Quartet*, where he devised the latter half of the third movement as if it were "the following willy-nilly of a ball which is rolling in front of you." But it took contact with Zen to clarify his aim in thought and to exploit it in action. The audible result was likewise primitive, the linear mutation of a process Cage set in motion while still in the midst of his traditional, tasteful way of composing; he then had deliberately to correct the end of the movement to make it fit his rhythmic scheme. Although he had selected the individual gamuts of the *Sixteen Dances*, his use of chance operations to arrive at a large number of determinations, rather than a single rule bringing about an automatic process, was a significant step forward. Chance operations thereafter became the signature of all of Cage's activities, so that *Sixteen Dances* qualifies as a turning point.

The piece was in another respect connected with the past, since Cunningham's request for emotive music linked it to the expressive interpretation of Indian philosophy which Cage was now transcending. As a transitional aim, he said, "I wanted to see if I could fulfill a commission for 'expressive' music while at the same time making use of chance operations."

His previous way of writing did not vanish at a stroke. In March 1951 Cage described his compositional technique as if none of the leaps of the previous months had taken place. "I take my sounds when I have decided what they are going to be," he said, "and place them in this background of silence. This reduces the structure of the composition to pure rhythm, nothing else." He asserts that "it was with *Sixteen Dances* that I entered – with confidence – the domain of chance." The concept of chance composition, however, crystallized while writing the piece; Cage launched into chance with some vigor but, as with many discoveries, it had first to be asserted among vestiges of the earlier system.

II

Sixteen Dances was first performed in Cunningham's program at the Hunter Playhouse on January 21, 1951. Work had long been under way on its successor, the *Concerto for Prepared Piano and Chamber Orchestra*. Begun the previous summer, it was completed in February.

The piano in this piece has fifty-three prepared notes which span the available registers, utilizing the usual bolts, screws and rubber stripping, plus for the first time a "plastic bridge" which produces microtonal pitch deviations. There are twenty-two players in the chamber orchestra, with no parts doubled except the clarinet; among the percussion instruments are a water gong, a radio, a metal container (such as a waste-basket), a wire coil in a pickup, an electric buzzer and a recording of a generator.

The *Concerto* is rhythmically simple and texturally thin; the speed is a constant half-note equals fifty-four. The rhythmic structure is 3/2/4/4/2/3/5. The large-scale structure is divided into three movements: 3/2/4 in the first, 4/2/3 in the second and 5 in the last. The structure of the first and second movements constitutes a palindrome against which the last movement stands in monistic isolation.

Whereas chance was added to the *Sixteen Dances* as Cage prepared it, the *Concerto* was intended from the start as a work using chance, and in part Cage used it to consolidate his discoveries. It can be seen as a musical allegory of his development over the previous half-decade. The instrumentation features twelve years of inventions, from the water gong and wire coil to the prepared piano. As Cage characterizes the piece, "I made it into a drama between the piano, which remains romantic, expressive, and the orchestra, which itself follows the principles of Oriental philosophy." In the first movement, as Calvin Tomkins quotes Cage, he "let the piano express the opinion that music should be improvised or felt, while the orchestra expressed only the chart, with no personal taste involved. In the second movement I made larger concentric moves on the chart for both pianist and orchestra, with the idea of the pianist beginning to give up personal taste. The third movement had only one set of moves on the chart for both, and a lot of silences."

Each cell on the charts was unique, disconnected, centered on itself; yet since the compositional system made the appearance of each cell equally likely, Cage also saw each as coextensive with the others. Chart technique thus made it possible to forge a first connection between sound and the Zen principle of interpenetration, although it is hampered by the monophonic texture to which the schema was committed.

The setting apart of the third movement in the rhythmic plan could be seen as prophetic, for in it Cage introduced the resource which would provide the cornerstone of his chance operations. For some time he had been teaching a sixteen-year-old high school student born in Nice, Christian Wolff. His father, Kurt Wolff, had come to the United States from Germany just before the Second World War and had established the Pantheon Press. One of the few people with a strong claim to have been taught composition by Cage in anything like the conventional sense, young Wolff was so much liked not only by Cage but also by Tudor and Feldman that he became a fully fledged member of the Bozza mansion set. "He was quite remarkable," Cage recalled, "and I believe I learned more from him than he did from me."

Remembering the generosity of Schoenberg, Cage did not charge Wolff for lessons. The young man showed his appreciation by occasionally bringing Cage the newest publication from his father. Knowing that Cage was keenly interested in Oriental philosophy, he one day brought along the new Pantheon English translation of the *I Ching*.

The origins of the *I Ching* lie beyond the reaches of historical record. Like all texts of such distant origin, whether the *Iliad*, the *Gilgamesh* epic or the *Vedas*, it is generally accepted that it emerged from an oral tradition. It emerged, too, from practical use, for the *I Ching* is among other things an oracle, whose two main sections deal with sixty-four oracular images and their commentaries.

A number of accounts exist to explain how this division came about. In Ancient China, one suggests, fortunes were told by casting a turtle shell into a fire. When the heat caused the shell to shatter, the soothsayer would interpret the pattern of cracks, just as in Ancient Rome the quest for fate led Roman seers to haruspicate and scry in the entrails of cows. Supporters of this reconstruction suggest that the cracks of the turtle shell were gradually taxonomized into sixty-four different patterns.

Rather less imaginative is the suggestion that the images developed out of the mathematics of the process. At first an oracle would be cast in binary form, yes or no. Over the centuries the possibilities were combined, first by putting together two casts, giving four possible replies instead of two (0/0, 0/1, 1/1, 1/0), then by linking three casts in a *trigram*, giving eight possible answers. In the form in which it settled, the pattern is made up of six casts, written as broken (— —) or unbroken (——) lines. The six casts together yielded one of the sixty-four possible combinations of the eight trigrams. These sixty-four oracular images are called hexagrams.

The person using the *I Ching* identifies by chance which hexagram should be consulted either by casting three coins or by drawing yarrow stalks six times, once for each line, building the hexagram from the bottom line up. The wisdom of the time saw all conditions as necessarily changing; the oracles do not represent states but tendencies in movement. A circulation is taking place, represented by the sequence of the symbols for each hexagram, from the most *yin* to the most *yang* condition – hence the alternative title of the work, the *Book of Changes*. One reads the oracle not to know if what one wants will come about, but to discern how to insert oneself into the flow of activity in order to live more harmoniously and thus more fruitfully. Whether one throws coins or draws yarrow stalks, the generation of hexagrams contains a provision that highlights the changeability of life: lines are moving or non-moving. If one or more of the six lines is moving, it is not only the hexagram generated which is consulted, but also (as referring to a situation close at hand) the hexagram created when all the moving lines are read as their opposite – a moving unbroken line becomes a broken line and vice versa.

Around the middle of the twelfth century B.C.E., King Wen and his son, the Duke of Chou, took the sixty-four hexagrams and related them to specific moral counsels. The *I Ching* became as much a book of wisdom as of divination.

The new Pantheon edition was a translation by Cary Baynes of a German translation by Richard Wilhelm. Wilhelm had been an ideal translator, for not only did he have command of the language but also practical experience of the *I Ching*. He had been taught how to use it in the years after the 1911 revolution in China. He studied the philosophy on which it rested with Lao Nai-hsuan in Tsingtao. The translation was made in consultation with his master, rendering it back into Chinese to check its accuracy; Wilhelm finished the work in Peking in the summer of 1923.

Cage had been shown the *I Ching* years earlier. Lou Harrison drew his attention to a copy in the San Francisco Public Library of the translation made by James Legge, which had been published in 1882. In an interview in 1971 Harrison said he had used it, in a way he did not specify, in the course of composing music. At a time when Cage, Harrison recalled, "was very turbulent and hunting and asking, I told him one day of the work that I had begun in Los Angeles (my manuscripts tell me that it was in 1943), in which I used the *I Ching* in a number of determinative ways." As Cage told the listeners at his Norton seminars in 1989, "I didn't at that time have a use for it." Now, at the beginning of 1951, he both better appreciated its philosophy, and found it fulfilled a practical need. "The moment I opened the book," Cage said, "and saw the charts and the hexagrams which were used for obtaining oracles . . . I saw a connection with the charts I had been using on my *Concerto*."

The new version of the *I Ching* was first published in 1951; the final movement of the *Concerto for prepared piano and chamber orchestra* was finished in February of that year. As the second movement is dated October 2, 1950, and allowing for the possibility of Wolff bringing an advance copy, the discovery by Cage of the *I Ching* can be dated to the end of 1950 and the beginning of 1951.

The third movement had been set apart structurally in the original plan; now Cage set its method apart, too, using the *I Ching* to determine the moves on the charts for both piano and orchestra.

As for the preceding movements, the chart had sixteen rows and fourteen columns, assembled from the charts already used. Cage was committed to this format, but as the product was 224, it was difficult to relate to the sixty-four of the *I Ching*. Unbroken lines in the *I Ching* cast represented the orchestra, and broken lines the piano. If the line cast was not moving, that cell of the new chart would be filled by the relevant cell from the orchestra or piano chart as appropriate. When a moving line was thrown, a new cell would be composed for the chart involving both; if an unbroken line moved to broken, the cell would begin with the orchestra and end with the piano. Moving from broken to unbroken, the reverse would occur. Cage made two additional charts of moves to determine the succession of selected cells.

The use of the *I Ching* chance operations made the *Concerto* not only a consolidation of his discoveries; it was also another major step. The allegory it embodied was up to date; indeed, in its final silent measures it was premonitory. The *Concerto* was premiered at the Julius Hartt School of Music in Hartford, Connecticut, with Cage as soloist and the Hartt Chamber Orchestra under Moshe Paranov.

Henceforth, the practical basis of all of Cage's work, his hallmark, the technique he sought to develop, was that of chance operations – usually generated with reference to the *I Ching*. The making of art non-intentionally was the way he put his world view into practice. Faced with the necessity of living *as a particular*, John Cage was finding a way to conduct his life that increasingly struck a workable balance between his various temperamental inclinations. With his study of Zen he had made a sudden leap in the adequacy of his thought. Now, with chance operations and the *I Ching*, he could make a similarly dramatic leap in the adequacy of his work. What he did could in turn clarify who he was, and how he understood it.

While the magic square required charts to be made in relation to each number, Cage soon discovered ways to relate the *I Ching* "to numbers which are larger or smaller than sixty-four so that any question regarding a collection of possibilities can be answered." Later he made use of the Gerber Variable Scale to divide any length into sixty-four parts.

Using yarrow stalks to build up hexagrams was too time-consuming for Cage's purposes; he instead used the coin oracle, casting nickels or quarters. The generation of sufficient hexagrams for a whole piece – especially one of appreciable size – was inordinately time-consuming even by this method. Cage would toss coins on even the shortest subway journey, to use time as efficiently as possible. "All kinds of strangers came over to me to say, 'What are you doing that for?'" he remembered. "Then we got into conversation and I learned something from them sometimes." He would inveigle visitors into casting for him. Years later he used a computerized version of the oracle. At no point, however, did he seriously consider replacing it with a random number generator. "I have confidence in the *I Ching*. It's the oldest book in the world," he told a reporter disarmingly in 1969. His confidence is, he admitted, "a value system, but based on nothing more positive in me than sentimentality . . . I'm full of these inconsistencies and see no reason why I shouldn't be."

Cage was applying the *I Ching* to generate chance operations for his music. It is unclear how much or how often he has resorted to its oracular function. To Daniel Charles he said that he used it not only in his music but in everyday life, "every time I had a problem. I used it very often for practical matters, to write my articles and my music . . . For everything." In one of the stories which make up his lecture *Indeterminacy*, he recounts how he once cast the *I Ching* for a very sceptical Richard Lippold.

For some years Cage has consulted the oriental astrologer Julie Winter – a rare nod in the direction that can tend to irrationality and superstition, to which the most prominent analogy is his sentimentality concerning the *I Ching* – but he is suspicious of divination. "I didn't like," for instance, "the drama or the melodrama associated with the Tarot. The hanging man and all that," whereas the *I Ching* is more concerned with empty counsel than with fate. "I use the *I Ching* when it is useful, just as I turn on the water faucet when I want a drink," recorded Cage. "I generally say, 'What do you have to say about this?' and then I just listen to what it says and see if some bells ring or not." Over the years Cage has resorted to it in this way less and less. He uses it when troubled, "but I haven't been troubled for quite some time – that is to say, I haven't been so troubled that I felt the need to ask it."

If the description is accurate, his first sight of the *I Ching* gave him the idea for a piece that, just as the *Concerto* overlapped and overtook the *Sixteen Dances*, immediately went beyond the limits of the *Concerto*. "Right there and then I sketched out the whole procedure for *Music of Changes*," said Cage, the new title playing on the alternative title of the *I Ching*. Thus began the long and gruelling composition of one of his longest works, at a time when his financial situation was at one of its all-time lows. "I ran over to show the plan to Morty Feldman, and I can still remember him saying, 'You've hit it!'"

III

Work on the *Music of Changes* began after the *Concerto* was finished in February 1951. The first part, just over three and a half minutes long, is dated May 16; the second, sixteen and a half minutes, August 2; and the third and fourth parts, both around ten and a half minutes in length, respectively October 18 and December 13.

The rhythmic structure of the piece is $3/5/6^3{}_4/6^3{}_4/5/3^1{}_8$. To make it more flexible, Cage decided to vary the tempi, selected from a chart by the *I Ching*. "At each small structural division," Cage explained in a 1958 lecture, "at the beginning, for example, and again at the fourth and ninth measures and so on, chance operations determined stability or change of tempo." He noted elsewhere, "Every few measures, at every structural point, things were speeding up or slowing down or remaining constant."

Cage designed every chart as eight squared, so that each could be related to sixty-four, to avoid the difficulties caused by the charts of the *Concerto*. In the charts for sounds, he placed sounds in odd-numbered spaces, and silences in those even-numbered. "All twelve tones were present in any four elements of a given chart," he explained, "whether a line of the chart was read horizontally or vertically. Once this dodecaphonic requirement was satisfied, noises and repetitions of tones were used with freedom."

The sounds of the piece include tone clusters (notated according to the conventions of Henry Cowell), slamming shut the keyboard lid, striking the bass construction bar, dropping the tip of a cymbal beater onto the frame, muting the strings, playing a glissando on the strings, and various effects using the pedal. As Cowell suggested, Cage seems to be attempting to discover how near to a prepared piano sound he can make a piano which has not been prepared.

To write each segment, Cage ascertained the tempo first, and the density of layers in a unit. While the *Concerto* had been monophonic, each unit of the new piece would consist of between one and eight independently composed layers. Cage could thus better seek the musical correlate of interpenetration. "The sounds enter the time–space continuum centered within themselves," he wrote, "unimpeded by service to any abstraction, their 360 degrees of circumference free for an infinite play of interpenetration." He would then compose the large phrase of each layer of the unit. If silence was indicated, he would measure the requisite duration and leave it blank. If a pitch was specified, he would write it down and then determine its duration, dynamic and timbre.

To reduce the frequency of repeating figures, half of the sound, duration and dynamic charts – either the odd- or the even-numbered ones – were designated "mobile" and the other half "immobile." In the mobile charts, each element was replaced by a different one as soon as it was used. This process of random replacement depended on two factors: whether a chart was mobile or not at a given point, and, in the time for which it was, which charts were used.

In determining durations, Cage did not use the *I Ching* but the Tarot pack. "I had the durations all notated in a permutation-like way," he explains, "starting from the smallest and going on to large ones that would be added to one another." Shuffling and dealing the Tarot, he could select a limitless number of additive durations, "which did have the character of starting with the shortest ones and moving toward the longest ones." "But," he observes, "that never really shows in the *Music of Changes*." It is interesting to note that Cage used another oracular resource rather than a secular pack of cards. He never used the Tarot again, however; it represents, like Joseph Campbell's shaggy nag story, a sore thumb, a rare concession to European impurity (in a technical rather than a moral sense).

After this process was completed the next layer was composed, and the process repeated until the unit was finished. Only sound with a role in the next phrase could cross into it. The amount of effort involved in generating chance operations for all of these parameters for a half-hour piece was enormous. "You must realize that I spend a great deal of time tossing coins," he wrote to Boulez, apologizing for the sketchiness of his letter, "and the emptiness of head that that induces begins to penetrate the rest of my time as well."

Chance in the *Concerto* had only applied to the pitches, so the range of chance operations in the new piece represented a great advance. Choice, it seems, still played a part; "the *Music of Changes* was composed," he says, when comparing its drafting with that of the *Sonatas and Interludes*, "by playing the piano, listening to differences, making a choice." Cage devised the pedalling indications. Sometimes the chance operations yielded impossible requirements, in which case the player is to use his or her discretion, so that chance generates the conditions in which choice must be exercised. Even as he composed the piece, Cage was charged by Henry Cowell with not fully liberating himself from his tastes, which gave him a challenge to address.

The compositional system yielded a number of instructive surprises. Cage expected the fourth movement, for example, to be more spacious, and for the sounds in it to grow progressively louder, but this did not arise. Despite the mobility of the charts, some figures repeat (as, for example, the second system of page 43 of the score).

Durations are notated in the traditional manner, but not grouped metrically, so that a sixteenth note, for instance, may stand by itself without the context of a previous note or a rest. To allow the juxtaposition of notes that resulted to be both notatable and readable, Cage represented a quarter note by a standard 2.5 centimeters, so equivalent durations would always last as long on the page. Durations which were metrically complex could thus be readily set within the metrical structure by working out their position on the page.

David Tudor practiced each section as it was completed. Fastidious as ever, he learned a new form of mathematics to convert the tempo directions into clock time. "It was a very difficult process and very confusing for him," Cage recalled. "Tudor applied himself completely to that music. At that time, he *was* the *Music of Changes*." Tudor presented the first part at the University of Colorado at Boulder on July 5, and again at Black Mountain on August 19. On December 16 the *New York Times* announced the first full performance. Judith Malina, who later went into movies (*Awakenings*, for instance), and Julian Beck had, encouraged by Cage, been leasing the Cherry Lane Theater on Commerce Street in New York City since August for their Living Theater, and it was premiered there on New Year's Day 1952.

Music of Changes initiated a period of stability in Cage's compositional technique, lasting perhaps a year, in which he explored the chart technique for *I Ching* chance operations, mostly through works for piano. The *Seven Haiku* and *For MC and DT*, from 1952, used the same charts as well as the same manner of notation. The *Haiku*, in keeping with the poems, are built around three measures of five, seven and five quarter notes each. The structure of *For MC and DT* is realized graphically, with the page as a "canvas" of proportionally notated time.

Like the close of the *Concerto*, the sixteen silent measures that open *Waiting* are premonitory, and the title can be read symbolically. The raw materials of the piece are repeated sequences, and durations are calculated as the number of their repetitions.

The *Two Pastorales* are dated November 9, 1951 and January 31, 1952. They use only two layers, giving a thinner texture than *Music of Changes*, requiring less virtuosity from the performer. The first served as music for a dance by Merle Marsicano, *Idyll*, which he performed at the YMCA at Lexington and 92nd on the date given on the score. Its rhythmic structure is $2/3^1_2/5^1_2$, realized by Cage as changes of speed. The pedalling directions were determined by Cage's taste; he uses them to highlight the decay of sounds.

Cage considered applying the chart technique to poetry. He wrote to Boulez, "I have also tried charts of words based on a gamut of vowels and then made poems by tossing (which means that I can extend the method to include vocal works)."

The high points of chart technique were achieved in the fourth and fifth *Imaginary Landscapes* and the *Williams Mix*. *Imaginary Landscape No. 4* resulted from a request for a piece by the new Music Society – and from Cowell's charge that the *Music of Changes* was not free of taste. Cage produced a four-minute piece for twelve radios, two players at each; one controlled the tuning, the other tone and volume. For the first time, Cage wrote the parts in proportional notation, developed from the equation of space and time in *Music of Changes* but dispensing with conventional note-heads. "My thinking," Cage claims, was that the work could further his abandonment of his preferences, "that I didn't like the radio and that I would be able to like it if I used it in my work" (although he had used radio before, in *Credo in US* and the *Concerto*). His principal aim, however, was further to liberate not only himself but also the compositional process from likes and dislikes. Using radio, he could not define the musical material – pitches and the like – in advance, only if and how sound was to be produced: the tuning, dynamic and duration of each radio sound, and the combinations of the twelve parts. These were the materials on which chance operated, and the audible result could be sound, static and silence. "I wrote the music for radios feeling sure that no one would be able to discern my taste in that," Cage records.

The idea for the piece went back some years. Like *4'33"* the following year – and like his general concern to eschew his likes and dislikes – it had been waiting to come to fruition, as thought and techniques developed. *Forerunners of Modern Music*, written in 1949, mooted the possibility of "a piece for radios as instruments" which "would give up the matter of method to accident."

Cage wrote the piece between April 5 and 27, 1951, while still in the early stages of writing the *Music of Changes*. The premiere was arranged for May 10, at the McMillan Theater of Columbia University – 8.30 p.m., admission free. Walking on East 43rd Street, a few blocks south of Radio City, Cage passed the G. Schirmer Music Shop and saw in the window an RCA Victor radio, neat, compact, "eight pounds in weight, thirty-five dollars each, with a golden throat acoustical system." The manager of the store agreed to lend twelve of them to Cage.

On the night of the first performance Cage set the radios onstage, murmuring in a stage whisper, "Ah, twelve golden throats." The audience was large. *Imaginary Landscape No.4* was played last, against the wishes of Cage, because a recent article by Virgil Thomson, suggesting links between the music of Cage and new developments in abstract painting, had stimulated interest in his work, making the radio piece an obvious peak to the program.

The length of the other compositions meant that the *Landscape* did not begin until midnight. Among the players were Beck and Malina, Remy Charlip, Lou Harrison, Richard Miller, the poet Harold Norse, Richard Stryker and others, mainly musicians. The audience was buzzing with anticipation. "Cage conducted with great seriousness from his score," recalls Norse. "The effect was similar to an automobile ride at night on an American highway in which neon signs and patches of noise from radios and automobiles flash into the distance." In and out of earshot drifted fragments. The word "Korea" recurred:

> In Korea. And on the central front, the enemy
> Fielder's choice Tommy Spillane is moving off base
> Now ladies, remember that when washday comes
> But mother, I can't tell

Among it all, to spontaneous applause, came fragments of a Mozart

137

violin concerto. "Picking up snatches of music and speech," Norse records, with lengthy silences in between, it had a disturbing effect." Reviewing the concert, Henry Cowell suggested that the late hour at which the piece was played ruined it, since most stations had gone off the air. "It was certainly not what Lou Harrison used to call a rabble-rouser," Cage conceded in a letter to Boulez. However, he challenged Cowell's claim that the piece amounted to a failure. "In fact," he corrected, "there were all sorts of broadcasts." The volume levels specified are all low anyhow. "I knew that the piece was essentially quiet through the use of chance operations and that there was very little sound in it, even in broad daylight, so to speak."

After the concert, a procession of helpers lugged the golden throats and the percussion instruments out to the sidewalk. Richard Lippold drove up in his hearse, which carried them away into the night.

Like many people in the first flush of revelation, Cage was enthusiastically proselytizing for Zen. Peter Yates characterized Cage at the start of the fifties as "stiff, soft-spoken, rather humorless, single-minded, coming into the room as if he were a boddhisatva, his feet a little off the ground." Jasper Johns recalls from a couple of years later Cage's disarming tendency to begin abruptly talking about Buddhism without any conversational cue. Everything he said was permeated by a philosophical angle.

His sudden shift in thinking alienated some former allies. As Cage delivered the *Lecture on Nothing* in 1949, he recorded, Jeanne Reynal had walked out, shouting, "John, I dearly love you, but I can't bear another minute." Hazel Johnson, who had met Cage at the Bennington Summer School in the early fifties and was then much taken with his work, was incredulous when she heard him again in the early fifties. "I didn't believe my ears. The whole reaction on campus was, 'he can't be serious,'" Johnson recalled. "It was all in this super-pontifical tone. 'Our new music is this. Our new music and dance.' Come off it. We know you. I mean this is John. I remember at a party I said, 'What do you mean by this? What's going on?' Then all this business about silence, silence, silence. What I didn't know then is he'd gotten into the Zen thing. Also," a charge rarely made against Cage, "he's an operator, and it was the thing that was in the wind."

Not everyone was put off by the sudden strength of his involvement with Zen. On the road in 1950 Cage and Cunningham visited Denver. Cage played the *Sonatas and Interludes*; Cunningham gave masterclasses at the McLean School. One of the women stunned him with her dancing; her name, it turned out, was Carolyn Brown.

IV

Brown, born Rice, had made her stage debut at the age of three as a flower, at the school of Denishawn dance run by her mother Marion in Fitchburg, Massachusetts. While in high school, she presented dance concerts for hospitalized soldiers. Luminaries such as Gladys Hight in Chicago urged her to pursue a career in dance. Her ambition, however, was to be a writer. She took a B.A. in philosophy at Wheaton College, was elected to Phi Beta Kappa, and only incidentally ran and choreographed the college dance group.

Having married a young engineering graduate from Northwestern in June 1950, soon after leaving college, she moved with him to Denver, where she taught dance and drama at a private school. Despite working at her literary career, she was increasingly embroiled in the world of dance. Brown took up with Jane McLean's dance company, which led to her enrollment in Cunningham's masterclass.

At a party following one of the Denver concerts, Cage was chatting in a group when a rather gaunt young man among them said abruptly, "Do you think your music has any relationship to the music of Anton Webern?" Cage was surprised; he came across few people with any knowledge of Webern, least of all in a provincial college like the McLean School.

The young man turned out to be the twenty-five-year-old husband of Carolyn Brown. Though his degree had been in engineering, Earle Brown had barnstormed as a jazz trumpeter throughout his college days, and gone on to study with Kenneth McKillop techniques for orchestration and composition based on those of Joseph Schillinger, and had studied composition and counterpoint with Roslyn Brogue Henning. Now he was teaching Schillinger technique in Denver. He was also studying contemporary art in depth, in particular the work of Alexander Calder and Jackson Pollock. Brown had made his first steps toward a style of composition which would furnish situations and logics analogous to the visual work he admired – attempts which were to lead by the end of 1952 to seminal work.

Cage and Cunningham found they had a great deal in common with Carolyn and Earle Brown. With Earle, Cage shared an interest in visual arts which was unusual among musicians and composers, and found his music of great individuality and interest. In Carolyn, Cage found a thoughtful mind sympathetic to his new interest in Zen. "We knocked a couple of cocktail parties apart by dominating the whole thing," Earle Brown recalls of their first acquaintanceship in Denver. "John and Merce and Carolyn and I talked a blue streak about philosophy and dance and music and art." Cunningham and Cage invited the couple to join them in New York so that they could all work together. The timing was fortuitous; the Browns arrived as Cage was in the midst of a revolution in his thought and some of his most path-breaking work, inaugurating one of his most fruitful relationships, and providing Cunningham with a virtuoso dancing partner who would work with him in the company for the next twenty years.

Cage has suggested that the arrival of the Browns in New York infuriated Feldman. "The closeness that I had had with Morty and David and Christian was disrupted by the advent of Earle," he has stated. Earle Brown insists that this is not quite accurate. Feldman did fall out with him, but not for several months; at first the couple were made very welcome. "Morty invited us to his house with a writer friend of his named Daniel Stern," Earle Brown recalls, "and surprised us by making baked scallops."

Feldman had a garrulous, dominating side; for instance, he had a strong territorial sense about Washington Square Park, which was near his apartment, insisting that they always sit on one particular side, and he puzzled the Browns by demanding to know who was their psychoanalyst, refusing to believe they could manage without one. At first, though, the Browns often saw him, and in his own way he was very friendly.

Robert Rauschenberg, the young painter from Black Mountain, had also come to New York. Since he and Cage had first met, he had married – Sue Weil, with whom he had fallen in love at the Académie Julien in Paris back in 1947. The wedding took place in 1950, and their son, Christopher, was born in New York on July 16, 1951; the marriage ended in divorce by the end of the year.

Meantime Rauschenberg was making blue photochromes – Carolyn Brown was one of the subjects. In the course of the year, among work on the *Music of Changes, Imaginary Landscape No. 4* and other pieces, Cage was the coproducer of a Rauschenberg work. "Cage was involved with this because he was the only person with a car who would be willing," remembered Rauschenberg. The painter glued together fifty of the largest sheets of paper in his possession and stretched them out on the street. Cage drove his A-Model Ford through paint and onto the sheets. "The only directions he had were to try to stay on the paper," Rauschenberg recalled.

Over the previous few years, the pioneering work of Cage with percussion, electrical instruments and the prepared piano had attracted increasing recognition and even acceptance. His name was becoming more widely known, the subject of newspaper cartoons and syndicated stories, though it was not until 1964 that he became the subject of a crossword puzzle clue. The work of the previous decade continued to attract attention, sometimes faintly commercial. Reviews were improving. His music was performed in South America; Herbert Eimert arranged a broadcast on Nordwestdeutsche Rundfunk; he was talked of in Japan. After the Korean War broke out, his *Three Dances for Two Prepared Pianos* was broadcast to Bali, "with the hope," Cage wrote, "of convincing the natives that America loves the Orient." Incidentally, this ploy fits into the context of government research into political uses of "humanistic" music against the Soviet Union. Cage noted laconically, "they were doing their work and I was doing mine. I wasn't paid for it."

The *Music for Marcel Duchamp* (1947) in particular, and the feel of the work of Cage in general, attracted interest from filmmakers. A writer in *Film Music Notes* had proposed in May 1949 that "some day a cartoon director is going to wake up to the fact that he is missing a sure-fire bet by not availing himself of the talents of Cage for the cartoon." In April 1951, while steeped both in *Music of Changes* and *Imaginary Landscape No. 4*, Cage was asked to provide music for a film on the work of Jackson Pollock. The directors, Hans Namuth and Paul Falkenberg, had thought to use Balinese music, but Pollock wanted something more American; his wife, Lee Krasner, approached Cage. As Cage later told Irving Sadler, "I couldn't abide Pollock's work because I couldn't stand the man." He recalled elsewhere, Pollock "was generally so drunk, and he was actually an unpleasant person for me to encounter. I remember seeing him on the same side of the street I was, and I would always cross over to the other side." This is probably the strongest expression of dislike by Cage on record. Cage refused Krasner's request but referred her to Feldman, who accepted it in return for an ink drawing.

Soon afterwards Burgess Meredith, who had attended the premiere of the *Sonatas and Interludes*, asked Cage to write music for a film he had produced and narrated on the work of Alexander Calder. The score won an award in the first Art Film Festival held in September 1951 at Woodstock, a town little suspecting what Cage would present there eleven months later. He was duly fêted at the awards ceremony, at Hunter College auditorium on 69th Street, on November 16.

None of this interest changed the fact that Cage was desperately poor. His parents' predictions years earlier had not been unrealistic: "maybe there is a connection between poverty and music," he noted. He sold the paintings by Mark Tobey which he had purchased so painstakingly. *Vogue* paid him fifty dollars in December 1951 for the use of his apartment for a photo session, for Horowitz and Duberman's "junior miss" fashions. The publicity material he designed for his own concerts and those of Tudor and William Masselos led to some graphic work for the textile designer Jack Lenor Larsen at 16 East 55th Street.

A danger Cage saw was that paid work would divert him from his true work as a composer. He remembered once "meeting a man who had a desire to be an artist. But not having any money, he took a job in order to make some in Hollywood. And his job continued, and he made money, but he never made any art things." By the turn of the fifties Cage resolved to force himself to earn money in extraneous employment only when he really needed it. "I could go a long time without working. I mean without getting a job," he recalled.

At the beginning of 1951 Cage spent two or three days trying unsuccessfully to find work. "So," he recounted matter of factly, "I decided not to look anymore, but to do my own work"; "to limit my work to my composition, not to look for another kind of work" – "and, if necessary, to die as a result."

Cage worked on the *Music of Changes* so close to that edge that he gave instructions to Tudor as to how the piece could be completed in the event of his death. To ameliorate his condition, if only a little, Cage sent out letters to everyone he knew, offering them shares in the piece. "Would you like to be rich when you're dead?" his uncompromising, unpromising copy demanded. He carefully inscribed the names of any takers in a book; total receipts came to around 250 dollars. When Cage was asked, in less harsh times, if his benefactors – especially his parents – had received their dividend, he replied, "not nearly enough."

This was, as he put it, his "heroic period." Working "out of line with the economy," "not paying any attention to not having any money led me to continue my work as I saw fit," he told the Harvard class. When years later a young composer explained he wanted to make a living, Cage replied, "You have to decide whether you want to make a living or whether you want to make music." "It is in living dangerously economically," he proposed in a letter from 1964, "that one shows 'bravery' i.e. socially."

"We were all in the same boat," according to Earle Brown. Rauschenberg was eating unripe bananas which he could pick up off the wharfs. The friends helped one another as and when they could. Cage bought a Rauschenberg in 1951 from his first show at the Betty Parsons Gallery; Earle Brown bought one of the black paintings for $26.30, since that happened to be the amount he had received that day as a refund from the telephone company.

V

Tape music was born with the fifties. Up until then the recording media had consisted of disc, wire and photoelectric means; since the Second World War, tape technology had developed rapidly. Magnetic tape had changed from a metal base – dangerous if it snapped while running – to plastics. *Musique concrète*, music derived from recorded sounds (juxtaposed, superimposed, played backwards, slowed down, speeded up), was first composed in France in the late forties, notably by Pierre Schaeffer, whose Groupe des Recherches Musicales became an institutional hotbed for electroacoustic work into the seventies, attracting composers from Luc Ferrari to Denis Smalley.

Karlheinz Stockhausen, a younger contemporary of Boulez who was likewise developing a serial music which led on from Webern, recorded a since-lost *Etude* in Paris, using concrete sounds, in December 1952. Back in Germany, pioneering work was carried out in electronic compositions, using sounds not only treated but also generated electronically and recorded on tape. It was Stockhausen who in 1953 put together what is often isolated as the first purely electronic composition, *Studie I*.

Cunningham made use of some of the new music as an accompaniment to his dances. In 1952 he choreographed *Collages I* and *II* to Schaeffer's *Symphonie pour un homme seul*, and the following year *Fragments* to tape works by Boulez, *Etude à un son* and *Etude 2*.

Cage felt a growing urge to experiment with tape, so when Jean Erdman called to ask if he would write an accompaniment for her dance *Portrait of a lady* – they had met less than a fortnight earlier when he had spoken on "Music for the Dance" at her school at 77 5th Avenue – he took it as his opportunity, and leapt to work with characteristic speed. In eighteen hours on January 12, 1952 he completed his fifth *Imaginary Landscape*, for any forty-two records, "the score to be realized as a magnetic tape." The piece was a collage of fragments re-recorded on to tape, "treated as sound sources, rather than being what they were." In *Imaginary Landscape*

No. 4 Cage had used radios in an attempt to overcome his dislike of radio; here he mostly used jazz records, partly because "the dance had a character that suggested popular music," partly to circumvent his aversion to jazz.

Imaginary Landscape No. 5 is another *I Ching* chart work, with a five by five structure, containing, not unlike the *Concerto*, an allegory of the compositional itinerary of Cage as he worked: "at the fourth large structural division, there is the sign M–I, meaning "mobility–immobility." This refers to the method of composition by means of the *I Ching*. Erdman danced to the piece at the Hunter Playhouse on January 18, in a program that included *Daughters of the Lonesome Isle*.

Cage wanted to compose a more complex tape work. His applications to the Ford and Rockefeller foundations were rejected; one of his contacts from Black Mountain came to the rescue.

As a student at Black Mountain, Paul Williams had become interested in minimal architecture – producing comfortable dwellings at the lowest cost. Soon after leaving college he married another former student, Vera. The young architect's inventor father had become a millionaire, unlike John senior, and when he died he left his son a substantial inheritance. Williams's first philanthropic act was to donate five thousand dollars to establish a "Project for Magnetic Tape" for the investigation of electroacoustic music.

The money provided a weekly stipend of forty dollars for the five members of the project team: Cage, Tudor and Brown (which alleviated their poverty somewhat) and Louis and Bebe Barron (born in 1923 and 1928). They divided their work between the Barrons' studio at 9 West Eighth Street in the Bowery, where field recordings were catalogued and spliced; Cage's apartment, where editing was carried out; and Colonel Richard Ranger's Rangertone Studios in New Jersey, where master tapes were dubbed from time to time. The one brief exception arose when Boulez came visiting; he stayed at the Bozza mansion, and Cage and Brown temporarily moved with the equipment into Cunningham's flat.

All materials for the project had to be paid for out of the stipends. Equipment was scarce. The Barrons had two tape machines; in his apartment, Cage laid out on the table razor blades, glass as a cutting surface, talcum powder and sticky tape.

In its short life the studio presented four works. A dance commission, *For Magnetic Tape* by Christian Wolff, was begun in March. For a film by Ian Hugo, the Barrons produced music they called *For an Electronic Nervous System, No. 1*; later, they would devise electronic music for the sci-fi remake of *The Tempest*, *Forbidden Planet*. The greatest effort went into starting work on a composition by Cage named after their sponsor, the *Williams Mix*. Remaindered tape cuttings from the piece were rather rapidly assembled by Earle Brown into his *Octet I*.

Cage, Tudor and the Browns recorded a variety of sounds as source materials for the compositions, then copied and catalogued them in the studio, eventually accumulating five to six hundred sounds. For the *Williams Mix*, Cage used a chart to generate a random structure of forty-six squared, divided 5/6/16/3/11/5. He planned a dense piece with up to sixteen layers of sound, two on each of eight tracks. A taxonomy was devised for the library material: A stood for city sounds, B for sounds from the country, C for electronic, D for manually produced, including musical, sounds; E for sounds produced by wind (songs were included here). Category F was for "small sounds" – sounds so soft that amplification was needed to make them audible. Each sound was then classed according to whether its frequency, overtone structure or amplitude remained constant (c) or varied (v). The notation Cvvv would thus refer to an electronic sound whose frequency, overtone structure and amplitude all varied throughout its length. Such operations led, for instance, to the inclusion of a snatch of Beethoven's Ninth Symphony. In recent pieces Cage had worked on accepting jazz and the radio; now chance operations gave him the opportunity to do the same with the "roll of toilet paper" – the composer to whom he most objected.

Since Cage was working in clock rather than metrical time, durational structure was based on inches of tape, as the *Imaginary Landscape No. 5* had been. In this he mirrored the activities of the European pioneers. Stockhausen, for example, measured out the serialized durations of his *Etude* in centimeters, an interesting example of the way numerical precision was used in chance and serial music for very different purposes.

The tempo was modified, as in the *Music of Changes*, by a factor of n, by which the proportions of the section were multiplied. The number of layers for each section was determined, then within this, a duration, and whether it was sound or silence: if a sound, chance selected the dynamic gradient by which it started (its attack), the way it decayed and which of the six types of sound was to be employed.

Lengths and specifications were carefully drawn at a one to one scale on quadrille paper. The tape was cut according to it, "like a dress-maker's pattern." As each splice was completed, the corresponding area of the score was marked with a red dot. Soon the score was peppered with cigarette burns and coffee stains. With a tape-speed of fifteen inches every second, each page lasts only one and a third seconds; the music as completed, which lasts just over four and a half minutes, runs to 192 pages.

Again, as in the *Music of Changes*, composition required hundreds of casts of the *I Ching*. One visited the Bozza mansion at the risk of being handed three coins and a sheet of paper. At this stage over a dozen people were involved, including Earle Brown, Cunningham and M.C. Richards. "The quantity of the work I had to do," Cage recalled, "was so immense that David [Tudor] learned all my composition techniques and composed ... along with me." He wrote to Boulez, "Tudor has been composing superpositions seven to eleven. A student from Illinois worked."

The student was Ben Johnston, who met Cage earlier in the year. Johnston had been asked to write music for a play at the university and the writer, Arthur Gregor, referred the result to Cage for his opinion. Cage said he found it interesting and recommended it be used. While the play was in production, he was asked at the last minute to give a lecture and take part in a panel discussion. After he delivered a talk on March 2, later reproduced in *Silence*, there was an outcry. Johnston introduced himself and invited Cage to his apartment for coffee; Cage suggested as they talked that he come down to New York in the summer so they could work together. "This was my first year of teaching, and I didn't have the time to do all the preparation," Johnston recalled. "When I arrived, and he discovered that I hadn't done any of the things he had asked me to do, he set me to work splicing tape for *Williams Mix*."

Tudor carried out little work on the splicing; Johnston worked only over the summer of 1952. It was Earle Brown who was the main assistant to Cage at this time. There was no direct subway service; Brown preferred to walk from his home in Greenwich Village to the Bozza mansion, and walk back, every day. The two men sat at opposite sides of a huge table with razors, tape and talcum powder, and cut and spliced for twelve hours a day with only an occasional break. "He taught me patience," Brown remembers. "John and I had these endless conversations – we talked about everything under the sun; and sometimes twenty minutes would go by and neither of us would say a word."

They discovered as they worked that different ways of cutting the tape affected the attack and decay of the tape sounds. Cage specified cuts to be used to exploit this, including free irregular cutting, even pulverizing, of the tape, marked in the score by a green plus sign. To Boulez he wrote: "The attacks and decays are specific cuts of the tape ... also 'cross-grain' use of the tape (which affects the overtone structure as well).

I have organized single and double cuts . . . and then use a '+' to indicate more complicated cuts and curves which are invented at the moment of cutting." The spontaneous cuts were another vestige of improvisation which in each successive piece through the fifties he strove to excise.

There had been problems with synchronization when preparing music for the Calder film; the editing of the *Williams Mix* caused serious difficulties. As the tapes made by Brown and Cage were different tracks which would eventually be synchronized, they would periodically be checked to see that corresponding parts matched, and there were often discrepancies. Once the men had discounted the idea that one of them was simply careless, they decided to test for differences in perception. Taking a single ruler and a single length of tape, each marked off an inch. The points did not coincide. Brown, it emerged, closed one eye to measure; Cage kept both open. Cage tried closing one of his eyes; Brown later began working with both open. The problem remained. Finally, they agreed that one person be made responsible for the final synchronizing splices. Then they realized that temperature and humidity caused the tape to expand and contract to a minute but significant extent.

In the light of his new way of thinking, Cage interpreted these difficulties as further inducement to abandon control, just as he had begun to celebrate the unreplicability of piano preparations. "I took our failure to achieve synchronization as an omen," he noted, "to go toward the unfixed, rather than to change my methods so as to make it more fixed."

One day, amidst the splicing, the telephone rang. "I think it was Pepsi-Cola," Brown hazards in retrospect. "They wanted him to write a jingle, or use his music for commercial purposes." It was actually a woman calling on behalf of the J. Walter Thompson Company. The business had been founded in 1864 and acquired by its eponymous owner fourteen years later; one of the first advertising agencies to operate internationally, by the fifties JWT was a giant, an adventurous user of scientific skills such as motivational studies in market research. Cage was handed over by the woman to one of the directors. "Mr. Cage," he asked, "are you willing to prostitute your art?" Hunger uppermost in his mind, Cage said, "Of course I am. What do you want me to do?" They arranged an appointment for Friday at two.

After hearing a few recordings, one of the directors said to me, "Wait a minute." Then seven directors formed what looked like a football huddle. From this one of them finally emerged, came over to me, and said, "You're too good for us. We're going to save you for Robinson Crusoe."

Cage and Brown generally finished work at around two o'clock on Fridays and went up to Columbia to hear Suzuki speak. Cage, Cunningham, Rauschenberg and the Browns would go to the movies together. Most Sunday evenings Cage would visit his parents, accompanied by the Browns and Cunningham, at first at their apartment off Fifth Avenue, later in Montclair, New Jersey, for dinner and a round of Scrabble. A three-hundred-page textbook by John senior, *Theory and Application of Industrial Electronics*, written with C.J. Bashe, had just been published by McGraw-Hill. The radar research of John senior had already raised the issue of technology, knowledge and common orientations, allowing different people independently to generate similar inventions. This was again true in the early fifties, when he worked on television technology. He produced an improved cathode ray tube, experimented with color transmission, and carried out preliminary work on projected television.

Like some of his other work, it did not lead to recognition or reward. RCA had already begun work with color; John senior tried to sue for royalties. One day he arrived at the Bozza mansion and announced, "I've just been in to see a lawyer and he thinks I can get retroactive royalties to all color television programs ever broadcast." It would have amounted to millions of dollars, even then, and he promised to buy his son and his colleagues the very best equipment for an electronic music studio. He did not win the case.

Feldman fell out with Earle Brown during work on the *Williams Mix*. Every so often when the master tape had been cut and spliced to a satisfactory standard, it was taken over to be copied at Colonel Ranger's studio in New Jersey. On the way home one night, Cage, Feldman, Earle and possibly Carolyn Brown stopped off at a diner for a bite to eat. Feldman criticized Boulez and his penchant for mathematics. Earle Brown defended the Frenchman, partly because of his own involvement with mathematics, as a scientist and an advocate of Schillinger techniques. Unknown to Brown, Feldman was taking his response as a personal attack. After returning to Manhattan and dropping off Feldman, Cage told Brown that he could tell his friend was furious. Feldman in fact ignored Brown for three or four years afterwards. At concerts, Brown recalls, he and his wife would enter the foyer, "and Morty would embrace Carolyn and cut me dead."

Cage was now on good terms with Edgard Varèse. "Varèse would walk all the way from the Village over to Grand Street and Monroe and climb the six flights to where I was working," Cage recalled. He came to rank with Henry Cowell as one of the composers of the previous generation most interested in the younger man's activities. During work on *Williams Mix*, Varèse visited Cage at the Barrons' studio "and we had a conversation about harmony ... and we both, in a spirit of pleasure, mirth, and so forth, agreed that anything that was worth knowing about harmony could be taught in half an hour."

The "Music for Magnetic Tape" project continued until early 1953, culminating in a concert featuring *Williams Mix*, the *Octet* by Brown, and other electronic works by European and American composers, mostly solicited by Cage. The concert was held as part of the University of Illinois Festival of Contemporary Music on March 22. Only the first two sections (5 and 6 of the rhythmic scheme) of the *Williams Mix* were ever laid down. It was not played in public until the Donaueschingen Festival in 1954.

VI

Cage first employed chance operations alongside means devised for his earlier, choice-based musical style. However, rhythmical structure, which had become senescent prior to Cage's engagement with Zen, was an uneasy bedfellow of chance. Likewise, the chart system, which Cage had begun to use only a few months before he turned to chance, was showing disadvantages. Cage's view of sound as a continuous field clashed with the way sound materials in the chart system were catalogued in separate boxes. He was concerned, too, to remove will as much as possible, and while with chance there would always be a framing problem with the manner and extent to which choice is involved in assembling the compositional materials, chart technique was specially problematic because it forced Cage to begin by choosing the possible contents of the work and only then bringing chance to bear.

Chance operations had shortcomings of their own. The length of time required for casting the *I Ching* – computerization was years away – was a special problem. One of the principal features of Cage's work over the next ten years was the quest for better ways to use chance. After the magic square, the Tarot and the first use of the *I Ching*, he would variously experiment with shuffling cards, tracing star charts, folding paper to isolate points, or highlight imperfections on its surface. After his phase of chart pieces from *Music of Changes* to the *Williams Mix*, Cage would try a point system rather than a chart system, then attempt to combine them to compensate for their respective shortcomings. In the *Music for Piano* he experimented with dot notation, and shortly began notations for live performance works using the chronometric time he had learned from Tudor's rehearsal technique for the *Music of Changes*, beginning with *Water Music* and most apparent in the series to be called the *Ten Thousand Things*.

Cage was the first artist to base his work on chance. However, he was far from being the first to employ it; several artists had used chance at some stage in the compositional process. Mozart wrote Dice Waltzes, in which the order of musical material was selected by chance – later, in *HPSCHD*, Cage was to employ them – and Bach wrote a random piece. In the twentieth century the Dadaist writer Tristan Tzara put together poetry from words cut out of newspapers and drawn from a hat; Duchamp made both musical and visual works by means of chance selections ("I must have been fifty years ahead of my time," he told Cage later.)

Looked at only historically, Cage's use of chance could seem derivative or opportunistic. The technique (the interest value of which was easily exhaustible) had been employed before; the more anguished times between the wars, for instance, gave the use of chance then a lively urgency. Yet such urgency scarcely applied to the complacent optimism of postwar America. Many of the ideas by which Cage explains his recourse to chance had also been ventured before, from classical times onward. There are so many precedents and no historical necessity.

That is one view, but one-dimensional. Another view could begin with Cage's own reasons for using chance operations. What is distinctive about his use of chance, and what redeems it, is the fusion of his deep and idiosyncratic motives and the seriousness with which he pursues them and puts them into action. Chance becomes a discipline used with integrity to play out trends in his character such as impersonalism, asceticism, accepting the world, and mystical aims.

The concept of dialectic existed before Marx and the concept of the unconscious was used prior to Freud. Marx and Freud transformed the concepts they took over in ways which made them generally useful. Cage used chance operations in a different way to what had gone before, but they have not become generally useful (there is no Second Los Angeles School of composers by chance); despite Cage's influence, his specific practices have not obtained currency. Their success does not emerge so much from chance operations being an appropriate response to social conditions, which by and large they had been for his predecessors, as from their over-arching suitability, which Cage in turn refined, for his entire personal network of life, work and thought. Chance was not the deadend for Cage that it had been for others: through it he could address the whole of his being. As a productive solution to tendencies and tensions in his work, chance operations did not lead to its ossification, but gave it a direction; it could always be coherent and possibly progressing.

Cage's achievements, as stated at the outset, are intelligible with reference to a unifying theme, both heuristic and apodeictic – Cage making himself through a self-clarifying, ever more adequate direction which locates his tendencies in a system of thought permitting him to realize them in actions, which clarifies the internal in turn. His experience of Zen gave him a world view which validated, located and synergetically reinforced his temperamental inclinations, and answered some of his questions; chance operations gave him adequate practical means. This is not to say that John Cage was in some way destined to discover Zen and compose by chance; simply that, whatever processes brought them to his mind, Zen and chance were far and away the best fit for the man he had become – a far tighter and wide-ranging fit than most people achieve. Whereas the greatness of a Beethoven or a Mozart lies in their ability to turn inwards and integrate their total humanity, the success of Cage, perhaps his greatness, lies in his adopting and adapting a global system to suit him perfectly.

Chance operations tear the rug from under all customary forms of music analysis. The attempt to understand music generally treats the structure, pattern and regularity of a piece at various levels and dimensions. One of the criteria for evaluation is how far a suitably novel balance is struck between form and content – not so simply formed as to be redundant, not so divorced from form as to be unrecuperable. Sometimes music is related to the intentions of the composer; one way to judge music is to decide the quality and integrity of the composer's aims, the extent to which the music fulfills them.

With a music of chance, such criteria either do not apply at all, or do so in attenuated form. As Cage observed in *Silence*, chance identifies the composer, but one cannot build on that "identification." Composition consists of setting up the processes which lead to the score or, as Cage later develops it, preparing the materials and specifying the processes a performer must go through to prepare for performance. Cage makes his "responsibility asking questions, instead of making choices."

The only way to talk about such a piece is to describe the chance processes used in its writing. There is nothing on which conventional analysis can seize; even psychoanalysis can only provide insight into the desire to use the method, not the work it produces. One must go back to look at *precisely what Cage has done*, or else simply play or listen – hence the otherwise puzzlingly pedantic prefaces by Cage to his writings. He was already concerned with pure form in his lectures of the late forties and early fifties, when he takes pains to point out the structural subdivisions into which, as with his music, he has divided the work ("here we are at the beginning of the thirteenth unit of the fourth large part of this talk"). This tendency reached its height in the *Lecture on Nothing*, with its fourteen repetitions of the same section, differentiated only by its number sequences.

Since Cage's work with chance operations is not amenable to customary approaches to music, what he is doing and can do is often misunderstood. One way to avoid such misunderstanding is to work at least once with chance operations oneself to produce some sort of work – textual, visual or musical, because this immediately clarifies the attitudes needed and the practicalities of the technique. As Cage once responded to a questioner from the audience, "Perhaps you would understand if you did it." However, a number of recurrent misunderstandings can be anticipated immediately. Cage did not take up chance operations out of laziness, so he could write music more easily. They constituted a discipline through which he could achieve the suspension of likes and dislikes essential to Zen. The traditional disciplines of Eastern philosophy are inward-looking: Zazen, Yoga. "I have never practiced sitting cross-legged, nor do I meditate," Cage relates, "because I did enough sitting and I'm still sitting now." He sought a discipline to open himself to Mind, to use Suzuki's terminology, through the world of relativity, and found in chance operations one which he would practice as he went about his activities.

"Chance is a leap," Cage suggested, "out of reach of one's grasp of oneself." He explained, "I write by using chance operations to liberate my music from every kind of like and dislike." "By flipping coins to determine facets of my music, I chain my ego so that it cannot possibly affect it." In *Empty Words*, Cage explained at greater length:

> Chance operations . . . are a means of locating a single one among a multiplicity of answers, and, at the same time, of freeing the ego from its taste and memory, its concern for profit and power, of silencing the ego so that the rest of the world has a chance to enter into the ego's own experience whether that be outside or inside.

152

Chance not only circumvents tastes in the compositional process, but provides material for performing and listening on which the suspension of preferences can be exercised, for what is about to happen can never be construed from what has already occurred. Performers and listeners, however, can come to know what will happen through repeated exposure. Chance leads to an openness to discovery, whereas, according to Cage, composition by intuition or inspiration does not permit one to learn anything. "What you need is not inspiration," Cage posited, "but you need some understanding of what questions would be productive of good answers." One can tell if a question is not good because the answers are not interesting. A radical question – one which gets at the crux of the matter – is not easy to devise.

At last Cage knew the answer to the question posed by Schoenberg when the latter had asked Cage all those years ago to identify the principle underlying the eight or nine solutions which his pupil had devised. Now Cage felt his mistake had been to take the principle as, like the solutions, a statement. "The principle underlying all the solutions acts in the question that is asked," he realized. "It was in fact his question that produced all of the solutions and he would have accepted that."

Chance operations, for Cage, make all things new. It is impossible to become an expert with respect to the unknown – that is, be able to apply facts, opinions and categories; one can, however, be skilled, by nurturing an empty framework, which allows the unknown to be seen as it is.

Another misunderstanding of chance operations is that they make the concept of a piece central – and most interesting – and that the actual sounds are unimportant. This may be one way for a practitioner to approach working by chance, but it is a rather impoverished one, and not that adopted by Cage. His technique is self-annulling; it cannot be seen and cannot be heard, for as we saw in relation to music analysis, it leaves no trace, nothing that can be construed. It is a discipline which will yield actual sounds, which are the important things – and one can thereby appreciate them for themselves, which is the other important thing.

A more challenging objection is that to appreciate the music in these terms, one needs to know beforehand what are Cage's aims. If one were to listen to the music and spontaneously hear the sounds themselves, then one would have no need of Cage's program; if one cannot do so spontaneously, one needs the theory to appreciate the experience, and perhaps then the theory would be sufficient in itself, the music superfluous. This raises questions about what really happens in the reception of Cage's work. However, just because Cage is not merely a thinker does not exclude him being very useful as a thinker.

It is easy to be confused by the project of abandoning likes and dislikes and conceptual structuring, which underpins Cage's advocacy of chance operations. This is a confusion rather than a misunderstanding because Cage does not give a clear message on these points.

Does the abandonment of likes and dislikes mean they no longer exist, or that we cease to give them priority? The answer is in three parts – what Cage thinks, what is actually the case and whether the two match up. Cage's own view was that "tastes, memory and emotions have to be weakened; all the ramparts have to be razed. As far as I'm concerned, I'm trying to release myself from them." Then he continued, "You can feel an emotion, just don't think that it's so important. . . . It's just like the chicken I ordered in the restaurant: it concerns me, but it's not important." As he told a reporter in Chicago, "we can like chocolate sundaes, but if they're out of them, we're not going to burst into tears." In another formulation, "I am willing to have emotions, but without being a slave to them." "The question is not *not to want*, but to be free with regard to one's will." The task is to apply one's self constantly to minimizing the presence of emotion – "trying to release myself" – rather than to achieve release once and for all.

The idea of abandoning conceptual structuring is subject to similar confusion. Does Cage mean we rid ourselves completely of it, or that it no longer dominates our mental life, or that it is simply given its proper place? The answer would again involve working out what Cage thinks and what is actually the case, and matching the two. As we saw in the third section of the previous chapter, Cage advocates unmediated experience over conceptual understanding, and believes it possible to avoid positing a conceptual relation between elements of reality. In *Silence* he proclaims, "I'm losing my ability to make connections because the ones I do make so belittle the natural complexity"; "seeing the second of two like objects, we no longer manage to remember the first."

The moments – few or many as may be – when one beholds the world in this way are profoundly enriching and conducive to wonder. It is also the case that a surprising number of complex activities can be carried out without the engagement of reflexive consciousness – particularly if one nurtures the ability; I may, for instance, want to reach the cafe up the hill, and do so with an utterly still mind, simply observing the cobblestones and the eaves of the houses, and for those minutes my body *is* my desire and decision to go up to that cafe. My walk, at another level, is the outcome

154

of my human development, which means that the details of my motility – which muscles move where and when – are remembered, and constitute a resource which carries me automatically at times like this. Often an activity depends on this non-reflexive action, as when one successfully performs a piece of music.

However, conceptual structuring has an important place in many other areas of life. It is needed not only to work out how to make a neutron bomb, or to calculate how big is the hole in the ozone layer, but also to allow one to reflect on complex situations in life such as coping with, let's say, a marriage breakup. What do I do, as A.J. Heschel says, when I come back from wondering at the stars?

Just as Cage seems to recognize that likes and dislikes do not vanish once and for all, so he sees conceptual structure and unmediated experience as a seesaw. With chance operations, for instance, there is a need to reach zero as far as expectations are concerned, and then, once a discovery is made, to renew that zero so that discovery can go on. Asked how this can be done, Cage replied,

It's a good question. It's exactly the problem that I face all the time, and it's very difficult because we have a memory. There's no doubt of it. And we're not stupid. We would be stupid if we didn't have memory. And yet it's that memory that one has to become free of, at the same time that you have to take advantage of it. It's very paradoxical.

On the question of intellect, possibly more than on the question of desire, Cage is vaguely inconsistent and prone to bombastic rather than simply precise statements. It is not possible to abandon all conceptual organization; one can only constantly strive to limit its use to its proper place. Cage puts it rather more definitely: "I only keep that amount of organization that is useful for survival." Language is useful for many forms of communication; later, again, Cage was to express rather unrealistic suspicions about it.

At other times Cage is more balanced. Some situations, he observes, require more organization than others. After he became interested in chess, Cage described it as "a balance to my interest in chance," for if one plays the game one enters a situation which is intrinsically organized. "Games are very serious success and failure situations," he observed, ". . . and if I make a wrong move with my knight, I lose." Likewise, if Cage is going to hunt and eat wild mushrooms, he classifies the finds into edible and poisonous, or he may die.

Elsewhere, Cage proposed, "Free the mind from its desire to concentrate." We need a little of everything. Different activities are more or less transcendent – that is, the extent to which desire and conceptual structuring can be set aside varies. Cage came to the conclusion that music could be exemplary because there more than elsewhere he could see a way that in it intellect and likes and dislikes could be excluded. "We can take the attitude of *moksa*, which is liberation from all those other concerns," he explains.

This does not mean that music reflects the purity of a goal from which the rest of life deviates, simply that it is in the nature of music to be able to transcend everyday concerns. It is by being precisely what it can be that music is exemplary – not of an attitude to life, but of life itself. "Writing a piece of music is not everyday life," Cage explains. "What one does in the making of a piece of music is not what one does when one cooks dinner or crosses the street. So there shouldn't be a desire to do in all of one's life what one does in the making of the music." For example, "If I'm not writing music but doing something else, I'm not going to follow the use of chance operations."

The avoidance of intention through chance operations depends paradoxically on intentionally setting up the parameters within which chance will operate. "My choices," Cage clarifies, "consist in choosing what questions to ask."

Although Cage proposes that there is no difference between art and life, the concert situation, with its fancy clothes, rows of seats, and musical instruments themselves, is a sufficiently exceptional situation for it to be specified as a particular part of life; and the distinction between it and the whole of life does not disappear in music such as that of Cage – it relaxes, fades, becomes movable, like steam on a window, which condenses and can be wiped away. As Noel Carrol observed, "Cage's noises are not like everyday noises"; they are samples – exemplifications – of everyday noises "in the way that tailors' swatches of material are symbols but at the same time physical samples."

As we have seen, the effect of Zen on Cage's work and thought was dramatic and rapid. This crucial, precipitate flurry occurred between approximately 1948 and 1953. In the years that followed, however, he continued to develop his new ideas and strove to make his actions more consistent.

When he first wrote by chance means, Cage noticed that he was hoping for certain results. "When I first tossed coins," he wrote, "I sometimes thought: I hope such-and-such will turn up." He consequently disciplined himself to give this up. "If we want to use chance operations," he explained, "then we must accept the results." Both the technique and the range of chance operations could be extended. Cage soon became aware, as we have seen, of the shortcomings of the charts, and tried to develop new means. The works of 1951–52 also show concessions to taste which he would try to avoid in later work. The notes to *Waiting*, dated January 7, 1952, include the instruction "prepared or unprepared if prepared (at pleasure)" (this instruction was removed when the piece was later published).

The transcendence of likes and dislikes was a constant struggle; initially a great deal of progress could be made, though, noting in the fifties his continuing tendency to evaluate, he stated, "I'm annoyed that I am doing so." The difficulty he had been experiencing in listening to familiar, classical music – at a party one evening, Cage winced when a recording of a Brahms symphony was put on in the background – eased, and he felt less seduced by its structure. "I begin to hear the old sounds as though they are not worn out," he reports, and he listened "to object-works . . . to Beethoven in a new way." For example, "I managed in the case of Mozart to listen enthusiastically to the held clarinet tones." Reflecting in 1989 on the possibility of hearing classical music as a collection of sounds each in their own right, Cage noted, "probably not very many people do it. But it can be done" by "paying attention, in the way of hearing things. Surrounded by space, instead of being tied together in what we call relations – or in any relations." One can change one's way of hearing by constructing each sound as proceeding from its own center.

Engagement with Zen also provided a structure for Cage in his attitude to social dealings. "Our lives are not ruined by the interruptions that other people and things continually provide," he stated. Neither interruptions nor our irritation at them need spiral into anger. What is irritating keeps us from ossifying, it shows us what we need to accept and develop next. Cage is "studying being interrupted." "Distractions? Interruptions? Welcome them," he recommended. "They give you the chance to know whether you're disciplined. That way you needn't bother about sitting cross-legged in the lotus position."

This reveals a no doubt practical but interestingly partial definition of discipline which focuses on passivity as the way to tranquility. What Cage seizes on, here as elsewhere, is acceptance. "Responsibility is to oneself," he wrote, "and the highest form of it is irresponsibility to oneself which is to say the calm acceptance of whatever responsibility to others and things comes along." Cage then characteristically reads this not as a call for resignation but for hope.

> What we are really confronted with, in any case, is ourselves. Whether you are in the lion's den, whatever, there is always access to a full life through the acceptance of the situation you are in. Rather than being pessimistic, I find a way to proceed positively. Pessimism and bleakness are not part of me.

This is a viable attitude, but Cage does not make of it an external standard to which one must live up, as Christianity has tended to do. "No 'should' and no blame," he wrote ("no blame" is one of the *leitmotifs* of the *I Ching*).

In keeping with this attitude, it was only reluctantly that Cage resorted to secretarial assistance. He considers his refusal to use an answering machine a social duty (which is interesting as, if it is reserved for use when one is absent, it allows more people to make contact), believing he should be accessible to others as "a matter of ethics." "If I notice that I'm disturbed if the phone rings and not giving my full attention to whomever it is, then I think that I am not doing my work properly," said Cage. "I should be able to be interrupted. I mean, it's being done well if being interrupted is not upsetting it. . . . I enjoy being at the telephone when I am there and I enjoy my work when I am *there*."

Cage explains his way of relating to other people in terms of Zen. "I think one of the most important teachings in Zen philosophy is that each being, whether sentient or non-sentient, is at the center of the universe." Therefore one meets each thing with reverence for what it is. Cage has linked this attitude with his use of chance operations, suggesting that purposelessness is employed "if only out of respect for other 'centers'." He once replied to a critic of his music, "If someone offers you a beefsteak, don't say it should have been a pork chop." One permits "each person, as well as each sound, to be the center of creation."

What he believes, and practices, is that emotions, preferences, and even conceptual connections should be kept to oneself. "My feelings belong, as it were, to me," he says, "and I should not impose them on others." They "mean something to me, but I don't want them to be imposed on another person . . . You're not demeaning feelings, but leaving them where they can function without hurting other people." In the introduction to his *Themes and Variations* he says, "Love=leaving space around loved one."

The ability to connect two things is a privilege of each individual, one which is not to be exercised publicly.

"I think that I have the right – and, in fact, the need – to be myself, as long as I live! . . . But I try to keep this fact of being myself *for myself*, that is, I try not to impose it on others." Doing so, "I do not disturb your center, nor you mine," and, said Cage, with a rare nod to liberalism, "This concept has grown where there has been democracy." "I think the Golden Rule, which is often thought of as the center, really, of Christianity, is a mistake: 'Do unto others as *you* would be done by.' I think this is a mistaken thought. We should do unto others as *they* would be done by."

A colleague reveals, "He's extremely opinionated in his views, but he won't tell you those views unless you really dig for them." "He says he likes my music," says Earle Brown, "but I don't know if he really likes it or not." Brown also recalls a concert that Cage attended which included Frederic Rzewski's *The Workers United Will Never Be Defeated*, a powerful, bombastic work with a political program. Since in all these respects the piece was diametrically opposed to Cage's approach, Brown wondered what he would say to the composer. With marvelous diplomacy, Cage shook Rzewski's hand and exclaimed, "Quel tour de force!"

Cage has more difficulty deciding whether he should intervene if players perform his work wrongly. The day after one appalling performance which he attended but did not interrupt, Cage said ruefully, "There's actually some kind of mistake in my make-up, that I wouldn't correct that wrong situation." He decided in retrospect that it would have been inappropriate to have stopped it with a shout; that he should have walked up to the front, interrupted the players, explained both to them and to the audience that the piece was being performed incorrectly, and attempted to tell them how it should be played.

A common theme runs through Cage's attitudes – economy. Like a martial artist, he tries to see each thing as it is and expends just enough energy to cause something to happen. It is noteworthy that what is ethically desirable – such as allowing other people to be what they are – is also what is most practical in terms of economical action. Cage has a wise humility which reflects what is practicable. Asked what he saw as the role of the poet in society, for example, Cage replied, "I don't think it makes much difference how I see it." Our responsibility is to lighten ourselves and open ourselves. "When we remove the world from our shoulders we notice it doesn't drop," Cage said. "If you let it, it supports itself."

VII

Williams Mix was a time-consuming project, and Cage made a number of great strides in his work and thought as he and his friends gradually assembled the piece in the course of 1952.

In the first half of the year, Cage produced a new, particularly theatrical work. The solo performer plays not only piano but also siren whistle and radio, and is called on to shuffle and deal seven playing cards, blow a duck call in a bowl of water, and prepare the piano on the spot with four objects in just over thirty seconds. (Cage does not specify the strings to be prepared; they need not even be played in what follows.) Moreover, the score consists of ten large sheets which are to be joined to make a single large poster, which, if visible to the audience, as generally it is, allows them to follow the proceedings in whatever detail they choose.

Other activities listed in the charts but not selected include lighting a "shire" match and blowing it out from behind closed teeth, lighting a cigarette, playing an ascending scale on a duck whistle and saying "Hello!?".

Cage's initial plan was to give the piece a mobile title, taking its name from the place of performance or, in a later version, from the date. It was first performed at the New School for Social Research at 66 West 12th Street in New York, and was played later in the year, on August 29, 1952. The piece was soon retitled *Water Music* and, as Cage claimed in an invitation to Nicolas Slonimsky, "unlike Handel's, it really splashes." Slonimsky attended a performance by Tudor, noting later that "it did not really splash, and I whispered my disappointment to my neighbor."

Following the use of proportional notation in *Imaginary Landscape No. 4*, *Water Music* was notated in chronometric time, multiplying numbers generated by the *I Ching* by factors of quarter, half or whole seconds to determine durations. The structure of the piece is ten groups of ten units, each lasting four seconds, yielding a total length of six minutes and forty seconds. Cage wrote in his notes. "Each forty seconds determines superpos. and how toss affects time: either 1/4 (sec.) 1/2 (sec.) or (1 sec.)."

Durations are specified using decimals rather than fractions: 3.2175 thus means three minutes, twenty-one and three-quarter seconds, .215 means twenty-one and a half seconds. This notation would be carried much further in the time-length pieces of the coming years known as the *Ten Thousand Things*.

Water Music includes various vestigial concessions to taste. The

160

opening instruction asks that the dynamics of the radio be "changed at the discretion of player within range of 5 and 6." Unused elements of the charts suggest that if the cigarette is called for, the performer may "smoke at will to"; the charts for superpositions provide that if the *I Ching* yields sixty-four, this should be read as "free sound 4th. superpos.) (joker)."

Over the summer of 1952 Cage was invited back to Black Mountain College by Lou Harrison, who was now head of the Music Department; enough time had passed, Harrison felt, since the Beethoven *débâcle* for his friend to reappear. With Cage came Cunningham and Tudor. Since the breakup of his marriage Robert Rauschenberg had been traveling – working for a construction firm in Casablanca, and then causing a brief furor in Italy with his sculptures, which he consigned to the River Arno before leaving; by this time he was back in New York, living in a loft on Fulton Street, and he joined his friends in North Carolina, too.

Cage and his companions commandeered the main dining room of the college for three-quarters of an hour to stage a diverse theatrical performance. A form scheme for the activities had been devised by chance means. A number of "disparate activities" occurred, sometimes simultaneously, sometimes in succession. Cage read one of his lectures from the top of a stepladder; Cunningham danced, both around and amid the audience; Tudor played the piano. Rauschenberg played scratchy records on a vintage windup Victrola with a horn loudspeaker; his "White" paintings hung from the rafters. Mary Caroline Richards, poet and potter, time-shared with the poet, and sometime biographer of Auden, Charles Olsen, on the upper rungs of another stepladder, and two other people projected slides and movies at various points on the walls. This "concerted action" has often been construed as the prototype for the multimedia "happenings" of the sixties. The audience, in Cage's words, "was seated in four isometric triangular sections, the apexes of which defined a small square performance area. It was later that summer that I was delighted to find in America's first synagogue in Newport, Rhode Island, that the congregation was seated in the same way – facing themselves."

TWELVE

I

"From Rhode Island," Cage recalls, "I went to Cambridge." There, at Harvard University, he discovered an anechoic chamber – an environment as soundproof and reverberation-free as was technologically possible. "In this remarkable room," proclaimed the *Harvard University Catalog* for 1949–50, "99.8 or more per cent of the energy in a sound wave is absorbed during a single reflection over a frequency range of 60 to 20,000 or more cycles per second."

Silence had long been an important facet of Cage's music, from its prominent place in the *Duet for Two Flutes* and *Sonatas and Interludes*, and the perhaps symbolic closing of the piano in *A Flower* and *The Wonderful Widow*, to its function in more recent works, for instance disrupting continuity in *Two Pastorales*; significantly, the longest durations in *Imaginary Landscape No. 4* pertain to the silences. Engagement with Zen made it philosophically interesting; Cage understood silence to be the manifestation in music of the nothingness he sought. He asked to sit in the anechoic chamber "with the intention of hearing what it was like to hear nothing. I literally expected to hear nothing."

Although the anechoic chamber anecdote is one of the best-known stories about Cage ("anybody who knows me knows this story," Cage said), it is not clear exactly when it took place. Moreover, two anechoic chambers were in operation at Harvard University at this time and it is not possible to establish conclusively which one was used by Cage.

The first formed part of the Cruft Laboratories of the Applied Engineering Department, on Oxford Street opposite Malinkrodt; it was a straight chamber of thick concrete, windowless, with only one, heavy door. Inside was 72,000 cubic feet of space, differentiated only by a narrow catwalk suspended above the floor on wires from the four upper corners; twenty thousand wedges of foam on the walls damped out sound and echo. This is the anechoic chamber whose acoustic qualities were quoted above. The Cruft chamber was constructed in 1943, mostly as a research tool for Frederick Vinton Hunt (1905–72), at first for testing acoustic equipment in wartime and later for more general sound and vibration research in both air and liquid. It was demolished in the late spring of 1971.

The second chamber was one of the psychology laboratories run by Stanley Stevens (1906–73) in Memorial Hall. The Hall had been built in 1878 as a commemorative monument to the Harvard men who died in the Civil War; in 1947 its basement and part of the first floor became home to the psychology laboratories. The psychoacoustic laboratory had been instrumental since the war in hearing-aid research. Its anechoic chamber was much smaller than the one at Cruft, tucked into a corner of the basement, adjacent to the woodshop and the men's bathroom.

Most accounts of Cage's visit specify a physics laboratory. It hardly matters; the uncertainty seems somehow appropriate. What is important is that when Cage sat down in the stillness of the chamber, he was surprised. Far from its being devoid of sound, he could hear two sounds, persistent and quite loud – a constant singing high tone and a throbbing low pulse. Cage supposed there was something wrong with the room. Puzzled, he quit the chamber and asked the engineer in charge why, if the room was soundproof, sounds were creeping in. "Describe them," the engineer demanded. Cage complied. The engineer told him they were not any fault of the chamber; they were the sounds made constantly by his own body – the high sound the ringing of his nervous system, the low noise his blood in circulation.

"I had honestly and naively thought that some actual silence existed," Cage recalled. "So . . . I had not really put silence to the test." Now he realized that silence, as he had construed it, did not exist. "Try as we may to make a silence, we cannot," Cage observed. "No silence exists that is not pregnant with sound."

If "silence" was to remain a valid concept, Cage had to redefine it in the light of his experience. Up to this point, his advocacy of the principle of non-dualism and interpenetration had not stopped him maintaining a division between sound and silence. Now experience had corrected him; he saw the split was in the head. The dichotomy had to be refined in such a way that its source was made apparent: intention versus non-intention.

"The situation one is clearly in," Cage averred, "is not objective (sound–silence), but rather subjective (sounds only), those intended and those others (so-called silence) not intended." Silence is the absence of intention. The experience of nothingness, which in sound is incarnated as silence, is not available like candy on the shelf of a store; it was to be entered or achieved by work on oneself – breaking the habit of unreflectively acting on the world or thinking about it, and thereby becoming a fruitful receiver of what was actually happening. "Silence is not acoustic. It is a change of mind. A turning around." Cage adds, "I devoted my music to it."

In view of his long and growing interest in silence, this can be seen as another instance of the way temperamental tendencies are brought over time to conceptual clarity and then to practical success. The visit to the anechoic chamber "gave direction to what was already in my inclination, not in detail." Indeed, "we had to conceive of silence in order to open our ears."

II

For at least five years Cage's involvement with Eastern philosophy, his penchant for silence, and, it is fair to say, his fondness for experiment had led him to consider the ultimate in musical audacity: a piece of music with no sounds in it. Only silence. At Vassar College back in 1947 – maybe in 1948 – Cage mentioned the idea in a speech, *A Composer's Confessions*, delivered as part of a festival involving a multidisciplinary ménage of artists and thinkers. His first feeling was that a silent piece would be "incomprehensible in the European context." "I didn't wish it to appear, even to me, as something easy to do or as a joke," Cage remembered. "I wanted to mean it utterly and be able to live with it." Then, in 1949, he saw a new series of paintings by Robert Rauschenberg: all-black and, especially, all-white paintings.

"I didn't want color to serve me," Rauschenberg had said in his usual matter of fact way. What fascinated Cage was that the white paintings brought home the point that, in Rauschenberg's words, "a canvas is never empty"; it acts as a landing-ground for dust, shadows, reflections. The canvasses were "mirrors of the air," not passive but, as Calvin Tomkins said, "hypersensitive."

The white canvasses gave Cage what he has frequently referred to as "the courage" or "permission" to compose his silent piece. "Permission" is an interesting word which occurs elsewhere in Cage's accounts of his work – Cowell and Carlos Chavez, for instance, "gave me the permission to enter the field of music" – and seems to indicate confirmation by other people of the possibility of being himself. Rauschenberg's canvasses were followed by the premonitory use of silence in the last movement of the *Concerto* and in *Waiting*; the anechoic chamber clinched the deal.

For Cage, a silent piece would be the ultimate in non-duality; the ultimate in non-intention; the ultimate elision of art and life, the vanishing point between listening to life and experiencing or living it. The piece he wrote, *4'33"*, was one of the earliest statements of his new approach, yet in it he made the quintessential statement of his position and direction in life. It is intrinsically self-annulling, like a porthole through which we can look at what is the case. "Few composers leave behind them such a testament," as Herbert Henck wrote.

Cage composed it in just the same way as he wrote his other works at this time, applying *I Ching* chance operations to rhythmic structure. Since no sounds are to be intentionally produced in the piece, the structure is illuminated only by the sounds which accidentally occur; as a flowering of his new ideas, it showed the old as simply a redundant concept which no longer bore a vital relation to what he was doing. Cage built up a three-movement piece by accumulating short silences of chance-determined duration. "I know it sounds absurd," he laughed years later, "but I may have made a mistake in addition." Cage's unchecked calculation came to four minutes and thirty-three seconds, which soon after the first performance – when it was misleadingly called *Four Pieces* – became the title of the work. It breaks its own boundaries completely, however; with gaps between the movements, *4'33"* from start to finish will always last longer than its title.

The first performance was scheduled for a concert Tudor was to present for the Artists' Benevolent Fund at the Maverick Concert Hall on August 29, 1952. The Bozza mansion set knew what was coming; they all shared their ideas as a matter of course. However, no one in the audience (many of them musicians from the New York Philharmonic on vacation) could have guessed that after an evening of avant-garde music of the usual sort – an extended tonal range, technological complexity, greater virtuosity – John Cage would present four minutes and thirty-three seconds of silence.

Anyone who listened would have heard the wind in the trees, then rain blown onto the roof and, in due course, the baffled murmurs of other audience members. After the final piece, Cage joined Tudor, and Feldman and Brown whose work had also been featured that night, on stage for questions. "There was a lot of discussion," Earle Brown remembers. "A hell of a lot of uproar ... it infuriated most of the audience." As Peter Yates tellingly observed, "The audience had come prepared to be shocked but not to be dismayed." A local artist finally stood up and suggested with languid vehemence, "Good people of Woodstock, let's drive these people out of town."

Cage presented a score of the work to Irwin Kremen, a birthday gift along with the black cherry ice cream they were sharing with Cunningham, Tudor and M.C. Richards at the New York home of Kremen's fiancée Barbara Herman. This score – dated August 1952 – was published in *Source*. It differs from the score subsequently published by Peters in that it is written in space–time notation, with an eighth of an inch representing a second of silence. The lengths of movements vary between the different versions: Kremen's manuscript gives 30″, 2′23″ and 1′40″, as at the premiere, while the published score specifies 33″, 2′40″, 1′20″.

4′33″ has been widely lauded as a cultural landmark for our times, "the pivotal composition of this century," as John McLure suggested in 1969. David Tudor claims "it was one of the most intense listening experiences you can have." Cage has continued to excite, perplex and enrage; contemporary music has moved on to new developments and controversies. Cage produced other work based on ambient sound. In the seventies he used the *I Ching* to find four places in Manhattan to visit and listen, and to determine a path through the University of Wisconsin campus which three hundred people followed in silence as a *Demonstration of the Sounds of the Environment*. Other composers followed suit. In *Listen* by Max Neuhaus, "an audience expecting a conventional concert or lecture is put on a bus, their palms are stamped with the word listen, and they are taken to and thru an existing sound environment." Neuhaus sprang this on audiences between 1966 and 1968, taking them to places such as power stations and the subway.

Yet Cage's tiny, empty piece which came first somehow sits on its own, unsurpassed, defying every attempt at a classification. Time and again, theorists debate whether it can be called music, and what that does to our definition of music. Despite the attention *4′33″* has received, Cage doubts "whether many people understand it yet." It is often referred to without people being able to quote the correct title: *1′33″* or *4′55″*; Henry Cowell in 1954 called it *4′36″* and Lejaren Hiller, later a collaborator with Cage, called it *4′44″*. Cage, whose new direction had cost him friends, lost even more after *4′33″*.

Cage treats the work reverentially. "The most important piece is my silent piece." He places it before everything else he has written, both in importance and in practice. "No day goes by without my making use of that piece in my life and work," he explains. "I always think of it before I write the next piece."

III

Cage had for years been trying to link music and spirituality in his work. After *4'33"*, which evinces this tendency quintessentially, it is possible to assess both the seriousness of his attempt and its pronounced and revealing idiosyncrasies.

As a youth Cage had thought seriously about a vocation in the ministry. His attitude to his work has often been seen as tending in a parallel direction. Calvin Tomkins, a very perceptive commentator on Cage, once compared him to a "missionary," and Jasper Johns calls him "part preacher, part teacher." Cage, commenting on his conviction that an urgent change is needed in our attitude of mind, told Roger Reynolds, "I could be likened to a fundamentalist Protestant preacher."

That Cage retained a place in his life for spirituality has always been clear: anyone who hears him talk, reads what he has written, or, arguably, listens carefully to much of his music, knows that susceptibility to "divine influences" is exactly where Cage's music is coming from. Yet Cage shows difficulties of both social and personal origin in living that out in the late twentieth century. Though grounding his work in a spiritual program, he feels gravely ambivalent about religion; and his spiritual strivings are focused in a very pure but narrow part of the spectrum of life.

Asked in 1989 if he felt a link existed between his religious leaning as a boy and his subsequent involvement with Zen, he flatly replied that he did not. There was not only no continuity, but also a discontinuity. If Zen was concerned with the same things as Christianity, "there's no need to go to the other. You could stay." Cage turned to the Orient, he explained, "for its flavor, and also for the fact that it has spoken to you, as the Western Church was no longer talking, so to speak." It had ceased to be vital; it had become doctrine. He recorded elsewhere how "when I was growing up, Church and Sunday School became devoid of anything one needed. . . . I was almost forty years old before I discovered what I needed – in Oriental thought. . . . I was starved – I was thirsty. These things had all been in the Protestant Church," the church of his ancestors in which he was brought up, "but they had been there in a form in which I couldn't use them."

When once asked if he considered himself a Buddhist, he said he considered himself a composer. When asked if he believed in God, he replied, "What a marvelous question. Certainly not in the anthropomorphic sense. My religious involvement has been with Zen Buddhism. . . . I couldn't have composed without its influence. Nirvana is some sorrow. Heaven is with us. These beliefs show up in my work rather than the stereotyped 'I believe in God.' I prefer 'Every day is a beautiful day.'"

"Stereotyped" is the crucial term here; Cage appears to be objecting to religion as an institution and as ritual practice, rather than to its spiritual object. He makes numerous disparaging references to religion, from the pun of *In the Name of the Holocaust* (=holy ghost) and a mock-biblical description of his visit to the anechoic chamber, to his blunt assertion, "It's as stupid as believing in God . . . We know . . . that God doesn't exist." In calmer mood, Cage looked at the arrangement of leaves on a tree and suggested that "no one, not even God, could have decided that."

Cage sometimes alludes to the lexicon of traditional religion, describing Mila Repa as a Tibetan "saint" or speaking of divine influences as all the things that happen in "creation". He wrote his songs on Ecclesiastes soon after he abandoned his vocation for the ministry. At other times his views seem diametrically opposed, as when he speaks of our mutual presence together in "chaos." One nurtures one's ability to respond to the world, he posited on another occasion, "following, of course, the general outlines of the Christian life," adding, "I myself tend to think more of catching trains than Christianity."

As quoted earlier, Cage has mentioned the feeling that he "had, so to speak, a guardian angel." "So to speak" introduces a hint of uneasiness, a feeling that the description is inadequate, which has the effect of distancing the idea of a "guardian angel" from its traditional connotation. Likewise, reflecting years later on Gita Sarabhai's formula, "to sober and quiet the mind, thus making it susceptible to divine influences," he suggested, "I might alter it slightly now and not state it so 'churchily.'"

There is thus an ambivalence in Cage's attitude to religion. He has tended, in particular, to separate the religious from the spiritual, and to relate Christianity to the one and Eastern thought to the other, sclerotized tradition versus vital discovery. Only in his brush with Meister Eckhardt did he approach a reconciliation of the two.

The manner in which Cage channeled his spiritual aspirations – which shows up most clearly in the development of his art – is idiosyncratic in both obvious and telling respects. His is not the only way to achieve the goal suggested by Sarabhai, nor even, in terms of his program, to integrate people into their daily lives. "I wouldn't say it's the best way to do it," Cage concedes, "but it is a way." His approach is transcendental – he left behind even the cycles of the seasons. It intimates the reality of the universe in its immanent, non-particularistic, ultimate dimension, in which it is an undifferentiated whole. This is a pure but in some senses extremely narrow part of the cosmic spectrum.

What Cage progressively disengages himself from is that at another level the universe is also composed of differentiable entities, human beings among them, whose regularities and passions can also nurture susceptibility to divine influences. A person breathes, and his or her heart beats too; the moon waxes and wanes, the tides come and go, and so, as Cage knows well, do the seasons.

Repetition and periodicity do not have to be seen as a military conspiracy; as Cage quotes René Char, "each act is virgin, even the repeated one." Non-Western music, for instance Kodo drumming or traditional African rhythm, uses rhythmical, orgiastic music which magically suspends time. Cage, on the other hand, has ceased to "like to tolerate" regular beats – "they don't seem natural to me. They seem too anthropomorphic." Similarly, some mystical orientations, notably Tantra and certain early versions of Hasidic Judaism, urge us to open ourselves to divine influences not in something transcendental, but in a pure earthiness of everyday acts in the world, such as sexual passion.

Eastern musical systems, Japanese, Balinese and Indian – gamelans, kotos, tablas or khêns – are carefully ordered in both pitch and rhythm. Frequently, the more aware of its spiritual function, the more precise is the discipline applied to rules and patterns.

The early Zen gardens, such as Daisen-In from the sixteenth century, sober and quiet the mind through stylized representation of the world; they are a place of contemplation – raked sand, for example, represents water. While it is true that later Zen gardens are quite abstract – Ryoanji, for instance – this is the outcome of historical development, just as in Central America Mayan textiles mutated gradually from depicting figures to presenting abstract images which had descended from them.

Art which is expressive in the traditional sense likewise has its own validity. It can reconcile us with our human frailty – not only in a spurious way – and integrate it; consider the richness of the last quartets of Beethoven. Cage's proclamation that he does not wish to put his feelings into his work is a personal as much as a rational decision.

Asked if he associates emotions with excess, Cage replied, "You could associate them with all kinds of things – with jealousy, hatred, fear, anger, sorrow" – negative associations. "All the good ones can be turned into bad. Most murders come from people who love one another. Love, in fact, is said to make people blind. 'I was blindly in love.' You could get run over. Emotions have long been known to be dangerous. You must free yourself of your likes and dislikes."

Cage's work is rich in its lessons on how to enjoy the world in all its imperfection. It tells us nothing about how to deal with our internal imperfections, nor how to confront, let alone enjoy, them. These are lessons in transcendental freedom; there is no concern here with existential freedom – the heroic, anguished application of the will to the complexities of life and the contradictions we carry around in our own heads. Cage applies will, but solely to circumvent the passions: the rocket using its fuel to escape from orbit to a stress-free space where fuel is unnecessary.

One important example of this very narrow purview of Cage is his virulent opposition to his idea of improvisation His earliest references are exceptions: the *Credo* of 1937 includes the suggestion that once a method of rhythmic structure has become widely accepted, "the means will exist for group improvisations of unwritten but culturally important music," citing Oriental music and hot jazz as examples. He tried this idea out with his experimental music class in Chicago, as described in Chapter 7. After this a prolonged aversion to any form of artistic spontaneity sets in.

Yet for many players the experience of improvisation is not at all personal; it is as if a certain sound has to be made at a particular moment or, more accurately, one makes it, with no gap between decision and action. Significantly, this requires physical coordination and often other levels of technique if it is to be realized adequately.

These rare prejudices of Cage lead him to miss completely what happens in improvisation. More seriously, he is not neglecting just one performance option, but the whole basis of successful musical performance. The sound-producing action is the same for both notated and improvised music.

Spontaneity is never a personal process. It is located, however, in space and historical time, so that it often appears as the wooden repetition of cliched responses, which is what Cage chooses to see when he looks at it. Spontaneity can be nurtured so that it is untrammeled. In Zen calligraphy, the split-second before the brush meets the paper is a moment of no-mind, *konton haikai*. In Zen archery, the release of the bow occurs spontaneously.

Intriguingly, Cage's *bête noire*, Jackson Pollock, observed that his frenzied action painting could only be faulted "if I lose contact."

Cage once posed the question, "How can I get a B♭ to come to me of myself, and not just out of my memory, tastes, psychology?" He notes that "in an utter emptiness anything can take place." "To see, one must go beyond the imagination and for that one must stand absolutely still as though in the center of a leap," but he does not seem to consider that this could provide a basis for improvisation. A rare exception is a suggestion, made in the course of a discussion of the performance of indeterminate music, that the performer could make the most appropriate sound produced in the best possible way for the particular instrument, "appropriate in the sense of being appropriate to silence."

As was observed in the introduction, everyone has to find a place to conduct his or her life between the poles of light and dark, unity and dispersion, calm and passion. In both his inclinations and his idiosyncrasies, Cage leans markedly to one end of the scale: the ascetic, the austere, the transcendent, calm, tranquility, emptiness, cheerfulness. One of the classic ways of addressing these tightropes is the distinction between Apollonian and Dionysian characters; the one for light, unity, restraint and calm, the other for darkness, dispersion, passion, excess. Those with mystical power are often described as having light in their eyes or the fire from within. The Apollonian approach, significantly, has been the tenor of Christian attitudes, especially in the Methodist tradition. As a tribute for Cage's seventy-fifth birthday, his friend Norman O. Brown discussed Cage in terms of this classical dichotomy.

Cage, argues Brown, is the Apollonian *par excellence*. In contrast to the mad action of Morris Graves, Cage states, "I wouldn't even dream of picking up an axe and smashing a stove to pieces. Nor would I throw myself on the floor." Brown notes that sobriety and quietness are the essence of Apollonian discipline. "Not disruptive, but cheerful." He explains, "Apollonian means the urge to perfect the separate life of the individual, to compensate for the pain of separate identity with the seductive pleasures of aesthetic enjoyment. . . . There is the Apollonian consciousness haunted by the question, Is life worth living? . . . and finding in aesthetic enjoyment an affirmative and cheerful answer." Apollo is the shining one, the god of light. Cage notes, "I was gifted with a sunny disposition,; and his music seems analogous to light, in the sense both of weight and of clear visibility. Apollo is, too, the god of boundaries, definitions, separations, clear and distinct ideas.

171

Brown's general thesis is borne out when one examines specific points. The Apollonian character cleaves to the idea of nobility and feels discomfort in the crowd. As seen in Chapter 3, Cage felt like a "criminal" and was "revolted" when he and his fellow pupils were asked to read the same text at college. Later, discussing his music, he comments tellingly that he has no wish to attempt to put his "emotions into someone else. That way you 'rouse rabbles'; it seems on the surface humane, but it animalizes, and we're not doing it."

Cage not only seems to circumvent his own emotions; his wish to be free of "constraint" also makes him wary of any situation where the emotions of a group may be unified by a common object. "I had just heard *The Messiah* with Mrs. Henry Allen Moe [wife of a director of the Guggenheim Foundation], and she said, 'Don't you love the "Hallelujah" Chorus?' and I said, 'No, I can't stand it.' So she said, 'Don't you like to be moved?' and I said 'I don't mind being moved, but I don't like to be pushed.'"

"Chance operations are an Apollonian procedure," Brown suggests. The Apollonian "I" asks the questions, "and the results of chance operations are univocal and unambiguous." Chance operations circumvent the anguish of uncertainty, "they are always impeccable."

By contrast, the approaches which Cage rejected over the years generally have a Dionysian flavor. *Four Walls*, as seen in Chapter 8, sought the stillness of rapture, and is thereby saturated with human concerns. The use of the Tarot pack in composing the *Music of Changes* had an impurity about it and touched on the absolute through the unconscious in a way which did not suit him. The same is true of the story of the miserable shabby nag by which Cage accounts for the close of the *String Quartet*. It is exceptional in that it is the only European folktale he quotes, and has a much richer feel than the Eastern stories he cites more often. He refers to it, sometimes in fragmentary form, many times: pages 148, 152, 167, 176, 180, 189, 192 of *Silence*, 102–3 and 138 of *A Year from Monday* and page 130 of *X*. The only other European folktale in Cage's life, also Irish (he has no Irish blood) and also from a collection by Joseph Campbell, gave the title to that other sore thumb, *The Perilous Night*.

With the advent of chance operations, he attempted to iron out all trace of his tastes, making mistakes along the way, such as the pedalling of *Music of Changes* and the *Two Pastorales*, the improvised slices of *Williams Mix*, the piano preparations of *Waiting* and the smoking option of *Water Music*.

The Apollonian tendency gives emotion and passion, especially in their complex form, little place. Just as spirituality as a living experience can be turned into the hollow politics and ritual of religion, so Apollonian leanings can be distorted into a fear of feelings. It is interesting that while Cage refers to his "supreme good fortune," which is a state, and describes himself as cheerful, which is an attitude, he does not say he is happy, which is an emotion. It is this shift from underplaying to repressing feelings which underlies the idiosyncrasies, inconsistencies and fissures in Cage's activities: his blindness to the paradoxical validity of improvisation is an extreme example, his rejection of regular rhythm an intermediate example, his ascetic and transcendental leaning or his discomfort in the crowd are more general instances. The attempt to take one pole and reject the other – repress the other rather than integrate it – never entirely succeeds. Repression does not mean removal: on the contrary, it means increased pressure. It bursts out. And the return of the repressed stands out, incongruous, like a sore thumb.

"John Cage," Norman O. Brown concluded, is "an extreme case of the artist, suffering the contradiction between Dionysian and Apollonian tendencies, a living oxymoron ... obstinately reasserting both sides of an unresolved argument, is not yet a dialectical fusion or coincidence of opposites." This is the irony of living as an oxymoron; one has to contain both poles, so one might as well live a resolution of them, even if final resolution cannot ever be achieved.

It is significant that in *The Bacchae* by Euripides, the fatal flaw of the obstinately Apollonian King Pentheus – the flaw that leads him, one against many, to be torn limb from limb by a crowd of women including his mother – is his refusal to give this god from foreign parts, Dionysos, his proper due.

The above points are observations not criticisms, intended to further the understanding of the path taken by Cage. John Cage is not wrong; he is simply John Cage. He had certain temperamental inclinations and, it seems, saw that his music, at least, could have a spiritual orientation. He found an existential placement, a world view which enabled him most successfully to put his native advantages and deficiencies to use. Which means Cage is not only for the birds; he is a bird, flown the cage.

sparrowsitA gROsbeak betrays *itself* by that peculiar squeakari- EFFECT OF SLIGHTEst tinkling measures soundness ingpleasa We hear!

IV

The media's burgeoning recognition of Cage's work came to a halt as he deepened his involvement with chance operations. Cunningham suffered, too, the general feeling being that he was a superb dancer who was letting himself down badly by his experimentation. Cage, however, retained a number of champions among the critics, especially Peggy Glanville-Hicks and, later, Peter Yates.

In very little time his new direction was threatening some of his more valued friendships. In their correspondence, he and Boulez lined up in ever more polarized positions – chance versus serialism, non-control versus control. In an exchange with Peter Yates, Boulez thumped the underside of a piano and barked, "It is not in the musical continuum." Cage gently ridiculed Boulez, citing the way he related music to literary features as an example of the way that in Europe "composers are continually mixing up music with something else." As they fell out, Cage feels in retrospect, he took their disagreements more personally than did Boulez, for the French are prone to vituperative arguments. During Cage's European tour in the fall of 1958 – after Boulez had published the article "Alea," which Cage felt both dismissed his own work and tried to take over some of its elements for the writer's own purposes – Stockhausen brought Boulez to the hotel room where Cage was staying. Cage is said to have refused to open the door. By the early sixties, after a final flourish of conflict when Boulez came to New York in 1962, they could no longer talk to each other.

Later in the fifties Cage went through a similar process with Karlheinz Stockhausen, who was also unable to reconcile himself with Cage's wish to abandon control and, on the other side of the coin, his avoidance of traditional musical skills and competencies. "A phenomenon that seems so completely beyond the pale," Stockhausen commented, "Cage represents, in his anarchic protest against the European tradition, the final destination of his own evolution – in a musical no-man's land. . . . A composer who draws attention to himself more by his actions than his productions . . . mixed up with a good measure of philosophical thinking." By the sixties they too could scarcely talk and, as one source put it, what Cage felt for Stockhausen was "as close as John comes to detesting someone."

At one level these disputes were between American and European culture. Yet to be born in America did not require a composer to be experimental (plenty of American composers were firmly rooted in the

European tradition), it simply made it easier, and on the other hand
no European was condemned to tradition: the music of Boulez and
Stockhausen is in many ways, and the obvious ones, highly experimental.
More significant were the different cues the composers took from the
modernist field of music. What Cage did in turning to chance operations
would have been impossible in another era: it depended on the availability
of a number of different sources (American experimentation, European
tradition, Eastern mysticism) and on a cultural psychology that made it
possible to take so abstractly transcendental a path – and later to be
lionized for it. At the social and cultural level, Cage picked up on an
undertone of modernism. Boulez, Stockhausen and many other musicians were likewise embarked on a task inconceivable in another era, yet it
was more obviously modernist, so humanist, so rationalist, so much a part
of the postwar climate. There was also, perhaps, something less rational
at work in the serialists' objections, what Jung refers to, in his introduction
to the *I Ching*, as the "terror of randomness": never has so much been
excluded, in thought and in practice, as in the modern West.

Many composers from the mid-fifties onwards began to eschew to a
limited extent conscious control, putting together parts of their music
without attempting to plan each detail in advance. This is due in part
to the example of Cage: often composers would use chance and, as will
presently be discussed, indeterminate techniques.

What characterized these experiments was the incorporation of non-
control within a controlled overall schema. Luciano Berio devised a
notational system using boxes, bracketing material which could be
played at will within the defined section. Iannis Xenakis began to
use statistical means to generate the details of his music, but within
a consciously determined pattern. "It is my privilege to control my
music, and my pleasure," he said. "That is my definition of an artist:
to control. . . . I admire Cage very much, as a man, but what is chance?
If you think you are using chance in his way, you may simply be acting
unrationally. The intuition of Cage is dangerous, a style and a mentality
of mystico-romantic improvisation, which agitates ignorant souls."

In part, much in the manner of John senior's inventions, such innovations were due to the spirit of the age as well as Cage. Stockhausen, for
instance, developed "variable," "polyvalent" and "statistical" elements
in his composition and notation through the fifties, but is insistent that
these came out of his own independent reading and thinking.

Boulez found his own way to a controlled use of chance, finding his
explanatory route by the discovery of a work by Stephan Mallarmé.

Taking the Latin term for a game of chance, *alea* (a very European thing to do), Boulez dubbed this musical resource "aleatory." Thereafter, aleatory elements have become taken for granted as a resource in a wide spectrum of compositional styles. Cage has found his work with chance operations brought under the same rubric, a conflation he resents, because their aims are completely different. Assimilation of his innovations, however, is only to be expected, not only because that generally happens with time, but also because they seem so personal to Cage, so set apart, so narrow, that it is not surprising that his direct influence on compositional technique is slight.

In the months which followed the premiere of *4'33"*, Cage was most concerned with finding some way to speed up the generation of chance operations. *Music of Changes*, his ongoing work with *Williams Mix*, and the tiny durations which made up the silent piece, all brought home how crushingly time-consuming was work with the *I Ching*. If *I Ching* chance operations were comparable to painting with oils, he needed the compositional equivalent of watercolor to enable him, at least sometimes, to write more quickly.

His first experiments involved paper, as a material rather than as a means to record information. In October 1952 he composed his first *Music for Carillon* for M.C. Richards, tackling the speed problem by using differently shaped scraps of paper which were folded, with some holes cut at the points of the folds. These were then used as stencils "at points in time space *I Ching* determined."

The template method was faster than the chart technique, but Cage wanted something even easier. In a series of short pieces, *Music for Piano*, he attempted to go beyond the stencilling idea. He wrote numbers 1, 2 and 4 to 19 in May 1953 and number 3 in June; number 20 is dated August 8. "I looked at my paper," said Cage. "Suddenly I saw that the music, all the music, was already there." He conceived of a procedure which would enable him to derive the details of his music from the little glitches and imperfections which can be seen on sheets of paper. It had symbolic as well as practical value; it made the unwanted features of the paper its most significant ones – there is not even visual silence. The procedure also raised questions concerning repeatability. The imperfections apply only to the master sheets on which one works. There are different imperfections on copies. When Cage first wrote articles assisted by the technique – in keeping with his tendency to write words in the same manner as his compositions – he relocated the paragraphs on publication for that reason.

Piece 1 was completed one system at a time. Cage set a time limit and marked as many imperfections on one sheet as he could in that time. A page with staves drawn on it was then set on this master sheet, and the imperfections traced on as pitches. Dynamics were then selected from *pianississimo* to *fortississimo*.

Piece 2, for Louise Lippold in her role as dancer, is divided by irregular strokes which group the notes, suggesting an attempt to reconcile the new technique with rhythmic structure. Normal, plucked, and muted notes are indicated; dynamics are left to the performer.

In the remainder of the series from 1953, the number of imperfections to be found was ascertained by means of the *I Ching*; that number was located and staves superimposed as before. Chance operations ascertained whether the note was to be played normally, plucked, or muted; a single coin decided if the stave was set in bass or treble clef. Duration, pedalling, tempo and dynamics were left free.

The new point-drawing technique had the desired advantage of speed; a new one-page piece could be composed in minutes. Its limitation was that it only yielded single pitches, not the constellations and chords of the *Music of Changes*. "The limited nature of this universe of possibilities makes the events themselves comparable to the first attempts at speech of a child or the fumblings about of a blind man," Cage wrote.

His first solution was to suggest that any number of the pieces could be played together, with the order and the superimpositions left to chance. This extended the musical embodiment of interpenetration, "events that are related to one another only because they take place at the same time." This is the first example of a provision which would be one of Cage's hallmarks; it is also the first notable sign of his tendency to amass quantity in music, by stacking events on top of one another, perhaps as compensation for a refusal to allow traditional ideas of quality in creation or expression.

Numbers 4 to 19 were performed by Cage and Tudor as an accompaniment to Cunningham's dance *Solo Suite in Space and Time*. Cunningham's plans, nurtured at least since visiting Cage in Paris, had finally come to fruition, and the Merce Cunningham Dance Company was established in 1953, with Carolyn Brown, Anita Dencks, Remy Charlip and Paul Taylor. From its inception Cage was administrative and musical director.

While still composing *Music for Piano*, Cage began a new series of complex pieces in which he hoped to combine the chart and point-drawing systems of composition. Returning to the principle of the superimposable piano pieces, he conceived a series of works which could be played individually or simultaneously.

Cage now felt that chance operations were incompatible with his existing type of rhythmic structure. In the new series he attempted a fresh approach, of open rather than closed rhythmic structure. Rather than a whole divided into parts, each piece would consist of the same overall structure of a series of independent units of equal size: thirteen parts with the proportions 3/7/2/5/11/14/7/6/1/15/11/3/15, adding up to 100, which squared gives 10,000. This structure, Cage states, "just happened," which perhaps suggests a chance origin, but whether by accident or design, ten thousand is an auspicious number; in Taoism and Chinese Buddhism it refers to the infinite or to the material diversity of the universe. "It just happened that the series of numbers which are at the basis of this work add up to 100×100, which is 10,000," said Cage in the speech which forms part of the series. "This is pleasing, momentarily: The world, the 10,000 things." The *Ten Thousand Things* became Cage's private code name for the whole series.

Leading on from its use in *Water Music*, chronometric time became the foundation of the notation for the series, and the pieces were identified by whatever duration they turned out to be. In May, Cage wrote *57¹/₂″* for a string player, then five other string pieces: *1′5¹/₂″* dedicated to Broadus Earle and dated June 14; *1′1¹/₂″ seconds* (as it is written in the manuscript), to Matthew Raimondi, dated June 28; *1′18″*, to Seymour Barab, June 29; *1′14″* to Walter Trampler, June 30; and *59¹/₂″* to Claus Adam, dated July 2. The first five of these would be incorporated into a single work for string player the following year. The works are for any four-stringed instrument; notation refers not to the sound to be produced, but to what is to be done – the location at which each string is to be stopped. Directions are provided for vibrato, bowing pressure and its location, making virtuosic demands on the player. Cage also calls for extraneous noises.

Cage worked briefly over the summer of 1953 on a tape piece which he intended as part of the series, using the library of sound materials he had accumulated for *Williams Mix*; he also sketched procedures for a vocal work. Neither were completed.

Later pieces in the series cite fractional durations which are both conceptually and practically problematic. After *59¹/₂″* came *34′46.776″* and *31′57.9864″* for piano, *45′ for a speaker* (1954), *26′1.1499″ for a string player* (1955) and *27′10.554″ for a percussionist* (1956).

In January 1954 Cage returned to the point-drawing system to compose

Music for Carillon Nos 2 and 3 as a birthday gift for Tudor. He located imperfections in one large sheet of cardboard and punched holes in it at these points, which then became notes for the piece. Transcriptions could then be made for the specific carillon to be used. For number 2, Cage read the cardboard from top to bottom; for number three, he read it again with the card turned upside down.

Tudor presented the first New York City performance of *4'33"* at the Carl Fischer Concert Hall on April 14, 1954. The movement lengths were the same as those at the Woodstock premiere. Only now did the piece receive substantial press attention. The *New York Post* presented a jovial but essentially sympathetic and perceptive notice (Nancy Seely, "You could have heard a piano drop"). The concert was referred and alluded to for months to come.

As she and her husband were living in Upper Montclair, Crete took the opportunity to attend. *4'33"* was in the first half of the program, followed by the *Music of Changes*. Just before the silent piece began, Crete whispered to her neighbor that it was "like a prayer." About forty-five minutes later, when Tudor finished *Music of Changes*, the neighbor leaned over and responded, "Good heavens, what a long and intense prayer." Earle Brown was present at the concert; his *Twenty-Five Pages* (1952) was being played in public for the first time. In the intermission, he saw Crete making for him. "John's mother and father always thought I was much more sensible than John," he explains. "And John's mother came over and said 'Now Earle, don't you think that John has gone too far this time?'"

V

The Bozza mansion was scheduled for demolition: a new twenty-million-dollar housing project was planned for the area, so in 1953 Cage and his neighbors had been served notice to vacate.

Merce Cunningham had lived for some time at 12 East 17th Street, "an average old five-story brownstone and brick house intended for average living," as James Britton, a neighbor at the time, put it later. "The few remaining crippled houses like ours were surrounded by monstrous many-sided business buildings." Confounded by the apparent impossibility of finding a habitable apartment at a price he could afford, Cage moved in for a few months. "Their floor was my ceiling," Britton recalled. "It sprang while Merce danced."

In December 1953 Paul and Vera Williams had asked Cunningham to place a small ad in his program: "WANTED, about 100 acres, hilly, mostly wooded, with stream or lake and house, up to 50 miles N.Y.C. Call Williams, WA6-4744." Paul Williams wanted to use his inheritance to purchase houses and land to set up a community with, in the longer term, a theater for music and dance and, as he told Cage, a tape laboratory to fulfill at last his hopes for an experimental music center.

They found an old farmhouse at the end of a treacherously rocky path, on Willow Grove Road in Stony Point, Rockland County, an hour and a quarter out of New York City. It became known as "The Land." The core of the community consisted of friends from Black Mountain: Paul and Vera Williams, Mary Caroline Richards, the sculptor David Weinrib and his wife Karen. David Tudor opted to join. In August 1954 Cage and the others moved in.

Paul Williams' plan was to build more houses so that the community could grow. His interest in minimal architecture meant he wanted to design unconstrained by the planning regulations of city developments. Over the next few years a system was established by which each member agreed to pay a monthly installment to Williams for thirty years. Each person could stay as long as they wished, but if they left could take nothing with them. As the new dwellings were built, the community grew in size; around eleven houses, a score of adults (among them George Ancona and Patsy and Lamone Davenport) and a dozen children. While not intended as an artists' colony, most people interested in the idea were involved with arts or crafts. As Cage would tell Daniel Charles, perhaps a little anachronistically, it was an experiment in substituting utility for property.

For $24.15 a month, plus a contribution toward the shared jeep, Cage occupied two small rooms, perhaps twenty by ten feet, separated by a narrow kitchen area. He lined the floor with cocoa-matting and suspended a wide, white hammock. When he first moved in, however, he shared the farmhouse with Tudor, Richards and the Weinribs, living in the attic with a wasps' nest for company. His life in the city had been surrounded by bustle but was private; the countryside was peaceful, but communal life gave him a shock. To retain some of the privacy he wanted, he immediately began walking in the nearby woods.

The profusion of mushrooms caught his eye; since it was August they were at their most abundant and colorful. Cage had tried wild-food gathering during his time in Carmel in 1934, with alarming results. Now he resolved to take time to learn properly about fungi. He collected and borrowed books, but at first found them confusing. He called the 4-H

Club in New City, a few miles southeast of Stony Point. A secretary said they would call back: when it began to look like they would not, Cage called the club again, and they suggested he ring Guy G. Nearing. "Come over any time you like. I'm almost always here, and I'll name your mushrooms for you," Nearing told him, and from then onward he became Cage's guide in the study of mushrooms and other wild edible plants. When the weather was too dry for mushrooms they would forage for lichens, about which Nearing had published a book.

Cage has recounted in his books some of the more unpleasant experiences which came out of his new interest. In his first spring as a wild-food eater he gathered skunk cabbage. His parents were visiting and he gave them some to take home; the rest he cooked for dinner for several guests. To emphasize his enthusiasm for wild food, he ate a particularly generous serving. Coffee and a game of poker followed; Cage fell ill with vomiting and diarrhea. The guests rushed him to the Spring Valley hospital, where his stomach was pumped and, as his blood pressure plummeted to fifty, he was given shots of adrenalin.

"In the morning," Cage narrated, "I felt like a million dollars. . . . I read a notice on the wall which said that unless one left by noon he would be charged for an extra day." He rang the bell to announce he was ready to leave. No one came. He shouted to a nurse passing outside that he had no money to pay for a second day. "In no time at all I was hustled out." When he returned home, he discovered his companions had not suffered nearly so much, and his parents had been warned before they had eaten any of the plant. Skunk cabbage, Cage subsequently discovered, is easily confused with hellebore, which is highly poisonous.

Vera Williams, concerned that her children might follow Cage's unfortunate example, told them that on no account were they to touch his mushrooms because they were all deadly poisonous. A few days later, deciding on steak for dinner, she opted for a garnish of sliced mushrooms. "When she started to cook the mushrooms, the children all stopped whatever they were doing and watched her attentively," Cage recorded. "When she served dinner, they all burst into tears."

Cage became pleasantly obsessive about fungi. He felt they acted as a counterbalance to his use of chance operations. But that does nothing to explain his eager acquisition of not only mushroom manuals, but a mushroom ashtray, a mushroom tea towel, a clip-on plastic mushroom and a large tie bearing a mushroom motif. In 1956 Morris Graves sent Cage a letter-painting from his home in Edmonds in Washington State; on a huge sheet of airmail paper there were six beautifully rendered varieties of mushroom and the words, "Dear John/ Yum yum? Morris."

Soon Cage was taking every opportunity to track down fungi. If he caught sight of any on the roadside as he drove by, he would pull over, which often attracted the attention of the Highway Patrol. Cage once took Cunningham and two other friends at least an hour off their route in search of morels which were not there. In later years gratuities to the coach driver for the dance company ran high, not only because of the antisocial hours required by touring, but also so he would stop if Cage saw mushrooms flashing by.

Within the first few months of this new enthusiasm, Cage was invited to contribute to a special issue of the *United States Lines Paris Review* devoted to humor. Asked to write about music, he produced *Music Lovers' Field Companion*, the first of many sardonic attempts to relate mushrooms and music which, as he later observed, are generally contiguous in the dictionary (although my newest puts "mushy" in between).

This interest in mushrooms subsequently grew into something of a money-spinner. Cage would win a quiz show thanks to his knowledge of fungi; he would teach courses in New York not only on the music of Satie and Virgil Thomson, but also on mushroom identification. In the late fifties he sold mushrooms he collected through Emile d'Antonio, who otherwise worked in advertising and since the middle of the decade had been chairman of the board of the Rockland Foundation. Dee, as he was known, sold the mushrooms to Creative Food Services, and Restaurant Associates, in New York, which supplied top-class restaurants such as the Four Seasons. This was sufficiently lucrative – in September 1959 alone Cage made $208.95 – that he splashed out fifty dollars to buy a secondhand mushroom dryer.

At the end of the first summer at Stony Point Cage continued work on the *Ten Thousand Things*. Between August and September he prepared *26' 1.1499" for a string player* with the assistance of Tudor, incorporating as pages 34 to 58, with slight changes, five of the six pieces he had written in New York City the previous year. *34' 46.776"* and then *31' 57.9864"* followed, both for prepared piano, both dedicated to his new landlords. The pieces were his last substantial work for the prepared piano. Only general instructions are given for the type of preparation and, following the live preparations in *Water Music*, they are to be adjusted in the course of performance. The notation breaks down dynamic into force of attack, its speed, and the distance of the attack from the keyboard – a division only just redeemed from being pretentiously cerebral by the formidable abilities of Tudor, who could more or less make the distinctions tangible.

Cage's new attitudes and his new techniques seemed to have opened the floodgates: his experimentation was broader, deeper, and proceeding faster than ever before – challenging definitions of beauty, music, or composition, changing the manner of notation, pushing back the frontiers of what a performer could do.

Cage finished the piano pieces just in time for his departure on a European tour with Tudor. On Saturday, October 2, 1954, they sailed from Manhattan on the *Maasdam*, bound for Cobh in County Cork, Southampton, Le Havre and Rotterdam. Cage was to deliver a speech at the Composers' Concourse in London later that month, and intended to write a text based on the structure of the *Ten Thousand Things*. On Sunday morning, a French ship, the *Tofevo*, collided with the *Maasdam*, which was forced to limp back to shore. A messy couple of days followed in which passengers, most of them – Cage and Tudor included – people of limited means scarcely able to afford travel in the first place, staged a sit-down protest in front of the South Sea murals in the ballroom. They protested against the laxness of the Holland-America Line in accommodating them aboard ship, providing for their expenses, or making alternative travel arrangements. Finally the company chartered a KLM plane for Amsterdam for the sixty "hardship cases," as a spokesman put it, least able to afford to wait for another ship later in the week. Among the sixty were Cage and Tudor.

On October 17, they presented the *Water Music* and the new pieces at Donaueschingen, and the new pieces again in Cologne on the 19th; on the 25th they played in France in a concert promoted by Pierre Schaeffer, then moved on to London in November. In hotels, in restaurants and on trains, Cage endeavored to complete the text he had intended to write on board ship. It was written in the same way as the other pieces, including its own set of ancillary noises – snores, slaps on the table, coughs, hisses, blowing the nose. This made it, Cage felt in retrospect, "a somewhat hermetic article." Chance had yielded a duration of 39′16.95″; this was too short a time for Cage to read the script aloud, so practicality made this speech an exception in the *Ten Thousand Things* series at a round *45′ for a speaker*. In a sense, Cage said in the course of the speech, "time . . . is the title of this piece," an example of a continuing interest in the relation between ideas and the concrete.

The new piano pieces were premiered in the United States in New York City on December 15.

VI

It was around 1954 that a short series of concerts of American and European music culminated in a party at Sari Dienes's studio on 57th Street. Cage and Feldman went along and met a young painter named Jasper Johns. Johns had been born in Augusta, Georgia, in 1930. Having left the army, he was working in a bookstore down the street while he developed his painting; he had just made the *Construction with Toy Piano*. Recently Johns had met Rauschenberg. The two artists were soon to become lovers; with Cage now knowing Johns too, Cage, Cunningham, Rauschenberg and Johns would often go out as a foursome. Their haunts included the San Remo bar in the Village. It was a rich interrelationship, in which they shared ideas, worked and socialized together. In their joint work for the Cunningham Company, it was Cage who would make the most judgments and decisions.

The four meshed in with a wider circle of gay artists around Emile d'Antonio, Cage's mushroom salesman. In 1955, in his capacity as chairman of the Rockland Foundation, Dee decided to promote a concert by Cage and the Cunningham Company at the Clarkstown high school in New City.

Cage had not long since completed a new series of *Music for Piano*, numbers 21 to 36 and 37 to 52. Like the series from 1953, they were composed by observing the imperfections in paper, but by a different procedure, and they included interior and exterior noises from the piano body.

On the night of the concert – October 15, 1955 – the police warned locals to stay indoors, for torrential rain was falling and roads were flooding. In spite of this the hall was packed with a mixture of local music-lovers, avant-garde artists and loyal camp followers. The New York converted were enthusiastic from the beginning; most of the Rockland County music-lovers listened in amazement for a few moments and then made to leave, only to find they were effectively trapped by the torrential rain. "It was even worse outside than in," Cage remembered.

Cage continued to spread the word across the country in more or less unlikely concerts. On October 23, at the New School for Social Research, he performed his music in an eclectic broadcast concert of *Music and Musicians of the Village* that set him alongside jazz and folk musicians, including Rocco Costello, Italian bagpiper, and his singing friend Patsy. From November 8 to 9 Cage was at UCLA taking part in seminars and discussions of student compositions, presenting a public lecture and performing with Tudor. In Santa Barbara in November he wrote *Speech* for five radios plus a newsreader reading from two newspapers or magazines. By November 18 he had moved on to Portland State College.

Cage completed what was to be the last of the *Ten Thousand Things* pieces, *27'10.554" for a percussionist*, on January 14 of the following year. The four lines of each page mark off four types of sound source: metal, wood, skin and others – "electrical devices, mechanical arrangements, radios, whistles etc." The vertical position of the notes does not indicate pitch but volume, suggesting virtuosic leaps of dynamic; the density of sounds is sometimes greater than is likely to be practicable, leading Cage to suggest that it be read "in any focus."

With Feldman, Cage arranged a concert at the Carl Fischer Hall in New York City for May 30. He completed a further series of *Music for Piano*, numbers 53 to 68, dedicated to Grete Sultan, which would be performed in the concert by her, Tudor, Cage and Maro Ajemian. Work by Wolff, the string quartets of Feldman, and the *Fünf Stücke* by Webern were also scheduled – the latter works to be played by the Juilliard String Quartet. Cage wrote to the Ampex corporation asking for the loan of sound equipment so that the *Williams Mix* and the *Octet* by Brown could be presented. "Unfortunately," Cage wrote to Jacques Barzun, "Ampex has not answered my letter requesting the use of machines and loudspeakers. Wishing, nevertheless, to involve the machine in some way in this program I am making a new composition for 8 radios – along a plan different than the one for my earlier piece for 12." Pains in his back resulted in doctor's orders to stay in bed, but Cage finished *Radio Music* in time for its premiere on the 13th.

In the fall of 1956 Cage began to present his first set of occasional classes at the New School for Social Research, which he would continue until 1960. This Composition of Experimental Music class was attended by some of the pioneers of experimental art in the next generation, who would form an avant-garde for the sixties: George Brecht, Al Hansen, Dick Higgins, Allan Kaprow and Jackson MacLow. Cage developed a pedagogical style based on exchange rather than on his authority: he would describe what he was doing, each student would describe what they were doing, and opinions but not evaluations would be swapped. This approach emerged from the rejection of traditional teaching methods that went back to his college days, and the idea of respecting other centers, which he gleaned from Zen.

"I told the people at the beginning of the class that my intention was to keep them looking not for familiar but for unfamiliar ideas," Cage remembers. "If they showed signs of not moving, I would try to irritate them to get them moving." The course

> generally began with my trying to bring the students to the point of knowing who I was, that is, what my concerns and activities were, and I wanted them to find out also who they were and what they were doing. I wasn't concerned with a teaching situation that involved a body of material to be transmitted by me to them. I would, when it was necessary, give them a survey of earlier works, by me and by others, in terms of composition, but mostly I emphasized what I was doing at that time and would show them what I was doing and why I was interested in it. Then I warned them that if they didn't want to change their ways of doing things, they ought to leave their class, that it would be my function, if I had any, to stimulate them to change.

Attendance at the class was not high, but few dropped out. The only point on which Cage insisted was that they produce work which could practically be realized, which usually meant in the small room in which the class was held, with its closet of percussion instruments, a broken-down piano, and anything the students brought with them. "Practicality has always seemed to me to be of the essence," Cage said again. "I hate the image of the artist who makes things that can't be done."

THIRTEEN

I

No piece of music can ever be performed the same way twice – this is as true of the *Emperor* concerto of Beethoven as it is of *Pli selon pli* by Boulez. The players shed new light on the work by their decisions. Sometimes these are major, such as the instrumentation and dynamic of the *Künst der fuge* by Bach (an example used by Cage), the choice of stops in organ music, or the interpretation of tempo markings; yet even if a decision is made and rehearsed, the intention to produce a certain reading never fully succeeds.

Cage had been noticing the uniqueness of musical events for years. "One drum is quite different from another," he said of his percussion music, "and instead of wanting the best drum, you have to take the drum you have." His attempts to replicate effects in preparing different pianos had taught him that no two pianos were the same; in *Double Music* it was extremely hard to control the attack of the temple gongs, which were set ringing by friction. Indeed, he had been incorporating variable elements into his work. For some of his early compositions, such as the *Sonata for Two Voices*, the *Composition for Three Voices* and the "Melody" of *Living Room Music*, the instrumentation is unspecified. The use of radio, from *Credo in US* onward, provides a sound-source without permitting prediction of what would be heard. More recently, his notational experiments, in the *Music for Piano* series – where tempo was left to the performer – or in the *Ten Thousand Things*, nurtured pronounced differences between performances.

The circle of composers around Cage had been exploring other ways to capitalize on the uniqueness of the moment of performance since the early fifties. Wolff began to write game scores in which the action of one player is conditioned by that of the others, throwing notes between one another like passes in basketball. The graph scores by Feldman had little sense of replicability: a five in the top register, say, might imply hundreds of possibilities. Earle Brown was making special inroads in this direction, with works such as *December 1952* – the first wholly graphic work since the staffless neumes of the middle ages – and *Twenty-Five Pages*, premiered alongside the New York presentation of *4'33"*, a score for piano of which the sheets could be arranged in any order and played either way up on its horizontal axis. These ideas were very much in the air. In 1956 Stockhausen released *Klavierstück XI*, a single large sheet bearing nineteen sections which are read in any order; an instruction at the end of each section determines the tempo, usually the dynamic, and sometimes other features of the section to follow. Cage discussed the work in a lecture from 1958. Otto Luening had experimented with controlled improvisation early in his career; Cowell wrote some pieces in which the performer could choose the order of musical events.

New music, then, was highlighting and exploiting the essential unrepeatability of musical performance. The development might be understood sociologically. Just as one spur to the development of abstract painting was the rise of photography, which monopolized (and transformed) the representative function which formerly belonged to painting, so as the recording of music mushroomed, music appeared which was founded on the uniqueness of the moment.

Although a pioneer of music for magnetic tape, Cage began to object to recordings of instrumental music. "Record collections," he fulminated, "that is not music"; they do not provide a "musical experience," though that appears to be their function. One night, as he has since recounted many times, Cage attended a performance of Stravinsky's *Firebird* conducted by the composer. A boy, who had obviously heard the suite on record many times, turned to his mother and said loudly and authoritatively, *"That's* not how it goes." On a different occasion, Cage heard a boy exclaim, "Why don't they turn the record over and play the other side?"

In the second half of the fifties Cage began to take a new and serious interest in writing music which could exploit its variable dimensions. This did not simply arise out of acknowledgment that music could work in this way; his line of thinking and his compositional development made it relevant. In this case, as elsewhere, his interest was deeply grounded in his general world view. It related to the emphasis in Zen on the present as our sole location and the only place of immediate experience, and suspicion of memory as sullied by connections with likes or dislikes; the feeling of repeatability is part of the myth of ownership.

Other composers attempted to use ideas of musical time which highlight the present, particularly Stockhausen, with his ideas of "group" and later "moment" form. In an article of 1960 Stockhausen wrote, "Concentration on the Now – on every Now – makes as it were vertical sections which penetrate across ... Eternity." Cage is much less cerebral about it, and thus is more concrete.

The term adopted by Cage for music premised on unrepeatability was "indeterminacy." While commentaries have often conflated indeterminacy with chance operations, the two are quite different, although in Cage's case they are rooted in the same rationale, and indeterminate materials are generated by chance means.

Winter Music, for between one and twenty pianists, was Cage's first major excursion into indeterminacy. It was written in January 1957 and dedicated to Rauschenberg and Johns. Tudor and Cage played it at the Hobart and William Smith College in Geneva, New York, on February 7, and at the Akron Art Institute on the 20th; then, joined by Masselos and Sultan, at the Fischer Hall on April 30.

In the course of the year Cage began his largest-scale work since the *Concerto*, the *Concert for Piano and Orchestra*. It is a hugely ambitious work, above all in the piano writing, which features eighty-four different compositional techniques over its sixty-four pages, with correspondingly diverse notations. Some are in the manner of the *Ten Thousand Things*, others the *Winter Music*; others presage the notation of works which he would write in the near future, *Variations*, *Fontana Mix* and so on.

Coomaraswamy's formula, "imitation of nature in her manner of operation," was uppermost in Cage's mind. On his rambles he had been struck by the profusion of nature, not least the plethora of diverse mushrooms. He took abundance to be the manner of operation he would imitate in his music. Instead of starting from a specific structural focus, as he had tended to do, he sought the widest possible focus, incorporating as many compositional methods as possible. Absence of structure blurs the difference between art and life. "The only thing I was being consistent to in this piece," Cage said, "was that I did not need to be consistent."

Nature provided, too, an image for indeterminacy. If one looks at a leaf, Cage suggested, it does not seek to impose a single viewpoint by which it is to be viewed. Music could operate in the same way, unlike the European view of the will of the composer compelling everyone to listen in the same way.

Indeterminate composition throws the activity of the performer into a new light. He or she becomes far more than an "interpreter"; their creativity is engaged on a much wider scale than in other forms of notated music. The function of the composer also changes. As Cage asked even regarding the *Music for Piano*, "What has been composed?" The composer's function becomes more and more obviously modest, to initiate or enable a musical event. Writing no longer marries form and content, for one or the other will be left out: content may be provided, for which the performer will supply form, or form may be given, within which the performer will manifest content. As we have seen, Cage had long been interested in clarifying the distinction between form and content. Moreover, indeterminacy calls the status of the composer into question. Why do these pieces become famous under the composer's name? Why are they even titled? Do such features arise only from a concern with private property and profit?

The relation between composer and performer likewise changes. To write an indeterminate work implies respect and trust for the performer. Interestingly, however, it may be that in the work of Cage it is the composer who makes the discoveries by composing the work from nothing but questions; in some form or other the piece exists for performers, and they must very deliberately, very intentionally, discipline themselves to prepare a performance. "By the time you've worked out all this material," asks the pianist Margaret Leng Tan, "can you really give a spontaneous performance? It's a discovery for him if he's hearing it for the first time, but it's not a discovery for me — because I've done it before."

So successful was the split between the generation of scores by Cage and their aural result that on at least one occasion he failed to recognize "his own" music. "This is nice. What is it?" Cage asked at a dinner party after a drink or two. His hostess exclaimed, "You can't be serious!"

II

Rauschenberg and Johns had been talking with Emile d'Antonio about the possibility of a retrospective concert of Cage's music. Dee had a wide range of contacts, and the two artists were making money by designing window displays; the rest of the money needed, they decided, could be raised by organizing a paying exhibition. "Finally we talked ourselves into it being practicable," Johns recalls.

When Rauschenberg presented the plan to Cage, he was flattered but reluctant to pursue it. He was loath to have his earlier music performed;

he was more and more inclined to focus his interest on what he had not yet written, or had written most recently. Furthermore, he was working intensively on the *Concerto* and so had little spare time. His friends assured him they would handle all the arrangements; David Tudor offered to select the program. The premiere of the *Concert* would be the climax of the event. Cage assented.

He set to work even harder on the piece to meet a deadline of May 1958. He nevertheless completed two other pieces, the *Haiku* and *Variations I*. Both are dated January 1958 and are dedicated to Tudor, the latter as a late birthday present. *Variations I* is the first of a number of indeterminate scores in which directions for performance are obtained by superimposing transparent plastic sheets; the significance of the figures on the sheets is to varying extents allocated by the performer. The transparencies developed out of the point-drawing system: instead of accumulating complexity in performance, by superimposing pieces, as *Music for Piano* had done, complexity is generated here in the compositional activity delegated to the performer, superimposing layers of notation and reading from them complex requirements.

The Twenty-Five-Year Retrospective took place in New York Town Hall on May 15, 1958. Alongside the concert, an exhibition of scores by Cage, including *Water Music, Haiku* and the *Concert*, was mounted upstairs in the Stable Gallery (Rauschenberg was having a show downstairs). Several pages of the scores were sold; Cage wrote them out again to keep the sets complete. After the preview on the 5th, the exhibition received great praise from critics.

D'Antonio, Johns and Rauschenberg, billing themselves as "Impresarios Inc," had arranged at Tudor's suggestion a program consisting of *Six Short Inventions* (1933), *First Construction* (1939), *Imaginary Landscape No. 1* (1939), *The Wonderful Widow of Eighteen Springs* (1942), *She is Asleep* (1943), *Sonatas and Interludes* (1946–48), *Music for Carillon* (presented for the first time, using a two-octave Schulmeid electric instrument), *Williams Mix* (in its first New York performance) and the premiere of the *Concert*. The event was recorded by George Avakian, and later released as a boxed set of records.

In a rare display of solidarity, the entire New York avant-garde assembled for the occasion. As usual, and intriguingly, for the decade, most of the audience were painters, followed proportionally by dancers; painters urged their dealers to buy up boxes. The beginning of the concert was received with general pleasure; as the works became newer, the occasional boo or catcall crept in and snowballed until the audience polarized into those who were vocally enthusiastic and those vociferously against. Despite the pieces having been carefully chosen, even the players' reaction to the *Concert* was mixed, particularly to the conducting technique, in which the conductor moved his arms like the hands of a clock to measure the passage of relative time. "Merce conducted and it was beautiful," recalls Johns. Tudor played piano, and Anahid Ajemian, sister of Maro and later wife of George Avakian, was one of the three violinists.

Afterwards Avakian talked with a painter from the audience who in 1913 had attended the notorious Paris premiere of *Le sacre du printemps* by Stravinsky. The old man felt the retrospective had featured the same amount of derision and more applause. Cage told the press, "I like all comments, favorable or unfavorable." He was touched by the solicitude of his friends, and stored away the good luck telegrams he had received from Remy Charlip and others; from his Chinese calendar he tore off and kept the 15th of May.

At the end of that summer Cage went to Europe with Tudor. At the Darmstadt course for new music in September, Cage gave the three lectures of *Composition as Process*, which included a discussion of indeterminacy. Among others he met there was Nam June Paik, a young Korean composer, artist, and founder and sole member of the Institute for Avant-Garde Hinduism. At the end of the month Cage was in Stockholm, and in his hotel room prepared a new lecture for the forthcoming World's Fair in Brussels. *Indeterminacy*, as he called it, was a series of stories (there were thirty for his first delivery), each of which is to be read in one minute, so that the longer the story, the faster it has to be read. "My intention in putting the stories together in an unplanned way," he wrote, "was to suggest that all things – stories, incidental sounds from the environment, and, by extension, beings – are related, and that this complexity is more evident when it is not oversimplified by an idea of relationship in one person's mind."

Cage presented the lecture at the Brussels exposition early in October, following it with a two-piano recital given with Tudor; Stockhausen attended. Cage would present it again at Teacher's College, Columbia, in the spring of 1959, and record it later that year in a single lunchtime session. After the Brussels reading, Cage and Tudor combined forces with Cunningham and the Browns; Bruno Maderna was booked to conduct Earle Brown's *Indices* for full orchestra as accompaniment for the Cunningham dance *Springweather and People*. It proved impossible to find an electric guitar, or some of the percussion instruments. Great effort was put into arrangements for Tudor to play a piano reduction as accompaniment. "At the last minute the authorities agreed," Cage narrated in one of the stories from an extended version of *Indeterminacy*. Just before the projected performance, the Pope died; Belgium being a strongly Catholic country, "everything was cancelled," with no hope for rescheduling.

On October 14 Cage and Tudor performed at the Galerie 22, playing *Variations I* and the premiere of *Music Walk*, which the *Rheinische Post* characterized as "the sensation of the day." The end of the month found them in Cologne, again joined by Cunningham and Carolyn Brown. While there, Cage called on Mary Bauermeister. Born in 1934, Bauermeister had first planned to be a scientist, but turned to painting in 1953; in 1961 she would become a student of Stockhausen, in 1967 his second wife. As Cage stood in her apartment, he recalled, "Nam June Paik suddenly approached me, cut off my tie and began to shred my clothes, as if to rip them off." Paik poured a bottle of shampoo over Cage's head. "Just behind him, there was an open window with a drop of perhaps six floors to the street, and everyone suddenly had the impression that he was going to throw himself out." Instead, Paik strode from the room, leaving all present frozen and speechless with terror. A few minutes later the telephone rang; it was Paik announcing that the performance of the *Homage to John Cage* was over.

Milan was a calm city in which to end the year. Luciano Berio (b. 1925) had set up an electronic music studio at Radio Audizione Italienne three years earlier in collaboration with Maderna, and Cage worked there at his invitation from November 1958 to March 1959.

Berio had married Cathy Berberian, a young American singer who had come to Milan on a Fullbright scholarship, yet it was Cage who first saw clearly her potential as a vocalist for experimental music. "You have that fantastic voice right here in your own house," he told Berio, "why don't you write something for her?" Berio began *Circles*, for female voice, harp and two percussionists – he finished it in 1960 – and Cage wrote with characteristic briskness the *Aria*, dedicated to Berberian, a score whose color layout defines ten styles of singing, with black blobs denoting ancillary noises in the manner of the *Ten Thousand Things*. Pitch was notated by the vertical position of the colored lines. It was the start of a lifetime career for Berberian, and she and Cage were to work together frequently.

Cage was increasingly interested in producing distinct works which might or might not be performed simultaneously. To go with the *Aria* he prepared the *Fontana Mix*, which legend has it was named after his Milanese landlady. The score is similar to that for *Variations I* – a mixture of transparent and opaque sheets, a straight line and a graph grid. A shopping list exists, written on the back of a formal invitation to a reception at the Belvedere which Cage had brought with him from Brussels: "Ink from Luciano," it says, "eggs butter coffee salt pepper," and below are sketched a number of lines of the sort he was to use in the score. *Fontana Mix* had been realized in many different forms over the years, but the best known is Cage's own, made in the Studio di Fonologia, using the score to determine which of an array of sound-sources was to be used, the manipulation of each sound-source, and the way it was cut and spliced onto quadrophonic tape. He finished this version, with technical assistance by Mario Zucchen, in February 1959.

III

Lascia o Raddoppia was a hugely popular television quiz show, presented by Mike Bongiorno, every Thursday at nine o'clock. The format was an American import. Each contestant answered questions on a subject of their choice. As the weeks passed the questions grew harder and the cash reward greater. Answer a question wrongly and a contestant dropped out, keeping half of their winnings; answer every question correctly for five weeks, one stood to win five million lire – then worth about eight thousand dollars. Thus it was that Cage became a prime-time Italian television personality.

He applied to answer, aided by an interpreter, questions on mushrooms, and each week he would perform a different piece before he answered the questions. In the first week he played the prepared piano solos from *Amores*, and went on to answer every question correctly. For the second he used transparencies to put together a new theater piece, *Water Walk*, which was reminiscent of *Water Music*. It is less durationally specific (its three-minute duration is notated only at five-second intervals) and not so virtuosic, while it is more flamboyant in its list of properties, many of them with liquid associations: roses in a vase, a stove and a pressure cooker, a rubber fish, a quail call; a Waring blender, a goose whistle, a bath tub, an exploding paper container and a bottle of Campari. "Why are you always laughing?" asked Bongiorno afterwards, playing to the audience with his customary mild sarcasm. "It's a situation that makes you laugh," Cage replied with apparent innocence, but perhaps a trace of defensiveness.

Having answered correctly again, Cage took off at the end of the week to visit Peggy Guggenheim in Venice (their quarrel of sixteen years ago was long forgotten), and wrote to his parents, "Spent the last four days in Venice with Peggy. She remembers you with much love. Has six beautiful dogs and we were photographed together for the newspaper. I collected sounds for next Tuesday's music."

The sounds which he recorded went into his presentation for the next show, *Sounds of Venice*. Still he answered correctly; by now he had attained celebrity status, and was besieged by autograph hunters and photographers and interviewed every day. The G. Bresadola Mycological Society made Cage an honorary member and sent, via Bongiorno, a catalog to their exhibition of the previous September. A little Italian girl gave him a good luck card, "Buonviaggio et buoni funghi." The press depicted him as a classic American, tall, square-jawed, "pleasantly reminiscent of Frankenstein." Cage was a curiosity not only as an American, and one who knew everything there was to know about mushrooms, but one who performed such curious music on such strange instruments. "Next he'll invent electronic mushrooms," quipped one reporter.

Asked if he was nervous at appearing a fourth time, with the risk of losing half his prize money, Cage replied that he did not feel the least bit nervous, for even if the worst occurred he would still carry away more than the value of a Guggenheim Fellowship.

"In the booth for two million five hundred and sixty thousand lire," Bongiorno announced, "we give you an envelope containing seven color photographs of mushrooms. You have to tell us: which of them represents the mushroom 'poliporus frondosus'? is it edible or not? does it grow on the ground or on trees?" Cage replied, "It's photo number seven. It's an edible mushroom and it grows on wood."

In the fifth and final week Bongiorno asked him to name every type of white-spored mushroom. Cage had prepared for this eventuality. From the glass isolation booth he began to slowly recite them in alphabetical order. Then he noticed the soundless gestures of the delirious audience, pointing at the clock above his head: he realized there was a time limit on his list. Yet he could not see the clock, and so carried on, with what seemed like careless languor, finishing with a fraction of a second to spare.

It is ironic that it took a television game show to give Cage his first financial break. After the necessary exchange transactions were deducted, he came away with six thousand dollars. Returning home in March, he was able to buy himself a two-thousand-dollar Steinway and a Volkswagen station wagon for the Cunningham Company at $2336.

Cage was soon on the road again, appearing on the panel at a conference on Zen Buddhism in American culture at Sarah Lawrence College on April 18. Meantime a letter had arrived from Gianfranco Mingozzi in Rome, requesting a number of full-face and profile photographs. His superior had seen Cage on *Lascia o Raddoppia*. Federico Fellini was considering hiring him for his new picture, with the projected title *La dolce vita*, though the filmmaker's interest went no further.

IV

Cage's first contact with Virgil Thomson was at the end of the thirties, when he had written to him from Seattle; they had then met in 1941. Relations had soured when Thomson told Cage after the premiere of *Imaginary Landscape No. 4* that it was not the sort of piece that should be performed before a paying public. "We had difficulty after that," Cage stated flatly. Yet for some time he had been involved with a book project concerning Thomson's music.

Over the years Cage was to write numerous tributes and *pièces d'occasion*, for example, on Johns, Rauschenberg and Nam June Paik, but the book on Thomson is unique, the only sizeable study by Cage of work and ideas other than his own. It is interesting, in view of Cage's dedication in his own work to impersonalism and his opposition to psychoanalytical introspection, that the project hit a reef when he decided he had to deal not only with Thomson's music but also his life; that, indeed, "there was no way in this case to separate one from the other." Cage stated, "I tried to explain changes in Virgil's music through changes in his life."

Thomson objected, feeling that the second chapter in particular was "definitely unfriendly," and asked Cage to cease work. A series of stops and starts ensued which left Cage uncertain where he stood. The book was taken over by a friend of Thomson, Kathleen O'Donnell Hoover; when Cage objected, Thomson announced he would carry out the purge himself. Cage protested that everyone knew his style of writing. They compromised on a third editor, Herbert Weinstock of the publishers Alfred A. Knopf. Finally, when proofs arrived from Yoseloff, the publishers, Cage found *The Life of Virgil Thomson* was credited to Hoover, and his contribution had been patently meddled with by the subject. "I found this objectionable and completely contrary to our understanding," Cage stated. From this point onward, they saw one another very little. The final straw came in the early seventies, when Thomson characterized Cage as "a pied piper on a one-way ticket to the gadget fair." Cage told a journalist, "This last argument has really hurt me."

Course number 424 at the New School for Social Research for 1957–58 had been Cage's class on the music of Thomson, which he gave with the continuation of the Composition of Experimental Music course, number 244, and a class on the music of Satie added at the last minute. The dispute over the book did not discourage Cage from offering the course again for 1959–60.

He taught it along with two other courses. The initial registration for his class on mushroom identification – "mushroom administration" as one chronology of his career put it – was a flatteringly unlikely forty students, but thereafter attendance fluctuated, sometimes dipping to a dozen. One of the women who attended eventually explained that adults enrolled for courses at the New School were eligible for discount airline fares to Europe. She, and many of the others, had browsed through the prospectus and found that the cheapest class was the one taught by Cage. He subsequently received a postcard from Europe from an ex-student who had spotted some mushrooms.

The third class that year was in Experimental Composition, which, like its predecessor, was renewed for the year that followed. Among those who enrolled for 1959–60 was a young Japanese composer called Toshi Ichiyanagi. The uncompromising individualism of the young man vividly reaffirmed the way Cage strove to approach education. When the winter semester ended, Cage felt he should summarize the progress made by his students by commenting on their work, suggesting to each the direction it might take, so that they could reflect on the suggestions over the vacation and come back keen for greater experimentation. At first no one demurred. Then, when he began to make observations on the music of Ichiyanagi, the young man stared into space over his teacher's shoulder and said flatly, "I am not you." For Cage this confirmed that "the teacher is best who studies with the pupils. They each have different things to learn. Let's hope they don't have to learn the same things. We can converse together then, rather than compete."

Cage's principal pedagogical involvement at the time – the nearest he came to a traditional pupil–teacher relationship since teaching Christian Wolff ten years earlier – was with Ben Johnston. As mentioned previously, Cage had met Johnston just before he began *Williams Mix*, and the young man had helped out with the piece over the great coin-tossing summer of

1952. Johnston had by this time received a Guggenheim grant to work at Columbia, but was frustrated by the protectiveness of Milton Babbitt over the electronic music facilities. Cage recommended he work with Richard Maxfield, but academic politics made it unfeasible. Instead, Johnston drove up to Stony Point once a month to consult with Cage. "It was really very valuable," Johnston observed. "He didn't stop me from doing what I was doing; he simply criticized – and very perceptively." Cage later helped Johnston secure a Fullbright scholarship so he could work with Pierre Schaeffer in France.

In January 1960 Cage completed his *Theater Piece*, performed at the Circle in the Square theater in New York on March 7 with Cunningham and Carolyn Brown dancing, Arline Camun singing (she had performed in the twenty-five-year retrospective), and three musicians, Tudor among them. In February the *Music for Amplified Toy Pianos* was completed, a new transparency score of eight sheets to yield directions for between one and five toy pianos. Between January and May he prepared *WBAI*, "material for making a mechanical program," used since principally for sound projection. At Richard Maxfield's studio in June, Cage made a nine-minute tape piece as incidental music for *The Marrying Maiden*, a play by his former student Jackson MacLow; its text was in part generated by chance means.

Then in July Cage completed *Cartridge Music*, for "amplified small sounds," a further transparency score from which the player or players assemble directions for making audible otherwise indiscernible sounds. To obtain this effect Cage increased the use of phonograph cartridges, which had been a feature of the second and third *Imaginary Landscapes*, to orchestral proportions, suggesting the players insert feathers, lengths of wire, toothpicks, pipe cleaners, small twigs, wire coils or nails. Early performances, for instance, featured a tiny Japanese cocktail parasol and a miniature Stars and Stripes. As with *Music for Amplified Toy Pianos*, the loudspeakers are to surround the audience. "All events, ordinarily thought to be undesirable, such as feedback, humming, howling, etc., are to be accepted in this situation," Cage wrote in the score.

Cage has said that one distinguishing feature of his work is its sense of theater. This points not only to the *Theater Piece* or the Zen vaudeville of *Water Music* or *Water Walk*, but also to the introspective but curious action of pieces such as *Cartridge Music*. Indeed, since Cage's music is intended to transcend emotion, it is what people see in the physicality of live performance which can let them project, almost without noticing it, the drama they are accustomed to find in a concert situation.

In October Cage was performing at Bauermeister's studio in Cologne. In January 1961 he was to speak in Brooklyn at the Evening School of the Pratt Institute. He used *Cartridge Music* to structure four different speeches which may be given in whole or part, on their own or with any two, any three or all four playing simultaneously, with any number of the speeches delivered as a recording. The burning questions among the students, Cage was told before his presentation, were "Where are we going? and what are we doing?" and these, he says, became the topics and later formed the title of the lecture. However, although this is how Cage accounts for the title, it is perhaps no coincidence that in 1897 Gauguin painted a large canvas called in translation "Where do we come from? What are we? Where are we going?"

V

In 1961 Cage took up his appointment as a Fellow in the Center for Advanced Studies at Wesleyan University. When, the previous year, he had received confirmation of the appointment, Crete had asked, "Do they know you're a Zen Buddhist?" It was the longest time he had been away from home since moving to Stony Point.

A seminar on "Approaches to Commitment" was held on February 23. Cage devised the *Lecture on Commitment* as a series of cards: twenty-eight, with texts of differing lengths, and twenty-eight more bearing different numbers. Shuffling both sets of cards, the first number-card gave the duration in seconds of the first text-card, and so on. The texts seem to be about commitment in tangential ways, but Cage seems overall to be suggesting that if we have free will, commitment consists of using it for setting ourselves in specific conditions. "We are as free as birds," he wrote. "Only the birds aren't free. We are as committed as birds, and identically." The birds, Suzuki might have said, live in Zen but not by Zen. As Cage recounted:

> Artists talk a lot about freedom. So, recalling the expression "free as a bird," Morton Feldman went to a park one day and spent some time watching our feathered friends. When he came back, he said, "You know? They're not free: they're fighting over bits of food."

Cage, as already noted, stands up for the birds.

In the course of the lecture Cage told of his studies with Goldfinger and with Schoenberg, how he left the first because he could not devote his life to architecture, how he promised Schoenberg five years later to devote his life to music, even though that meant devoting his life to beating his head against the wall of harmony.

After the seminar Cage told a reporter, "I'm more interested in arousing the realization in each person of the central nature of his own experience than I am in controlling him with respect to mine." This became the byword for the activities he instigated with students. At the '92 Theater he presented, for instance, LaMonte Young's *Poem*, which uses a telephone book to generate the directions for a performance involving everyday objects which can produce prolonged sounds. As described by a student reporter, "radios crackled, chairs, benches, brooms, tables were pushed around the floor, gongs sounded, students yelled . . . even a fire extinguisher was set off . . . (until it ran dry)." Cage told the young reporter, "Art has continually had the function of awakening people to the life around them."

While at Wesleyan Cage came to know a number of people, including Victor Butterfield, president of the university, and another Fellow at the center, Edgar Anderson, from the University of Washington, with whom he went foraging in the woods. He met Richard K. Winslow, who despite favoring a quite different compositional style, and despite his alarming habit of suddenly singing quietly, became a fierce champion of Cage's work. Cage, reciprocally, assisted Winslow, spending three twelve-hour days, for example, copying up Winslow's *Ikon* for its premiere at Wesleyan the following week. Another new-found friend was Norman O. Brown, a psychoanalytic historian and theorist, and uncompromising clear thinker, who had been at Wesleyan since 1946. Born on September 25, 1913, Brown was optimistic and libertarian like Cage, but in other ways was an unlikely compatriot, committed to a diverse, passionate, Dionysian view of life quite opposed to the orderly asceticism to which Cage devoted his artistic energies. "I'd rather be drunk than sober," Brown declares.

In the course of the fellowship Cage again tried to realize his twenty-year dream of founding a center for experimental music, again with no success. The University Press at Wesleyan, however, with the encouragement of Winslow, undertook to release the first collection of Cage's writings, aptly entitled *Silence*, which remains the outstanding source document of Cage's best-known *prises des positions* up to 1960. It was published on October 26, 1960 to interested but often puzzled reviews.

Cage was also now a published composer. In March and April 1953 he had corresponded with Universal Edition in Europe concerning the possibility of publishing *Music of Changes* (Alfred Schlee borrowed a copy from Stockhausen for the company to look at), but this had come to nothing, as had his offer of the *Sonata for Clarinet* to *New Music* years earlier. Only *Amores* had been made commercially available. Yet since moving to Stony Point, Cage was finding it difficult to supply his work to those who wanted it. He took his music to Schirmers. Mr. Heinsheimer there said that Cage's music would only give them a headache; the one piece he liked was the *Suite for Toy Piano* from 1948, but even then he told Cage that the title would have to be changed. Cage replied there was no need, since he was taking the music back home with him.

Then, while he was preparing the tape for *The Marrying Maiden*, Cage set down his pen and resolved to do nothing more until he found a publisher. He looked through the section on music publishers in the *Yellow Pages*, and his eye fell on the number for the C.F. Peters Corporation. Walter Hinrichsen had established the New York office in 1948, and a string player Cage knew had told him how interested Hinrichsen was in American music. When Cage called, Hinrichsen, adventurous yet thorough, told him very cheerfully that his wife had for some time wanted the company to publish Cage's music; that day they met for lunch and signed an exclusive contract.

While Cage worked at Wesleyan, the Montreal Festivals Society commissioned from him a work for full orchestra. Almost ten years earlier he had found a ready-made source for chance operations in the imperfections of paper; now he found a new source in the dots of light in the heavens. Cage designed a complex compositional system using Czechoslovakian star maps which he had discovered at the Wesleyan Observatory, employing transparencies and chance operations to select stars, which would be traced as notes, and to determine their combinations. He tried the work out on a small scale in March 1961. After he had finished a three-octave arrangement of the *Music for Carillon No. 1*, he used the star maps of the *Atlas Coeli* to make *Music for Carillon No. 4*. Cage would return to the star maps as a source for chance operations in later work, and their use, and his manner of notation, would be alluded to by other composers, for instance Stockhausen in *Sternklang* (1971).

The projected title of the Montreal piece was *Atlas Eclipticalis*, after the great circle of stars around the sun. Cage planned eighty-six parts, all or some of which may be played, consisting of four pages of five systems each, each system lasting sixty seconds. Each of the parts is dedicated to a friend or colleague, among them Mary Bauermeister, Luciano Berio, Morton Feldman, Toshi Ichiyanagi, Mauricio Kagel, Richard Lippold, Nam June Paik, Steve Paxton and Karlheinz Stockhausen. Cunningham and Tudor are dedicatees of the timpani parts; Cage's parents, interestingly, given his appreciation of *Don Giovanni*, of the second trombone. Ichiyanagi helped with some of the manuscript preparation, and as parts were completed, the work was performed in various ensembles.

The full premiere, performed simultaneously with *Winter Music*, was conducted by Cage at the International Week of Today's Music at Montreal on August 3, 1961. A performance in Venice, which was attended by Stravinsky, provoked a near-riot. An old man smacked his chair with his walking stick, barking, "There, now I'm a musician too." Asked if the tumult compared to that of the premiere of his *Le sacre du printemps*, Stravinsky grandiloquently replied, "There has never been a scandal like mine."

VI

Early in 1962 Richard Lippold was commissioned to make a sculpture for the lobby of the Pan Am building, to the rear of Grand Central terminal in New York. As he had no wish for his work to be bathed in muzak, he recommended that Cage be asked to supply some form of sound installation.

Cage thought that it would be most practical to use "things right there": the supply of muzak, for which Pan Am already had a contract; the loudspeakers built into the walls; and the television screens with photoelectric cells, which would trigger the playing, pulverization and filtering of muzak. As the cells would never be activated in the same combination twice, the aural result would vary constantly. For several months the proposal was considered; the Bell Telephone Laboratories on Murray Hill were consulted. Finally the plan was rejected; as a compromise, Lippold was given silence in the lobby.

Cage turned fifty that September and his friends clubbed together to buy him the massive two-volume work by V.P. and R.G. Masson, *Mushrooms, Russia and History*. The twenty-four signatories are Norman O. and Beth Brown, Merce Cunningham, Ralph Ferrara, Jasper Johns, Elaine de Kooning, Minna Lederman, Louise and Richard Lippold, Lois Long, Susan and David McAllester, Paula Madawick and Tucker Madawick (Lois Long's children by her first husband), Guy Nearing,

M.C. Richards, David Tudor, Paul, Vera and Sarah Williams, Richard K. and Betty Winslow, and Christian Wolff.

With Ferrara, Long, Guy Nearing and Esther Dam, Cage founded the New York Mycological Society. In an early expression of his anarchist leanings, the initial rules, since rescinded, made no provision for a president. The founders felt records needed to be kept, so a secretary and a treasurer were required, but nobody needed to be in charge; all decisions were made cooperatively. The New York society was just one of a number of mushroom societies to which Cage belonged in the sixties; he was Eastern vice-chairman of the People-to-People Community Program Committee on Fungi, receiving a plaque for his outstanding contributions to amateur mycology in 1964, and around that time he joined the Czechoslovakian Mushroom Society.

A couple of weeks after his birthday Cage and Tudor traveled back to Seattle and the Cornish School – and Morris Graves, who came to their concert there and banged the seat in front of him three times to express his approval. Then they moved on to the University of Hawaii for the 28th. The following month, they embarked on a six-week concert tour of Japan, in the course of which Cage was able to visit Suzuki. In Tokyo on October 24 he wrote – and simultaneously performed – *0'00"*, dedicated to Toshi Ichiyanagi and Yoko Ono (they were then still married). *0'00"* is a "solo to be performed in any way by anyone," yet despite the ring of licence, it is one of Cage's pieces where discipline is in the forefront. The main instruction reads, "IN A SITUATION PROVIDED WITH MAXIMUM AMPLIFICATION (NO FEEDBACK), PERFORM A DISCIPLINED ACTION." The first performance was an amplified writing of the manuscript, as we know from an indented note added the following day. *0'00"* is a very direct framing of the everyday; its subtitle is *4'33" (No. 2)*.

Cage also refers to the piece in terms suggested by Hidekazu Yoshida. Yoshida seems to have been a friend who both possessed a Zen approach to the world and appreciated the appropriate attitude in Cage. Once when discussing Herrigel's *Zen in the Art of Archery*, Yoshida observed that, apart from the heroic masters who can hit a bull's-eye blindfolded, there is a renowned archer who had never hit the bull's-eye, even in broad daylight. On another occasion, Yoshida suggested that the three lines of haiku correspond to nirvana, samsara and specific individual action, completed by non-action. Cage applied this to his work, thinking of *Atlas Eclipticalis, Variations IV* (which was not written until the following year) and *0'00"* as a trilogy corresponding to the lines of haiku.

Cage was to present the piece in a number of different ways over the following years – the score demands that no two performances be of the same action – drinking a glass of water ("we could simply decide to drink a glass of water," as he said in the "Lecture on Nothing") or answering his mail. It was a simple piece to notate, another form of performance watercolor, which would be mirrored in named works such as *WGBH-TV* (1971) and numerous, perhaps somewhat expedient, performances in the eighties when work pressure cut down on the time available for preparation of new materials. The idea for *0'00"* had been cooking for some time; Cage had told a reporter in Canada the previous year that he had a plan to set up a kitchen on stage and have women preparing food with contact microphones on their sleeves, so their movements made their cooking a concert.

From December until the new year Cage worked at Stony Point on *Variations III* – another transparency score – and further into 1963, on *Variations IV*. The highlight of 1963 was the world premiere of Satie's *Vexations*, a piece Cage had discovered in a drawer during his time in Paris in 1949. As early as 1950 he had mooted the possibility of performing it. His interest in Satie had continued to grow. "It's not a question of Satie's relevance – he's indispensable," Cage had written in 1958.

Most people who had heard of *Vexations* considered it a typical Satie joke. Cage took it quite seriously. "If you think about it," he told reporters, "there are a lot more than eight hundred forty repetitions in life – like paying the telephone bill, for instance." He arranged the first performance to begin at the Pocket Theater on Third Avenue at six in the evening on September 9.

VII

There were several people in the audience when Viola Farber, otherwise a dancer with the Cunningham Company, began to play; by eight o'clock there were twenty-two. Without a break, Robert Wood moved his left hand onto the keyboard to play the bass as Farber vacated the seat. Wood was followed by MacRae Cook, then by John Cale (soon to form a rock band). Cage himself took the fifth shift, then was succeeded by Wolff, David del Tradici, Tudor, Philip Corner, James Tenney and Joshua Rivkin.

Early in the morning of the 10th, Cage slept on a mattress in a downstairs drawing room. In the lobby, survival rations were set out –

coffee, chicken broth, pastry and peaches. Cage expected the audience to go in and out, suggesting, when he first raised the idea of a performance, "you'd drop in on it like a serial." Among the audience was a high proportion of beatniks, but Sari Dienes was there from the start, and Max Neuhaus listened in from nine until three the next morning. A music student revised an accountancy exam; the *New York Times* staff writer fell asleep. A young man named Saul Stollman left, afraid of being hypnotized. Occasionally the player would nod and strike a bum note; "the presence of human frailty becomes an integral part," Cage observed.

The last session again belonged to Farber, this time sporting a rose in her hair. She rounded off the piece at 12:40 on September 11. Champagne flowed, but not the conversation. Cage drove back to Stony Point feeling, he said, a changed man. "We all realized," he reflected afterwards, "that something had been set in motion that went far beyond what any of us had anticipated."

As with many of his projects, Cage had nurtured the idea for some time, during which he had devised a number of ancillary schemes. He had planned a similar performance piece of his own – to find a cracked Mischa Elman recording of the Dvorak *Humoresque* and play it continuously for thirteen hours. The audience would have been allowed to enter without paying, but charged as they left: the sooner they departed, the higher the fee. This unrealized idea not only suggests *Vexations*, which soon followed, but the crackly records used in *Europeras III* and *IV* twenty-five years later.

Uncharacteristically, John Cage's compositional CV for 1964 is blank. Other matters were keeping him busy. He had to deal with the death of John senior, at home at Montclair on January 4; he was seventy-eight. Cage encouraged his mother to visit the family back in Los Angeles. "You'll have a good time," he urged. "Now John," Crete replied, "you know perfectly well I've never enjoyed having a good time."

Atlas Eclipticalis was scheduled for its New York premiere on February 6. Feldman had said some time earlier, "To catch on to us, what the public needs is to get it from Leonard Bernstein," and Bernstein it was who was going to conduct the New York Philharmonic in a concert aimed at making new music more accessible: *Atlas* and Earle Brown's *Available Forms I* were combined with the *Four Seasons* by Vivaldi and the Tchaikovsky *Pathétique* symphony.

In rehearsal, Bernstein encouraged a responsible and serious approach to the pieces, and coached the players on reading the parts, for the notation of the Cage work was quite unfamiliar. In *Atlas Eclipticalis* there was the added complication of new technology; Max Matthews of the Bell Telephone Laboratories had built a sound system to be operated by James Tenney, who had played in the *Vexations* premiere. Contact microphones led from each of the instruments and were fed into the console, mixed according to chance operations and distributed over six channels.

As in *Concert*, there was no conductor as a governing agent; indeed, the chronometric conducting of the earlier work was taken over by a mechanical conductor made by Paul Williams – a metal box on a stand, with a rotating arm to define the placement within the eight-minute duration of the piece, and colored lights to mark its subdivisions.

The opening concert was sold out. *Atlas Eclipticalis* was prefaced by an experiment in score generation by computer from a British machine called Pegasus, and a free improvisation by the orchestra (not perhaps the best preface to the music of John Cage). As soon as the Cage piece began, the Philharmonic audience began to mutter in protest, and presently to walk out. By the time eight minutes had elapsed half the audience had left, and in doing so made it impossible for the faithful and the agnostic to go on listening. By the time the works by Feldman and Brown were performed, only a third of the audience remained.

The program was repeated three times. On the Sunday Crete attended and found herself next to a woman who was especially vociferous in her disruption of *Atlas*. When the piece ended, Crete turned to her and stated, "I am the composer's mother." "Good heavens!" replied her neighbor quickly. "Your son's music is magnificent! Would you tell him, please, how much I loved it." Cage commented afterwards, "Don't you love it – even courtesy is a conditioned reflex."

Stockhausen came to the second performance. Cage found now that not only was the audience reacting against the new pieces, but when he and his friends took their bows, the orchestra was also hissing them. On the third night, during the performance of *Atlas*, the orchestra laughed and talked among themselves, played scales or melodies instead of the notes in their parts, sang or whistled into the contact microphones; some stamped on the electronic equipment. Bernstein seemed unable to control the situation. Afterwards, Cage spoke to Carlos Mosely, the president of the Philharmonic, and to the union representatives of the orchestra; Bernstein addressed the whole orchestra and castigated them for their behavior.

Problems with performers bedevilled the work of Cage before and after the Philharmonic débâcle; it had been at its worst among the large, uncommitted numbers required for orchestral concerts, and avoided completely only with individual players close to Cage – Masselos, Ajemian, Tudor, Tan. The Venice performance of *Atlas*, as mentioned, provoked a near-riot; the presentation at Texas Tech on May 4, 1964 featured a trumpet player busking selections from *Annie Get Your Gun*. The 1972 premiere of *Cheap Imitation* would lead to a similar shambles; and when the Los Angeles Philharmonic performed *Renga* in 1977, the players smirked, giggled and exchanged jokes, one of their number writing to the *Los Angeles Times* to say "no musical training is necessary for this . . . quasi-intellectual trash: . . . only the ability to make noise for thirty embarrassing minutes. I felt ashamed to sit on stage and be a part of *Renga*." Even in 1990, at a festival in Glasgow, Scotland, where Cage was the featured composer – and consolidated to some extent his status as an elder statesman – at least one player in a performance of *Atlas Eclipticalis* kept his part shut and played whenever he felt like it.

The Philharmonic incident provides insight into the expectations of Cage and those of orchestral musicians. The latter had no tradition or precedent for the piece – it was not just different, it was opposed to everything they were accustomed to performing – so they had no idea of why the piece was as it was, or how to approach its performance, and perhaps felt it was dangerously nihilistic. Among the Philharmonic players was Saul Goodman, a celebrated timpanist and author of a standard teaching method on the subject. The way this accomplished musician described the piece serves to indicate how poorly it was understood:

> Now instead of music we had a graph to follow. . . . As it was explained to us, as the line went upward on the graph, you were supposed to improvise something going up, and as the line went down – or downward as we say – you were supposed to play something going down. There was no rhythmical structure; you could play anything you wanted, you could improvise anything you wanted.

Such errors show less a lack of commitment and interest than the realities of professional orchestral life, in which time is scarce, even for the newest pieces. Without an understanding of what Cage hoped to achieve, much of what was happening seemed wilfully arbitrary. The parts did not take traditional considerations of instrumental balance into account, so a player might find what he or she played utterly engulfed by another. Moreover, the chance mixing of the input from the contact microphones left the players baffled and irritated to find that what they played might not be heard. "Even if you were making your choices with diligence," Earle Brown observes, "you might be turned off. Maybe you were heard. Maybe you weren't . . . That sets up a psychological condition in which they say, 'What am I doing this for?'"

The ferocity of the response may have been a surprise, but some kind of objection from the players was easily predictable. It is revealing that Cage refused to compromise his aims, and that he remained optimistic that players could, if not should, take a livelier interest and have a more open mind. In this one principled exception to his empiricism, Cage lets his optimism override what can be seen in the world. "I think he expects people all to be enlightened," Earle Brown comments. "Ninety-eight Buddhas in an orchestra." In this refusal to compromise, Cage allows himself the luxury of "should" rather than "is". Henceforth, however, it was clearer to Cage that his music needed to be better understood to be properly performed, and this later led to the practical step of demanding extra rehearsal time, which helped the players become involved in the music.

April was a gentler month: Cage traveled with Johns and Lois Long to Hawaii, having been invited by the Music Department to take part in an East–West colloquium – he the West, Toru Takemitsu the East.

Cage was growing interested in the work of Marshall McLuhan and of Buckminster Fuller. He had known Fuller since *Le piège de Méduse* at Black Mountain in 1948; over the years the wide-ranging thinking of Fuller took off – the C60 carbon molecule was to be dubbed a Buckminsterfullerene. By 1968 Cage would say "the work and thought of Buckminster Fuller is of prime importance to me," and Fuller's ideas, especially concerning "space-ship earth" and the global utilities network, have remained important ever since.

Likewise Cage was attracted strongly to the ideas of McLuhan. On the surface a celebrant of the instantaneity of the electronic age and the mass media, and the ensuing "Global Village," McLuhan was a traditional, religious man at the core, and for him, as for many, fame came through misunderstanding what he was about. His apotheosis came in a cameo role in Woody Allen's *Annie Hall*.

While in Hawaii Cage had an experience that confirmed for him the optimistic view of social progress these two men shared, and which prompted him to closer involvement with it. The university is at the southern end of Oahu, the island on which Honolulu stands. Cage, Johns and Long were staying at the northern end, separated from the university by a mountain range. As they passed each day through the tunnel connecting north and south, Cage noticed that on top of the mountains were crenellations, like those of European castles in the middle ages. "They had been used," one of the locals explained, "for self-protection, shooting poisoned arrows on the enemy below." By the time of Cage's visit, scarcely a century later, the range had been tunneled through, and both sides shared the same resources in peace. "We are, as Fuller has pointed out," Cage concluded when describing what he learned from this story, "an island on the earth. It's all one piece of land; it can be connected."

Cage's thinking on these matters led him to begin a celebration of the ideas of Fuller, *Diary: How to Improve the World (You will only make matters worse)*. The first installment was begun in 1965 for publication the following year; Cage wrote a dozen more until 1973 when, feeling less hopeful about the likelihood of world improvement under the Nixon administration, he abandoned one halfway through and did not complete it until 1982.

When he first told his mother that he was writing about world improvement – it was 1967 – she said, with characteristically unexpected severity, "John! How *dare* you? You should be ashamed! I'm surprised at you." He asked if, in view of the condition of the world, there was not room for improvement. She said, "There certainly is. It makes good sense."

The principal reason that Cage did not finish a piece in 1964 was that, as he told an inquisitive friend, "in 1964 I wrote letters." He was working with Cunningham on what was agreed would be a make-or-break world tour for the dance company, which meant constant correspondence to make bookings and raise money. In the middle of the year the six-month tour began: seventy engagements, beginning in Strasbourg and Paris (to mixed reviews), then Venice and Vienna. The one-week booking at the Sadler's Wells Theatre in London was received so enthusiastically that three more weeks were added at the Phoenix on Charing Cross Road, which promptly sold out. The tour continued in Scandinavia, Czechoslovakia and Poland, and ended in the East: Japan, India and (on November 3) the unlikely honor of a Royal Command Performance in Thailand.

On its return the company took a well-earned sabbatical. Viola Farber had to stop dancing altogether due to injury; Rauschenberg resigned from his job as artistic director after falling out with Cunningham. The company was heavily in debt. Yet its reputation had snowballed, spurred particularly by the success in London. The following year the

Cunningham Dance Foundation was formed, and new members joined the company. Jasper Johns became artistic adviser; because of his other commitments, he did not travel with the company and would often delegate commissions (a notable exception was his set for *Walkaround Time*, based on the *Large Glass* by Duchamp). Tudor remained the company musician and Cage the musical director, augmented by Ichiyanagi and a young electronics whizzkid, Gordon Mumma.

VIII

Early in 1965 Alvin Lucier invited Cage to present a concert at Brandeis University. He accepted, on the condition that the concert also included works by Lucier and Christian Wolff.

The Music Department at Brandeis was preoccupied with developments in serialism and Lucier hoped that his invitation would act as a corrective. He expected, however, that the department would tend toward indifference, so he arranged for the concert to take place in the Rose Art Museum on the campus, under the auspices of Sam Hunter.

Cage elected to perform *0'00''*, and announced that he would prepare a new work for tape loops. In a note to Lucier, he requested that at least eighty-eight tape loops be made, "as many as there are keys on the piano." He had no preference as to what was on the tapes – he later requested that splices be made without the person splicing knowing what was on them either – but said he would like to hear a "non-pop version someday." Then Cage sent descriptions of splicing techniques, following procedures devised for *Williams Mix*: horizontal and vertical splices at different angles, producing sounds with varied attacks, played forwards, backwards, upside-down and sideways.

On a flier advertising the concert, Cage tried to work out a title. Below "Rose Art Museum: John Cage and Alvin Lucier" he wrote Beau Arts Mix, then replaced the first letter with an R, added an x, crossed off the s: Reaux Art Mix. Turning the paper on its side, he tried Reau Ar, breaking off suddenly – the title, he decided, would be *Rozart Mix*.

The university had lodged Cage in the Faculty Club. Lucier and his students had completed just over half of the minimum of eighty-eight loops he had requested, so he spent a good part of his time assembling the remainder in the guest room. "Anybody who knew John Cage at that time knew how much he disliked air-conditioning," Lucier recalled. "I remember him remarking later that, because of having to spend so much time in it, he had finally learned to enjoy it."

The Rose Art Museum was small but roomy, built on two levels connected via a small landing by an open stairway that enabled each level to be visible to the other. The concert was presented on May 5. Before the audience entered, Cage began to perform *0'00"*, answering letters at an amplified typewriter, seated in a very squeaky chair which he had brought with him from New York to be amplified. Now and again he quaffed water, amplified by a Second World War airplane pilot's microphone strapped round his throat.

The Lucier piece, *Music for Solo Performer*, followed. After a lull in his work as a composer, Lucier had begun making the first incursions into bio-music, making audible the physiological processes of living things. Using equipment loaned by Edmond Dewan, a physicist at the nearby Hanscombe Air Base, he was experimenting with ways of converting brainwaves into sound. Lucier had been loath to try this out in concert in case it failed, but Cage was characteristically insistent and enthusiastic.

Electrodes were attached to Lucier's scalp to pick up alpha waves. The alpha current was amplified, routed through a low-pass filter and played over speakers, which set off resonance in a number of percussion instruments: drum heads ringing in sympathetic vibration, metal instruments struck by the rapidly moving loudspeaker cones. A threshold switch, when triggered, fed in a stereo recording of accelerated alpha. Lucier's task was to attempt consciously to control what is normally an automatic brain function: he had to try to avoid either looking or visualizing, for any visual distraction would cut off the alpha waves.

As the piece went on, the smallest speakers, stripped from automobiles, were blown apart by the enormous amplification, but their ruptured cones continued to emit clicking sounds; one fell off its drum and flapped around the floor like a dying fish.

Next came *For 1, 2 or 3 People* by Christian Wolff, with Lucier on amplified bowed cymbal, Wolff with electric guitar, and Cage playing a saw. It contrasts markedly with anything by Cage; like a number of pieces by Wolff, as we saw when discussing indeterminacy, its success depends on instant reaction to the unpredictable choices of the other players, involving a dangerous proximity to improvisation and an interpersonal spontaneity which Cage would never countenance.

Rozart Mix ended the concert. Lucier and a number of the Brandeis graduate students picked up loops, threaded them on the recorders, and extended them around the mike stands. Some removed shoes and socks to wade through the shallow pool on the ground floor bearing loops. The tapes ran, occasionally breaking, sometimes replaced, until most of the audience had left.

Throughout the postal exchange by which they had set up the concert, Lucier had been puzzled by Cage's insistence that he be sent xeroxes of all the correspondence. Several months later, Henmar Press sent him the score for the *Mix* which consisted, he discovered, of their letters with some additional notes. While *0'00"* is performance for a busy man, this was an early instance of scores for a busy man – recycling handwritten notes rather than laboring to produce a new, neat version of instructions.

Later in May, Cage stayed with Jasper Johns at Edisto Beach, and there wrote "Mosaic," an article for the *Kenyon Review* about Stein's edition of the Schoenberg correspondence, which they had sent him in March. He related the whole book (each letter, the jacket, biographical notes, contents list and indices) to sixty-four, letting the *I Ching* tell him which part of the book he was to discuss and for how many words. "The editors will have to like it or lump it," he had said over lunch while still at Brandeis.

A commission from the French–American Festival resulted in *Variations V*, presented at the Lincoln Center on July 23 with Cunningham and his refurbished dance company. The aim of the work, Cage wrote, "is to implement an environment in which the active elements interpenetrate . . . so that the distinction between dance and music may be somewhat less clear than usual." He had set out to find ways that sound could be affected by the movement of dancers. With the help of Tudor he discovered many, but only two turned out to be immediately practicable. One consisted of a dozen metal antennae, five feet high and about an inch in diameter; when a dancer came within range of its active radius of about four feet, sound was triggered. The other source was a series of photoelectric cells aligned with the stage lights, which were intended to set off sounds when the dancers broke the path of the light. They failed to work at stage front so, at the last minute, they were placed at the base of the antennae. "Adapt to physical circumstances," wrote Cage.

Billy Kluver, who was working on laser research at the Bell Laboratories – he had collaborated with Jean Tinguely on the *Homage to New York* – made the ten photocells, wired up to activate ten tape-recorders and ten short-wave radios. Cecil Coker designed a transistorized control circuit which was built by Whitford Wittnebet. Films and video images by Paik and Stan VanDerBeek were projected; the work also made use of some of the earliest percussion devices by synthesizer pioneer Robert

Moog. "Non-focused," Cage noted. The complexity of his projects and his growing reputation meant that Cage's work with other people was not so much collaboration as delegation, and no doubt he was aware of its advantages.

While the score for *Rozart Mix* was written as the idea crystallized, *Variations V* is, as it describes itself, an "a posteriori score," dedicated to Mary Sisler and written at Stony Point between September and October. The number of words for each comment in the score was determined by means of the *I Ching*. "Changed function of composer," Cage notes, "to telephone, to raise money."

IX

Over the winter of 1965–66 Cage often found himself at the same parties as the Duchamps. He had first met Marcel Duchamp in 1942, soon after he and Xenia arrived in New York; Cage had written music, too, for the Duchamp sequence of the film by Richter in 1947. Their paths had occasionally crossed since then. In the fifties Cage saw him on McDougall Street in Greenwich Village. "He made a gesture I took to mean O.K.," Cage wrote. Probably at the invitation of Duchamp, Cage joined him and others in an apartment in the Village. "The talk turned to dope," Cage recalled. Duchamp opined that dope would never become a serious social problem: people would not take it any more than they now drank Cointreau or *crème de menthe*.

Duchamp was a keen player of chess. Edward Lasker, an American master, ranked him one of the top twenty-five chess players in the United States in the twenties and thirties. He refereed a blindfold chess match in the fifties in which Max Ernst took part. Cage worked with both of them on an exhibition at the gallery of one of Duchamp's chess pupils, Julien Levy. "The Imagery of Chess" featured paintings, music and chess design, including *Chess Pieces* by Cage.

"I didn't wish to bother him with my friendship, though I admired him," Cage remembered. Duchamp showed every sign of disliking music; "he objected to an art," Cage notes, "in which people scraped on cat-gut." Yet the way Cage had developed in the fifties made Duchamp even more interesting to him. Back in 1913, Duchamp, with his sisters Yvonne and Magdeleine, had produced the *Musical Erratum*, drawing notes of the scale at random from a hat and writing them down; they produced a piece which consisted of random isolated pitches with no indicated durations. When Cage and Duchamp met in Venice in the early sixties, Cage said, "Isn't it strange, Marcel? The year I was born you were using chance operations." The other smiled and said, "I must have been fifty years ahead of my time."

Now, suddenly, contact with Duchamp took on a sense of urgency. "I saw him every night, four nights in a row," recalled Cage, "and I noticed there was a beauty about his face that one associates, say, with coming death or, say, with a Velasquez painting." "His complexion looked more like that of a painted portrait than that of a live person; I deduced that he wasn't going to live long," Cage observed elsewhere. "I realized suddenly that I was foolish not to be with him, and that there was little time left."

Cage "marched up" to Teeny Duchamp – born Alexina Sattler, who had married Duchamp in 1954 – and asked whether she thought her husband would teach him chess. She said she thought he would. Duchamp checked only that Cage knew the basic moves, then said yes. They made an appointment for Cage to go to his home, and they met once or twice a week from then onward if circumstances permitted. "I was using chess as a pretext to be with him," Cage recalled. His aim was to be in the company of Duchamp as often as possible, to let things happen rather than to make them happen. Remembering how Schoenberg had told him to mind his own business, Cage never asked Duchamp about his work. "We got to know Marcel not by asking him questions," he stated, "but by being with him."

Since his game was much weaker than that of Duchamp, Cage generally played with Teeny. Duchamp sat smoking at the other end of the room and would periodically glance at their game and make criticisms, "and in between take a nap. He would say how stupid we both were." "Don't you ever want to win?" he barked at Cage. "He didn't say it was likely, but he said it very accusingly," Cage recalled. "I was so hurt that I was wondering whether to leave altogether. The next day when we met he was all smiles and friendship. I think that Teeny had said something to him." "I was so delighted to be with him," explained Cage, "the notion of winning was beside the point." He was delighted, too, when he heard that Duchamp, on being asked what kind of relationship they had, replied, "We're buddies."

The two were alike in many respects. Duchamp was endowed with a Cartesian inventiveness; "doubting everything," he once said, "I had to find something that had not existed before." He felt, like Cage, that it was easier to comply with other people's requests, because afterwards one is free. Their apparent shared interest in chance masked very different perspectives; "your chance is not the same as my chance," Duchamp warned (without addressing Cage specifically), for he saw chance as an expression of the subconscious personality. On other matters they obviously diverged. Duchamp tended to consider the ideas for a work, the *Large Glass* for example, more important than their realization. "He spoke constantly against the retinal aspects of art," Cage notes, while "I have insisted upon the physicality of sound and the activity of listening." He continued, "You could say I was saying the opposite of what he was saying," then added with tellingly curious rationality, "Yet I felt so much in accord with everything he was doing that I developed the notion that the reverse is true of music as is true of the visual arts."

Cage produced *Variations VI*, for "a plurality of sound-systems," in March 1966; it was a puzzle piece consisting of a supply of symbols on transparent material: triangles for loudspeakers, half-circles for sound sources, and bisected short lines for components such as amplifiers, preamps, filters and modulators. "Let the notation refer to what is to be done," Cage specifies, "not to what is heard or to be heard." He also makes a concession, rare in the sixties, to improvisation. "Towards the end of activity," he writes, " – not having preconceptions," he specifies, " – any other (and any number of) interpretations of this material than here given may be used."

On the road between Rochester in New York State and Philadelphia, Cage prepared *Diary: Audience 1966* for a presentation in New York in May. With characteristic self-discipline, he ascertained at the start of each leg of the journey how many words were needed for the next statement of the text, formulated it and revised it in his head as he drove, pulled over and wrote it down, checked the length of the next statement and drove on. By the time he reached Philadelphia, the piece was finished.

Later in the year came *Music for Carillon No. 4 #2*, and the premiere of *Variations VII* "for various means" at the Nine Evenings of the Armory Show sponsored by Experiments in Art and Technology; it routed sounds from a restaurant kitchen, an aviary, the street and a subway toll station. Cage toured with Tudor and Gordon Mumma with the Cunningham Company, presenting throughout 1966 and 1967 *How to Kick, Pass, Fall and Run*, a set of stories in much the same mold as *Indeterminacy*, which served as an "irrelevant" accompaniment to a "cheerful" dance. "Sitting downstage to one side at a table with microphone, ashtray, my texts, and a bottle of wine, I tell one story a minute, letting some minutes pass with no stories in them at all," wrote Cage. "Some critics say that I steal the show. But this is not possible, for stealing is no longer something one does."

In London the three musicians often ate in an Indian restaurant Tudor had found near Euston railway station. One night at the Saville Theatre, Cage met a young composer called Gavin Bryars, and took a couple of his pieces for a new project, a collection of scores and score excerpts Cage was assembling to demonstrate the profusion of modern music notations.

The Soldier's Tale by Stravinsky was conducted by Lukas Foss at the Lincoln Center on July 15. Instead of choreographing the work, or hiring actors to tell the story, the parts were shared out between three composers. The narrator was Aaron Copland and the soldier was played by Elliot Carter. The Devil, who wins the day, was played by Cage.

"Everyone thought I was well cast," Cage comments drily. The *Village Voice* described "John Cage as a perfect devil." "He devoured his part, breathing fire and smoke and coloring his lines with great intensity," enthused the *New York Times*. "It was Bela Lugosi cum Boris Karloff and the audience loved it."

Stravinsky was in the audience and enjoyed Cage's performance. It is not clear who suggested they meet, but some days later Cage called on him in a hotel on Fifth Avenue. Stravinsky turned out to be an extremely interesting and witty man, and their conversation was very pleasant. "You know," Cage confided at one point, "the reason I never made an effort to see you before was because I was so partisan and so devoted to the work of Schoenberg." Stravinsky replied, "The reason I've never liked Schoenberg's music is because it isn't modern." Cage's response is not recorded, but looking back he reflects that the old Russian "was quite right."

Stravinsky's remark reminded Cage of Schoenberg's habit of presenting a series of notes to his class and describing how they have been used by Bach, by Beethoven, by Brahms, and, referring to himself in the third person, by Schoenberg. He thought of himself, in other words, as the next step in a tradition. and felt a reticence and to some extent fatalism about the direction suggested by his discoveries.

Cage, as we have seen, had learned from Schoenberg never to make a change unless it became necessary, but this does not presuppose a similar attitude to tradition. Thinking about it years later, Cage felt closer to Stravinsky in the wish "to make a discovery rather than reassert tradition." Cage was not depressed by innovation; for him, invention was the keynote, but it was never whim. He strove to take himself and his art just seriously enough, neither flippantly nor too

Lucretia "Crete" Harvey.   John Milton Cage senior.

John Cage, California, c. 1918.

With John senior and G. A. W. Cage, c. 1916.

In Detroit, 1918.

KNX Radio, Hollywood, c. 1930.

Graduating from high school, 1927.

Working on *Sonatas and Interludes*, 1947.

The anechoic chamber, Cruft Laboratories, Harvard University, late 1940s.

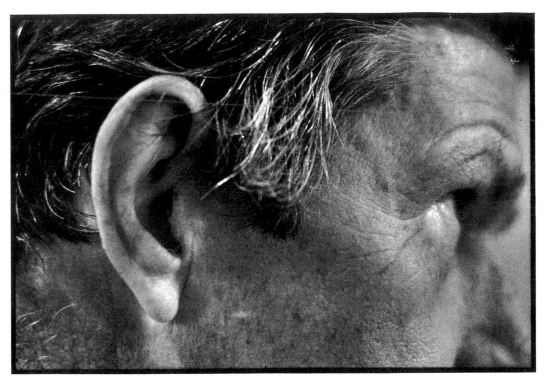

Happy New Ear.

3 HEADS = ⊙ ; 2 HEADS AND A TAIL = — ; 2
TAILS AND A HEAD = -- ; THREE TAILS = ⊙.
— AND -- ARE UNCHANGING, WHILE ⊙ IS
READ FIRST AS -- , THEN AS — ; AND ⊙
FIRST AS — , THEN AS -- . SIX TOSSES PRO-
DUCE A HEXAGRAM WHICH IS READ FROM ITS
BASE UP.

UPPER TRIGRAM → LOWER ↓	☰	☷	☵	☶	☳	☴	☲	☱
☰	1	34	5	26	11	9	14	43
☷	25	51	3	27	24	42	21	17
☵	6	40	29	4	7	59	64	47
☶	33	62	39	52	15	53	56	31
☳	12	16	8	23	2	20	35	45
☴	44	32	48	18	46	57	50	28
☲	13	55	63	22	36	37	30	49
☱	10	54	60	41	19	61	38	58

KEY FOR
INTERPRETING THE HEXAGRAMS.
FOR EXAMPLE: ☶ IS 7 ; WHEREAS ⚌ 36,
CHANGES TO 2.

Manuscript fragment for the *Music of Changes* (1951).

Examining mushrooms
at Stony Point,
1954/55.

The Golden Throat radio,
of the type used for
*Imaginary Landscape No.
4* (1951).

In search of fungi, 1958.

Flying high with Karlheinz Stockhausen, 1958.

About to perform *Music Walk* in Düsseldorf, c. 1959.

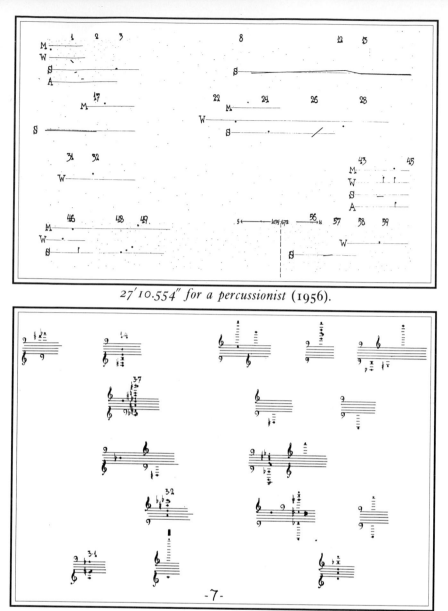

27′10.554″ for a percussionist (1956).

Winter Music (1957).

Doodles from Milan, 1959.

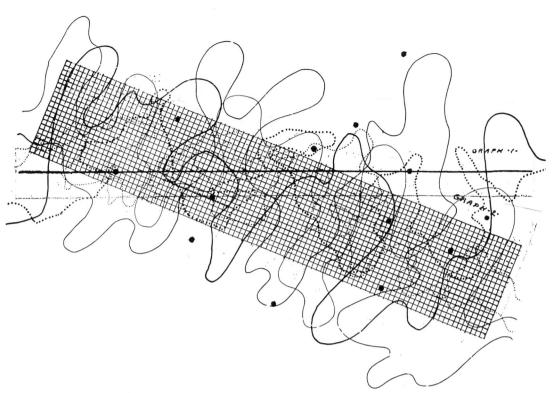

One available superposition of *Fontana Mix* (1958).

With Suzuki in Japan, 1962.

With Cunningham, early 1960s.

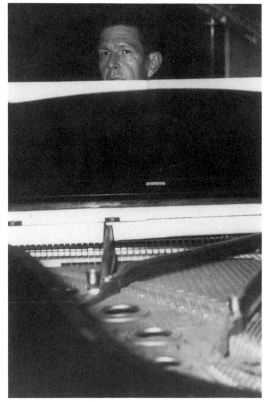

Performing in Japan, 1962.

"Unfortunately — European harmony."

In the early 1970s.

The third page of the score of *WGBH-TV* (1971).

Foraging for mushrooms, early 1970s.

Rehearsing the *Etudes Australes* with Grete Sultan, 1979.

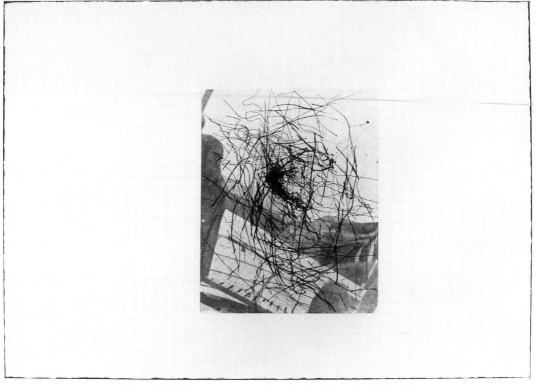

Day 6 of *Seven Day Diary* (*Not Knowing*) (1978).

On the Surface (1980–82).

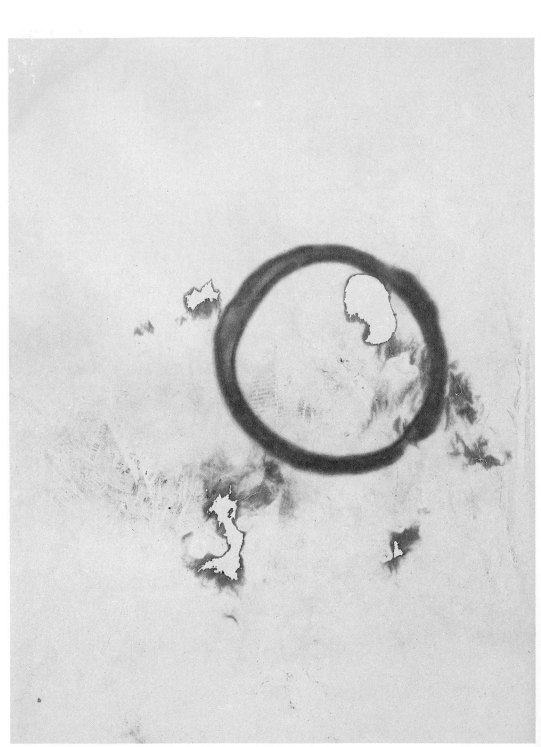

No. 41 of *Eninka* (1986).

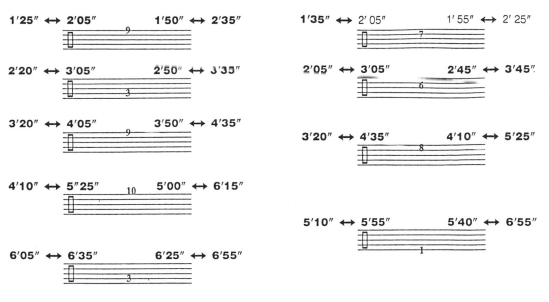

Excerpt from *One⁴*.

A 1988 performance of *Europeras I* and *II*.

Cage and Norman O. Brown, Wesleyan University, 1988.

Painting at Mountain Lake, 1988.

ponderously, and his seriousness did not look backwards, but forwards, sunny side up

His friendship with the Duchamps burgeoned. They requested a complete list of music by Cage. In September 1966 Cage spent two weeks with them at their summer home in Cadaques on the Costa Brava.

The following year the necessary cash and pledges were secured by friends and patrons of Cage for him to take up a place as composer-in-residence at the University of Cincinnati. A new collection of writings, *A Year from Monday*, was published later in the year. He was increasingly considered for awards, from the prestigious to the spurious, and was informed he had been elected a Knight of Mark Twain, "in recognition of your outstanding contribution to American scholarship by your silence."

For the first time money was not a worry; Cage committed a good part of it to providing for his mother, as he had earlier done so for his father, becoming her sole support. Crete had suffered another heart attack in 1965 and presently, to the great regret of her son, she became a resident of a nursing home.

By now a generation of composers had risen under the influence of Cage. Max Neuhaus (b. 1939) had trained in percussion with Paul Price at the Manhattan School of Music. He composed but was best known as a performer, producing his own version of *Fontana Mix, Fontana Mix-Feed*, in 1967. The Englishman Cornelius Cardew somehow managed to be a devotee of both Cage and Stockhausen (he worked out some parts for *Carré*) before turning to an ostensibly proletarian style in the last decade of a truncated life.

As we have seen, Cage worked with Ichiyanagi, Johnston, Mumma and Lucier, and had met Gavin Bryars in 1966. A performance of *Imaginary Landscape No. 4* at the University of California, Berkeley, in 1959, was coordinated by LaMonte Young, with a young Terry Riley on the tenth radio. The new generation set up their own ensembles and associations; Fluxus, or the Once Group, variously featured Neuhaus on percussion, Mumma on horn, Robert Ashley on piano and David Behrman playing violoncello, and Mumma, Lucier and Ashley formed the Sonic Arts Union. A scribbled note survives bearing the number CH32368 and the legend "Mr. Higgins," suggesting Cage knew Dick Higgins by 1956. Certainly, by the mid-sixties Cage was in regular contact with young people in New York and had arranged a series of weekly meetings at Higgins's townhouse. John Brockman, who attended, recalled, "The evenings had no particular agenda, it was

217

simply Cage leading a discussion. He would throw out some ideas and the talk would go around the room." "Everyone in the room was erudite, filled with intellectual hunger, intellectual desire," Brockman continued, perhaps a little romantically. "Most of them went on to brilliant careers."

FOURTEEN

I

The sixties were the years of youth, adventure and revolution; boldness and progress mingled with chaos and excess. For some people, though not so many as it seemed at the time, drugs expanded the mind; for others they were a novel distraction in confused lives. For some, not so many as it seemed either, it was a time of political awakening, with new agendas and sudden opportunities: Cohn-Bendit and Malcolm X and Martin Luther King. For others politics was a pose, or a vast drive-in for their own projected inadequacies.

Musicians likewise differed in the clarity and depth of their ideas and motives. The avant-garde double act of Nam June Paik and Charlotte Moorman is a case in point. Paik had cut a dashing figure and a necktie in the *Homage to John Cage* at the apartment of Mary Bauermeister. To Dick Higgins, Paik dedicated a *Danger Music* consisting of the instruction, "Climb into the vagina of a living whale." *Playable Music No. 4* consisted of the imperative "cut your left arm very slowly with a razor (more than ten centimeters)." After the first performance a spectator called for an encore.

Moorman, a highly talented cello player with a classical background, began from the early sixties to perform string music by Cage. Her realizations were characterized by dramatic, often destructive gestures; in *26'1.1499"*, for instance, ancillary sounds included breaking a Pepsi-Cola bottle and smashing a pane of glass with a hammer.

Together Moorman and Paik produced *Variations on a Theme by Saint-Saëns*, consisting of Moorman playing that cliché for cellists, *The Swan*, until halfway through she climbs into an oil drum five feet tall and filled with water, climbs out and finishes off the piece dripping wet. The *TV Sculpture* involved tiny working television tubes devised by Paik as the

219

sole covering for Moorman's breasts, giving a new literal meaning to the term boob-tube. These kinds of activity made them a controversial pair; lawsuits blossomed into test cases for the limits of artistic censorship.

Art need not, and probably should not, be comfortable; frenzy and the energy of madness can work as well for concept art as they do for the Native American shaman. The Dionysian in all its forms is as valid as the Apollonian, but only insofar as it furthers the integration of our humanity. To do this it has to have soul; it has to have direction, and those who are its harbingers will know, even if only vaguely, what they are about. It is possible to look at the wild work of Paik and Moorman, and see in Moorman a chaotic energy and an unfocused brilliance, in Paik an evident power, directed to abstract tantrums that tend toward nihilism.

When people come across Cage's work for the first time, they are often put off, or attracted, by its showmanship: hitting the piano, the theatricality of *Water Music* or *Water Walk*, the sarcasm of taking thirty or forty stories and calling them *Indeterminacy: New Aspect of Form in Instrumental and Electronic Music*, or preparing in advance six answers to your questions. As Conlon Nancarrow once observed, "Cage is pretty good at putting on performances." What saves his work is that one can trace behind it a seriousness of intent. In the sixties Cage sometimes forgot about sobering and quieting the mind: thumping piano stools with rocks, slamming an iron pipe onto the piano body, stretching a singing Yoko Ono half across a keyboard. He would only learn to play with fire later on.

II

At a reading in Port Royal, Kentucky, the poet Wendell Berry introduced Cage to the *Journal* of Henry David Thoreau. It was a new departure for Cage and was to influence his work and thought for years to come. By November 1967 *Focus* told its readers he "is currently reading the complete works." The following April Cage enrolled as a life member of the Thoreau Society. Writing to Walter Harding, an officer of the society and biographer of Thoreau, he describes how "I am enjoying and sharing with my friends the books about Thoreau. And last night, ... [I] continued my reading of the *Journal*. It turned out to be that magnificent walk in the moonlight in volume two."

It was the first time Cage had given close attention to Thoreau. He had been moved as a college student when he had read *On the Duty of*

Civil Disobedience. At the inception of the New York Mycological Society he had invited W. Stephen Thomas to talk about "Henry David Thoreau: Amateur Mycologist." But none of this signalled special interest, no more than the fact that he had read *The Leaves of Grass* by Walt Whitman to combat homesickness in Paris as a youth (he felt no special attraction for Emerson, the other writer in the transcendentalist triumvirate).

Thoreau (1817–62) is generally seen as an uncompromising idealist, devoting himself to the important matters of life by concentrating on the details of simplicity and avoiding the confusion of superfluous activity. For two years he lived in a simple hut set among trees mere moments from the sandy-shored New England lake at Walden, which gave its name to his best-known work. There he wrote:

> I went to the woods because I wished to live deliberately, to front only the essential facts of life . . . I wanted to live deep and suck out the marrow of life . . . and, if it proved to be mean, why then to get the whole and genuine meanness of it . . . ; or, if it were sublime, to know it by experience.

To each thing he gave the concentrated attention it merited, to "steadily observe the realities only," as he put it in *Walden* – in the words of Cage, "keeping his ears and eyes open and in his daily work being present at each moment." As Lewis Mumford suggests, "Thoreau sought in nature all the manifold qualities of being; he was not merely in search of the likenesses or distinctions which help to create classified indexes and build up a system." His experiences taught Thoreau "this, at least . . . that if one advances confidently in the direction of his dreams, and endeavors to live the life which he has imagined, he will meet with success unexpected in the common hours." When at the end of his life a relative asked if he had made his peace with God, he replied, "I wasn't aware we'd ever quarreled."

The distaste Thoreau felt for regimentation and spurious activity made him one of the prototypical American anarchists. "If a man seems out of step," he observed, "perhaps he is hearing a different drum." His refusal to pay taxes, in part a protest against the Mexican War, landed him in prison for a night in 1846.

His writings, in particular *On the Duty of Civil Disobedience* ("'That government is best which governs not at all'; and when men are prepared for it, that will be the kind of government which they will have," later the source for one of the texts in Cage's *Song Books*, 1970), had an influence on political activity disproportionate for its length, inspiring Mahatma Gandhi and Martin Luther King. The bibliography of Gandhi's *Hind Swaraj* cites two Thoreau titles; in 1919 he peddled copies of *Civil Disobedience* on street corners.

Cage found Thoreau a major source of inspiration. From *Song Books* (1970) onward he became a fountain of source material, whether in the form of words, as in *Empty Words* (1974) or graphics, for *Renga* (1976) and later for Cage's own visual work in *Seventeen Drawings by Thoreau* (1978). Cage was influenced, too, by his social and political ideas, becoming in the next few years a self-proclaimed anarchist.

What, finally, attracted Cage so strongly to Thoreau, and produced so much work in its wake? Each time Cage connects strongly with an artist or thinker – Schoenberg, Duchamp, Thoreau and later Joyce, or Rauschenberg, Johns, McLuhan and Fuller – the attraction is not only based on manifest correspondences of ideas, local, rational choices, the strength of argument, but also on broader similarities, which one sees in little temperamental links. Cage might have met Robert Rauschenberg, had a few interesting conversations, and never seen him again; but both had arrived at a position where they had a great deal to offer one another. So with Thoreau, Cage could have read the *Journal* on Berry's suggestion, enjoyed it, and picked up Emerson, but the different paths of their life and thought meant he found in Thoreau's work "every idea I've had that's worth its salt."

III

Amid the dizzy optimism of the sixties, Cage became more enthusiastic about the benefits of technology than at any time since his *Credo* in 1937. For Cage "the electronics age is extending the power of the body and mind. Electronics is fast becoming an infinite universal power. . . . We are leaving the Renaissance and going into an Electronic Age."

He extended the fascination he already had for small sounds into an interest in making audible the microcosmic world. "Sound is vibration," he told a reporter from *Newsweek*, "everything is vibrating. So there is no earthly reason why we can't hear everything." He proposed, "If we push beyond the limits of perception, there is a chance that perception itself will be extended." We could listen to the sound of DNA, Cage suggested, or pick up the sound of a mushroom producing spores: "mushrooms are making sounds and we should be listening to them." On another occasion he applied the same idea to an ashtray: "When I went into the anechoic chamber, I could hear myself. Well, now, instead of listening to myself, I want to listen to this ashtray , . . I'm going to listen to its inner life thanks to a suitable technology." Such listening could be given a ceremonial form. "Imagine people bringing objects to a central place," Cage suggested. "You would be able to listen to their offerings."

Early in 1968 Cage realized *Reunion*. A number of sound-systems which operated continuously were prepared by Tudor, Mumma and David Behrman. The sounds varied according to the position of pieces on a specially prepared chessboard built by Lowell Cross of the Polytechnical Institute in Toronto. The gates switched by the pieces triggered a passage of music by Cage, Tudor, Mumma or Behrman; since the sound-systems operated all the time, even the reappearance of a move would lead to a different sound.

Teeny Duchamp looked on while Cage and Marcel Duchamp played the game. The evening began with a large audience. Cage and Duchamp adjourned after several hours when the house was empty. Next morning they finished the match; Duchamp had given himself the handicap of a knight, but still beat his pupil.

Reunion might be considered as the third part of *4' 33"*, just as *0' 00"* was part two. Cage told Daniel Charles that his first silent work "involved one or several musicians who made no sound. The second one . . . indicates that an obligation toward others must be fulfilled, in a partial or complete manner, by a single person. The third one involves gathering together two or more people who are playing a game in an amplified context. A bridge or chess match, or any game at all can become a distinctive – another essentially silent – musical work."

Electronic music studios were proliferating all over the Western world. Early performance instruments were beginning to appear, such as those by E M S, whose patchboards are now regarded with nostalgia; Brian Eno has recalled waving a signal generator about in his first performances.

The most impressive developments of the decade following *Fontana Mix* had come in the field of computer applications. At the forefront of computer composition was Lejaren Hiller, Jr. Initially a chemistry student, Hiller had moonlighted as a musician at Princeton in the late forties under the tutelage of Milton Babbit and Roger Sessions. For the next eleven years he earned a living as a scientist, first at du Pont and subsequently as a lecturer at the University of Illinois. In 1955 – although he was not to work in music full-time for a further three years – he and Leonard Isaacson began, and presented the following year, the four-movement *Illiac Suite* for string quartet: the first score to be generated by the huge machines and punched cards that constituted state-of-the-art computer technology. Hiller referred to the *Suite* as a group of experiments, significant as a technical breakthrough but with little artistic merit of its own. His claims for computer composition were correspondingly modest, seeing it as a heuristic aid to understanding the principles behind the aesthetic features of music. "My objective in composing music by means of computer programming," he stated, "is not the immediate realization of an aesthetic unity, but the providing and evaluating of techniques whereby this goal can eventually be realized."

Despite such modesty, the experiment attracted a great deal of popular attention, and led to Hiller moving to the Music Department of the university. There, in 1959, in an attic room across the road from the Music Building, he set up the University Electronic Music Studio – the second major institutional studio after that at Columbia. His work ran in parallel with that of others, such as Johnston, Salvator Martirano and Kenneth Gaburo, without them ever constituting a group or school.

While Cage was still in Cincinnati in 1967, he and Hiller resolved to carry out a joint project. As Hiller recalls, Cage telephoned him and said, "I'd like to do some computer music with you. Is there any chance I could come to Illinois?" According to Cage, Hiller rang "and said he could arrange for me to do a piece using computer facilities and would like to know if I was interested in doing it." Either way, Hiller engineered an appointment for Cage at the Center for Advanced Studies, which gave the benefit of a salary without imposing teaching duties. He became an Associate Member of the Center for 1967–68, and the post was renewed for the following year.

Cage took an apartment, number 303, at 401 Edgebrook Drive in Champaign; it was a long, narrow room level with the treetops. Hiller had deputized Gary Grossman to program the machine, but, Cage recalled, "When I got to Illinois, the programmer that he'd chosen for me was nowhere to be found. So I spent about two weeks doing nothing, and Jerry finally said that he would do the programming."

The two men set to work with two projects in mind. The first, a technically ambitious work which never came to fruition, was the *Ten Thunderclaps*, also provisionally titled *Atlas Borealis*. The thunderclaps came from the ten one-hundred letter words which form some of the few non-syntactical elements of James Joyce's *Finnegans Wake*. Cage imagined "the transformation of a live orchestra and chorus into a genuine hurricane." He anticipated the use of a string orchestra, possibly adding winds toward the end. The piece "will be composed in the same way as *Atlas Eclipticalis*, from astronomical maps. But the string instruments, like the chorus, will use special equipment with microphones to transform the sounds actually emitted so that they fill up the envelopes of rain falling." Or, as explained in the *Mushroom Book*:

Voices singing Joyce's Ten Thunderclaps
transformed
electronically to fill actual
thunder envelopes; string players playing star
maps transformed likewise to fill
actual raindrop envelopes

Cage envisaged that the materials on which the rain seemed to be falling would recapitulate the history of technology: on water, on earth and on metal. "The last thunderclap will represent the electronic technology of our era," as he saw it, finding there an echo of McLuhan. "At that stage, rain may no longer fall on anything whatsoever, but simply sound in the air – and that is why I will perhaps make use of wind instruments in the last section."

Unable to produce the piece in Illinois, Cage would nurture hopes of realizing the project for many years. By the end of the eighties, however, he had abandoned the idea. He no longer wished to deal with the institutional setup which would be necessary for such a large work (although he did work at IRCAM for *Roaratorio* and at the Brooklyn Center for *Essay*). He also felt that others were busily exploring the possibilities offered by electronics, and the area in which he could be most innovative was among traditional acoustic instruments. The development of sampling techniques meant his ideas could have been implemented with considerable ease, but he had wanted to effect the transformation with live performers and real-time electronic transformation, "which is more like magic."

The second project of Cage and Hiller came to fruition as one of Cage's largest-scale undertakings, and its catalyst was an unlikely source. Antoinette Vischer was a dumpy middle-aged woman from Basel in Switzerland who was on a lively crusade to commission new music for the harpsichord. By the time Cage was in Illinois she had over forty pieces, from composers as diverse as Berio, Brown and Duke Ellington. For some time she had been badgering Cage for a piece. He was slow to respond; he had already declined a similar request from Sylvia Marlowe. "I've always hated the harpsichord," Cage explained. "It reminds me of a sewing machine."

He and Hiller sat in a trailer at the back of the Hiller family garden discussing the commission, and their ideas grew gradually grander. They saw the possibility of situating the very limited dynamic and timbre of the harpsichord in the complexity of a huge mixed-media event, which would find multiplicity in quantity: a number of harpsichord solos, tapes, and various visual elements. The work would be on a scale which could only be attempted using a computer: it would be called *HPSCHD*, the computer handle for "Harpsichord," which is how it is pronounced.

In *HPSCHD* Hiller's use of mathematical probability and Cage's religious use of chance could meet. Hiller worked so hard and contributed so much to the project – including, for instance, the KNOBS program which accompanied the commercial recording, consisting of chance-derived directions for tone and volume settings for the listener's stereo – that he came to be credited as co-composer, making it the most extensive collaboration by Cage up to that time (even the collaboration on *Double Music*, a much shorter piece, had been by mail and long-distance telephone). "We worked very easily together," Cage remembered. "I'd always been interested in his work because he has such an unpredictable mind." Around the time of the premiere, Hiller noted, "Every single note was a mutual decision. It was a rather unique instance that two composers' endeavors were so intertwined that you can't tell them apart."

As we have seen, the biggest single practical problem Cage faced since the turnaround at the start of the fifties was the generation of sufficient chance operations. The new work would require 18,000 tosses of the coin. Hiller proposed that they employ a random number generator. Cage insisted that they retain the *I Ching*. Salvation appeared in the form of Ed Kobrin, another composer and coincidentally a colleague of Mumma. As Hiller observed, hexagrams are notated in binary fashion, and Kobrin wrote a program in Fortran which directly simulated the mechanism of the *I Ching*, even down to printing out the shape of the hexagrams. Vast numbers of chance operations could be generated within seconds.

Faced with the option from then onwards of using mass-produced, computer-generated chance operations, Cage found that "if you have a question for which you want a great number of answers, then it is economical to use the computer. But if you have a question which you want only one answer to, then it's better to do it yourself." Some years later Cage installed a portable computer in his home which would, among other things, generate hexagrams, and he could keep an advance stock of printouts, "so I have a great supply of answers to questions which I have not yet asked." After computerization made *I Ching* chance operations abundantly available, Cage developed, or returned to, more conventional notation. The transparency techniques, used in such pieces as the early *Variations*, and "watercolor" chance techniques, such as locating imperfections in paper, were less frequently used.

The first task for Cage and Hiller was to generate pitch material for the tapes. Fifty-two tapes were made, each using a different scale, dividing the octave into between five and fifty-six tones (amusingly, the chromatic scale was omitted). The composers then defined a field of intonational deviation – half the distance between any two tones – so that each tone had two fields, one with reference to the tone above, the other to that below. The upper and lower fields were each divided into sixty-four parts, so that they could be related to the *I Ching*, giving 129 variants, including the tone itself, on any tone. In this way, chance operations separated out and operated on 885,000 pitches for the tapes.

Each of the pitches was then assigned a duration. A timbre was selected with sine, sawtooth or square wave characteristics; an attack and decay time was ascertained, and a maximum amplitude. Routines were used from Matthew's Music IVB program. An IBM 7094 and the ILLIAC II, which had been used for the *Illiac Suite* and was here used for the last time before decommissioning, had to be linked up both for composition and synthesis of the tape. The programs written by Hiller frequently surpassed the capacity of the computers, which to some extent neutralized chance. Cage remembered, "We could only integrate a very few chance operations."

The aural result was extremely complex. "Seventeen tapes mixed together gave us chamber music," said Cage. "When, say, thirty-four tapes had been combined, the result had the density and quality of an orchestra. But all fifty-two tapes together sounded like something never heard before." Once superimposed, the tapes, built up from the rational operations of computers, were quite devoid of order. "Disorganization," Cage observed, "can result from the accumulation of organizations having fine differences."

To obtain the material for the harpsichord solos, a number of piano works were selected from a range of composers spanning two hundred years of musical history – Mozart, Beethoven, Chopin, Schumann, Gottschalk, Busoni, Schoenberg and (counted as one) a piano sonata by Hiller and *Winter Music* by Cage – and chance and statistical programs made selections based on their distribution of pitches. In all, the solos ran to 581 pages of manuscript.

The diverse visual elements which would be screened at the same time as the performance were arranged by Ronald Nameth, cinema instructor in the Art Department of the university. A young graduate student in art, Calvin Sumsion, arranged for the projection screens to be partially transparent, so that the projected images would mingle with each other.

For Cage, the progressive division of the octave on the tapes was reminiscent of the magnification of work with a microscope, so he suggested to Nameth that a telescope would be a suitable visual complement and that a possible theme was space travel. *Flash Gordon*, with Buster Crabbe, and *Voyage de la lune* by the turn-of-the-century French director Georges Méliès, were both shown. NASA sent around forty films; there were also around a hundred cartoons projected.

IV

In the spring of 1969 Cage's mother died. Cage scattered Crete's ashes, like those of her husband before her, from a beautiful hilltop in part of the Ramapo Mountains near Stony Point, asking that in turn the same happen to him after death. Then, in midsummer, he held a wake for her, a picnic on the rocks beside his glass-walled house.

The Assembly Hall of the Urbana campus was a circular space surrounded by a corridor with glass walls. "I had always admired that hall," Cage said, "and imagined that it would be a wonderful location for a ... musical event." There, on May 16, 1969, the first performance of *HPSCHD* took place. The following Sunday, Apollo Ten was launched.

The performance ran from half-past seven until midnight, with tuttis of tape at half-past eight and eleven o'clock. 3M in St Paul had provided forty-nine Wollensak tape machines; after the event ended they thanked Cage effusively, because he had ensured that they were returned factory-fresh.

David Tudor's solo was derived from a computer-generated twelve-tone gamut, Antoinette Vischer's from the waltzes written by Mozart in which dice determined the succession of events. William Brooks and Ronald Peters played the same dice-game with passages substituted occasionally from other compositions by Mozart – Brooks with the treble and bass keyboards linked, Peters with them independent. Yuji Takahashi and Neely Bruce likewise performed the dice-game with the nine-composer historical sequence substituted, and with their treble and bass keyboards respectively linked and independent. The final soloist,

228

Philip Corner, was briefed to perform, or practice live, any compositions by Mozart.

Seven pre-amplifiers were used, 208 computer-generated tapes, fifty-two projectors, sixty-four slide projectors, eight movie projectors, 6,400 slides, forty movies, a 340-foot circular screen and several eleven by forty foot rectangular screens.

Assembly Hall could seat sixteen thousand spectators. *HPSCHD* was attended by about six thousand, making it easy for them to circulate, giving them different perspectives on the sounds and sights. "We wished only for bicycles," reported one reviewer, "in order to circle the hall faster and faster in a wild attempt to hear everything at once." Members of the audience clustered around the harpsichord players. Some lay on the floor; a woman breastfed her baby, and a reporter was asked if he was a performer. Circle dancing broke out spontaneously, "adding," in Cage's interpretation, "their own theater to the whole global theater they had been given." In a cunning marketing ploy, the Nonesuch recording was available for sale at the premiere. Cunningham and Johns came along; Andy Warhol planned to, but had fallen ill. Citing his new enthusiasm, Cage told the *Chicago Sun-Times* that "When Thoreau went to Walden, it was an attempt to minimize the circumstances of his life and to see whether it was glorious – if it was, to publicize it. I went to the computer two years ago with the same idea."

Even more than the *Concert*, *HPSCHD* highlights a relationship between Cage's asceticism and his enthusiasm for an at times chaotic abundance. "I've always been more interested in quantity than in quality or value or intention," he claimed around the time of performance, "and in the last year I've been curious about the opposition between quantity and quality." He saw multiplicity as a way to avoid a false sense of unity, false in that "unity doesn't recognize the abundance of things."

This is interesting in that most people with the spiritual sensibility that Cage often displays see the world as an orderly unity, whereas he highlights diversity. The relation of multiplicity to asceticism in Cage's work is epitomized by the contrast between the narrow characteristics of the harpsichord and its complex, mixed-media setting in *HPSCHD*. Perhaps Cage needs to compensate for having no latitude in dealing with the passions – no opportunities to fill his work with qualitative subtleties, self-expression or spontaneity – by generating a richness that is only quantitative, stacking narrow, ascetic elements in the most rudimentary multiplicity.

While still in Urbana, Cage received a telegram from Teeny Duchamp.

Marcel had died. One morning he had bought a book by Alphonse Allais, and was reading it when his guests had left after dinner. Then he had gone to clean his teeth: his wife heard a thud, and he was dead. Cage placed the telegram on his coffee table and retreated from it to the far side of the room. "It was a loss that I didn't want to have."

Alice Weston proposed that various artworks be made in memory of Duchamp, and Irvine Hollander suggested that as part of this project Cage might prepare a series of lithographs. He pursued the idea in collaboration with Calvin Sumsion; together they devised a series of eight plexigrams, each consisting of eight panels of plexiglass with silk-screened words and fragments of words in various typefaces, all selections determined by chance operations. Eye Editions published an edition of 125, made under the supervision of the workshop run by Hollander. Seeking a title, Cage remembered a comment Johns had made when Weston had asked him for a contribution: "I don't want to say anything about Marcel." (Johns felt he had said quite enough in his sets for *Walkaround Time* a year earlier.) Cage and Sumsion titled their work *Not Wanting to Say Anything About Marcel.*

It was a landmark for Cage's involvement with visual art. While by no means his first visual work, it was his first commission as an artist rather than as an artisan, and, while able to benefit from the seriousness with which his music was beginning to be taken, it succeeded in attracting serious attention in its own right.

Notations was also published, a selection of the scores he had been collecting for a number of years for the Foundation of Contemporary Performance Arts to show the diversity of notation in contemporary music. Cage collaborated on the publication with Alison Knowles. The collection included manuscripts by Stravinsky, Babbit, Feldman and Milhaud, and, thanks to the intercession of Yoko Ono, John Lennon.

V

In the fall, Cage took up his position as artist-in-residence at the University of California at Davis (David Tudor had held the post in 1966–67, when Stockhausen was a visiting professor of composition). He had visited the campus briefly on January 20, when he had played *Sonatas and Interludes* in a daytime concert ("bring your own lunch").

The Davis campus had started out as an agricultural college, built in 1908 in the wake of the Populist movement. Legislation at the end of the fifties, encouraging the growth of the universities, led to its expansion, and a flush of funding and the university's self-promotion led to opportunities such as that given Cage.

Cage offered a special group study class, Music in Dialogue (course number 198), concerning the "inter-relations among the arts." In practice it was an experiment in learning guided by the *I Ching*; materials in the library were selected by chance operations, as then was the division of those attending into discussion groups. No distinction would be made in the class between students and non-students; nobody would know what they were going to study.

Various pieces by Cage were performed during his residency; *Winter Music* and a recorded concert of *Variations IV* in October, *Sonatas and Interludes* in December. The main event was announced as an "environmental collage" for November 21. When the woman who administered university concerts asked how it was to be billed, Cage suggested *Godamusicday*. This amused her, but her husband, who worked for the university in a legal capacity, was not impressed. "Profanity is forbidden," he cautioned. "Nothing might be printed that might come to the Governor's notice." Pursuing his current enthusiasm, Cage recalled how Thoreau once needed a guide to the Maine Woods, and when he asked an old Native American if he knew of anyone who might help, was told, "Me will . . . me wantum moose." In Thoreau's account the guide said, "Me sure get some moose." The exposition was advertised at the Mewantemooseicday.

Different parts of the campus were set aside for diverse activities; films were shown, a new Cage work, *33¹/₃*, for records, gramophones and audience participation, was performed, and he gave four readings of the *Diary*. Several events featured the work of Satie, who was of continued interest to Cage since the staging of *Vexations* in 1963; Satie's furniture music was presented, and at the Putah Creek Lodge at five o'clock Cage organized a wine recital of his music, including the *Trois poèmes d'amour, Nocturnes* and *Socrate*. Cage had arranged the first movement of the *Socrate* in 1944 as the accompaniment to a dance, *Idyllic Song,* and it was a central example in his infamous lecture at Black Mountain on the structural means of Satie, Webern and Beethoven. More recently, Cage and Arthur Maddox had arranged it for two pianos, and had presented it in that form at the University of Illinois on July 20; Cage intended to use it in the new year as the accompaniment for a new dance by Cunningham.

In Room 101, a small, austere sixty-seater, Cage arranged a performance of *Vexations*. Due to the scale of the undertaking he had

231

recruited everyone who could play the piano, but he coached each player individually and insisted on a great deal of discipline. For this performance, tempo was crucial: every repetition was to last exactly one minute and twenty seconds. The players were each to arrive twenty minutes ahead of the time they were due to begin and were to sit to the left of the piano in contemplative silence, then, when the time came, they could slip onto the piano stool without breaking the remorseless flow. The vacating performer would sit to the right of the new player and keep count: fifteen repetitions in twenty minutes. Cage played first, at six in the morning, immaculate in his concert suit and Bond Street shirt; the hall was packed, and remained so for most of the day. He performed, another of the musicians recalls, with "a great deal of elegance and precision", which inspired others to do the same. One pianist, Michael Furnoy, "attempted very subtle variations in touch, which Cage enjoyed thoroughly."

In December Cage heard from Satie's publisher: he was not to make further use of his two-piano version of *Socrate*. This was potentially disastrous, as Cunningham had already choreographed on the basis of the structure and phrasing of the piece. As he had in other ways before, Cage solved the problem by accepting the new limitations but thereafter cleaving as close as he could to his first plan. He conceived a piano solo which would preserve the structure and phrasing of *Socrate*, but would use chance operations to determine pitches, transpositions and continuity, thus circumventing the copyright problem but retaining all the markers on which Cunningham was relying. Cage called Cunningham from Davis and told him in one swoop both the problem and his solution: the new score, he said, would be called *Cheap Imitation*. Cunningham opted to call the dance *Second Hand*. The finished piano score is dated December 14.

Cheap Imitation was the first work by Cage for years to consist exclusively of conventional notation. At the time he reflected that it distracted him from the continuous quest for ever more radical indeterminacy. It was not, however, to prove an aberration (following the computerization of *I Ching* chance operations). Critics were intrigued; it was, one suggested, "the most musical thing he has created in a long time."

Early in 1970 Cage and Cunningham traveled to the University of California at Santa Cruz, thanks to a grant from the Carnegie Foundation, to offer their views on planning for the performing arts in what was still barely a five-year-old campus. Norman O. Brown had been Professor of Humanities there since 1968, having left Wesleyan in 1962 and taught

232

in the meantime at the University of Rochester. Paul Lee, a professor of philosophy, invited Cage to spend the day hunting mushrooms with Alan Chadwick, a remarkable gardener whose background included Shakespearian acting, the study of Rudolph Steiner, and practice of French Intensive Biodynamic Horticulture. They were accompanied by two garden apprentices and the poet Robert Duncan. Cage was particularly taken by Chadwick and his work. He told Lee that it had been one of the most wonderful days of his life, and thought he might donate his considerable library of mycological texts to the university.

Life at Stony Point was beginning to disenchant Cage. The community had grown bigger and more anonymous; he did not even know some residents, and plans were mooted of increasing the size of the community as much as possible. He felt it was becoming a shanty-town; the garbage uncollected, roads left unmaintained. "I feel a little like I'm being pushed out," said Cage. He also felt he was becoming "immoral," because his frequent trips abroad meant he did not use what he possessed. To be "an absentee landlord" was "in our age" a "transgression of morality," though it is difficult to see how Cage could avoid being an absentee if he continued to tour while maintaining a home base.

He remedied his discontent with Stony Point, however, in September 1970 by moving in with Cunningham to his basement flat at 107 Bank Street in Manhattan, near Abingdon Square in the West Village. His new neighbors were Yoko Ono and John Lennon. At the beginning of the sixties, when she and Cage first met, Ono had been married to Ichiyanagi, but since then she had left him for a visionary American, and was now the controversial partner of a world-famous Beatle. When Lennon first came to the United States he sent a bunch of roses to Cage at Ono's behest, and contributed, as mentioned earlier, a page of song material to the *Notations* collection.

Cage found that when the couple brought back tapes of their day's work in the studio, he could hear them better than they could; at his request, Lennon stopped using wall-mounted speakers. Ono and Lennon occasionally visited for dinner. One night Cage called them up to offer a sample of his latest Mexican dessert; Lennon was so impressed – he had a very sweet tooth – that he asked for the course which preceded it, and gradually worked his way backwards through the entire menu.

VI

Between March and June 1971 Cage was engaged in writing *Sixty-Two Mesostics re Merce Cunningham*, utilizing both his graphic skills and his growing interest in chance-generated texts; it is a piece which can be viewed, read and (in its musical version for "voice unaccompanied using microphone") heard.

Cage had long been fond of incorporating hidden structures in his work; in his entry to the Los Angeles High School Yearbook for his senior year, his summary forms an acrostic:

Recreation: orating
Occupation: working
Mischief: studying
Aspiration: to earn a DD and Ph.D
Noted for: being radical (West Coast Background)

In Edwin Denby's loft on 21st Street, Cage once wrote a birthday note in prose, and highlighted the letters which made up the name of his host as they appeared among the words. In a number of occasional pieces he subsequently wrote, he began to spread the words over lines, as in poetry, and arranged the letters which were highlighted under one another, forming a spine which spelled out the name or word – not solely down the left margin, as an acrostic, but in any place in the line, which was then aligned. For example,

> to Become
> fRee:
> nOt
> to knoW
> whether we kNow or not

Norman O. Brown, the subject of this example, suggested the term "mesostic."

Cage began to work with mesostics on a grander scale than single-stanza tributes for birthdays and the like. The *Sixty-Two Mesostics* constitute his first mesostic writing designed for concert use. He built the work from chance selections of syllables and words from *Changes: Notes on Choreography* by Cunningham and from thirty-two other books

234

most used by the dancer in his work. Letraset typefaces and fonts for each letter were also selected by chance operations. Cage decided not to leave spaces between letters, either horizontally or vertically, "The poem would then have a spine," he felt, "and resemble Cunningham himself, the dancer." In performance, each mesostic is vocalized in one breath followed by silence, giving attention to each letter.

WGBH Television in Cambridge asked Cage to come to Massachusetts in September to make a telecast. The station was well known for its adventurous programming, and had broadcast *Sonatas and Interludes* back in April 1960. Cage had received a letter from Eva Smercheck asking if he would contribute an item to the Caledonian Woman's Club benefit auction for retarded children. He sent back the score for the work he was about to realize, *WGBH-TV*, written on the back of her envelope (and, just as the correspondence with Lucier became the score of *Rozart Mix*, reproductions of the envelope became the published score). "Recurring statement for WGBH Telecast," wrote Cage, " 'music is being written, but is not finished yet. That's why there isn't any sound'. Camera focuses, without moving, on work table. No face – just ms, hands, pen etc."

For the recording Cage busied himself writing orchestral materials for a new version of *Cheap Imitation*, which he had been preparing since the beginning of the year, making his work into a performance, just as for *0'00"* he would often answer letters. One of the engineers who worked on the broadcast good-humoredly recalls thinking, "Who the fuck is this guy and when's he gonna finish?"

In the course of the year Cage also began work on a collaboration with Lois Long and Alexander Smith, to be called the *Mushroom Book*. He had issued his invitation to Smith on October 28:

Lois Long is making a series of lithographs . . . and I am making texts (as strange as some of my music) to be published with them. Over each illustration will be a Japanese tissue (not a fancy one) on which we would like to put your naming of the mushroom(s) together with any remarks about the species you'd be willing to make. My texts attempt to touch upon the many varied interests I have and are handwritten in five different litho crayon intensities (and there are superimpositions, making much unreadable). They will therefore be printed also on the tissue overlay, enabling the reader, if he's so inclined, to go hunting in my handwritten page.

– "as though he were hunting for a mushroom in a forest," wrote

235

Cage in the advertising pamphlet for the volume. Hollander's workshop hand-printed *Mushroom Book* between August 1971 and May 1972 for publication on July 1. The first and third of the ten lithographs by Cage also served as endpapers to his book *M*, published in 1973.

Cage escorted in person the first shipment of his mycological collection to the University of California at Santa Cruz, with Norman O. Brown coordinating, at the beginning of December 1971. The idea grew in his mind that ultimately the collection should be housed in a garden chalet rather than the central library, and that it should be possible for every book to be withdrawn from the library and taken into the field. "I wish to emphasize," Cage wrote to the curator Rita Bottoms, "my desire that the books be placed in a botanical situation rather than a conventional library situation." He explained in a subsequent letter, "From my own experience as a mushroom hunter and user of mushroom books, I know that the books should be placed closer to the earth from which mushrooms come rather than protected from it on restricted library shelves."

Barely was the collection on its way than Chadwick, the original inspiration for the archive, left the university. "There was a very fine gardener-botanist teaching there whom I liked a lot," Cage recalled. "I no sooner gave it than he left, so there was really no reason for the gift." Gradually, his collection of some three hundred books and numerous mycological ephemera, including the tie with the mushroom motif and the letter-painting from Graves mentioned earlier, arrived at the university and, Chadwick now gone, remained in special collections. Cage was to send a letter later in 1972 chiding the university for not freeing the collection from standard regulations which restricted evening and weekend use, which he had emphatically requested. When changes were made in availability, he commented that they "made me happy" and, with revealing simplicity, "I wanted you to know that I love you all and didn't want to make you miserable with my last letter."

VII

With the dawn of the seventies, Cage was increasingly interested in – and vociferous about – social and environmental issues. He no longer confined his enthusiasm for technology to its practical application in music, but talked at length of his belief in the positive impact it could make on all areas of life. Cage spoke, too, of his engagement with political philosophy, particularly his own interpretation of anarchism.

As an inventor's son, Cage had always been enthusiatic about technological development; his optimistic expectations about its benefits for music had grown in the mid-sixties and now, with the influence on him of McLuhan and Fuller at its zenith, he expressed the conviction that technology could solve the problems of the world. In his various pronouncements, Cage suggested and celebrated techological solutions to incredibly diverse problems and situations, speaking with the brevity of secure conviction.

"We've got the automobile. No sense in leading horses around. Let 'em go where they will. Fix it so if they're thirsty there's something for 'em to drink." The globe can be freed from the scarcity which has framed history, producing "an environment" (he cites Norman O. Brown) "which works so well we can run wild in it." Cage proposed that the world food problem could be alleviated by making our newspapers edible. And to alleviate overpopulation, we might follow the suggestion of John Platt, that contraceptive substances be added to staple foods, so people would have to go deliberately to special stores if they wanted a child. In McLuhan's terms, the world was now a "global village," and what was needed was planning on a world scale. Pursuing his conviction of the importance of minimal organization, Cage proposed that planning apply, to use Fuller's concept, to a network of global utilities. A global voltage should be established. Utility must, as he had said for some time, be substituted for property; disposing of ownership, substituting use.

Cage speaks highly of Fuller's project for a Dymaxion Airocean World Map, big as a football field, where players can try out "How to Make the World Work" to "facilitate attainment, at the earliest possible moment, by every human being of complete enjoyment of the total planet Earth."

Nothing is artificial, Cage claimed. Advertisements are all good. Traffic lights could be installed which could read traffic flow, so the "go" signal would not show if there are no automobiles waiting for it. The Soviets had been researching techniques for electronically induced sleep by which their cosmonauts could secure the equivalent of eight or nine hours' sleep. Even pollution would make us rich.

Cage opined that the benefits of technology would bring about a situation in which each person would need only to work a couple of hours per year. The apparently inevitable increase in unemployment could be construed as a positive rather than negative trend. Education could then teach us how to make good use of our leisure time, rather than to prepare us for work which it will be hard, and unnecessary, for us to find. To show that such developments are practicable, Cage pointed to developments at the time such as those at the Olivetti company in Italy. There, he claimed, industrial accidents had been wiped out; staff were trained how best to use their leisure time, and retired at the age of forty-five.

A number of statements by Cage moved from his customary non-intellectual position to an anti-intellectual one. "The Renaissance was characterized by the printing machine," he stated, "but today children watch TV with ease but have a lot of trouble reading. Literacy will no longer be a measure of social status."

The main reservation Cage expressed concerning technology at this time regarded the highway system which, following the critic of modern industrial society Ivan Illich, he dubbed a "false utility." However, we would all be able to communicate by videophone.

These views can be readily criticized, not because artists should not discuss such matters, nor because visionary thinking is wasted effort, but because they are not adequately explained and because they generally fail to have a bearing on how social change occurs. Cage does not construct an argument, but uses the points like artist's materials. He often makes a passing reference in a mosaic text like *Diary*, with nothing to substantiate, elaborate or qualify his expectation. Moreover, uncompromisingly optimistic expectations scarcely work with the New York Philharmonic Orchestra, and do not go very far on a macrosocial, let alone global, scale.

Such criticism is not intended to invalidate Cage's words; it is to make clear that if they have value in themselves the proposals are pretexts or slogans or color for the artistic palette. They are not in any way coherent economic, ecological or social thinking. Cage's optimism, even naivete, is exemplary – uncompromising expectations rarely travel very far, but are needed because of their clarity and their productive forcefulness – but its practical effect here, in some contrast with the case of music, is zero, because it fails even to touch how the world actually changes.

A clear example of this inadequacy is Cage's attitude to unemployment and staff redundancy. For him, they are causes for celebration rather than concern. "We're glad to hear unemployment's increasing." Invention has reduced the necessity for work, "so you really have to put your mind to it to figure out what to do. You have to create, not foolish jobs, but . . . a use of your time . . . that you can devote yourself to." From May 1984 until March 1985, coal miners in Britain engaged in strike action in protest at major proposals for pit closures and job losses. For Cage practicality was central – mining was not necessary in the eighties, according to Fuller.

He pointed to his own example, and those of Fuller and of his father, of people who had been self-employed. But, whether or not the strike stood a chance of succeeding, or should have done, the miners were fighting for their livelihood, and in many respects for a community way of life. It was fatuous to suggest that destitute miners could set themselves up in ways that resembled those of the American intelligentsia.

To set against the example of his self-employed father, one may turn to a different story told by Cage. "Dad . . . was given a job irrigating (a job that'd kept several men busy every day all day long). He looked the land over, made something, dug something (can't remember which). No further work was necessary. Seeing he had nothing to do, they fired him." This is the complex reality with which those who would change society must reckon.

Alongside the celebration of the effect he anticipated technology would have on society at large, Cage began for the first time to speak frequently about political ideas. "Our proper work now if we love mankind and the world we live in," he proposed, "is revolution." It would not be a difficult process. "We have only one mind; radical change is therefore simple," he wrote. "The revolution," he stated elsewhere, "will be simple, like falling off a log."

It is never clear, however, exactly what the revolution of which Cage spoke at the beginning of the seventies would consist of. The nearest he gets to details is probably the following:

The revolution that we want will not deprive us of our individuality. This must be increased and intensified. What we want is a change in the means by which we live. At present the controls are coercive . . . the hope is that the present coercive and bureaucratic powers of our society will dwindle, wither, and fall away.

At the start of the decade, Cage was avowedly interested in the thoughts of Mao, a preoccupation which would briefly infiltrate his music, such as in the orchestral version of *Cheap Imitation*. At the suggestion of Norman O. Brown, he read *China: The Revolution Continued* by Wheelwright and McFarlane. By the end of the decade, however, Cage had abandoned his interest, feeling that since Mao had died, "They're doing more or less what everyone else is doing."

What predated his interest, and outlasted it, was a credo of anarchism. It went back decades as an inclination; indeed, Richard Kostelanetz has suggested that Cage is a "thirties leftie" far more than he is a Zen

Buddhist. "Zen and chance and everything else came afterwards," Kostelanetz proposed. "They are merely icing on the anarchist cake." It was not until the mid-sixties, however, that Cage began to describe himself as such – saying by 1966, "I'm an anarchist." From then on it was a point which he would often make, and which set the tone of his increasingly frequent pronouncements on political and social matters.

Unlike Thoreau, Cage continues to pay his taxes. "I do it in order to be free of the things the government could do to me in revenge," he explained. "I want to be able to continue my work so in that situation I do what the government requires, but no more . . . Many, many people are interested in what I am doing, so I must continue." On the other hand, he declines to use his vote, and looks forward "to the time when no one votes." When, by the eighties, "the presidential business was a contest between two movie stars" – Cage referred to Ronald Reagan and Paul Newman – "we . . . see that democracy had sunk to a level that ought to be questioned . . . It made me think how nice it would be to have Greta Garbo as president."

"Anarchism is fully practical," Cage opined. "We don't need a president. We can get along perfectly well without the government." What is needed instead, as he frequently proposes, "is a little intelligence which we don't have at all." We should remove social controls to points at which they escape our notice. All that is required by way of organization is a residual state to coordinate a network of global utilities. "If the object is to reach a society where you can do anything at all," suggested Cage, "the role of organization must be concentrated on the utilities."

One source text on anarchism to which Cage frequently refers is *Men Against the State* by James J. Martin. Cage met the author at his home, so he could acquire the last copy then available. However, although Cage defines himself as an anarchist most vocally, he uses the term in a highly idiosyncratic way. Just as Cage's thinking on music is transcendent and idealistic, and his ideas on the uses of technology and social change are abstract and idealistic, too, so Cage's "anarchism" is unconcerned with social practice, not reasoned or expressed in terms of action to change the world. It is transcendent, abstract, idealistic. People who call themselves anarchists are usually actively critical of government and what they see as other unnecessary social structures, and often take more radical lines in posture, policy and action than Marxist or Communist organizations. By contrast, Cage has deliberately eschewed involvement in direct action – a march, a protest or suchlike. He gathers information – in the early eighties, for instance, concerning Werner Erhard's hunger project (at the advice of Fuller) – but will not do anything directly aimed at changing an existing state of affairs.

"I've made lots of statements of a social nature," Cage said. "They're all rather anarchistic." He comments, "I don't do anything to promote the government. Nor do I do anything – well, I guess I do something – to stop it. In the dedications to my books I speak against government. Every now and then, I say something specifically against the government of the United States."

During the crisis which preceded the Gulf War in 1991, Cage opined, "I think our pretence of being the proper policeman for the world at large is unfortunate. I think many other nations feel that our presence now in Arabia needs no help, since we have sufficient determination to be policemen. But now we're poor policemen and we would certainly suffer a great deal." Such statements, however, are of personal opinion, rather than clamoring for change. "I was recently asked to sign a petition against atomic energy," Cage recounted in 1978. "I wrote back saying I wouldn't sign it. I wasn't interested in critical or negative action. I'm not interested in objecting to things that are wrong."

"I don't think critical action is sufficient . . . even if it's right," he states. "Protestors just fan the flames of whatever they're protesting." This is partly an extension into politics of the ethical approach one can draw from Zen Buddhism: keep one's ability to make connections to oneself. The approach Cage takes is clearly shown in his comments on Cornelius Cardew, who by the early seventies was taking a rabidly polemical stance against activity which failed to fit his ideology. "What Cornelius was doing didn't help the Revolution as much as he would have liked . . . And it also didn't help music," Cage suggested. "Instead of doing his own work, he got involved in attacking other people who were working. So that he didn't do himself any good, or them any good."

The stance taken by Cage is not only ethically appropriate, but also what is practical. Cage suggests one strive to "alter the nature of whatever circumstances you have the capability of altering." One response to a state of affairs or a practice with which one disagrees is to "discourage it through your lack of interest in it." "When you see all those detergents and things," Cage suggested, "just don't buy them anymore. Embarrass the government out of existence, by not accepting their offer of letting us vote." What one can alter above all, however, is not what other people do – one can simply discourage that – but what one does in one's own work, and if one changes other people, it is not by interfering with their work, but by example.

Cage makes anarchism his own; he makes it fit the most to the least rational levels of his character. When he observes that "my activity is anti-institutional", his objection to institutions and to organization is reasoned, *and* it exemplifies a temperamental reluctance to dirty his feet, *and* incarnates his Apollonian distaste for the crowd: "I work best as an individual, not as one sheep in a herd of sheep."

The limitations of Cage's anarchism are very much those of his general social concerns, and they cluster around his uncompromising idealism. It is all very well speaking of Spaceship Earth, but who is steering it? Having said that, Cage may be surprisingly realistic about some aspects of social change, not underestimating, as do most social theorists, the gradual way ideas percolate, nor overestimating the effectiveness of dramatic political action.

For decades Cage had seen parallels between musical activity and social situations or aspirations. As early as *Credo*, he had suggested that "Schoenberg's method is analogous to a society in which the emphasis is on the group and the integration of the individual in the group." When Cage redrafted the speech in 1940 he made further interesting points which are early examples of his refusal to engage in critical or negative activity:

> Some composers today are writing music of a conventional nature, but with the purpose of helping to bring about a better state of society. When this better social order is achieved, their songs will have no more meaning than the "Star-spangled banner" has today. We will then realize our need for the new music which will have been written by composers who didn't help fight, but who were aware in a general way of, and sensitive to, the continual series of world events.

When he began to speak of anarchism, Cage started to construe indeterminate music as its exemplification. Writing about the various *Etudes* which he undertook later in the seventies, he proposed that "pieces of music can be taken as models for human behavior, not only proving the possibility of doing the impossible, but showing, too, in a work performed by more than one person, the practicality of anarchy." As discussed earlier, Cage saw art as a sphere of activity in which likes and dislikes could be most thoroughly given up; likewise, art can be an experimental station in which "one tries out living" because it is purer, not as complicated by conflicting concerns. Thereby, Cage suggests, it is historically advanced. When it was put to him that ethical standards

242

should be sustained until such time as "we are ready" to discard them, Cage assented, "but if we wait until that time, that time will never come. Therefore we begin with that time in the fields where it is possible to do without such standards, such value judgments, to prepare the way – and art is one of them."

Responding to students in England in 1989, Cage suggested:

Imagine that the music that you're writing is not music but is social relationships, and then ask yourself whether you would want to live in that kind of a society that would have that kind of music in it . . . I make a music situation in which everyone is on his own, and that can be difficult, unless you believe it – unless you believe the need for it.

For a short time it appeared that Cage was subsuming music within a program of social action, rather than letting it stand as an activity in its own right. Even in the early sixties Earle Brown had been able to suggest to Cage – and he agreed – that his friend was not so much interested in experimental music as in experimental sociology. Cage was leaning toward the position that what was urgent was not art, but society. Through the sixties, social terms – particularly "utility" – increasingly appear as the criterion for the evaluation of art; Cage praised, for example, Ichiyanagi's "*useful* works." "Music (not composition)" became his focus; the composer, he said, simply facilitates an enterprise. He suggested that success be defined in social rather than in aesthetic terms, that, for instance, the work can include action on the part of others; he tried this out by organizing events – at the University of Michigan at Kalamazoo among others – in which all who attended took part. The aim was not simply "audience participation," which maintained the dichotomies, but a music by everyone. "The sooner I get on unemployment compensation the better off I am," Cage suggested.

This line reached its height in the following statement from *A Year from Monday*:

The reason I am less and less interested in music is not only that I find environmental sounds and noises more useful aesthetically than the sounds produced by the world's musical cultures, but that, when you get right down to it, a composer is simply someone who tells other people what to do. I find this an unattractive way of getting things done.

243

Cage made this, sensibly, a personal rather than universal statement; his choice of phrase ("simply someone who tells other people what to do") sets the emotional tone that leads to a reader's assent, and it avoids either the position that the traditional composer role is an attractive way to achieve results, or the more flexible position that whether or not that role is attractive depends on the people and work involved. The English composer Roger Smalley observed: "Personally, one of my life's greatest pleasures is to do what Beethoven tells me to do via the notes of his piano sonatas. I don't feel coerced either. If Cage really wants to 'get things done', perhaps he should try to get himself elected to an administrative position or become a social worker."

Perhaps Cage's stance in previous years had been less risky and more productive: "nothing is accomplished by writing a piece of music." Smalley suggested:

> Cage's music is as unlikely to make its listeners free as listening to Shostakovitch's symphonies is likely to make them communists or the Ninth Symphony into brothers. ... You might be humming a tune from the work – or you might be *thinking* about freedom, brotherhood, communism etc – or you might be wondering whether you can get to the pub before it closes – but isn't *action* what's really needed to change the world?

As the sixties gave way to the seventies, Cage had stretched beyond the bounds of the project he had embraced in the previous decade. For a while his showmanship was given freer rein; his enthusiasm for technology was renewed, and applied not only to music but also to the problems of the world; above all, the focus of his pronouncements shifted toward social and political matters, particularly his version of anarchism, which changed his vocabulary for discussing music and seemed for a time to subsume it as his paramount concern. One may feel that these changes showed Cage overstepping his limits as a composer. One may feel, in a more subtle and less judgmental formulation, that he was trying something else out and, arguably, that his success was limited: his showmanship teetered on the edge of excess, his social and political pronouncements stand as rhetorical fragments rather than arguments on the matter with which one could concur, and are sustained with what is in politics a questionable idealism. None of which need contradict Norman O. Brown's suggestion that his willingness to overstep the mark is an act of "valor and courage."

244

VIII

Scarcely had Cage said "I am less and less interested in music" than he was writing more and more music, for more conventional instrumentation, using more conservative notation. He felt less interested in electronic work because so many people were carrying on good work in that area that he could be more creative elsewhere. Between 1971 and 1972 he produced a version of *Cheap Imitation*, which he had first made for piano in 1969, for an orchestra of twenty-four, fifty-nine or ninety-five players.

Cheap Imitation "stands in complete contrast to my indeterminate works," Cage noted as he worked on it. "It has a beginning and an end. It has three parts." In a characteristically unrevealing appeal to facts, he noted, "That's all a result of my great love of Satie." The orchestral version was commissioned by the Koussevitsky Foundation, which had been asking him for an orchestral piece for some time. Cage let practicalities define the boundaries within which chance would operate. He first listed which orchestral instruments could play each phrase of the piano version. When the inventory was complete, he asked the *I Ching* how many of the possible instruments should play and then which ones; how many notes of the phrase, which ones, and how each should be articulated. The conductor, Cage stipulated, should have no function other than as a coach during rehearsals; he or she should not direct the performance. Thereby the piece does not solidify into an object. "The work returns to itself to make itself," as Cage put it. "It became a current, a flux."

Between February and March 1972 Cage toured with the Cunningham Company. Carolyn Brown announced her resignation, with good timing, since the company was going to rest after the tour, but Cage was unusually upset. Dining one night in Grenoble, a little the worse for drink, he said to her plaintively, "You're not *really* going to leave Merce, are you?"

At the Albany studio in April he made *Birdcage*, "twelve tapes to be distributed by a single performer in a space in which people are free to move and birds to fly," ascertaining the duration, arrangement and modulation of selections of tape by means of the *I Ching*.

Gaudeamus, the Dutch musical organization, had scheduled the first performance of *Cheap Imitation* for early May, using the twenty-four essential parts. When Cage arrived in The Hague on the day of the premiere, he discovered that the players were rehearsing the piece for the first time. It was too difficult to prepare for their performance in the concert, so that evening an open rehearsal of the first movement was given, and the following day, which was supposed to feature a repeat performance, the orchestra stumbled through two of the movements.

To make up for this disaster, Gaudeamus proposed that *Cheap Imitation* be presented a few weeks later in the Holland Festival, and formally assured Cage that it would be fully prepared. When he arrived on the day of the performance, he found that the final rehearsal was again the sole one. Most players were looking at their music for the first time, and the conductor had been switched to "a former pupil of Boulez" (as Cage put it) who asked, "I think this work has three movements; is that true?" Cage listened to a few half-hearted attempts to play the opening phrases, then interrupted. "I spoke to the musicians about the deplorable state of society, not only of musical society," he related later. "I added that I was withdrawing the work from the program of the concert planned for that evening, and that I congratulated myself for having come up with . . . something capable of opening the ears of orchestra musicians." It obliges musicians to listen to one another, Cage claimed, which they rarely do. "I had offered them something with which to make music, and not, as is practiced today, something with which to scrape together a little money," he reflected. "I am convinced that they play other music just as badly as they play mine. However, in the case of *Cheap Imitation*, there are no climaxes, no harmonies, no counterpoints with which to hide one's lack of devotion."

Interestingly, in view of his radical individualism, he does not suggest here that this lack of devotion be blamed on individuals; "it is to be blamed on the present organization of society: it is the *raison d'être* for revolution." "To play your music," one of the players told Cage, "you have to change your mind with regard to music itself. How can you expect ninety-six people to do that?" To which Cage subsequently observed that in view of the state of the world every one of us must change our minds.

This was the same problem Cage had encountered with the New York Philharmonic performance of *Atlas Eclipticalis,* and his response was the same – to carry on in whatever direction he saw as necessary, and to expect the best of performers. After the Gaudeamus fiasco, however, Cage insisted on a minimum rehearsal requirement for *Cheap Imitation*: the musicians were to be given their parts at least a week before the projected performance and must learn the melody – at least the phrases in which they participate – and be able to play it as presented, for instance without re-notating double sharps and flats. In the week prior to performance, an orchestral rehearsal lasting one and a half hours was to be held every day. If any player did not know his or her part, they should be dismissed, and if as a result there were less players than the quorum of twenty-four the performance was to be cancelled.

IX

Arthritis had troubled Cage increasingly since 1960; doctors could only suggest aspirin and he had reached a point when he was taking a dozen a day. He tried acupuncture, which helped a little. His wrists were so inflamed that he had to fit a new, specially enlarged strap in order to wear his watch, and the pain progressively hampered his piano playing, which was one reason why the pieces which he wrote for his own use were for voice. When a new orchestral piece, *Etcetera*, was premiered in Paris in January 1973, a renowned Chinese physician walked across town to give a consultation. After careful examination, he told Cage that acupuncture could give only palliative relief. "What you need is to have your blood tested and then to make a change of diet," he advised. "Someone will have to do that for you." Cage asked the doctor to name his fee; he replied that he wanted nothing, because he had not helped.

Over forty years after they had first met, Grete Sultan and Cage began work in 1974 on a new, virtuousic work for solo pianist. For a month Cage unsuccessfully wrestled with the piano, attempting to find a new approach that would seize Sultan's attention; then he decided, as he later would in preparing violin works for Paul Zukofsky, to learn not from the instrument but from the player. The way Sultan played, he noted, could be interpreted as a duet for two independent hands; he catalogued all the intervals and their possible combinations that could be played by a single hand. Each hand had its own two-stave part in the score.

Thus were born the *Etudes Australes*. For pitch material, Cage turned again to star maps. The density of notes is sometimes so great that it is difficult to read their succession; in her own copy Sultan measured and drew lines by which the sequence could be clarified. Some of the figurations generated were so complex they would not fit in the space available in the proportional notation and so appeared, identified by letters, in magnified form at the back of the score.

The *Etudes Australes* were the first of three sets of virtuoso etudes. They embody Cage's renewed interest in more traditional instrumentation and notation, and they come out of a new attitude to social issues and the way music can further social concerns. By the mid-seventies world events had in one sense struck him dumb, turning him, as he said of Fuller, from a prophet of Utopia to Jeremiah; the revolution no longer seemed as simple as falling off a log. His music began to stress less the Marxist collectivism of a music made by everyone, than a turn to the heroic example of the virtuoso, in whose brilliance Cage saw the chance to show that the impossible was possible.

I had become interested in writing difficult music, etudes, because of the world system which often seems to many of us hopeless. I thought that were a musician to give the example in public of doing the impossible that it would inspire someone who was struck by that performance to change the world.

Writing *Mureau* (1970), the *Sixty-Two Mesostics re Merce Cunningham* (1971) and the various texts of the *Song Books* at the turn of the decade had led Cage to conceive of a large-scale text determined by chance, at the interface of music and poetry. As seen in Chapter 11, as soon as Cage conceived of composition by chance he was considering applying the same processes to texts. *45' for a speaker* is derived in part from chance-determined selections from his previous writings, and the voice solo accompanying the *Concert for Piano and Orchestra* was a pot-pourri of prose and verse from cummings, Joyce and the *Huang-Po Doctrine*, to Goethe and the *Lakavatara Sutra*:

mud-luscious, I U, E–H, Glory, W, Shem. In Feld und Wald, sur le feu avec du beurre ... UB, intricate imperfect various, U, LNL, Tell mé, tell me, tell me, elm!

"Communication wiithout language!" Cage had proposed in the *Diary* for 1966 – "We'll still speak: a) for practical reasons; b) for the pleasure of it; c) to say what should/shouldn't be done." By the end of the decade he was concerned with "experiments away from syntax." The rejection of structure he was expressing in his anarchist ideas, and had been playing out in his music, was paralleled by a suspicion of language; as early as *45' for a speaker* he had proposed that "it was by means of words we became subservient", and now he began quoting with approval Norman O. Brown's proposition, "syntax is the arrangement of the army."

Cage found historical precedent in the classical Oriental languages, which featured no or little syntax. Suzuki, he knew, had made an early translation of Dante's *Divina Commedia* which lacked syntax. Although later a stylish writer of standard syntactical English, Suzuki had learned

248

the language first from books; as a young man he had solemnly told the students at the provincial school where he taught that "I have two legs" was in English "two legs in me are." Only on his first visit to the United States had he realized that the English he taught bore no relation to that of anyone else.

Since at least 1965 Cage had known and admired a particular haiku by Basho. What interested him in particular was that the absence of syntax made it possible to understand the haiku in English in a variety of ways. The published translation by R.H. Blythe rendered it as "the leaf of some unknown tree sticking on the mushroom"; the composer Toru Takemitsu suggested to Cage that it could be read as "mushroom does not know that leaf is sticking on it."

The Oriental scholar William McNaughton told Cage that the classical Chinese language can be classified into "full words" and "empty words." A full word has a specific, in a loose sense referential, meaning; nouns, verbs, adjectives, adverbs, are full words, though which of these forms the word takes cannot always be determined. Empty words are conjunctions, particles, pronouns, which refer only to other terms: a, at, it.

Using the overtones of the latter "to suggest the emptiness of meaning that is characteristic of musical sounds," Cage created a text between 1973 and 1975 which he called *Empty Words,* turning again to the *Journal* of Thoreau and through a laybrinthine system of chance operations, extracting a text which over four long sections moves from words and whole phrases –

notAt evening
                right can see
                    suited to the morning hour

– to letters and silences:

t hltht shh swh e atveth mf   *d*n   nd e aie
                        ean   byo   odo

Cage vindicates his claim made years earlier that English can be saved by its "high percentage of consonants and the natural way in which they produce discontinuity."

He recommends that the work be read, as he himself performed it, in an all-night concert, timed to end with the dawn. Schoenberg used to say, he recalled, that music should be played at night, not in the afternoon.

As the text effaces itself and the sun rises, the doors and windows of the place of performance should be opened to remove any hindrance to the sounds stirring outside entering in. It was a new, epic allegory of Cage's attitude to art: "opening doors so that anything can go through."

By the mid-seventies the progressively more qualified way Cage thought about social issues turned toward ecological matters. He gathered information about wildlife refuges, subscribed to the *East-West Journal*, and contacted the Franco-American anti-whaling organization, Project Jonah, copying from them a lengthy list of environmental organizations. In interviews he expressed concern about toxins in vegetables, and presently began to distill water at home and add seawater essence to restore its mineral balance. On tour he anticipated with pleasure visits to countries, such as Scotland or Iceland, where the air was clean and the water fit to drink. Cage continued, however, to abjure active politics, feeling that the Green parties "have some good ideas, but I'm very suspicious about power."

He noted that ecological concerns could only be tackled through unsettling compromises with the current situation. Talking of Fuller, as a parallel case, Cage observed that

> he's obliged, for instance, to drive to the airport and to fly from here to Australia, and the lecture he gives is against the use of the very energies which he has just used. That's the kind of situation we're involved in, and it makes us . . . well, we're not hypocritical – it makes us – it's more like helplessness . . . If Fuller didn't give his talk, no one else would give that talk. So I guess he decides to give it, and to take the airplane that someone else is going to take in any case.

As Cage's arthritis worsened he grew increasingly interested in the promise of alternative medicine. In 1974 or 1975 he consulted his astrologer, Julie Winter, as he had done, and would subsequently do intermittently. It seems remarkable that he does so, since the weight of his personality seems to lie in a different direction, toward the rational and the ascetic. Yet some of Cage's words and actions accommodate a magical view of life: his mention of a guardian angel, his idle play with the tree branch while first waiting for Buhlig in 1932, and a throwaway comment in the late seventies, "I often make mistakes: I was born early in September." Julie Winter, says Cage, "helps me with the complexity of circumstances I find myself in": on this occasion she told Cage that he would suffer pains that doctors would be unable to explain, and that he would receive help from an unorthodox doctor who would change his diet.

A number of musical works from the mid-seventies onward share the mood of nature and ecology – the organic simplicity of *Empty Words*, the rhythms of the breath and of the night, the voice and the dawn; *Child of Tree* (1975) and *Branches* (1976); *Inlets* (1977) and *Litany for the Whale* (1981). *Child of Tree* and *Branches* are percussion solos or optionally, in the case of the latter ensembles, using ten unpitched instruments chosen by the performer, made exclusively of plant materials; they might include claves, tapping sticks, log drums, seed maracas, hyoshigi and the like, or even just dried leaves and twigs. Players are obliged to use one or several pod rattles from the Mexican poinciana tree, and a number of cacti; the sound of their spines being plucked is rudimentarily amplified with the customary record player cartridge.

X

Child of Tree and *Branches* stand out as the first time in Cage's mature work that he had encouraged improvisation. As already seen, he strove from his earliest use of chance operations to excise any sort of spontaneous decision, and by the sixties instances such as the optional free interpretations of *Variations VI* were exceptional. "The thing I don't like about, or didn't like about improvisation, was that it was based on taste and memory, and it didn't get the improviser to the point where he encountered a revelation," Cage explained. Through the new pieces, "I have thought of a variety of ways of improvising that begins with a notion that gives a problem to the improviser to solve as he plays." The title *Child of Tree* was taken from the passage in *Finnegans Wake* which forms the text of *The Wonderful Widow*. Its eight-minute duration is divided by the player according to an *I Ching*-cast, and instruments are allocated to the different parts by the same technique, each instrument appearing only in one part of the composition. Cage then instructs – like the *Electronic Music for Piano* and *WGBH-TV*, the score is just a xerox of his handwriting – "Using a stopwatch, the soloist improvises, clarifying the time structure by means of the instruments. This improvisation is the performance. The rest of the work is done ahead of time." The only other comment Cage makes is that the player should try to avoid producing sounds in performance from any source other than the instruments.

"If you divide the time of an improvisation into sections you can then divide the sounds that are available for the performance into a similar

251

number of parts, and that fact of having a space in the time where certain sounds will go, and they won't go into others, will give an interesting something that could interest one as a problem as he was playing freely," explained Cage. As a performer, one does not know the plant materials, "You're discovering them. So the instrument is unfamiliar. If you become very familiar with a piece of cactus, it very shortly disintegrates, and you have to replace it with another one which you don't know. So the whole thing remains fascinating, and free of your memory as a matter of course."

Branches must always follow performance of the *Child of Tree* solo; it may simply be an "eight-minute variation" on the preceding, using a selection of the ten instruments ascertained by the *I Ching*, or be improvised by any number of players, each following *Child of Tree* after a number of minutes determined by chance operations.

Inlets, devised in Seattle in September 1977 for a dance by Cunningham designed by Morris Graves, is a third piece based on improvising within a structure. It is scored for sound-sources with a similarly organic flavor – twelve conch shells filled with water and graduated in size, divided equally between three players; a conch blower (as for the *Third Construction*) using circular breathing; and the sound of fire, preferably made live. The intentionality of the improvisation is interfered with by the nature of the instruments. "You have no control whatsoever over the conch shell when it's filled with water," Cage observed. The air chambers of the shell fill with water and empty unpredictably when one tilts it, "so the rhythm belongs to the instruments, and not to you."

In these three improvisational works it is possible to see Cage, having developed his very narrow compositional direction in great discipline for twenty-five years, beginning to incorporate on his own terms the features which were incidental, and he had thought inimical to, his project. This may in part be because he had worked his way around to such incorporation being possible, and perhaps in part because being twenty-five years older meant he had less internal pressures to combat.

The bicentennial of the United States was celebrated in 1976, and among the festivities came a number of commissions for Cage, involving so much work that he left the Cunningham Company for a year. The *Quartets I–VIII* are scored for an orchestra of twenty-four, forty-one or ninety-three instruments, and derive their title from the rule Cage established that at any given time only four musicians play simultaneously. With each phrase a new quartet is formed; sonority varies constantly. The score is derived by chance operations applied to eight eighteenth-century hymns and churals by the American composers William Billings, Jacob French and Andrew Law ("these American tunes, hymn tunes and what not . . . don't interest me," Cage had said in 1965).

Seiji Ozawa arranged a commission for the Boston Symphony Orchestra, of which he was guest conductor, which Cage fulfilled by writing *Renga*, seventy-eight parts derived from 361 drawings from the *Journal* of Thoreau. A renga is a classical form of Japanese poetry. In classical Japanese culture, a high value was placed on impromptu verse; rengas were improvised by poets in groups, each person writing a line in succession. They functioned to open the minds of poets, listeners and readers to relations other than those usually intended or perceived.

Renga may be played simultaneously with a "musicircus" Cage called *Apartment House 1776*, which features four solo vocalists performing the music of four key ethnic groups at the time of Independence: Protestant and Sephardic songs, the calls and hollers of African slaves, and an American Indian chief singing and rhythmically slapping his belly. "Many people became annoyed simply because I superimposed the spiritual songs of four different people," Cage observed. "Yet if you engaged them in a discussion on ecumenical thought, you'd probably find that they agree with the idea that there are different ways of approaching God."

The two pieces were performed together at the 50th Festival of the International Society for Contemporary Music in Boston on October 27. Jeers accompanied the first chords. Within the first fifteen minutes people began to walk out, and the air was filled with whistles, catcalls and both genuine and derisory applause. "I thought it would be a cheerful piece, and that it would be a celebration of the bicentennial – which I think it is. I'm always surprised that more people didn't recognize it as having that character," noted Cage. The incomprehension echoed that which had greeted pieces such as *The Perilous Night,* and had first led him to question the principle of expressive music. "Many people faced with sad music laugh, and faced with witty music start crying," he reiterated. "It seems to me that music doesn't really communicate to people. Or if it does, does it in very, very different ways from one person to the next."

The bicentennial pieces reveal Cage's relation to his native country. From *Other People Think* to *Lecture on the Weather* (1975), and his book *M*, with its dedication "to the USA, that it may become just another part of the world, no more, no less," Cage, latterly an avowed anarchist, had no interest in the United States as a political or economic boundary; indeed, his world view was opposed to such parochialism. Yet his attitude to his art is characteristically American: the inventiveness, the pragmatism, the optimism. He felt close in spirit to quintessential Americans such as Ives and Thoreau. The same country that produced the Pragmatist philosophers was home to Cage. "Music," he once wrote, "is simply trying things out in school fashion to see what happens."

Cage had first read selections from *Finnegans Wake* as it had appeared as work in progress in Eugene Jolas' *transition* magazine from April 1927 onwards, and when it had first been published in full in 1939 he had bought a copy from a department store in Seattle. He had not read the work in its entirety – "I was 'too busy' ", Cage recalled – but he used it for the libretto of *The Wonderful Widow of Eighteen Springs* in 1942, and it popped up in his text for the voice solo to *Concert* and in the plan for the *Ten Thunderclaps*; "HCE" (Here Comes Everybody) is mentioned variously, starting from the beginning of the fifties.

During 1976 Elliot Anderson, who edited the journal *Tri-Quarterly* at Northwestern University at Evanston, Illinois, was preparing a special issue, *In the Wake of the "Wake"*, and asked Cage for some kind of contribution. Cage was already declining invitations and avoiding tours because of his work on the Boston commissions, and so said no. Anderson persisted. As on a number of other occasions, Cage felt it would be as quick to comply with his request as continually to interrupt his work in order to refuse.

He opened *Finnegans Wake* at random – page 356 – and began writing mesostics using the name of Joyce as a string until he reached the end of the chapter. Norman O. Brown suggested the omission of punctuation. The twenty-three mesostics which resulted satisfied Anderson's request.

Having taken a new look at the book, Cage had some reservations about its dependency on English and its maintenance of syntax, but his interest was fired. He began collecting and reading books about the *Wake*. "I was caught in *Finnegans Wake*," he wrote. "I found myself from time to time bursting into laughter."

His work for *Tri-Quarterly* also gave him a new, serious approach to mesostic writing. "It was a discipline," he wrote, "similar to that of counterpoint in music with a cantus firmus." In his usual constructively obsessional way, he made an index of the syllables used to represent a given letter of Joyce's name. "I am native to detailed attention," he observed. Cage proceeded through 1976, among all his other work, with what became *Writing Through "Finnegans Wake"*, 682 pages of mesostics extracted from top to bottom of the book. Unusually, he "wrote because I decided to" – for years he had worked to commission or, as he put it, through the "invitation" of others "even though the project seemed somewhat idiotic and time-consuming." Before the year was out, Bill Bueno, Cage's editor at Wesleyan University Press, had suggested that the text was boring and unreadably long, and Cage began *Writing for the Second Time Through "Finnegans Wake"*, using his index in a system which avoided repeating a syllable for a given letter of the name. This resulted in a text around a third of the length of its predecessor which he finished by May 1977.

FIFTEEN

I

Cage's physical state was increasingly shaky. For two years he had accepted that, following a case of blood poisoning, the toes of his left foot were dead. Then the numbness began to affect his right foot. His doctor suggested "sophisticated tests," which failed to provide an explanation. His wrists were now so swollen from arthritis that he could no longer pick up a glass with one hand.

Between January 23 and February 6, 1977 Cage was in Paris promoting *Pour les oiseaux*, which Editions Pierre Belfond had just published. It was a collection of interviews with Cage by Daniel Charles, whose interest in his subject dated back at least to his 1964 manuscript, "L'esthétique du "non-finito" chez John Cage." "I am for the birds," Cage had told a reporter, "not for the cages in which people sometimes place them."

Media interest was high and his schedule strenuous. The night after a particularly grueling interview for television, filmed in an unheated basement, Cage could not sleep due to a new pain behind his left eye. Doctors said the pain stemmed from an abscessed tooth whose root had been removed years earlier. He underwent new root canal work. The pain returned. Having for some years taken a dozen aspirin a day, Cage was now taking a form that explodes in the stomach. His doctor smiled wanly and said unhelpfully, "Pains come and go." He continued complaining to his friends, but stopped paying doctors for the privilege.

Back in New York, Cage was lurching along Thirteenth Street when a long black limousine drew up alongside. Yoko Ono climbed out. Cage described his predicament. "You must go to Shizuko Yamomoto," she urged. "She will change your diet and give you Shiatsu massage."

Reminded of the predictions of both Julie Winter and the Chinese physician in Paris, he immediately made an appointment with Yamomoto.

256

She described to him the macrobiotic diet, a system of food choice and preparation based on an Oriental perspective on total health. The ingredients and their presentation suggest an austere, vegan variation on conventional Japanese cuisine: rice is the staple food, substituted on occasion by other whole grains, followed in descending amounts by vegetables, beans, sea vegetables, seeds, nuts and occasionally fruit. Many of the supplements and condiments are of Japanese origin, among them nuka pickles, umeboshi plums, tamari and miso, particularly used to make miso soup.

What most distinguishes the macrobiotic diet from other health regimens is that, rather than consisting of a fixed list of foods to be consumed or avoided, it provides a structure which applies to the whole range of available choices, an orientation which many adherents of the diet extend to a whole cosmology. The polarity of yin and yang, as manifested in the *I Ching*, becomes the way to understand human well-being in macrobiotics. Different foods and different ways of preparing them have different balances of yin and yang; fish is a yang ingredient and baking a yang technique, for example, while green leafy vegetables and steaming are the opposite. Health is achieved by balancing the one against the other; illness comes from a bodily imbalance stemming from a failure to balance yin and yang foods in accordance with our needs. The modern Western diet, in particular, combines extreme forms of food, for instance the extreme yin of coffee, tea, sugar and milk and the extreme yang of meat products. Advocates of macrobiotics propose that one consciously, and eventually intuitively, balance yin and yang in one's diet, by using foods toward the center of the continuum: rice, beans and vegetables are neither especially yin nor especially yang, just slightly inclined toward one rather than the other.

Until he met Yamomoto, Cage cooked as much as possible according to the traditional canons of *haute cuisine*, following, in particular, the books of Julia Childs. The food he had mentioned in his writings was generally lavish, brimming with butter, cheese and cream – Alan Watt's meat and truffle pie, Lois Long's fried chicken. In the mid-sixties Cage listed his favorite party dish as beef bourgignon. Faced with the prospect of a strict macrobiotic regime, "for two days I lived in shock. I ate almost nothing. I couldn't imagine a kitchen without butter, or a dinner without wine."

Through an assistant, John Lennon sent him six cookbooks; Cage procured the schedule of classes for the New York East-West Center winter program. Norman O. Brown's wife Beth suggested a granola without sugar which he ate dry. In less than a week the pain behind his left eye disappeared. After a month his toes began to loosen up. The swelling of his wrists receded, though they remained misshapen, and he stopped suffering from constipation. His weight dropped from 280 to 245 pounds. He also noted remarkable broader effects: "Your energy asserts itself the moment you wake up at the beginning of the day. It remains constant. It doesn't go up and down, it stays level, and I can work much more extensively. I always had a great deal of energy, but now it is extraordinary. At the same time," he added, "I'm much more equable in feeling; I'm less easily agitated." Cage said the diet made him more active than at any time since, specifically, 1952 – the year he presented *4'33"*.

His all-round improvement so amazed him that he remained faithful to the diet from that time onwards. He now continues it even on tour, taking with him a Panasonic rice steamer, an electric wok, some macrobiotic packet meals and some bancha tea bags. He frequently cooks macrobiotic dinners for his guests; when dining out he prefers to take his own food along.

Cage was becoming increasingly health-conscious. He had been smoking three packets of cigarettes a day – lighting a cigarette is one of the directions in *45' for a speaker,* and is featured in *Communication* and the charts for *Water Music;* Cage tells a smoking story in *Where are we going? and what are we doing?*. He stopped by seeing himself divided into two people, one who knew he had stopped, the other who did not. Every time the one who did not know picked up a cigarette, the other laughed until he put it down. After starting the macrobiotic diet Cage also cut out alcohol – his old favorites were wine, beer, Guinness and whisky (his penchant had been for eight-year-old Talisker). Occasionally he allowed himself a shot of vodka after dinner; he has sometimes tried champagne at receptions, but finds now that it tastes alien to his palate.

Macrobiotics provided a new slant on Cage's growing concern with nature and ecological matters. Big business and agribusiness, he stressed, damage our meat, vegetable and water supplies. "These are the problems that should be addressed rather than the protection of one country against another," Cage suggests. "A quick change in food intake will affect the health of the whole society. Drastically."

With its Oriental origin, its asceticism, and its application of yin and yang from the most immediately practical to the most obscurely cosmological, the macrobiotic diet fits in very well with both Zen and with the temperament of Cage. Yamomoto's first advice reminded him of Suzuki: "Eat when you're hungry. Drink when you're thirsty." Yet

Cage feels the diet did not influence his work in any major way because it had already been affected by the ideas which informed the diet. "In other words," he explained, "I accepted the diet you might say aesthetically before I accepted it nutritionally." He does, however, express concern at the dualism which one can find in the division of yin and yang.

As well as contributing to Cage's health, macrobiotics meant he was extending his tendency for ascetic discipline to his diet. It seems symbolic that his one extensive admission to his gustatory passions, *Where are we eating? And what are we eating?*, was written in 1975, not long before he gave up every food he describes himself then as eating. The time is also interesting because in his work, beginning say with *Child of Tree*, he was forging a new *rapprochement* with elements he had long excluded. However, he feels that he does not adhere to the diet as strictly as he might; he uses herbs, spices and lemon juice to give a distinctive flavor to each dish, and sometimes eats a whole bowl of fruit. One day Cage was being massaged by Yamomoto. "Don't take the diet too seriously," she urged. Cage was shocked by her apparent flippancy. It was not until two weeks had passed that he came around to asking her what she had meant. "When you're with friends," she answered, "you can eat a potato."

II

Under what he called the "patent tutelage" of Paul Zukofsky – the virtuoso who had premiered, among other works, *Centering* by Earle Brown (1973) – Cage began to take a new look at writing for the violin, in the same way that he had worked with Sultan on *Etudes Australes*. "I study," Cage wrote, "not how to play the violin, but how to become ever more baffled by its almost unlimited flexibility."

Zukofsky had recorded *Six Melodies* and the *Nocturne*, and, after seeking the advice of Earle Brown, decided that the best way to secure new music for the violin from Cage was to offer a commission, rather than to hope something would appear. Cage called him a few weeks after he wrote and declared that he was too busy with *Renga* and with *Apartment House 1776*, but once they were completed he would be happy to produce a new work.

Early in 1976 they met to discuss the project. The first fruit of their joint investigation was a solo violin version of *Cheap Imitation*, completed in 1977, following the versions for piano and orchestra of 1969 and 1972 respectively. "Two birds with one stone," Cage had said at the beginning of the decade, "maybe even three." He and Zukofsky agreed it would be a useful preliminary to a larger project, giving them the experience of working together. At first they planned a version for violin and piano, but that came to seem both fussy and unnecessary. Once they had settled on the idea for a solo violin arangement, only a few alterations, described in a preface to the score, were made to the piano version, beyond a global transposition up a third. The *I Ching* was asked questions concerning the melodic line and sometimes the accompaniment of Satie's *Socrate*: which of the seven white note modes is used and from which of the twelve chromatic notes it begins. In the first movement the *I Ching* selects the note of the given transposition except where the note is repeated. In the other two movements, original interval relations were kept for a half measure; in the opening measures and their subsequent reappearance they were preserved for a whole measure.

The performance instructions are very precise. Cage exploited the pitch continuum offered by the unfretted strings of the violin by specifying Pythagorean intonation, sometimes stretching pitch by up to forty cents in the upper register. He requests "a paradoxical *legato* or a 'philosophical' *détachée*"; dotted slurs indicate, uncommonly, phrases. In another concession to the tastes he expunged in the fifties, Cage suggests that tempo (in the third movement) may be slower according to personal preference; and for the first time since the *Composition for Three Voices* of 1934, he includes Italian instructions such as "quasi col legno."

Cheap Imitation laid the foundations of the work which followed it immediately, the enormously challenging *Freeman Etudes*, named after Betty Freeman, the patron from the West Coast who commissioned them. As he had for *Atlas Eclipticalis* and the *Etudes Australes* among others, Cage used star maps. Learning from his experience with Sultan, he clarified the space–time notation by running two lines under each stave, one divided into seven segments of equal length, the other marking the exact position of each event notated on the stave. In a manner again reminiscent of his work on the piano etudes, Cage sat with Zukofsky and worked out the chordal possibilities available on the violin: which pairs of notes could be played at the same time, then, from any of those which were selected, which third notes and, very occasionally, which fourth notes could be added. The resulting catalog was so exhaustive they considered publishing it.

The difficulty of the music heartened Cage. "Some of it will be absolutely impossible," he stated. Extending his views on the way music can further social concerns, he added, "We face at the present moment the possibility of doing the impossible by means of technology, and we're not certain exactly what to make of technology, so I'm letting the piece indicate a need."

As Zukofsky put it, "The *Etudes* are both fascinating and frustrating for many reasons. They are the most difficult music I have ever played, yet they are also extremely violinistic. They have endless phrasal possibilities, none of which were intended in the creation." A danger of this new generation of Cage works in which more traditional notation is used is that for those working with the score, including performers, they become superficially closer to the requirements of other musical styles; the minute specifications of the *Freeman Etudes* suggest other kinds of contemporary music, and the verbal comments invoke more traditional idioms. Yet the new pieces remain works by Cage, composed by chance, and decisions on how to prepare for a performance are better made by concentrating on this rather than on the notational features, an approach that would risk obscuring the differences between Cage's work and that of others.

Working in close collaboration with Zukofsky in 1977 and into 1978, Cage completed sixteen etudes. A further sixteen were planned, but he shelved the project because the second sixteen looked set to be too difficult even for the prodigious abilities of Zukofsky, and the prospect of producing them by electronic means did not attract Cage.

III

Kathan Brown had studied etching at the Central School of Arts and Crafts in London, and in 1962 had set up her own small studio, the Crown Point Press, in the Bay area of California. Brown had a vision of placing traditional etching techniques at the service of new art ideas; the press would be the perfect tool for artists, providing equipment and technical expertise to enable, but never to limit, the process of creation, producing art through conservative procedures but extending far beyond them.

In the middle of the seventies the artist Tom Marioni, Kathan Brown's husband and an admirer of Cage's work, suggested that she invite him to work at the press. It would be a risk – the press was usually made available to artists whose main work was visual, and the only previous visit by a composer had not been very productive – but Brown decided to take it. Cage accepted immediately, remembering, he said, a missed opportunity in the fifties to trek with Gita Sarabhai in the Himalayas. "I had something else to do," he recalls. "When I was free, Gita was not. I have always regretted this. The walk was to have been on elephants; it would have been unforgettable."

The invitation from Kathan Brown shows how success can breed ever broader success. As Cage became more widely respected, a wider range of resources was unlocked for him. The opportunity to make etchings was a special pleasure. Visual art was the last serious alternative vocation to music which Cage had considered as a young man. He had produced works with visual connotations – the *Constructions* and *Imaginary Landscapes* – and his excursions into film music had accompanied the sequences by Duchamp and the documentary about Calder. Despite his dedication to music, he continued to have brushes with visual work. His scores attracted attention as graphics, from the exhibition in the Stable Gallery at the time of the twenty-five-year retrospective to a presentation of *Renga* at the Museum of Modern Art in 1977, with exhibitions at the Fine Arts Center of the University of Rhode Island and at the Galerie Schwarz in Milan in 1971. In the fifties he had produced designs for Larsen and for the concerts of himself and his friends; in 1969 came his collaboration with Calvin Sumsion, and in 1971 work on the *Mushroom Book*.

Cage had in Gounod and, indeed, Schoenberg, examples of composers who were painters, and the writer William Burroughs was turning to painting. Yet Cage still felt an intense need to excuse his engagement with visual art in view of his promise to Schoenberg to devote his life to music. "Schoenberg himself did other things," he notes. "I still think I've remained faithful. You can stay with music while you're hunting mushrooms. It's a curious idea perhaps, but a mushroom grows for such a short time and if you happen to come across it when it's fresh it's like coming upon a sound which also lives a short time."

On New Year's Day 1978 Cage arrived at the Crown Point Press in Oakland to begin the *Seven Day Diary (Not Knowing)*. The same *modus operandi* was at work in this new sphere as in his music: producing the artwork non-intentionally through the use of chance operations. He first had to gain acquaintance with the various techniques and resources which the etching process involved, guided by the advice of Kathan Brown and the printmakers Lilah Toland and Stephen Thomas. The subsequent inventory could then be subjected to chance selections.

Despite the concessions he had recently made to improvisation in his music, Cage approached the visual field with caution. He was anxious to avoid "gesture," by which he meant personal, habitual reactions (this had formed the basis of his criticisms of improvisation, of jazz and of surrealism): "something connected with the knowing aspect of the person, as in a signature – when you sign your name, you just do it by habit." He tried out solutions such as, at first, avoiding looking at the plate as he made a chance-determined number of marks, with Lilah Toland keeping count.

The artists among Cage's friends were effusive in their praise of the result. Jasper Johns asserts that Cage has a highly developed visual and graphic sensibility. Some critical voices felt a kind of cultural con-trick was at work, not least because they could not believe Cage could be a visual artist as well as a composer and writer. Nevertheless, the next edition of *Who's Who in American Art* featured him, with no reference to his musical work, as a "printmaker."

Cage went on into 1978 producing as much music as ever: *A Dip in the Lake*, *Variations VIII*, and a piece for conch shells and tape, *Pools*. He produced *Some of "The Harmony of Maine"*, a forty-five-minute piece for organist with six assistants (two on each register), for his associate Gerd Zacher, who had years earlier recorded versions of *Variations I* and *III*. While still working on the *Freeman Etudes*, Cage made *Chorals* for Paul Zukofsky, an austere, microtonal study based on one of the pieces in the *Song Books*, and described by the violinist Malcolm Goldstein as

a set of nine melodies which have their origin in nine keyboard chorals by Erik Satie. Chance procedures determined the choice of pitch as well as what strings are played: the rhythm is also derived specifically from the Satie chords. The nine melodies thus created contain single and double note stops in a variety of microtonal relationships, as well as nuances of string timbre.

For KRO in Amsterdam, Cage produced a ten-hour radio event, *Sounday*, and, assisted by Juan Hidalgo and Walter Marchetti, *Il treno*, "variations on a theme by Tito Gotti" in the form of "happenings" on three excursions for "prepared trains" on June 26, 27 and 28.

In the midst of this work Cage moved with Cunningham from their loft on Bank Street to a new apartment, in what had been the B. Altman department store, on the West 18th Street at Sixth Avenue. It was light and spacious; Cage installed about sixty plants. He was also delighted at the street noise, so much so that he has deliberately avoided double-glazing the windows. "I love living on Sixth Avenue," he once remarked. "It has more sounds, and totally unpredictable sounds, than any place I've ever lived. The traffic never stops, night and day. Every now and then a horn, siren, screeching brakes – extremely interesting and always unpredictable." The Fire Department is on 19th Street, and their vehicles frequently circle the block, down Seventh Avenue, under Cage's window and up Sixth. Inside the building there are loud percussive sounds from the pipes in the skylight, so loud they can wake him from sleep. "Now," Cage observes, "I don't need a piano."

Cage had followed his first sudden engagement with Zen by a slower, continuous attempt to develop it and make it more consistent; now he learned to avoid being disturbed by the traffic sounds at night by transposing the sounds into images "so that they entered into my dreams without waking me up." As with his insensitivity to loud noises and the like, this adjustment shows Cage's extraordinary control over his response to external conditions (how far it is a natural talent and how far an ability he has developed is an open point.) As he described it:

> I translate the sounds into images, and so my dreams aren't disturbed. It just fuses. There was a burglar alarm one night and I was amazed because the pitch went on for two hours, was quite loud. It seemed to be to be going slightly up and slightly down. So what it became in my dreams was a Brancusi-like shape, you know, a subtle curve. And I wasn't annoyed at all.

Cage had suggested to Cunningham that the time had come to retire. He had calculated that if he retired to, say, Bolivia, the cost of living there would mean he could exist frugally on what he had already earned, and, he told his partner, there would be the added advantage that no one would be interested in modern music. One day, after they had lived in their apartment for some time, Cage looked out of the window on to the avenue. In its new function as the Avenue of the Americas, Sixth Avenue has the name of a different South American state featured on the street lamps of each block. Opposite the Altman store, the sign read "Bolivia."

On New Year's Day 1979 Cage returned to the Crown Point Press for his second visit. Having acquired a feel for the parameters available to him, he sought, as he had at a similar stage in chance music, to make the process increasingly complex. Paul Zukofsky, he told the printmakers, played violin as if he had six fingers; virtuoso etchings were possible too. In the project Cage began that year, Lilah Toland recalls, Cage kept "asking us to climb mountains." For *Changes and Disappearances* Cage and the printers frequently stayed up until two or three o'clock in the morning, preparing the 299 color mixes required by the chance operations. As in his music, Cage sought to incorporate what are customarily excluded as technical errors. Whereas the edge of a plate is generally wiped, a chance operation determined whether or not it should deliberately be inked. Foulbites, the accidental glitches caused by acid eating into unintended parts of the plate, were highlighted. The project was so complex that Cage continued work on it right through to 1982; he achieved, Lilah Toland feels, "more intricate beauty than he could consciously have set out to do."

In January 1979 Cage also made time to compose *Hymns and Variations* which, leading on from the processes employed in the *Quartets*, is derived from "subtractions" from "Heath" and "Old North" by William Billings, scored for twelve amplified voices singing, as usual in Cage's work, without vibrato. On February 1 he read the fourth part of *Empty Words* at the Whitney Museum. In the course of the year he completed another set of virtuoso studies derived from astronomical maps, the *Etudes Boreales*, and a new, large-scale project was in the air.

IV

Klaus Schöning worked for WDR in Cologne, where he produced *hörspiele*, substantial works and music specials by a wide range of international artists. Having been impressed by *Sounday* the year before, Schöning invited Cage to write music to accompany a broadcast of *Writing for the Second Time Through "Finnegans Wake"*. Cage accepted; he came up with the working title *Roaratorio*, which he felt evoked the world of the *Wake*, and then found it actually appears in the book.

Thanks to his work with the Cunningham Company, Cage knew a young engineer named John Fullemann, who came to mind as a potential assistant. Fullemann had studied phenomenology, history and music at Yale, and had worked with Lucier in the late sixties (a concert in which they both featured, at Wesleyan in May 1968, included compositions by Fullemann); now he was designing and building recording studios in the New York area, and had worked as a sound consultant for the dance company since 1976. The invitation from Cage caught up with him in a hotel room in Puerto Rico: he read the letter out loud, enthusiastically, and told Cage he accepted.

Cage's first thought was that *Writing for the Second Time* could be accompanied by a tape collage, based on the sounds mentioned by Joyce in the book. When he finished listing them, he had over four thousand items. To compound the problem, Cage discovered a new book, *A Finnegans Wake Gazeteer* by Louis Mink, who lectured in philosophy at Wesleyan. The *Gazeteer* lists the places mentioned in Joyce's book. "It was natural," Cage felt, "to add recordings of ambient sound from places in the *Wake* to the sounds already listed." He wanted to record at least thirty seconds of sound from each location. It seemed unlikely that Cage and Fullemann could complete the work in the time available, but Cage recalled his father's conviction that "can't" shows you what remains to be done. "If you don't have time to accomplish something, consider the work completed once it's begun," Cage suggested, explaining his attitude. "It then resembles the Venus de Milo, which manages quite well without her arms."

The task was large, and in a deft handling of different offers which characterized the artistic entrepreneurialism of his later career, Cage simplified it by condensing several other commissions and invitations into the piece. Taking up an offer from Boulez and Max Mathews, he decided that studio work could be carried out at IRCAM, the major electroacoustic center run by Boulez and located under the Centre Beaubourg in Paris. The finished work could fulfill not only the request from Schöning, but also the commission for an evening of music from the Festival d'Automne in Paris for their project "Autour de Merce Cunningham."

Cage thought that along with the text and the tape might go a third element, a circus of Irish folk music in the manner of *Musicircus*. Helen Schneyer suggested he contact the singer Joe Heaney. Fullemann, his wife Monika and Cage caught up with him in Norwich, England, at the end of April 1979. Cage gave Heaney the best description he could of the project, though he admitted that a great deal was still undecided. The singer accepted, and referred Cage to the piper Seamus Ennis.

The following month, in the midst of his tour with the Cunningham Company, Cage met Schöning in Lyon. Schöning agreed to arrange for letters to be sent to radio stations around the world to ask for sounds from the places mentioned in the *Wake*. One of the WDR staff, Peter Behrendsen, searched the station sound library for suitable materials.

Schöning wanted to know if they ought to postpone the project. Feeling that "two negatives make a positive," Cage again urged that they should do as much as they could. However, he noted, "I needed to find a way to proceed without becoming frantic or nervous." Basically the solution was to be arbitrary organization. The catalog of sounds was divided into categories; June 15 to July 15 would be spent gathering sounds in Ireland, June 15 to August 15 in the studio at IRCAM, assembling the tape.

"We went to Ireland and enjoyed every minute of it," Cage reminisced.

"Like the rest of the world it is magnificent and the people are a pleasure." He and the Fullemanns worked long hours gathering sounds, driving around Ireland in the couple's old Volvo. Ciaran MacMathuna, in charge of folk music at Irish Radio, made suggestions for musicians: Paddy Glackin for the fiddle, Matt Molloy for the flute, and the blind bohdran player Paedar Mercier and his son Mel. Cage concurred with Heaney's suggestion of Seamus Ennis for the pipes, and they found him at his trailer home, which was named, after a ballad, "Easter Snow." Cage contacted the other musicians in turn and each agreed to perform. "When I picked up the phone I thought I was talking to E.T.," Paedar Mercier recalls.

At IRCAM, the engineers were amazed to find that Cage and Fullemann began work immediately; most visiting artists took their time to acclimatize to the new environment. Their first task, accomplished in a day, was to record the mesostic text section by section. Rehearsing at odd moments in Ireland, Cage had rejected the idea of a mock Irish accent for his delivery, and plumped for a singsong intonation reminiscent of *sprechstimme*. The recording they made of *Writing for the Second Time* became the ruler by which they could place the taped sounds. "Somehow we were able to put up with it without losing our minds," Cage wrote. "The repetition of it took the place of musical theory." As they laid down track after track, Cage felt he both knew what had to be done yet had no expectation of the result: the Zen notion of purposeful purposelessness.

Roaratorio was completed on schedule and broadcast to a rapturous reception; it won the Karl Czuka prize for the year. The work has been subsequently performed live on numerous occasions, with different combinations of instruments and changes of personnel (for instance, Liam O'Flynn played the pipes after Seamus Ennis died); Cage read the text, and sometimes the Cunningham Company danced. A score was written up by Cage while in Scotland at the Edinburgh Festival in September 1979. Like the score for *Variations V*, it was written after the piece was completed, but it is more than the score to *Roaratorio*; the text functions as general instructions to convert any book into a piece of music, following the processes Cage applied to *Finnegans Wake*. The score is titled ——, —— *Circus On* ——. The first blank is the title (here *Roaratorio*), the second an article and adjective (*an Irish*, in this case), the last the title of the book from which it is drawn. Others have since produced versions drawn from local newspapers and a Scots version entitled *Realibogie – A Jacobite Circus on King James VI's Daemonologie.*

267

In January 1979 Louis Mink, the author of the *Gazeteer* used by Cage in his catalog for *Roaratorio*, wrote with some observations on Cage's mesostic writing. After reading *Writing for the Second Time Through "Finnegans Wake"*, Mink had concluded that Cage might be said to be writing impure mesostics; a pure mesostic, Mink proposed, would not let either letter appear between two of the word that formed the string.

Cage found this intriguing and tried out pure mesostic writing in *Writing for the Third Time Through "Finnegans Wake"*. Like the first, the third was not published, but was succeeded in 1980 by a *Fourth*, which follows the pure mesostic rule but resembles *Writing for the Second Time* by not permitting the reappearance of a given syllable for a given letter of the name.

Later in 1980 he began a *Fifth*, entitled *Muoyce*. Just as *Mureau* stood for Music-Thoreau, *Muoyce* stands for Music-Joyce; it is not written as mesostics, but moves according to chance operations from one part of the *Wake* to another. Like *Mureau* and *Empty Words* it omits sentences, containing only phrases, words, syllables and letters; punctuation is left out and, at frequent chance-selected points, the space between words is closed up.

Another literary project that year was *James Joyce, Marcel Duchamp, Erik Satie: An Alphabet*, a monologue intended by Cage for live delivery. It might be seen as an extension of the imaginary dialogue with Satie which he had written in 1958. Cage says he based his imagined staging on Fuller's idea that to give proper consideration to something one should begin not with one but with five ideas. He classified the possible staging by working out the possible combinations of the ghosts of Duchamp, Joyce and Satie with "non-sentient beings" (a perhaps obscure Zen reference which is his heading for stage properties) when a minimum of one and a maximum of five could appear onstage at once. The possibilities were thus each ghost alone, each with one to four non-sentient beings, the ghosts in the possible pairings with up to three other beings, or all three ghosts with one or two non-sentient beings.

The work is an alphabet in that Cage used chance operations to look up alphabetical entries in dictionaries and encyclopedias in his preparation for the work; the number of possible combinations of the ghosts and non-sentient beings also happens to come to twenty-six. However, "the piece is not an alphabet," as Cage states; the text which he wrote within these strictures "is a fantasy," a fantasy of the modernism his ghosts represent. He wanted "to remove the punctuation, so to speak, from our experience of modernism, to illustrate it with something like its own excitement." In the sudden leaps of his imagined staging, Cage makes "all those magical situations of buildings moving in and out quickly ... from one place to another, without any effort." This is a fantasy for the electronic age, of which an example in music might be *Stressed Space Palindromes* (1976–82) by Gordon Mumma, where high-speed doppler shift circuitry of his own design simulates the resonant characteristics of a room that changes rapidly in size and shape. Cage notes of his *Alphabet*, "that's the – electronic immediacy we're moving toward."

Alongside this extensive literary activity, Cage further extended his rapprochement with musical improvisation in *Improvisation Three (Duets)* and a fourth *Improvisation*, the *Fielding Sixes*, for which John Fullemann designed equipment which would continuously vary the playback speed of the three cassette machines employed in the piece. *Fielding Sixes* was premiered as the accompaniment to a Cunningham dance, with designs by Monika Fullemann, and was revived by the Ballet Rambert, designed by Mark Lancaster, in 1983. *Litany for the Whale* was completed in New York in July 1980, for two unaccompanied voices, singing as usual without vibrato. The piece consists of a recitation of the word "whale" sung with each letter pronounced separately (to D,C,B,G,A), alternating with responses made from different combinations of the letters. It suggests Cage's concern with ecology, but in a different way to that of *Child of Tree, Branches, Inlets*, the recordings of the weather for *Lecture on the Weather* or of the dawn over Stony Point which he used in *Score (40 Drawings by Thoreau) and 23 Parts* (1974). Where in those pieces his interest came across in the sound material he employed – the ambient recordings, the organic sound-sources – the *Litany* comes unusually close to being a statement.

In September Cage made what was now his fifth visit to the Crown Point Press. Realizing that *Changes and Disappearances* could be completed in his next couple of visits, he began to plan a new series of etchings. When he first lived in Seattle – probably in the course of 1939 – Cage had spent ten cents on a ticket to visit, with Graves and others, a small aquarium in the market near Puget Sound. Even if the tanks appeared empty, he was admonished, he should wait and watch. After a few moments, a clam came up from the bottom, broke the surface, and having taken some air sailed down again to the bed; its arrival disturbed others, who sailed up in turn, creating a magnificent clam tattoo.

Cage decided to call his new print series *On the Surface*, which evoked a comment made by Thoreau in his journal, "all sound is nearly akin to silence, it is a bubble on the surface which straightaway bursts. Cage wanted to achieve the visual equivalent of extreme quiet, which in turn he associated with the white writing of Tobey, and so wanted to find a group of plates with virtually no image on them. It occurred to him that he might use pieces of scrap copper, cut to shapes determined by the *I Ching*, so that the images would consist only of the shape of the plates used, and the random configuration of scratches which came with the copper, some of which would wear away in the course of repeated use. This was another acceptance of what was usually technically excluded, akin to the incorporation of foulbites and unwiped edges in *Changes and Disappearances*. Cage positioned the plates in relation to thirty-five equal horizontal sections, the top line of which became an imaginary horizon – or surface – which dropped down a section with each successive print. The plates were positioned and angled by chance; if one reached the surface, Cage divided it before it was used again, cutting it from the point where it hit the plate edge to a chance-selected point below the surface on the perimeter of the plate. What happened was that the thirty-five prints of the series began with large shapes which gradually decreased in size and increased in number.

Susan Barron had first studied music, but had been introduced to photography by the landscape photographer Art Sinsabaugh; she had begun two years of training at the University of Illinois at the tail-end of Cage's residency in 1969. In 1978 she studied in France with Paul Strand. Following her teachers, her specialism came to be landscape work. When Cage saw some photographs by Barron, he was delighted, in view of his own enthusiasm for abundance, by the way they overflowed the frame with detail, and he offered to write a text to accompany them in a limited edition.

His first plan was to marry his customary literary technique with one of his perennial themes and write mesostics on the names of the seasons. He shortly rejected that scheme, then one day in The Hague, looking out of a theater window on to a playground with a city street beyond, he thought of writing mesostics which in a sense photographed what was going on below with the empty evocation of haiku. This would have been an interesting concession of spontaneity – he did not usually create his textual materials, let alone do so on the impulse of perception – but he felt, as he was looking out over an urban view, he would not come up with anything appropriate for landscape photographs.

Finally he settled on a technique he had used before, for the libretto of *Solo for voice 35*, which appears in *M* as *Song*; each line was selected by the *I Ching* from the *Journal* of Thoreau:

The air delicious, thus we are baptized into nature
fall into the water
or lost, torn in pieces, frozen to death
thunder and lightning

The result, ten years on, was *Another Song*:

Bridging of the river, in the night, obstructing
apple tasted in our youth
state as when.

The collaboration was published by Callaway Editions in April 1981. That fall, the same publisher brought out the *Mud Book* by Cage and Louis Long.

Meantime, in August, Cage joined Cunningham and Chris Komar in presenting the International Dance Group for professional choreographers and composers, at the University of Surrey in Guildford, England. From nine until half-past ten every morning, Cage spoke informally about an aspect of his work. Then, after a half-hour break, he took a further hour and a half to prepare mesostics relating to what he had improvised earlier. He chose ten terms to serve as mesostic strings which would circumscribe his main concerns: method, structure, intention, discipline, notation, indeterminacy, interpenetration, imitation, devotion and circumstance. "Those seem to me to be the most important things," Cage stated later. "They omit, curiously enough, the word *invention*, and the word *non-intention*, or even such things as chance and so on, which mostly come in under the word *discipline*." Cage spoke each day on a different term except for, amusingly, "discipline," which ran for three talks, meaning that a correspondence could be made between the ten terms and the twelve days of the course. On the first day, Cage completed six mesostics in the allotted time and so, with characteristic imposition of discipline, adopted six mesostics as his target for the remaining days.

The mesostics Cage wrote were subsequently published as *Composition in Retrospect* and delivered on a number of occasions as a speech. Both title and content constitute a new concession to autobiographical testimony.

> the past must be Invented
> the future Must be
> revIsed
> doing boTh
> mAkes
> whaT
> the present Is
> discOvery
> Never stops

Any participant in the workshop could choose to sit in on the writing session, which thereby became a performance, rather like *0'00"*. From studying being interrupted, Cage was more and more turning to studying being frenetic, trying to turn time pressure into art.

Cage presented *James Joyce, Marcel Duchamp, Erik Satie: An Alphabet* again in 1981, and on September 25 gave an all-night performance of *Empty Words* from Real Art Ways in Hartford, Connecticut. From November 5 to 7 he attended the eighth Computer Music Conference, that year held in Denton, Texas, where it was organized by Larry Austin, the former editor of the journal *Source* whom Cage knew from his time in Davis. A revival of *HPSCHD* was presented at the conference, and Cage delivered *Composition in Retrospect*.

By the 22nd he had arrived in Pont-à-Mousson, near Metz, where the Orchestre Philharmonique de Lorraine was presenting the premiere of his *Thirty Pieces for Five Orchestras*. In this Cage was making his first, but ambitious, use of a new way of organizing chance operations which he would develop in works such as *Music for . . ., Two, Five, One* and other pieces using time brackets: multiplying simple means to reach a complex situation. He had found a new, lighter, more economical way to achieve the multiplicity he sought.

In preparing the score, Cage drew on the same images and techniques which had generated his *On the Surface* etchings the previous summer. "I enjoyed that work so much," he explained, that he decided to write the orchestral piece in an analogous way. He cut the music paper up in chance-determined ways and placed templates at points selected by the *I Ching*. All of the paper was potentially sound; the space between the staves would represent the ledger lines of one instrument or another, so every chance determination would specify a sound.

Whereas in etching, Cage noticed, the top of the paper was important and downward motion interesting, the same processes applied to music made the horizontal more interesting than the vertical, because the former corresponded to time. "I discovered that a horizontal line which determined graphic changes," he explains, "to correspond, had to become a vertical line in the notation of the music." The direction of the chance operations and what they referred to had to be altered accordingly.

The Metz premiere gave Cage one of his best experiences up to that point in working with an orchestra. Remembering the disaster with the orchestral version of *Cheap Imitation*, he had insisted that the contract stipulate ten three-hour rehearsals devoted solely to the piece. The result was doubly heartening. "About three-quarters of the way through rehearsals," Cage told Stephen Montague soon afterwards, "the musicians obviously became interested in what they were doing. So interested that they wanted to hear it. Every time they had a chance they would leave the group and go out and listen . . . The performance was excellent!"

In the course of 1981 Cage and Cunningham made time to extend their home. They bought the vacant apartment which adjoined theirs and had the wall between the two knocked in, adding a new door to the roof of the building. With more space available, Cage increased his plant collection to over two hundred.

Cage made his regular visit to the Crown Point Press in January 1982. *Changes and Disappearances* and *On the Surface*, begun in 1979 and 1980 respectively, were both completed, and he started a more simpler series, *Déreau*, which in many ways functioned to assimilate the lessons of his etching work up to that point. From February 25 to May 2 the Whitney Museum of American Art exhibited his scores and prints.

Meantime, from January 29 to 31, Cage was in Toronto presenting *Roaratorio*. He presented the work in London in May during a European tour with Grete Sultan. On the 10th of that month he presented *A House Full of Music*, a circus of non-professional music made by eight hundred schoolchildren, for the Pro Musica Nova in Bremen. And on September 5 back in the United States *Fifteen Domestic Minutes* for National Public Radio combined in a single broadcast performances in Denver, Los Angeles, New York City and Washington, D.C., thanks to a satellite linkup.

It was the year of Cage's seventieth birthday; many engagements were planned as celebrations. At Symphony Space in New York on March 13, 1982 "Wall to Wall Cage" was presented, a combination of individual and circus performances by associates such as Cunningham, Jackson MacLow, Cage's publisher Don Gillespie, his agent Mimi Johnson, the pianist Margaret Leng Tan (recently acquainted with Cage but increasingly presenting his work) and Cage himself. The audience was enthusiastic, but obviously already converted. At the Cabrillo Music Festival in California from August 16 to 25 *Dance/4 Orchestras* was premiered, a piece he had begun the previous year. For celebrations in mid-September at the Walker Art Institute in Minneapolis, Cage wrote *Postcard from Heaven* for between one and twenty harps. It was presented again on the 23rd in a celebration at the American Center in Paris. Earle Brown, who with Frederic Rzewski was present, recalls how visually spectacular was the concert; first the huge mobile and percussion setup for Brown's own *Calder Piece*, then "twenty harps, going off into the distance."

V

The Ryoanji garden was built in Kyoto about 1490: a flat plain of raked sand, with five clusters of stones rising from nests of moss; two groups of two stones, two groups of three, one group of five. By the time it was constructed, the Zen garden functioned to distill rather than represent reality, forming, thereby, an abstract focus for contemplation. Cage had visited the site during the tour he made with Tudor in the fall of 1962, and at the time he suggested to a Japanese friend that the emptiness of the sand would allow the stones to have been planted at any point in the space.

As the eighties began, Cage was growing interested in stones. He would draw up at the roadside to look at stones just as formerly he had scrutinized mushrooms. "I collect them for my garden from all over the world," he would tell Lisa Low in 1985. They incited his sense of wonder. "There are so many faces to this particular rock," he once remarked, "that it's like an exhibition of several works of art."

In 1983 Cage produced a new graphic work, *Where R = Ryoanji*, using the same number of stones as the Ryoanji garden as templates, which he drew around with pencils whose weight was selected by the *I*

Ching. The freehand use of pencils marked a new concession to gesture. Chance determined the number of stones to be used on each occasion, their placement, and the number of times each was to be drawn around The resulting drawings look fragile, as if with time light will make them fade, but chemically they are completely stable. That same year Cage crafted the twelve, rich images of *Weather-ed* (color photographs realized by Paul Barton), and, at the Crown Point Press, *HV*, thirty-six monotypes printed from soft materials – foam, jute, batting and felt. The title stands for horizontal and vertical, referring to the rectilinear structure by which he had positioned the fragments.

In September Cage completed his second string quartet, *Thirty Pieces for Spring Quartet*. It constitutes a quintessential example of his musical individualism. The four parts are without a coordinating score. Each player rehearses alone. In performance, each sits not in the usual tight proximity but far away from the others – at equidistant points around the audience, in an arc in front, or in an irregular fashion. The Kronos Quartet, to whom the work was dedicated, gave the first performance in Darmstadt the following year.

Around this time the mechanics of Cage's work were much simplified by the acquisition of his own IBM personal computer, on which he could run a new computer simulation of the *I Ching*, *I* by Andrew Culver, to replace that of Ed Kobrin, and a progam by Jim Rosenberg, *Mesolist*, to permit computer-assisted mesostic writing. Cage first made use of this in writing through Allen Ginsberg's Beat tour-de-force *Howl*, then applied it to an untitled text which he had received from the Australian poet Chris Mann. After writing through the text extracting mesostics, in ways akin to his treatment of *Finnegans Wake*, he used an excerpt for a short vocal piece, *Eight Whiskus* (1984), taking the opening line of Mann's text, "Whistlin' is did," as the mesostic string, and generating music for it which has a folk-like feel. This piece became the first of a series of solo vocal pieces which includes *Sonnekus* (derived from Genesis in the Hebrew Bible) and *Selkus* and *Mirakus* after Duchamp.

A thousand children aged between four and twelve took part in a workshop Cage gave in Torrino between May 4 and 20, 1984, building on his work with children on *A House Full of Music* two years earlier. The Olympic games that year were to be held in Los Angeles, and a great deal of music had been commissioned in celebration; Joan LaBarbara, for instance, who sang a lot of Cage's work, wrote *Time(d) Trials and Unscheduled Events*. From Torrino, Cage traveled to Cologne, where he produced his own commemoration of the Games at WDR,

HMCIEX, using a folk music from the 151 countries which recognized Olympic committees. "I wanted the feeling of 'Here Comes Everybody'", explained Cage, "and that's what the title is – the 'H.C.E.' of 'Here Comes Everybody' alternating with the letters of the word 'mix'." KUSC, Los Angeles, broadcast the work as part of the Olympic Arts Festival contemporary music program.

On July 12 Cage presented *Empty Words* in Lincoln, Massachusetts, and while in the area fitted in a visit to Walden Pond. Cathy Berberian had died; in the course of the month Cage wrote a new vocal work in her memory, *Nowth Upon Nacht*. He specifies that it be sung after *The Wonderful Widow of Eighteen Springs*; its text also comes from *Finnegans Wake*. Opened by a slammed piano lid, the text is sung with some rhythmic force in the high part of the vocal range, then the piano lid is slammed shut; it invites an emotional interpretation, by listener and performer, making it as near to expression – of rage – as Cage had come for decades. Generally only bad performances of Cage's music fill its tranquil happenstance with emotion, but in *Nowth Upon Nacht* emotion is as an ever-present element.

At the end of the following month, from August 30 to September 2, Cage was in attendance at a one-man show of his visual work at the Fruitmarket Gallery in Edinburgh, Scotland.

He began in 1985 at the Crown Point Press where he produced three series of etchings, *Ryoku*, *Mesostics* and *Fire*. *Ryoku* employs tracings of six of the stones used for *Where R = Ryoanji* over small, chance-located triangles and tetrahedra. *Mesostics* and *Fire* take elemental forces as their theme. The nine collages of *Mesostics* consist of papers glued into place along a common axis; the works can be displayed horizontally or vertically. Cage altered the papers by burying them in earth or soaking them in tea. In the third series of the year, he quite literally played with fire. The thirteen monotypes were made by burning a pile of newspapers on the press bed; as the flames licked to their peak, dampened etching paper was lowered onto the flames and turned through the press. As the fire was extinguished, it left behind its vestige of flame and smoke. Each sheet emerged with a sorched golden-brown background, sometimes with singed edges, giving an atmospheric field on which to print the etchings. The extent of the smoke made the inks appear relatively light or dark, and sometimes the firing would transfer fragments of newspaper. Each print was branded using the base of one or two Japanese iron teapots and, later in the series, large industrial piping, in *I Ching* – determined positions.

Fire is part of the process of incorporation with which Cage had been involved since the mid-seventies. In his music, he was introducing improvisation on his own terms. In his visual work, he had begun cautiously, but his use of stones and pencils contained a concession to gesture. With *Inlets* we hear the sound and in *Fire* we see the mark of fire. These changes show Cage admitting the sides of life excluded by his temperament and choices; now, in later life, he was not necessarily overwhelmed or overbalanced by them, but could admit them on the terms of who he already was.

Later in the year Cage wrote a twenty-minute piece for orchestra with voices, *A Collection of Rocks*, and *ASLSP*, a piano piece, to be played "as softly, long and slowly as possible," its title suggested by the last paragraph of *Finnegans Wake*. There were also sequels to the vocal pieces of the previous year, *Mirakus²*, *Selkus²* and *Sonnekus²*.

In August he created a work "in celebration of the work of Jan Arp on the occasion of the centenary of his birth" for the virtuostic percussion ensemble, Les Percussions de Strasbourg, bearing the pithy title: "But what about the noise of crumpling paper which he used to do in order to paint the series of 'papiers froissés' or tearing up paper to make 'papiers déchirées'? Arp was stimulated by the water (sea, lake and flowing waters like rivers), forests." This comes from a letter written by Greta Ströh, manager of the Arp Foundation, as part of an ongoing correspondence with Cage concerning the project. The score consists of ten parts, of which any number between three and ten may be used to make a performance of any desired time length (any number of repetitions may be made). Each player uses at least two, and preferably more, scarcely resonant instruments of different materials, and sound-sources which parallel the resources mentioned by Ströh: paper to be crumpled, torn or shaken like a thundersheet, pouring water or bubbling water. "The parts," Cage writes, "should be given some life by means of slight but not obvious changes of dynamics." There is no conductor; each player follows his or her own quarter-note count. As with *Thirty Pieces*, the players may be stationed around the audience, or among them if they are not seated. If the players are on a stage, they should not be close together.

Since the previous year Cage had been working on a series of pieces, *Music for . . .*, the title to be completed by adding the number of players performing. Two types of material appear in each part. There are single continuous tones, played softly and repeated at will; then there are sequences of tones, not to be repeated, consisting of diverse pitches, intensities, sonorities and durations presented in proportional notation.

Both kinds of section are contained within time brackets, which specify a duration within which the player can decide individually when to start and finish the material; the details of the music and the approximate time in which it will appear are chance-determined but this finalization in the moment is spontaneous. The result, as Cage puts it, is "a music that's earthquake proof."

Like an Oriental house made with sliding doors and panels, the different instrumental parts do not coincide in any fixed way. "Each player should prepare his part by himself and learn to play it with his own chronometer," Cage stipulates. "There shall be no joint rehearsal until all the parts have been carefully prepared." They are then to be played with each player being his or her own center, not forming a group. "The players may sit anywhere within the auditorium with respect to the audience and to each other." *Music for* . . . thus develops the musical individualism and the controlled spontaneity in Cage's work, extending his transcendentalism toward, as he increasingly began to conceptualize it, a "music without place" that reflected our social uprootedness in modern society.

Cage had tended throughout his career to draw parallels between musical idioms and social situations or aspirations. Art for Cage forms "an early warning system," the function of which is to prepare us for the world of tomorrow. The absence of place, or of security, was a new sociological parallel which increasingly he used to discourse on his work. "I think the whole harmonic structure of Western music is based on having a home," says Cage. "Wandering away from it and then coming back to it. A key, a mode, or a kind of repetitive music as we experience now, gives a sense of place. I think that's gone and what we're dealing with is an absence of that." In society, "the various aspects of all of the things that we have had, we don't customarily have any more. We're frequently on the move; things that we used to take for granted, such as home and family and so on, are gone."

These changes are paralleled by a disorientation in music, Cage says, "a feeling of not knowing where you are in sound, but rather floating; of there being no terra firma. I found an absence, not knowing where one is in the sound." Even notes generally seen as the same in different octaves cannot be associated, due, in practical terms, to displacement across the registers. This absence of place was appearing in the work of others; one composer Cage mentions in particular is Walter Zimmerman. In his own music, he felt it emerged from his new, effective way of using chance operations, multiplying simple means to achieve a complex situation, which he had begun around the time of *Thirty Pieces for Five Orchestras* (1981).

Both musical and social homelessness, as Cage puts it, are "in the air, so I think [the music]'s preparing us to be . . . homeless eventually." For Cage, music, society and the psyche of each individual are in transition. The question is what we should or can protect – not even the home offered by one's own psyche, Cage suggests. It is "more a question of how we can deal with their absence." The absence of place in music both incarnates this and develops our ability "to *do it.*"

Cage was working out his interest in the Ryoanji garden in music. Since the time he made the *Where R = Ryoanji* drawings in 1983 (and *A Collection of Rocks* in 1985), he had been preparing a series of superimposable works for single instruments, named simply after the garden. Each two pages of graphic notation, he explains, are a "garden" of sounds which should be "brushed" by the performer in and out of the field of hearing in a manner reminiscent of calligraphy, "as much as is possible like sound events in nature rather than sounds in music" (he called for the same approach in *Music for . . .*). The huge scoops and glides described by the graphics subvert the usual way the instruments present themselves since, particularly for the wind instruments, they have been designed to produce discrete, precise pitches.

Most remarkable is the percussion part, which is the one obligatory element in any performance of the work; it consists of conventionally metered quarter notes and quarter note rests. It was the first prominent use of pulse and meter for thirty years, and as with many of his recent experiments in incorporating aspects of art he had previously avoided, Cage was using them on his own terms, trying to find a way to circumvent their shortcomings. "What I wanted to do," he explained, "was to find a way not to know what the beat was, even though what I'd written would be measured. Make the measure long (twelve to fifteen beats), only five of which were to be heard. Slow the tempo down to sixty. You can't, in metrical terms . . . understand what you're hearing any more than you can when you listen to ambient sound."

Coincidentally, Cage's vanished landmark in this direction was about to be revived. Margaret Leng Tan, who had taken part in "Wall to Wall Cage" in celebration of his seventieth birthday, had discovered the score of *Four Walls* in 1984, and in 1985 presented it at the Asia Society with new choreography by Sin Cha Hay.

Along with his extensions into gesture, improvisation and meter, Cage was beginning to show an interest in redefining harmony so that it could be incorporated into the "music without place" which he was developing; the first suggestion of this movement appears in the *Thirteen Harmonies* for violin and keyboard, dating from 1986. Cage had noted with interest recent work by his longstanding colleague James Tenney, bringing harmony, as he puts it, "to a new open-ended life." "If this is harmony," Cage told Tenney, "I take back everything I've said – I'm all for it." In his own work Cage began to seek "a way of writing harmony which doesn't have rules." He says, "I'm finding a harmony. I discover that everything is harmonious and, furthermore, that noises harmonize with musical tones. And that gives me – I can't tell you – almost as much pleasure as the macrobiotic diet."

Etcetera 2/4 Orchestras, also written in 1986, updates the social allegory of Cage's music; at first a collection of soloists, the orchestral players may from time to time volunteer their services to one of four conductors, and subsequently leave the group and play again as soloists. The scoring further explores the stretched metrical time used in the percussion part of *Ryoanji*. Cage also produced *Haikai* for gamelan, and on June 8 played in concert with the improvising jazz mystic Sun Ra.

The discoveries Cage made in his work were thus characterized more and more by synthesis. The twenty-five years from, say, 1950 might be seen as the progressive period, often of strict clarification of his thinking and musical procedures, and the way they related. He had attempted to iron out all trace of his tastes, any semblance of the Dionysian. From the middle of the seventies he increasingly incorporated the elements in art which did not fit in with this main picture; improvisation, gesture, periodicity, harmony, the fire he used in his etching work. With ideas such as the "absence of place" in music, Cage was also further refining the way he construed what he did.

The rapprochement with improvisation developed further in a piece which Cage wrote in 1987 for Robert Black. A professional double bass player with a classical background, Black became interested in the new Steinberger bass guitar, which he learned of from his students, among whom it was much vaunted. He corresponded with the Steinberger president about the possibility of commissioning a showcase piece. With that agreed, Black approached Cage. Some months later Cage made time to meet Black; he was impressed – intriguingly in view of his comments years earlier on "looking at" the score of the *Concert* – by the sparse, clean and clear visual design of the instrument. Two months later he again asked to see the bass. A week later, the *cĊomposed Improvisation for Steinberger Bass Guitar* arrived for Black in the mail.

As with *Child of Tree*, the score consists of verbal instructions (this time typed) which provide the performer with a set of conditions within which to improvise. An eight-minute duration is divided into fifteen-second sections. Chance selects two from these thirty-one points in time (the thirty-second of the chart, 8″, is disallowed). The performer then takes the earlier of the two times. The times from the section which follows it up to the penultimate section (7′45″) become the frame from which chance selects two more times.

For instance, the two timings selected might be 45″ and 4′15″. The other two times are selected from times between the one following the former time (which would be 1″) and 7′45″. One might end up with 1′30″ and 6′15″. In a link to his use of time brackets, Cage has these latter two figures define not fixed starting and stopping times, but time brackets. The first section always begins at 0′0″, and runs until the first selected time, here 45″; the second begins at any time between the first and second times, (45″–4′15″); it finishes any time between the third and fourth times, (1′30″–6′15″); the third and final part lasts from the latter figure (here 6′15″) to the end (always 8′).

The performer then ascertains how many events, between one and eight, occur in each of the three parts, and a range within which the number of notes in each event must fall – each event will consist of not more than or not less than a number between one and sixty-four or, "if such latitude is not useful for the purposes of improvisation," a fixed number can be ascertained. All four strings may be used, but a different chance operation is made for each, to determine the range within which the notes of each event are to be played. "In memoriam Marcel Duchamp," these ranges are chosen by placing the numbers one to twenty-five (corresponding to the frets on each string) in a hat and drawing out two for each string. Chance also selects the settings for volume, equalization, and the pickup to be used for each event. A single, emphatic Bartok snap pizzicato is obligatory: chance determines its location by part and then event. When these specifications have been made, they constitute the "problem" around which the specific activity of the performer is open.

The Steinberger piece may be performed solo, or with either or both of two *cComposed Improvisations, for Snare Drum Alone* (the first of the three to be written) and *for One-Sided Drums with or Without Jangles*. The latter similarly consist of text instructions to furnish a set of conditions for improvisation.

In the course of 1987 Cage worked on a chance-modified film

of a chess match he played against Teeny Duchamp, *Chess Piece*. In September the Los Angeles Festival celebrated his seventy-fifth birthday with a week of concerts and events; on the 9th, at the Tom Bradley Theatre, Cage read his prize speech from high school, *Other People Think*.

VI

Once in Amsterdam, a Dutch musician said to me, "It must be very difficult for you in America to write music, for you are so far away from the centers of tradition." I had to say, "It must be very difficult for you in Europe to write music, for you are so close to the centers of tradition."

Cage learned, principally perhaps from Schoenberg, to respect the seriousness with which change was approached in the European tradition; but in his restlessness, his inventiveness, his pragmatism, Cage is American through and through.

With the exception of an avowed enthusiasm for Mozart's *Don Giovanni*, opera seemed to Cage to suggest the worst of Europe, reeking of romantic grandeur, expansive self-expression and, as a social event, conservatism, elitism and exclusivity. For all his interest in theater, it was never a style he had made his own. In the late forties Cage had been deterred in his plan for an opera based on the story of Mila Repa. That this determined man was deterred by an absent library book shows that he was quite ready to abandon expressivity and narration; it is not clear if the opera was ever begun.

In the mid-eighties Cage made an idiosyncratic, rather sardonic excursion to the citadel of European high culture in preparing *Europeras I* and *II*. There is no plot or other way of unifying the action. Cage prepared twenty-four scenarios using all the mannerisms of traditional plot synopses, but building them from fragments from other operas, producing unexpected and sometimes hilarious juxtapositions:

Dressed as an Irish princess, he gives birth; they plot to overthrow the French. He arranges to be kidnapped by her; rejuvenated, they desert; to him she has borne two children. He prays for help. Since they have decided she shall marry no one outside, he has himself crowned emperor. She, told he is dead, begs him to look at her. First,

282

before the young people come to a climax, he agrees. Accidentally, she drowns them.

Orchestra players perform fragments of operatic parts; nineteen vocal soloists sing operatic arias. As with the imaginary *mise-en-scène* of *James Joyce, Marcel Duchamp, Erik Satie: An Alphabet*, stage directions were selected by chance from Webster's unabridged dictionary; Cage designed the costumes and decor. The *Europeras* developed his characteristic concern with theater and circus. The coexistence of different activities, which was the cornerstone of his work with Cunningham even before the term interpretation was in his vocabulary, was extended across the media: lighting, decor, properties, costumes, stage action, singing, playing, and the program booklets. "For example," Cage notes, "the lighting doesn't illuminate the action; it does its own work."

"What I wanted to do," he explains, "was to have the programs such that if twelve people were sitting in a row each one would be looking at a different opera." From time to time the action is disrupted by what Cage dubbed the "Truckera" – a few seconds' snatch of a three-minute tape consisting of a forty-eight track stack of chance selections from recordings of traditional opera. This unpredictably obliterates the audibility of everything else going on, "as if," Cage observes, "you were shouting to someone on the opposite side of the street and a large truck passes by." The tape was produced in the course of an hour-long "Live Opera Mix" at the studios of WKCR, the student-run station at Columbia University, on July 27, 1987. *Europeras I* and *II* were prepared at the invitation of Heinz-Klaus Metzger and Rainer Riehm, with the assistance of Andrew Culver, and premiered in December at the Schauspielhaus of the Städtische Bühnen, Frankfurt, after arson at the Frankfurt Opera delayed the planned November opening. "For two hundred years the Europeans have been sending us their operas. Now," said Cage provocatively, "I'm sending them back."

At the Center for Computer Music in Brooklyn College in 1988, Cage made the *Essay* with the assistance of Frances White, Kenneth Worthy and Victor Friedberg, by manipulating a recording of himself reading a writing through of *Civil Disobedience* by Thoreau which he had prepared. Despite the use of the computer, the piece involved protracted labor and a dedication akin to that of the *Williams Mix*. Cage also began to write a series with number titles, beginning with *Two* for flute and piano, and continuing that year with *Five* (voices and instruments), *One* (ten systems of piano chords of varying dynamic selected by chance) and *Seven* (for flute, clarinet, percussion, piano and string trio, extending perception by "almost imperceptible" sharpenings of pitch). As in *Music for . .ʹ.* and the *Ryoanji* pieces, Cage typifies the manner of attack as "brushed" like an Oriental ink drawing, producing a music analogous to the concession to gesture in his graphic work.

Cage traveled extensively. From February 22 to 27 he was in residence at Wesleyan University for a celebration of his work and its influence as a belated commemoration of his seventy-fifth birthday. Despite suffering from influenza, he attended all of the events, mixing stoicism with his customary dedication. A large number of old friends and former collaborators took part. Those speaking included Norman O. Brown, Neely Bruce and Daniel Charles; Rita Bottoms and Deborah Campana, who ran the mycological collection at Santa Cruz and the John Cage Archive at Northwestern University respectively; Don Gillespie, Billy Kluver, Jackson MacLow, Keith Potter, James Pritchett (musicologist and husband of Frances White) and Richard K. Winslow. Among his composer friends, Lucier, Wolff and Pauline Oliveros attended. Gordon Mumma spoke and blew the horn for *Atlas Eclipticalis*; Earle Brown chaired the seminar on "Cage and Other Composers." David Tudor had planned to attend but could not; he had recently been involved in an auto accident. Pieces performed included the *Song Books, Inlets, 0'00"* and *Rozart Mix*, with a handful of pieces by other composers such as Lucier's *Music for solo performer*. Michael Pugliese performed the *Etudes Boreales* and *Ryoanji*, joined by the singer Isabelle Ganz. Margaret Leng Tan played *Four Walls*, with Ganz singing the vocal interlude; it was the first time Cage had heard the piece performed. A "Gigantic Cagean Disco" was mounted one evening, with three bands and two disc jockeys performing simultaneously.

Ray Kass taught watercolor painting at Virginia Polytechnic, and directed a workshop at Mountain Lake up in the Appalachians. Kass had studied with Greenberg and knew Morris Graves, writing a study of his work, *Vision of the Inner Eye*. He envisaged a workshop in which the use of local materials would produce art with the flavor of the locality.

When he had seen the *Where R = Ryoanji* series in 1983, Kass had been moved to suggest that Cage might like to experiment with watercolor painting at Mountain Lake. Later that year Cage went into the mountain studio, taking time for walks along the stony banks of the New River and forays with Orson K. Millar, Jr., and his wife Hope, in search of fungi. The results of Cage's experiments had been sufficiently interesting for him to agree in principle that he would undertake a series of paintings at the workshop. He sympathized, too, with the regional leanings of Mountain Lake, the dream, as Ray Kass puts it, of a time "when everyone in the Appalachians will have a picture of John Cage alongside their buckshot."

Cage finally scheduled his visit for the week of April 3 to 10, 1988. The New River is, ironically, one of the oldest courses in the Western hemisphere, and from the banks of the Richmond segment Cage picked fifteen stones, the same number, again, as those at Ryoanji. The stones, Cage decided as he prepared his scheme of chance operations, would be placed on the paper on whichever of their sides had the biggest surface area. The *I Ching* would determine the stones to be used, the choice of rag or mulberry papers, paper size, color mixes, the number of strokes and their size, and so on. At the suggestion of Tom Marioni, Cage opted to use feathers instead of brushes. Each morning, beginning on the 4th, was devoted to obtaining prescriptions from the *I Ching*, and the remainder of each day to fulfilling them, aided by Kass and several student assistants. Then, in the evenings, the team would discuss the lessons of the day's work, and the opportunities and developments they could suggest for the following day. It was a dialogue of chance and choice which refined the *I Ching* operations and thus the visual results.

In the first series, Cage was delighted with the ways his brushed tracings captured the characteristics of the rocks, but felt that the transparent wash glazes had an unfortunate effect, gathering in puddles which blotted the mulberry parchment. In the second series, he preserved open fields by choosing between a smaller number of rocks. In the final, fourth series he opened up more variables, including a wide range of brushes – for one image, the *I Ching* specified 195 paint operations. Cage produced fifty-two watercolors in all; as with his visits to the Crown Point Press, it would not be his last trip.

The work Cage carried out at Mountain Lake was typical of his endeavors in the eighties: the exploration of a new area that included approaches he had long avoided. As with the pencils of *Where R = Ryoanji*, he had been concerned that brushing with a free hand would make his work gestural; he took the risk, experimenting with "considered improvisation" in a manner which parallels his musical work. In one of the paintings of the third series, Cage included a mandala image he had dreamed the previous night. Some of his friends took such influences very seriously – Johns had begun his first flag painting because of a dream, and Feldman was a devotee of psychoanalysis – but for years

Cage had turned away from such a direction. Now he had become so secure as an Apollonian in the world of relativity that he could at last incorporate, rather than accidentally betray, glimmerings from the Dionysian realm of the Absolute.

VII

In the fall of 1988 Cage made his third major departure of the year. C. C. Stillman had decades earlier given money to Harvard University to set up a chair of poetry in memory of Charles Eliot Norton (1827–1908), a scholar widely read in the fine arts and literature. The Norton professor was to be resident for a year at the maximum salary for a Harvard lecturer, and granted reasonable freedom of travel. He or she – so far, in practice, he – was to give at least six lectures on poetry, "interpreted in the broadest sense, including, together with Verse, all poetic expression in Language, Music or the Fine Arts." It became customary that the lecture subjects for each year alternated between literature and the fine arts, including music. The Norton lectures have thus featured not only T. S. Eliot, Jorge Luis Borges, Gilbert Murray and Lionel Trilling, but also Bernstein, Hindemith, Copland, Stravinsky, Carlos Chavez and Roger Sessions. Reinhold Brinkman and Christoph Wolff proposed that Cage be the next incumbent.

So, almost forty years after his visit to the anechoic chamber, Cage returned to Harvard as a professor of poetry. It was one of an increasing number of honorary lectureships offered to him – in 1980, for example, he had been elected Regents Lecturer for the University of California at San Diego. For the title of his lecture series, Cage extended the mesostic strings of *Composition in Retrospect* from ten to fifteen: method, structure, intention, discipline, notation, indeterminacy, interpenetration, imitation, devotion, circumstances, variable structure, non-understanding, contingency, inconsistency, performance, one through six. When the lectures came to be published in 1990, commercial convenience reduced the mouthful to *I–VI*.

Cage composed a source text by making chance selections from *Composition in Retrospect*, from Thoreau's *Walden*, from one of the first texts on Eastern philosophy which influenced him, *Neti Neti* by L. C. Beckett, from Emerson, McLuhan, Fuller and Wittgenstein, and from the newspapers *The Christian Science Monitor, New York Times* and *Wall Street Journal*. He liked to refer to the source text as the "Bolivia Mix," after his abortive retirement plan, and it reads rather like the scenarios for the *Europeras* in that whole phrases are juxtaposed, making relatively meaningful and therefore humorous connections, particularly from the newspapers:

A police officer and a gunman issued a statement warning that human error was primarily responsible for the tax-fraud charges in the Persian Gulf. Unprecedented efforts for both attacks appeared to be edging towards talks in Geneva.

The fifteen terms of the title were used as mesostic strings; chance selected the number of repeats for the mesostic string within a section. Unlike his writings through, which extract mesostics from top to bottom of a text, the *I Ching* determined which parts of the source text were to be used, and where within that the mesostic word should be found. The computer program would then add words up to the value of forty-five characters on either side, which Cage trimmed at will. Each of the six lectures was composed of around 2,500 lines, which lasted approximately the scheduled hour.

In some mesostics by Cage, particularly his earliest attempts and, subsequently, when writing short occasional pieces for friends, the discipline of the string makes a puzzle which he solved by writing something which both makes sense and provides the necessary letters:

aViary without birds
(airplanE
fRom frankfurt
to basEl), hostess
recogNized me,
Asked for a poem

The mesostics of the Harvard lectures are of a different type; the words which illuminate the string are chosen by chance from a source text which was itself composed by chance, and the only choices made by Cage concern the extent to which the wing-words extending on either side of the string are to be trimmed. There can be, he had stated years earlier, a purposeless writing; the *I Ching* provides, as he envisaged in *M*, a language which can be enjoyed without being understood. This was the keynote of the writings through and particularly of a number of texts he had prepared for the eighties: *Themes and Variations* in 1982;

Mushrooms et Variationes, written when he was asked to give a talk during his brief visit to the Mountain Lake workshop in 1983; *The First Meeting of the Satie Society*, prepared between January and March 1985 and made available on the Art Com electronic network, subsequently published; and *Anarchy*, written for delivery at Wesleyan in the January before his lectures began. His work at Harvard, Cage explained, constituted the next step in an ongoing series which explored a way of writing which, though coming from ideas, is not about them, yet somehow unintentionally "brings new ideas or other ones into existence."

> In the nature of the use of chance operations is the belief that all answers answer all questions. The nonhomogeneity that characterizes the source material of these lectures suggests that anything says what you have to say, that meaning is in the breath, that without thinking we can tell what is being said without understanding it.

The unambiguous, optimistic, non-intellectual position of Cage is as implicit here as it has ever been; the purposeful purposelessness that finds the world meaningful beyond the symbols we use to discourse on it.

In publishing the lectures, Cage gave an exhaustive description of how they were produced. One may ask why he tells us that he ran fifteen files of sixteen words, that "the question would be asked fifteen times for each lecture how many times between one and twenty-eight (2 × 14) is the string to appear?" Whatever the reasons Cage has for doing so, for the reader it can be a reminder that chance composition excludes the qualitative judgments and linkages to mental states that are usually made about work; it requires that each thing be seen for what it is. One has to observe what has been done, or else simply read or listen.

The mesostic strings are structured elements which discipline the composition. Unquestionably – and significantly – the lectures are more rewarding as a spoken, and thus social, experience; if read aloud the strings go unnoticed. In performance, the content of a mesostic work will never reveal the structure.

Sometimes, as with the scenarios for *Europeras*, the chance juxtapositions make sense: "Thoreau is into being played." The *I Ching* tends to throw up more conjunctions and articles than in normal speech, and they come into corresponding prominence. Just as in *Speech* (1954), in which the same news keeps coming back, like *leitmotifs*, phrases reappear, generally in localized areas of the text. Cage characteristically insists that there are not repetitions in the strict, motor sense; the phrases return in different contexts and relationships, "very musical in effect I think," he says, and no more repetitive than to hit a woodblock a few seconds after it was struck before.

At the end of every section of each lecture, a single mesostic would be constructed by a chance selection of the words used in the preceding section, in the manner of a lecturer making a passing summary of what had just been said. The only exception to this rule was if a number 1 was selected by the chance process, in which case a word-for-word reiteration would occur; this happened once in each of the last three lectures.

In the Norton lectures, Cage again produced work which exemplifies rather than expresses its subject. As a professor of poetry he did not talk about poetry but, as part of his development as a writer, wrote it. One effect of doing so was to defamiliarize the lecture situation; the unusual experience of a usual format may stimulate others to think. This aspect of the lectures was shared with those he delivered as far back as the late forties. "If a lecture is informative," Cage told Roger Reynolds years earlier, "people can easily think that something is being done to them, and that they don't need to do anything about it except receive. Whereas, if I give a lecture in such a way it is not clear what is being given, then people have to do something about it."

It would be interesting to see what Harvard students jotted in their lecture notes. The sessions were magnificently boring; "you have the opportunity with these lectures," Cage suggested, "to discover or to pay attention to something that isn't interesting." Christian Wolff attended several of them; overall the attendance dwindled. One member of the audience described the experience as physically tiring, hypnotic, with reiterated words "like flashes of light, as they returned at different times in different combinations." Another recalls, "I was struck by its innumerable interesting juxtapositions – its free and creative energy, its meditative and centering qualities. Everything was so beautiful – each moment was so beautiful. There was no pretence, nothing overly calculated. It really worked. It was a powerful and transporting experience." Cage delivered the text with a "most temperate, peaceful, serene voice," or, as someone else heard it, "very expressive and very lovely but a little forlorn."

Since the lectures were unconventional, Cage agreed to present a standard seminar in Paine Hall a week after each one. As with most impromptu question-and-answer sessions, they meandered, and repeated questions he had been asked many times before, but the excerpts published as a foot-of-page addendum to the lectures serve as a good example of his charm in public dialogue, and give a rounded representation of his preoccupations at the end of the eighties.

While the Norton lectures were in progress, Cage prepared and appeared in two radio events at WGBH-FM, at its studios on Massachusetts Avenue, only minutes from the university; it was from here that he had made his telecast in 1971. The events were presented in October 1988 and the following April. On the first day Cage arrived six hours early because he had taken a cheap-rate flight on his senior citizen's pass. He bypassed the reception desk because a security guard had recognized him from a previous visit. "Can I work somewhere?" he asked. "It doesn't have to be quiet." His producer enquired if he would be concerned if it was quiet. "That's fine, too," he replied. They left Cage in the studio where the recording would take place.

Hours later a lighting team arrived to set up for an interview with him. He had vanished. The producer noticed that the cover was missing from the Bechstein piano which stood in the studio. They found it in the corner, with Cage wrapped up inside. Cage had been working on *101* and, he said, "it sent me to sleep."

Cage appeared live in the studio and telephone lines were opened. Dialling a certain number, listeners could speak to Cage; dialling another, they were invited to perform themselves, whether playing music, reciting poetry, or whatever. An amalgam of all simultaneous events was mixed according to *WBAI* and broadcast live.

VIII

Along with his usual belongings when he set off for the Crown Point Press early in 1989 (the Norton lectures still in progress), Cage brought some materials for a projected series: a suitcase filled with thirty stones, fifteen small and fifteen large. A porter caught sight of this aged man, frail, he figured, because he could scarcely carry one of his smallest suitcases. The porter offered him some help. "What on earth do you have in here?" he demanded when he tried the small suitcase. "Feels like a case full of stones." "That's right," answered Cage. He put them to use in *Nine Stones*, which furthers the investigations of his visual work and his growing comfort with concessions to gesture in a number of ways. Stones, in a position ascertained by means of the *I Ching*, were traced at fifteen points by freehand strokes of a chance-determined selection of twelve small or twelve large brushes, on to a background of smoked paper.

Cage also produced *Global Village* from the plates used to modify an earlier work; the title came from his feeling that the visual result suggested the isolated skyscrapers of a central American city horizon. The third series he made on that visit was *Empty Fire*, an interesting title considering the totalizing direction of his work.

In the course of the year Cage continued the number series he had begun in 1988. *101* for large orchestra, which had sent him to sleep at WGBH, was performed at Symphony Hall in Boston on April 6; it was a joint commission from the Boston Symphony Orchestra and the Fromm Music Foundation at Harvard. He also completed *Two²* for two pianos, *One²* for a pianist at between one and four pianos, written for Margaret Leng Tan, *Three*, for three recorder players using between them sopranino, soprano, alto, tenor, bassett, bass and great bass recorders, and *Twenty-Three* for strings. *Four*, for string quartet, utilizes his fondness for spatial separation. As in the first pieces of the series, Cage stresses that the instrumentalists should play not as if they were turning the sound on or off, but as if they were brushing it into existence. He wrote, too, a short piano solo, *Swinging*.

For Cunningham's dance *Inventions*, Cage produced *Sculptures Musicales*, a title derived from Duchamp. The score is to be realized using sound-sources with an invariant envelope – sounds which start "hard-edged," continue without growing softer or louder, and then abruptly stop, "so that," Cage says, "the piece is a succession of what you might call turned-on sounds, that, like burglar alarms, are just turned on and continue until they stop." The sounds are separated in space, "producing a sculpture which is resonant." Cage left it to the company musicians, led by Tudor, to select the specific sounds which they would use to fulfill these criteria.

At the end of October Cage visited London for the opening of a three-way exhibition at the Anthony d'Offay Gallery which celebrated the work of Cage, Cunningham and Johns; he thereby could enjoy a by this time rare opportunity to spend time with Johns. The following month Cage was featured composer at the Huddersfield Contemporary Music Festival in England. Among the pieces presented was a performance by Irvine Arditti of the *Freeman Etudes*. The previous summer Cage had heard Arditti play the *Etudes* in fifty-six minutes. In Huddersfield he cut it down by ten minutes. The composer asked him why he had played so fast. "That's what you say in the preface," Arditti replied, " – play as fast as possible." The duration of the regular tactus, Cage had specified, should be "as short a time-length as his virtuosity permits" (which one may infer is determined by the fastest rate at which the most difficult passage could be played). Three seconds is listed as a realistic estimate, based on work with Zukofsky, which, at 1,344 measures altogether, implies a performance lasting just over one hour and seven minutes.

The dexterity of Arditti suggested to Cage that it might at last be practicable to write the second half of the *Freeman Etudes*. He resumed the work in the course of 1989, but found immediately that he could not remember the details of the chance operations he had used. Yet he wanted the second series to remain faithful to his original conception and, indeed, to extend it, multiplying the number of questions asked. Cage passed on his notebooks to James Pritchett, one of the speakers at the Wesleyan celebration the previous year, who had been working at Princeton on Cage's use of chance operations to the extent that, Cage says, "he's learned to know exactly how I felt better than I do."

The multiplication of questions was designed to make the music more complex both compositionally and in performance. When there are more notes notated than can be played, Cage asks that as many as possible be played. Performers may, he suggests, "have to ignore, say, a whole page of notes, because in the time given it's simply not possible." This provision is reminiscent of the suggestions in work from the fifties, such as the *Ten Thousand Things*, that passages may be played "in any focus" or that discretion may be used if the notated aggregate is difficult to play. In no way, however, did Cage see it as an incidental part of the compositional process; he described it as a further step toward a music which is "getting along," as he puts it, "permitting a performance that omits a lot of the music that's written."

Cage increasingly related to his old friends in new ways. After seeing Jasper Johns at the d'Offay Gallery, he met Boulez in Huddersfield. "We can speak and talk a little," he felt, "but we're not the close friends that we were." He was growing closer again to Christian Wolff – who had frequently driven over for the Norton lectures – with only the geographical distance between them stopping them meeting frequently.

Two more *Europeras* has been commissioned, to be premiered at the Almeida Festival in London the following year and with a subsequent European tour. *Europeras III* and *IV*, while clearly related to the first two, and bringing with them features such as the "Truckera," stand in relation to them as chamber to grand opera. In *Europera III*, live singing with stage business determined by chance is accompanied, not by orchestra, but by two pianists playing from the standard repertoire, and by a handful of performers at old-fashioned gramophones with automatic feed dating from the fifties, which play old recordings of opera chosen by Cage with great care for the first performances. For the premiere tour, most of the gramophone operators were themselves composers. In *Europera IV* the staging consists of a singer, a gramophone and a dusty table lamp.

The use of gramophones suggests *33¹/₃* from 1969, or even *Credo in US*, but the flavor is very different. Cage's work was beginning to allude to his awareness of mortality, without it ever taking over as an expressive theme; *Nowth Upon Nacht* had been an example. Such an awareness could be seen as an additional feature of his use of fire. In *Europeras III* and *IV* the voices of Cage's youth, or young manhood, now long-dead, crackle out at us across the years in a decentered chorus. "The needles last for a long time," he says of the record players. "They have a beautiful sound. It's very touching." Singers can fall ill, as he also notes by way of account, "so I thought of record players taking their place, and I thought of giving a concert version of an opera." The gramophones can be interpreted, too, as an allegory of post-modernism, used as they are by a handful of young composers manipulating recordings from the classical world.

In 1990 Cage was a featured composer, alongside Nigel Osborne, Wolfgang Rihm and James McMillan, at the biennial Musica Nova festival in Glasgow, in Scotland. For his public lecture there on September 20, he delivered an autobiographical statement (like *Composition in Retrospect*, a concession to the validity of reminiscence), interpolating the speech he had already prepared for a conference on Zen and American Art which had been organized by Jeri de'Paoli for October back in the United States.

During his brief stay in Edinburgh at the time of his one-man show at the Fruitmarket Gallery in the summer of 1984, Cage had met members of the Scots folk band, the Whistlebinkies. He spent a day listening to them work through their repertoire of traditional folk instruments: the clarsach, side drum, the Scots fiddle, lowland bagpipes and wooden flute. Subsequently Cage corresponded with their flautist, the composer Edward McGuire, on the possibility of a circus of Scots music from the six players. The idea was that of his circus of Irish folk musicians in *Roaratorio*: each musician was to play as an individual, rather than as part of a group. What resulted was the *Scottish Circus*, premiered at Musica Nova. Without the additional thick texture of tape and voice which is used in the Joyce piece, the effect of the performance is spacious; tonalities are superimposed non-intentionally as players weave in and out. It can readily be criticized, on the other hand, as essentially a parasitic work: the input from Cage was minimal – he simply "signed" it, not unlike a Duchamp readymade – and so is dependent on a folk tradition with a lengthy lineage which, arguably, it denatures.

With the *Scottish Circus* as an apposite example, it could be argued that Cage's work exhibits a number of features which are both philosophically central and fruitful in their results – the spiritual program of "sobering the mind", the production of the artwork through chance operations – and that other features, such as the use of autonomously existing material (American hymns, folksong), or seeking richness and complexity by piling layers on one another, are neither central to his thought nor able to stand as particularly interesting or useful when they form the mainstay of a piece of work.

Cage's visit to the Crown Point Press in 1991 produced *Smoke Weather Stone Weather*. He traced around stones using softground, spitbite or sugarlift aquatint, employing a wider palette than for *Stones*. The paper was from Japan, handmade from natural fibers such as mulberry, bamboo and banana. Cage smoked every sheet, shifting each a little as it ran through the press, so the tracings of the stones he used were placed slightly differently from sheet to sheet. This disregard for what is known as "register" was related by Cage to making music without a conductor. The resulting prints were visually ambiguous and atmospheric. "It is difficult to know," commented Cage, "whether one is looking at smoke, stones, or seaweed, so that it all becomes as if it were a dream of some kind." The new series demonstrated further how his determined asceticism had acquired a wash of inclusiveness.

SIXTEEN

I

In the course of the eighties Cage became aware of the effects of aging. He suffered with sciatica and encroaching arteriosclerosis; a stroke left the movement of his left leg restricted. In February 1985 he broke his arm, leaving him unable "to carry much work" and with unsteady handwriting. His doctor recommended that he should not carry luggage; he began to carry it in a luggage carrier, but still found stairs a problem. Yet at the same time his pursuit of the macrobiotic diet gave him excellent general health. "I am gradually learning how to take care of myself," he told Stephen Montague. "It has taken a long time. It seems to me that when I die, I'll be in perfect condition."

Cage had been conscious of old age approaching ever since the onset of arthritis. Back in 1969 he had been claiming, "I'm on my last legs." In a letter to Hans Otte in 1971 he wrote, "I am not as well physically as I was ten years ago," and in 1973 he told Jan Hodenfield of the *New York Post*, "age is a special thing that really takes place." At this point in his life Cage made himself seem, if anything, prematurely aged; "even though I'm sixty years old and arthritic," he wrote in 1972, "I manage to play *Cheap Imitation*." "I'm getting old," he wrote in the same year. "In the winter I'm afraid of the ice." The *Diary* for 1973–1982 contains a number of anecdotes about old age; Cage began to use senior citizen concessions on transport and the like. As mentioned, evidence of his awareness of mortality can be found in his work – in *Nowth Upon Nacht* or the third and fourth *Europeras*. The fire which he began to incorporate in his visual work in 1985 is not only the fire he has set aside for so long – the fire of passion – but also fire as transitoriness and fragility.

Asked what was his biggest disappointment, Cage replied that he found the question uninteresting. "I have nothing to complain about," he said.

"I've enjoyed it, the whole thing." The prospect of death lost its sting as it grew nearer: as Cage puts it, "You see that death is not so bad after all." Back in 1970 Jacqueline Bossard had asked him how he would like to die. "That's a mystery the solution of which interests me very much," he replied. Early in 1990 Cage was asked the same question.

I have no control over that. And I can't even use chance operations! I simply have to be willing to do it the way it happens.

And I wonder if I will . . . We have no way of knowing. There's so many things that can happen.

Whereas previously Cage had felt protected, as if by a guardian angel, because he had work to do, he began to feel (by at least 1976) "that I might die in an accident or something . . . I have the feeling . . . that I've done more or less what I was obliged to do." Out of this, as he explains, came a sense of gratitude for each extra day. Asked by the magazine *Art News* to list his vices, he described them as collecting, and spreading himself more thinly. "I'm becoming interested in more things," Cage noted. "The older I get the more things I find myself interested in doing. It seems perfectly natural to open out to every single thing I possibly can do because I'm not going to be here much longer." He observed, "I'd better hurry up and be interested in whatever I can. There's no fooling around possible." He recalled the motto of Xenia's childhood club: no silliness.

Cage had become with age if anything a more eager worker, concerned to use his time more efficiently and fruitfully. He wanted to live the fullest days possible. His interest in technology had led him to describe in one of his diaries the electronic techniques used experimentally for Russian cosmonauts with the aim of reducing the time they needed for sleep; now he wished they were available to him.

With advancing years at last came recognition. Through the eighties he became a national monument in American culture, an icon of the avant-garde, an elder statesman not only of music but also of the world of modern art. Previously he had been subject to critical rejection, not to mention poverty. Now he was listened to and resources were mobilized for him, yet there was the growing danger of slavish acceptance. So many possibilities began to be opened up that the risk arose of taking on a schedule which might squeeze out the production of new work.

"I think he saw the vacuousness of fame in the seventies," one of his longstanding associates observed. "It almost seems like he's taken in by it now. It's very hard to be creative under such a schedule." The more in demand Cage became, the less time remained for new work, particularly for talks and presentations. Though convenience had not been the main reason, such economy was germinal to his reuse of passages in speeches in the late forties and fifties, and to his quest for fast methods of chance composition; later, as we have seen, he made scores out of his correspondence (*Rozart Mix*), jotted them down by hand without recopying (*Electronic Music for Piano, Child of Tree*), even on the backs of envelopes (*WGBH-TV*). As early as 1962 Peter Yates stated that "he had planned to compose a lecture . . . but had no time for it; instead he told them how the lecture would have been composed."

As Cage grew older and his fame spread, the demands on his time increased. "Every birthday that ends in a 5 or a 0 is cause for a celebration of some sort," Cage wrily observed in 1986. "When you have celebrations going on all over the world, it usually takes a year before and a year after those birthdays to get them all in. That leaves me with a year or two every five years to do my work."

Since audiences are rarely expert, Cage has for many years answered the questions with the same stories: my father was an inventor, Schoenberg used to send us all to the blackboard, Shizuko said don't take the diet too seriously. The various ways in which he recycles material begin to seem less of a freely chosen technique than a shortcut. Presentations increasingly involved material prepared for other purposes: reading the *Europeras* scenarios, or the "Bolivia Mix." Cage has frequently made his work activities into his performances. Invited to address students at Cal Arts in May 1986, he prepared a desk with writing equipment and a cooking timer, amplified the timer and set a contact microphone on the table. At long intervals he would read brief excerpts from the scenarios to the *Europeras*, which were then in progress; apart from this, his address consisted of the sight and sound of his writing and the ticking clock. Frans von Rossum asked him afterwards what he had been doing. "I was writing the bassoon part for my opera," Cage replied. "I had to use my time well and, because there was no chance to prepare a lecture, I decided to continue."

Such performances are akin to the "disciplined action . . . fulfilling . . . an obligation to others" in *0'00"*, or the sight and sound of *WGBH-TV*, yet they seem more desperate; what was added at Cal Tech was the ticking of a clock, making music of the problem.

Cage has tried to prune the calls on his time. In a letter from early 1971 he wrote, "I give as few concerts and accept as few engagements as possible," and he raised his lecturing fees to make this practicable. Yet the problem did not go away: he seems almost trapped by others' requests, implying he would like to stay at home and work but cannot.

Over the years he has begun to feel at home in the old Altman store. "I know the dishes in which I cook and I know the plants that are growing there, that I put around," Cage explains. "I look forward to being at home." Once traveling became difficult, "it's easier for me to be at home. Certainly, at home I can do better work." He feels a need for time and some space if he is to come up with new ideas. "I think, for instance," he suggested, "that I need to be at home for . . . at least three weeks with an empty head before any idea will come into it. This is an old romantic Renaissance idea, but I still have not found a way to travel around the world and have ideas." Yet he had become convinced that home is the whole world – McLuhan's global village. Rather than concluding that even in the global village he might have a need to spend some time in his own front room, he explains the discrepancy by suggesting that his feelings are lagging behind the reality of modern life. "We have changed from one culture to another with respect to traveling," Cage concludes, "but in this sense, as in many others, we tend to have one foot in a previous culture and the other in a new one."

Cage's travels result from a choice to travel as much as possible rather than as little as possible, which makes his reservations about it interesting. If one tots up the number of journeys he made between April and October 1990, for instance, he stayed in at least eighteen different places, including his home; between November 1990 and May 1991, sixteen. As a very rough average, then, Cage chose in that year to stay in a different city, often a different country, every ten days.

He has long been justly renowned for his openness and approachability. From the mid-eighties onwards, as he became particularly concerned to use his time wisely, while the demands upon it increased, he began to allocate less time than formerly for meeting people, and became more selective about those he would continue to see.

II

Four³, a thirty-minute piece for four performers written in May 1991, further developed the use of time brackets. Four activities interpenetrate with the given brackets: silence; the sound of one of twelve rainsticks (which might be seen as a nod to the simple ecology of *Child of Tree* and a citation of ethnic music); a sine tone or violin harmonic; or chance-determined variations on the *cantus firmus* and counterpoint of *Vexations*. The latter are performed very slowly and quietly on two pianos, spaced far apart (perhaps one inside and one outside the hall). There is to be no coordination between the two. The work was written as accompaniment for a new dance by Cunningham for his company, *Extended Lullaby*. It ends with the curtain to the dance or, for a concert performance, blackout.

From Yvar Mikhashoff, a frequent performer of Cage's music, including the tour of *Europeras III* and *IV*, came a commission for *Europera V*, an hour-long score for pianist, two singers, lighting and tape. It premiered in Amsterdam on May 21 and later in the month went on to Ghent and Bergen.

At the Spoletto Festival in Charleston, South California, at the end of spring, *Sounds of Venice* was put on for the first time since it was made for *Lascia o radoppia*. A longstanding copyright problem, which concerned recurring snatches of the fifties hit *Coma Prima*, had been resolved by making a blanket payment. John Kennedy, director of an ensemble specializing in the experimental music of the forties and fifties, Essential Music, performed it live with a relay onto monitors to preserve its character as a television piece.

In August a major exhibition of graphic works by Cage from the Crown Point Press and elsewhere was mounted at the Munchen Pinakothek. Other commitments ruled out a return to Mountain Lake; an exploratory visit to Les Ateliers UPIC, the computer music studio in Massy near Paris set up by Xenakis, was postponed until the following May.

1992, Cage's eightieth birthday year, began as he had booked it to go on. On the evening of January 8 he arrived at the Crown Point Press for a two-week stint, feeling fit apart from his sporadic back trouble. Within the fortnight Cage had completed three new series of etchings, *HV2*, *Variations III* and *Without Horizon*. The first of these is associated by its title with *HV* from 1983, and thereby implies horizontal/vertical. The plates used by Cage were small fragments which he found dotted around the studio; he arranged them "improvisationally" in a horizontal or vertical direction to fit tightly within the dimensions of the paper. The color of each geometric area was determined by means of the *I Ching*, using between one and six of sixty-four pigments or inks to hand. Each plate was covered with a lightly etched aquatint to protect it and hold the tone; this inclines the prints toward pastel hues.

Variations III relates to two earlier series of visual *Variations* made by Cage at the Crown Point Press beginning in 1987, using his now characteristic smoked paper and an *I Ching*-determined number of brands from a red-hot iron ring or iron bar. At his request, the paper was not plattened prior to printing, leading to creases which give the prints a three-dimensional effect. The series consists of fifty-seven images, a number suggested by the amount of Roma paper available at the press. Cage carried the number over, as a convenient limitation, into the third series of his visit: in *Without Horizon* he drew around fifty-seven edges of thirteen of the stones he had used for earlier works. Chance operations were used to ascertain which edge was to be traced, which of thirty-six brushes or other traditional or improvised drawing implements were to be used, and which technique was to be employed (drypoint, sugarlift, hardground, softground or spitbite). Cage used twelve different black pigments on ("coincidentally") fifty-seven pieces of handmade, smoked paper.

After his visit to the press, he made a brief trip to Seattle, then spent a week in Stanford as a Marta Sutton Weeks Distinguished Visitor at the Humanities Center. An exhibition in the Art Gallery had begun on December 10 and continued until February 9. Cage and Kathan Brown gave an informal talk on January 27, followed by music performed by, among others, Gordon Mumma. Norman O. Brown appeared in a panel discussion the following day on the place of Cage in American culture. Later in the week the composer performed *Muoyce, James Joyce, Marcel Duchamp, Erik Satie: An Alphabet* and (on January 28 and 30) *Here Comes Everybody: Overpopulation and Art, Part I* and *Part II*, a reflection of his social and political concerns in an up-to-date form.

Cage employs "Overpopulation and Art" as a string for forty fifty-percent mesostics. Unlike the last few excursions into mesostic-based lectures, the text, while it does not develop arguments at length, makes statements in the usual sense of the term:

> Of . . . niksa gligo wrote from Zagreb to say
> the ugly jugoslaVian war is not
> bEtween people
> it has been bRought about by
> that Part
> Of government'n'army that's concerned
> with serbian Power
> let oUr friends
> and aLl others know the truth this's not
> ethnic nor civil wAr

                nor differenT
          ways of thInking this's an imperialist
                    pOlitical
            aggressioN

                    Are you
                    iN to fax
                    anD
          electronic mAil
                    aRe you
                in Touch hce

There are also, for the first time, affirmatory allusions to sexual politics ("overcome the patriarchal thinking," "discussions about sex overcoming repressive structures").

In the course of the previous decade Cage's thinking on social matters had become less hopeful, turning him, as he said of Fuller, from a prophet of Utopia to Jeremiah. "We are under the control of precisely those things that the arts would like us to become free of; and we are under that control almost hopelessly," Cage felt. "I hate to say something like that because I haven't had much training as a pessimist. But I think it's evident from the media and the news that something like that is happening." World affairs are conducted in foolishness; what is needed, suggested Cage, is a little intelligence, which is scarcely in evidence.

"Perhaps it will change," he opined, "but after some awful pain, which will be a world pain. Then people will finally realize that something has to be done. But the Lord knows what form the pain will take." "And," Cage concluded for the first time, "music has little effect upon this situation."

III

Cage knows that his works will outlast him. "I'm afraid they will," he has stated. At times he implies it is regrettable. "I've now done so much work in so many different directions that it would be very hard to ... get rid of it now. Even for me, say I decided I wanted to get rid of it, that would be impossible – there's too much, and now too many copies." He foresees that after his death a decline in interest will take place, and subsequently a revival. He has little interest in posterity, but a clear idea of what will happen.

His focus of interest, as ever, is with what is in his power – what he does now and next. "My own concern now is to live as long as I can," he explained, "to do as much work as I can, and to let my work that is already finished live, so to speak, its own life."

Cage has lived through a time when the "avant-garde" meant what it said. As the twentieth century nears its end, there is no avant-garde of which to speak: the term has come to refer to a mid-century movement, and not to each successive advance on received artistic wisdom. Indeed, arguably times from the eighties have been recuperative rather than revolutionary.

Cage remains keen to discover and promote the work of young composers. Since he does not have a stereo system, he does not listen to tapes, but he enjoys new music in concert. In the work of Walter Zimmerman, he notes a similar absence of place to that which he finds in his own music. While presenting the Norton lectures Cage had met William LePage from Baltimore, whom he considered "a very gifted young composer"; he seriously considered making the young man his assistant.

It is Cage's view that the future of music is open-ended and diverse. In keeping with his respect for other centers, he celebrates the variety this entails. He predicted in the sixties "an increase in the amount and kinds of art which will be both bewildering and productive of joy." When he was a young man, he says, there were only two serious directions available for a musician: Schoenberg or Stravinsky. Today "the main stream has gone into delta. And beyond that into ocean. Now you can go in any direction at all, even your own." He suggests, "Music, instead of going in one direction, is going in many unpredictable directions. There are more people composing and more ways of composing. They seem to me to be increasing in number. That's what I mean when I say that I don't know what's happening. Now I think it's more like a French pastry situation – you don't know which way to go."

Whether or not it is going somewhere, art will continue to change. "History will be a cycle of changes," proposes Cage. "I like to think of history as remaining the same all the time. Having a richness of differences in it – all of the time." One can find, in recuperative times, a certain lack of integrity and engagement among artists, which leads to partial and rather cosmetic syntheses; meantime flashes of clarity and originality continue to appear. Cage has arguably exhausted the mines of non-intentional art; maybe he has not. He both shows and proposes that each person proceeds with his or her work as they see fit. Whatever

302

happens, it will not be what we expect, which is why life can be so enjoyable.

IV

"The situation of being constantly on the brink of change, exterior and interior, is what makes the question that has been asked difficult to answer. One never reaches a point of shapedness of finishedness. The situation is in constant unpredictable change." Asked to predict his most important legacy, Cage suggested it might be "having shown the practicality of making works of art non-intentionally." That may be the bequest of Cage as Cage. Around his work polemics will rage. Arguments will continue about categories – about what it means for our ideas of beauty, of music, of the task of music analysis. Studies will go on, concerned with the social, cultural, historical location and significance of his work. This will gloss the ineluctable, invisible way a place will be accorded for Cage's work and thought.

There is also the legacy of Cage as a human being. There is a generally applicable message in what he has done. "Put your faith not outside of yourself," counseled Cage, "but inside yourself and in your energy and put that as close to zero as possible. Work from your own center." It is not "essential" to be an artist, he reflected. "People can be plumbers or street cleaners or be like artists if they do their work as their lives; what and how they do makes how they live, and gives them the love and pleasure of living."

Cage's integrity is exemplary: his commitment and discipline, the continuity between his ideas and his life, the spiritual grounding of his work. When he is considered simply as a human being, his position has its shortcomings as well as its advantages, but he not only nurtured his strengths but also capitalized on his weaknesses. Some facets of his personality are excluded; they have been evident, but have not destroyed what he does. His ideas and practices have gradually been made adequate to, and have clarified, his inclinations. It is this personal, internal success which is his broadest, unshakable bequest.

How this has come about is, as ever, ineffable, however many facts one collects or collates, however much time one expends on breaking down and building up theory, however many friends one interviews and libraries one visits. Every dimension has its place, and each person develops an understanding of the relations between those dimensions as they work through their lives. Chance and choice: the facts of Cage's upbringing, his broader socialization, his juncture in history, the cultural climate, the serendipitous meetings – the factors of intrinsic faculties, will, determination, freedom and grace.

"Where do you think we're headed now?" Cage was asked. "I think," he replied, "that each day we . . . we wake up, huh? . . . headed towards a better situation than we hear in the news." Cage reminds us that life is both mysterious and "productive of joy." One of his widest lessons is thus ethical – in the classical sense of proposing a technology of the self, a way of relating to oneself and one's actions.

Supreme good fortune! We're both alive. "It's not futile to do what we do," affirmed Cage. "We wake up with energy and we do something. And we make, of course, failures and we make mistakes, but we sometimes get glimpses of what we might do next." Life is so good once one gets one's desires out of the way and lets it happen of its own accord.

"Nichi nichi kore ko nichi," as Cage quotes, "each day is a beautiful day."

Lincoln and Southampton
1991–92

SOURCE NOTES

Interviews and discussions between the author and John Cage or his associates are not credited here, except where the context makes attribution ambiguous; they are identified in the text by the use of the present tense before the quote (for instance, "says Cage," "explains Brown").

Titles and publication details for the works of authors named below will be found in the Bibliography. For books by Cage, the following form has been used (full details appear in the Bibliography):

EW	Empty Words (1979)
FB	For the Birds (Cage and Charles, 1981)
M	M (1973)
S	Silence (1961)
YM	(A Year From Monday 1967a)
X	X (second edition, corrected, 1987)
I–VI	I–VI (1990); punctuation has been added to excerpts from *I–VI*.

Preface
p.5   What is to be said: Appleton and Perera, p.326.

p.9   I once asked Aragon: Cage talking in Glasgow, Scotland, September 20, 1990.

Prelude
p.12   I have a horror of appearing: *New York Times*, September 3, 1972.

     I spend most of the day ... It's not that I have my nose: Montague, 1985.

     If I, for instance, have: Darter, 1982.

p.13   Chess is not the place: Cage talking at the Tate Gallery, London,

January 19, 1991.
I like it better: *I-VI*, p.306.
Get out of whatever cage: *M*, p. 212, *FB*, p.239.
I'm devoted: Reynolds, 1962.
If my work is accepted: Cage in Gena and Brent, 1982, p.170.
we get more done: *S*, p.220, see also *M*.

p.14   Two people making same: *M*, p.8.
I am not interested: *Art and Architecture*, April 1960.
he had what has never appealed: Kostelanetz, 1988, pp.13–14.
The world, for Cage: *X*, p.158.
there is no reason why: *I–VI*, p.233.
I have the feeling: Sumner et al, 1986, p.21, ellipses original.
the gift of a sunny disposition: *YM* p.x.
supreme good fortune: *M*, p.69.

p.15   the ten ox-herding pictures: see Reps, 1971.
The question is: *YM*, p.113.

One

p.17   I'm an Englishman: Montague, 1985.
was named a trustee: *Tyler's Quarterly* V, p.171; see Freeman's
biography of *George Washington*, vol.1, pp.494–5.
fought in the Eighth: see Gwathmey.

p.19   a man of extraordinary puritanical righteousness: Goldberg, 1976.
Sadie: on Aunt Sadie see *X*, pp.160, 161, 163, 166, 168, 169.
I've never been able to remember his name: *X*, p.160; *M*, p.102.

Two

p.20   a touch-key finder: patent no. 943108, December 14, 1909.
radio powered by alternating current: Cage in Kostelanetz, 1988,
p.2.
Cowell . . . called it his favorite drink: *I–VI*, p.323.

p.21   it would assume a charge: Cage in Cordier, 1973.
The problem then to be solved: author interview with Cage.
spoken of his father, generally as an inventor: the earliest reference
seems to be *Rockland County Journal News*, September 21, 1955.
Cage's father went bankrupt: Goldberg, 1976.
held in the name of his wife: Earle Brown, interview.

p.22   court reporter: see Gena and Brent, 1982, p.154; on Crete's career,
see Binheim, 1928.
a good one between bad people: Cage in Peyser, 1976.
I see a boy it is a good boy: in the Cage Archives at Northwestern

University, Evanston, Illinois; reprinted Charles, 1978, p.73.

He hasn't any conceit: preserved in the Cage Archives.

first examples of bussing: *Los Angeles Times*, March 28, 1976.

p.23 the place was full: *Los Angeles Times*, March 28, 1976.

Cage recalled that the pavement . . . while he revived: *S*, pp.263, 88.

p.24 I love this machine: *S*, p.85.

The general feeling: Tomkins, 1968a.

but I became more interested in sight-reading: Goldberg, 1976.

Music the Whole World Loves to Play: It has not been possible to trace a tutor with this title. The nearest approximations are Harold Dixon, ed., *Music the People Play*, from the early years of the century, and three collections edited by A.E. Weir and published in the Whole World series by Appleton: *Piano Pieces the Whole World Plays* (1916), *Modern Pieces the Whole World Plays* (1917) and *Concert Pieces the Whole World Plays* (1923). For the historical background, see W.A. Fisher, *150 Years of Music Publishing in the United States*.

For a while I played nothing else: Tomkins, 1968a.

p.25 These were still the pioneering days of wireless: on the history of early radio, see John Dunning, *Tune in Yesterday* and George H. Douglas, *The Early Days of Radio Broadcasting*.

p.26 The Dream Factory bought into radio: see Michele Hilmes, *Hollywood and Broadcasting*.

p.27 Cage began his radio career: see *YM*, p.132, and Fleming and Duckworth, 1989, pp.272–4.

Three

p.28 I had what was called a beautiful touch: Fleming and Duckworth, 1989, p.15.

as a teenager Cage played Chopin: *Christian Science Monitor*, March 9, 1970.

p.29 teachers putting needles down: *I–VI*, p.58.

Progress in such a way as to imply: *YM*, p.109.

what Hans Keller referred to: Keller, 1980, p.19.

I believed that what they said: *I–VI*, pp.196–7.

I remember having a kind of sinking feeling: Tomkins, 1968a.

I didn't have the desire: Fleming and Duckworth, 1989, p.17.

I can't keep a tune: *YM*, p.118.

he cannot recall melodies: Fleming and Duckworth, 1989, p.16.

p.30 The whole pitch aspect of music eludes me: Gillmor, 1976, p.19.

they were jealous . . . The real Boy Scouts . . . were very

ostentatious and pushy: Fleming and Duckworth, 1989, p.273.

p.31   he allowed it to be reprinted: in Kostelanetz, 1971, pp.45–9.

mentions it in his later writings: for instance *EW*, p.5.

the notion of turning the other cheek: Lanza, 1971.

The feeling is not familiar to me . . . a guardian angel: Goldberg, 1976.

Built in 1921 . . . : see *Southwestern Builder and Contractor*, September 16, 1921, p.15, col.1.

p.32   fascinated . . . in and around the church: *S*, p.271.

Reverend Tettemer: Los Angeles City Directory 1930, p.2386; see 1931, p.2609.

There are many . . . and father: *S*, p.271.

Neither of us knew anything . . . more than I do!: *Christian Science Monitor*, September 9, 1972.

p.33   Verlaine Medawering . . . and grimy pages: 'The Immaculate Medawering,' *Manuscript*, January 10, 1930, pp.11–14, 31.

writing is one of the ways: *Ka Leo Hawaii*, April 17, 1964.

I merely proved that I possess: Kostelanetz, 1971, p.52.

I was in the predicament: *Ka Leo o Hawaii*, April 17, 1964.

p.34   a hundred students could read a hundred: see *M*, p.61.

it "revolted" him: Tomkins, 1968a.

we could all sit . . . the same thing: *Los Angeles Times*, March 28, 1976.

If I could do something so perverse: Tomkins, 1968a.

I got an A: ibid.

Does not plan: Kostelanetz, 1971, p.52.

Four

p.35   I was struck first of all: Tannenbaum, 1985.

I preferred the flamboyant: "flambuoyant" in the original, *YM*, p.113; see *S*, p.261.

For between six weeks and a few months: Cage gives various accounts in, for example, *YM*, p.114, *S*, p.261, Tannenbaum, 1985.

Ernö Goldfinger: on Goldfinger see *Architectural Review* CLXXIII no. 1034 (April 1983), pp.44–8; CLXXVIII no.1064 (October 1985); James Dunnett and Gavin Stamp, *Ernö Goldfinger: Works 1* (London: Architectural Association, 1983). An Ernö Goldfinger Archive is held by the Royal Institute of British Architects.

p.36   measuring the dimensions of rooms: *S*, p.261, *YM*, p.113.

took only one or two lessons: depending on the account one follows

– Fleming and Duckworth, 1989, p.16; Tomkins, 1968a, p. 79;
Peyser, 1976, p.56.

p.37   I found myself at an intersection: *FB*, p.131.
Mallorca: *I–VI*, p.135.
if other people could do things like that: Gillmor, 1973.
he also wrote an *Allemande*: *S*, p.234.
songs from Ecclesiastes: Frans van Rossum discovered them in 1989.

p.38   dissonance was as *comprehensible* as consonance: Schoenberg, 1964, letter 192, p.218.
This was not intended as a hegemonic style: ibid., letter 204, p.236.
he was writing as he had: ibid., letter 95, p.124.
twelve-note *compositions*: ibid., letter 143, p.164.

p.39   a contained electrostatic field . . . and drinking water: *M*, p.137.
Since the black days of 1929 . . . eleven million in 1932: figures from Brogan, 1986, pp. 527, 534, 528, 531.
I didn't want to be a professor: *FB*, p.69.
I promised to learn faithfully: White, 1978.
In this way I taught myself: Gillmor, 1976.

p.40   I came out of these lectures: White, 1978.
those twelve tones were all equally important: Gillmor, 1976.
absolutely fundamental character of time: *FB*, p.71.
especially in music . . . to it: *S*, p. 273, *FB*, p.71.

p.41   Since then, I have always considered time: ibid.
Buhlig was a wonderful, cultivated man: Tomkins, 1968a.
It was love at first sight: Kostelanetz, 1988, p.7.
no silliness: *S*, p.271.
She was put off a little bit: Kostelanetz, 1988, p.7.
She said she'd have to think: Tomkins, 1968a.

p.43   I washed all the dishes . . . chop wood: *YM*, p.88.
pp.43–4 she looked the other way . . . and left the hall: ibid.
squintings at the landscape: Tomkins, 1968a.
What was interesting to me then: Adam, 1989, p.50.
Buhlig had meanwhile decided: *FB*, p.70.

p.45   When I first met John Cage: Cowell, 1952, pp.123, 124.
Henry Cowell looked: *FB*, p.70.
In the thirties we didn't take Bartok: Hertelendy, 1982; cf Cope, 1980, *S*, p.71 and *YM*, p.41.
Adolf Weiss: see Weiss, 1958.
He was such a bitter: Fleming and Duckworth, 1989, p.26.

one should never consider one's compositions: for example, *YM*, p.22.

Weiss got very angry: Montague, 1982.

p.46   washing walls: interview. See *S*, p.268.

I saw the same people: Gagne and Caras, 1976.

Five

p.47   He wasn't tall and he had very poor taste: Goldberg, 1976.

I didn't study music: Fleming and Duckworth, 1989, p.27.

1933: Goldberg, 1976.

p.48   public fantasies ... he never came to "study" with him: Keller, 1980.

I studied counterpoint at his home: Tomkins, 1968a.

I saw in him an extraordinary: Hertelendy, 1982.

Studying with him meant believing: Gagne and Caras, 1976.

Cage marched indignantly: Goldberg, 1974.

about nine solutions: interview; Dufallo, 1989.

p.49   he simple ascended: ibid.

He once instructed a student to play: *YM*, p.46.

a long fugue subject: Peyser, 1976, p.57.

he had named, among others, Lou Harrison: Schoenberg, 1964, letter 202, p.234.

p.50   has absolutely nothing in common: Griffiths, 1981, p.4.

I enjoyed it, but where are you going: *S*, p.264.

p.51   I'd read Cowell's *New Musical Resources*: quoted Peyser, 1976, p.56.

I was moving bits of colored cardboard: Kostelanetz, 1988, p.8.

p.52   That set me on fire: ibid.

He started me on a path: Fleming and Duckworth, 1989, p.19.

I was not inclined towards spiritualism: Peyser, 1976, p.57.

p.53   I stand by my work, always: Schoenberg, 1964, letter 131, p.154.

In that case I will devote my life to beating: *S*, p.261.

p.54   Maybe this is what I've been doing: Tomkins, 1968a.

I had studied harmony with Weiss: typescript c. 1940 in the John Cage Archive, Northwestern University.

The reason that I couldn't be interested: Gagne and Caras, 1976.

saw the *New Music* publication of percussion: typescript c. 1940, op. cit., italics added.

My purpose in teaching you: various sources including interview; *YM*, p.45; Goldberg, 1976.

Six

p.56   an annexe which held the radio station: Fleming and Duckworth,
        1989, p.271.

p.57   Morris Graves: see Kass, 1983.

p.58   read "the Ondt and the Gracehopper": *EW*, p.133.
        Six feet four, mind a whirlwind: *EW*, p.103.
        One day he drew up to a luncheonette: *YM*, p.138.
        hamburger or a lettuce sandwich: ibid.; *EW*, p.102.
        A crowd gathered, expecting: *YM*, p.138.
        The Purification of Cardinal Pacelli: *EW*, p.99.
        had a great effect on my way of seeing: Kostelanetz, 1988, p.174.
        He would continually stop to notice something: *FB*, p.158; see also
        M, p.187 and Kostelanetz, 1988, p.74.

p.59   It was the first time that someone else had given me a lesson:
        FB, p.158.
        Waiting for the bus . . .: *M*, p.190.

p.60   what was needed was a music of noise: *M*, p.xiii.
        All sounds are useful in music: *Vassar Chronicle*, March 21, 1949.
        directing their search towards those fields: *Quest*, February
        16, 1940.
        the particular part moving a step forward or backward: on
        this technique see Griffiths, 1981, pp.4–5, with an analysis
        of the *Trio*.
        whereas, in the past, the point of disagreement: *S*, p.4.

p.61   emphasize the structure at the beginning: Peyser, 1976, p.58.
        musical structure is geared to lengths of time: Griffiths, 1981,
        p.11.
        may have suggested to Cage an analogous process: ibid.
        It's not the rhythmic structure that I was concerned with: Dufallo,
        1989.

p.62   silence can be specified only as a duration: *S*, p.167.
        Curiously enough: *S*, p.79; see *M*, p.24.
        I'm always introducing silence: Montague, 1985.

p.63   find another word: *S*, p.190.
        organization of sound: *S*, p.3.
        "experimental music" troubled him: *S*, p.7; Cage notes there that
        he changed this view by the fifties.
        imitate traditional instruments: *S*, p.4. The Israeli composer Josef
        Tal, for instance, recalls attempts made in 1920s Berlin to play
        Haydn quartets using primitive oscillators (interview with Mark

Doran, lent to the author by the latter).

Marinetti had used sound effects: Ernst, 1977, p. xxviii.

p.64   which should give rich possibilities: Cage to George Antheil, September 17, 1940.

I believe that the use of noise: *S*, pp.3–4, edited according to Cage's manuscript in the John Cage Archive.

Art shows us how to adapt: Measham, 1976.

People may leave my concerts: quoted in *Time*, February 12, 1943.

p.65   using records on the turntables as instruments: see *I–VI*, p.169.

Imaginary Landscape No. 1: on the piece, see the thesis of William Duckworth.

p.67   the formalist approach of constructivism: see *Whitman College Pioneer*, January 11, 1940.

Paul Griffiths has suggested: Griffiths, 1981, p.11.

I am doing everything I can: Cage to Antheil, September 17, 1940.

p.68   did not have the resources: Kostelanetz, 1988, p.10.

Seven

p.69   I knew that wouldn't work for *Bacchanale*: Tomkins, 1968a; compare Peyser, 1976, p.58.

what was wrong was the piano: Dufallo, 1989.

He used a darning egg: *EW*, p.7.

He got an idea by knowing my own things: Cowell, 1952, p.54.

p.70   I was delighted to notice: *EW*, p.8.

Notation became a way: *FB*, p.160.

I invited Mark Tobey and Morris Graves: Montague, 1985.

p.71   a few lines to Syvilla Fort: from *EW*, p.10.

p.72   the recreation project: see Cline, 1939.

p.73   I was not allowed to make any sound: Gena and Brent, 1982, p.170.

I got along best with the Chinese: White, 1978.

Before I knew it, I was hearing music: *I–VI*, pp.64–5.

I think the teachers in the real school: *I–VI*, p.66.

p.74   The more egos you have, the better chance: *FB*, p.142.

p.76   It doesn't take much skill to smash a beer bottle: *San Francisco Chronicle*, July 28, 1939.

I can only say that we went thru all this: *Chicago Daily Tribune*, March 2, 1942.

newest rage among the musical intelligentsia: *Chicago Sun*, February 20, 1942.

American Magazine: July 1942, p.71.

p.77   I wanted to produce a musical continuity: *FB*, p.193.

p.78   *The City Wears a Slouch Hat*: see Fleming and Duckworth, 1989, pp.276–7.

We would come to New York. Cummings, 1974

p.79   Oh, it's you: *S*, p.12.

making it suddenly as "brilliant" as Paris: Dufallo, 1989.

Somebody famous was dropping in: Tomkins, 1968a.

I might become an artist after all: ibid.

the first duty I felt: Dufallo, 1989.

I knew that if she said that: ibid.

p.80   we didn't want your husband's work . . . as an insult: ibid.

She didn't turn any lights on: Shapiro, 1985.

but his presence was such that I felt calmer: Goldberg, 1976.

p.81   John Steinbeck . . . took the couple: *FB*, p.217; Kostelanetz, 1988, p.12.

On December 7, 1941: I owe the two anecdotes which follow to Brogan, 1986, pp.582–3.

Had I been drafted, I would not have refused: Lanza, 1971.

p.82   *The Wonderful Widow*: see *EW*, p.133.

p.83   I discovered that no matter: Cummings, 1974.

Amores is intended to arouse: *Time*, February 12, 1943.

Amores strikes perhaps the last note in the romantic era: Lou Harrison in *Modern Music*, May 1944, pp.236–7.

Eight

p.84   one young speaker . . . was censured: Norman O. Brown to the author, January 30, 1992.

everyone was so busy with his own schedule: Dufallo, 1989.

p.85   chic Sutton Place: see *Junior Harper's Bazaar*, June 1946, reprinted in Kostelanetz, 1971, pp.84–5.

my mother had the idea: *FB*, p.38.

something that was together: Adam, 1989, p.26; Tomkins, 1968a.

a set of whispers about some unknown plot: Lou Harrison in *Modern Music*, May 1944, p.236.

a big piano piece I wrote in the forties: recounted by Gordon Mumma, conversation, November 1990.

p.86   deft . . . has an ancillary meaning of "quiet": *Shorter Oxford English Dictionary*, vol. I, p.509, col. 3.

p.87   a willow in its flexibility: ibid., vol. II, p.2552, col. 1.

It must have been around 1945: *FB*, p.116.

I was never psychoanalyzed: *S*, p.127.

I always had a chip on my shoulder: ibid.

the things we know about Freud: 1972 file in the John Cage Archive.

p.88 and then in the nick of time: *S*, p.127.

I had poured a great deal of emotion into the piece: Tomkins 1968a; Peyser, 1976, p.59.

p.89 performed for me the function: Kostelanetz, 1988, p.13.

Gita Sarabhai: see *S*, p.127.

had been attracted by . . . Nbudi music: *M*, p.132.

the similarity . . . to the *tala*: note for the disc recording of the 1958 Retrospective Concert.

The solution of rhythmic structure: Fleming and Duckworth, 1989, p.40.

p.90 the purpose of music is to sober and quiet the mind: see *S*, pp.158, 226; *EW*, p.181; *X*, p.131.

And I believe it is true: *UCLA Daily Bruin*, November 11, 1955.

this *was* the proper purpose of music: Tomkins, 1968a.

art arouses religious emotion: quoted *YM*, p.56.

This is the traditional reason for making music: O'Driscoll, 1982, p.79.

All art . . . has shared this same basis: Tomkins, 1968a.

Music is edifying: reprinted in *S*, p.62.

p.91 imitate nature in her manner of operation: *S*, p.100; *YM*, pp.18, 31 and cf 59.

Our understanding of what this means . . . changes: *YM*, p.3.

At the center was tranquility: Mazo, 1983.

p.92 My first reaction was to express this idea: Peyser, 1976.

On this evidence, Cage could have been one: program to the Huddersfield Contemporary Music Festival, England, 1989.

Contemporary reviewers compared the writing: *New York Herald Tribune*, May 20, 1947.

Activity involving in a single process: *S*, p.63.

p.93 to four of his close friends: *YM*, p.73.

measured to fill exactly: *FB*, p.193.

Woody Guthrie . . . wrote: letter of July 10, 1947.

Nine

p.94 to integrate a man's total faculties: *Black Mountain College Bulletin*, VI, p.4.

p.95 He knew in his loneliness and in his courage: letter from Cage to *Musical America*, December 15, 1950.

With Beethoven the parts ... had been deadening to the art of music: quoted in Tomkins, 1968a.

p.96   I do something that resembles the lack: ibid.
       It was marvelous when I first met Rauschenberg: *FB*, p.157.
       backing away to leave, they discovered: *EW*, pp. 96–7; Kostelanetz, 1988, p.14.

p.97   Nancarrow ... attended: Gagne and Caras, 1976, p. 293.
       the first eight, the twelfth and the last sonatas: Dunn, 1962.
       constant use of the pause: Virgil Thomson in *New York Herald*, April 15, 1946.

p.98   Cage was very near to producing: Griffiths, 1981, p.20.
       As one practitioner has put it: Margaret Leng Tan, interview.

p.99   "Oh no," Milhaud corrected: see Tomkins, 1968a.

p.100 I couldn't help but be stupefied: *FB*, p.180.
       The circle around Boulez: Peyser, 1976, p. 60.
       Schoenberg had requested a grant: Schoenberg, 1969, letter 200, pp.231–3; see MacDonald, 1987, p.48.
       It was savage: *EW*, p.80.
       the respectable Schoenbergian credentials: Peyser, 1976, p.61; the lecture by Boulez is reprinted in Boulez and Cage, 1990, pp.41–8.

p.101 talked seriously of ... founding a dance company: see *Le Parisien*, August 17, 1949, p.2.
       identical with the dance: *S*, p.88.
       now maintains that dance and music should: *Dance*, March 1946, p.53.

p.102 An old shoe would look beautiful: *YM*, p.133.

p.103 He's built up a group: Cowell, 1952, p.95.
       Had you heard Marya Freund: *S*, p.126.
       the old proportional principle: Griffiths, 1981, p.22.
       Tibetan saint: Montague, 1985, p.212.

p.105 a person cannot be more than single: *S*, p.64.
       the *String Quartet* is "about" the Indian notion: Gagne and Caras, 1982.
       An Irish hero whose mother had died: *YM*, p.138.

p.106 the following willy-nilly of a ball: Gagne and Caras, 1982.
       the inclusion there of rigidly scored: *S*, p.25.
       it's a kind of music which doesn't depend: Gagne and Caras, 1982.

Ten

p.107 He is neither a monk: Sargeant, 1957.

p.108 from the late forties, until at least 1957: ibid.
a spell at the University of California at Berkeley: see Miles, 1990.
He loves to go to the movies: Sargeant, 1957.
1952 has been corroborated: by Earle Brown, in interview with the author.

p.109 Suzuki never spoke loudly: *S*, p.262.
He remembers three lectures in particular: ibid.
good if you were looking for a guru: W.T. de Bary, interview.
he had heard Nancy Wilson Ross: interview; *S* p.xi.
Zen in English Literature: *S*, p.143.
in a circle that included Joseph Campbell . . .: see *YM*, p.72.
reservations about Cage's apparent use of Zen: *FB*, p.107.
I didn't study music with just anybody: Fleming and Duckworth, 1989, p.27.

p.110 they fulfilled for him the function of psychoanalysis: interview; Tomkins 1968a; Kostelanetz 1988, p.13. The earliest traced observation by Cage of Zen taking the place of psychoanalysis is the *Muncie Star*, August 6, 1958.
In every sense: *YM*, p.35.
Each moment presents what happens: *YM* p.107; *I–VI, p.428.*
There is no rest of life: *S*, p.134.
Whether that is right: *S*, p.144.
a "mistake" is beside the point: *S*, p.59.
I think there's just the right amount: *S*, p.93.
We are all heroes: *S*, p.134.

p.111 to *accept the situation*: *FB*, p.56, italics original.
I don't think we're really interested: *Panorama-Chicago Daily News*, May 10, 1969.
to see each thing directly as it is: *S*, p. 276.
To kick a composer: *M*, p.25; *FB*, p.25.
writing music is not the same: *FB*, p.59; cf *S*, p.6.
You're not listening to it: Jasper Johns, interview.
you can't repeat anything exactly: *FB*, p.48.
if we thought we owned it: *S*, pp.110, 184; *YM*, p.106.
Unimpededness . . . Interpenetration: *S*, p.46.
Every individual reality, besides being itself: Suzuki, 1934, pp.66–7.
the essential nature of light: ibid., p.78.

p.112 You and I are inherently different and complementary: *M*, p.216.
Opposites are correlatives: *M*, p.3.

attainable only by transcending: Suzuki, 1934, p.128.

From the beginning of man's life: *Movie Magazine*, July 1962.

Every something is an echo: *YM*, p.78.

where we are: *S*, p.117.

No one loses nothing: *YM*, p.108.

Yes and no are lies: *M*, p.3; *EW*, p.11.

yes *and* no, not either/or: *YM*, p.79.

Toward the end he laughed gently: *YM*, pp. 67–8.

I'm not bothered by contradictions: Fleming and Duckworth, 1989, p.38.

the emphasis instead is on the here and now: *S*, p.46.

realizable only when all traces of causation: Suzuki, 1934, p.128.

The truth is that everything causes: *YM*, p.17; *M*, p.205.

When one says that there is no cause: *S*, pp.46–7.

p.113   People say, sometimes, timidly: *S*, p.111; *YM*, p.111; see *S*, p.x.

pass the potatoes: Ray Kass, telephone conversation.

Progress is out of the question: *S*, p.140.

a narrow-minded concept: *Buffalo-Courier Express*, March 2, 1965.

inactivity is not what happens: *S*, p.140.

you just start looking: Gillmor, 1976.

no need to cautiously proceed: *S*, p.47.

a "mistake" is beside the point: *S*, pp.170–1.

means . . . that an action has been made: Cage, transcript dated 1972.

p.114   Now take the way of painting . . . that kind of activity: ibid.

During one lecture Suzuki sketched an egg-like shape: the reconstruction of Suzuki's speech comes from interviews with Cage and the latter's description in *I–VI*, pp.242–3, and Furman, 1979.

what Eckhardt called the ground: *I–VI*, p.242.

Traditional arts and practices of Zen: see Hoover, 1978.

p.115   I don't want it to *mean* anything: *New York Post*, June 10, 1958.

Pay attention but stop short: *X*, p.53.

nothing needs to be connected to anything: *S*, p.229.

Separation works to protect us: *YM*, p.101.

I can accept the relationship between a diversity of elements: *FB*, pp. 78–9.

They apply to the world of the absolute: Turner, 1990.

p.116   It is only irritating to think one: *S*, p.185.

boredom takes over only if we arouse it: *FB*, p.49.

Each thing in the world asks: *YM*, p.148.

The mind can give up the desire: *S*, p.32.

open our eyes and ears: *YM*, p.146.

To accept whatever comes: *YM*, p.105.

Our delight lies in not possessing: *YM*, p.107.

secure possession of nothing: *S*, p.132.

Looking for something irrelevant: *M*, p.61.

your pleasure will be more universal: Low, 1985.

p.117   a poor piece. I wasn't quite aware: Gagne and Caras, 1982, pp.70–1.

to act is miracle: *S*, p.170.

Discipline is giving yourself: *Register*, May 14, 1961.

the question is not what should I do: Kostelanetz, 1971, p.13.

If the mind is disciplined: *I–VI, p.427.*

our will itself is obedience: Heschel, 1951, p.203.

The mind has nothing in it: *S*, p.190.

a man once stood on the brow: *S*, pp.117–18, 167, 176–7; *YM*, p.109.

p.118   What we do, we do without purpose: *S*, p.155; see *M*, p.57; *YM*, p.10.

Now that I'm enlightened, I'm just as miserable as ever: *S*, p.193.

no difference, only the feet: *S*, pp.88, 161, 167; *YM*, p.95.

essentially a cause for joy: *YM*, p.111.

Here we are: *S*, p.195.

Anything is a delight: *S*, pp.151, 110.

Nichi nichi kore ko nichi: *S*, p.41; *X*, p.151.

p.119   Unfortunately European thinking: *S*, p.46, cf pp.148, 166; *YM*, p.101.

One then decides whether he enjoys it: *YM*, p.96.

Vargas Llosa: 1987, p.221.

the belief that one may own: *S*, pp.111, 153; *YM*, p.105.

I can imagine a world without art: *S*, p.46; *YM*, pp.107–8.

It is almost impossible to remain alive: *S*, p.136.

p.120   Sounds are no longer just sounds: *S*, pp.116, 165; *YM*, p.96.

if a sound is unfortunate enough: *YM*, p.97.

what are important are relationships: ibid.

Harmony, so-called: *S*, p.152.

sounds are not just sounds, but are Beethoven: *YM*, p.97; see *S*, p.41.

There is all the time in the world: *YM*, pp.97–8; *S*, p.179.

When a composer feels a responsibility to make: *YM*, p.105.

A fugue is a more complicated game: *S*, p.160; *YM*, p.57.

p.121   Does being musical make one automatically stupid: *S*, p.49.

that is what is meant by the word: *S*, p.90.

At all costs must inspiration: *S*, p.189.

I would rather live: *I–VI*, p.412.

p.122   That's what I call self-expression: *S*, p.269.

There is no inner meaning: *Hartford Times*, March 14, 1951.

It's very hard to give a single sound: Dufallo, 1989.

Close your eyes and listen: *Montreal Star*, August 3, 1961.

if it is not interrupted by the things that happen: *S*, p.245.

Music is music now: *S*, p.161.

Art serves to the extent: *Music Magazine*, July 1962.

Art and our involvement in it: *YM*, p.42.

Make art useful to every person: *Music Magazine*, July 1962.

Left to itself art would have to be: White, 1978.

The function of art at the present time: *FB*, p.81.

a view of the arts which does not separate: *YM*, p.32.

I wouldn't say we are interested: *New Yorker*, July 24, 1971, p.64.

as a sort of experimental station: *S*, p.139.

If their ears don't get stretched by me: *New York Herald Tribune*, June 13–14, 1964.

they are apt to go into daily life: *Christian Science Monitor*, March 9, 1970.

p.124   I saw him and expressed the view that I had made . . . had to do my own thinking: Tomkins, 1968a.

p.125   What nowadays . . . is Zen?: *S*, p.xi.

are subsequently reflected in the music: Ernst, 1977, p.xxx.

Critics who in general link: *FB*, p.222.

I had been brought up on the twenties: Kostelanetz, 1988, p.13.

Surrealism relates to therapy: Gillmor, 1976.

blamed: *S*, p.11.

Eleven

p.126   wanted a music which would express emotions: *FB*, p.41.

I was wondering how to achieve a clear graphic: *FB*, pp.104, 43.

The elements of the gamuts: *S*, p.25.

While notating the sounds and aggregates of sounds: *FB*, p.104.

I reached the conclusion that I could compose: Tomkins, 1968a.

p.127   I do not deal in purposes: *S*, p.192, and see p.17.

the following willy-nilly of a ball: Gagne and Caras, 1982.

I wanted to see if I could fulfill: FB p.41.

I take my sounds when I have decided: *Hartford Times*, March 14, 1951.

it was with *Sixteen Dances* that I entered: *FB*, p.41.

p.128   *Concerto for Prepared Piano and Chamber Orchestra*: see Pritchett, 1988.

I made it into a drama: *FB*, p.41.

let the piano express the opinion: Tomkins, 1968a.

p.129   He was quite remarkable: *FB*, p.43. On Wolff, see the relevant essay in Revill, 1992.

p.130   very turbulent and haunting and asking: Harrison, interview recorded April 15, 1971.

p.131   I didn't at that time have a use: *I–VI*, p.237.

The moment I opened the book: Tomkins, 1968a.

p.132   to numbers which are larger or smaller: Kostelanetz, 1988, p.17.

Gerber Variable Scale: *FB*, p.109.

Using yarrow-stalks . . . was too time-consuming: *I–VI*, p.247.

All kinds of strangers came over: *Panorama-Chicago Daily News*, May 10, 1969.

I have confidence in the *I Ching*: ibid.

every time I had a problem: *FB*, p.43.

one of the stories which makes up . . . *Indeterminacy*: *S*, p.66.

I use the *I Ching* when it is useful: Montague, p.212.

I generally say: White, 1978.

p.133   but I haven't been troubled for quite some time: ibid.

Right there and then I sketched: Tomkins, 1968a.

playing on the alternative title: see *FB*, p.80.

I ran over to show the plan to Morty: Tomkins, 1968a.

At each small structural division: *S*, p.20.

Every few measures, at every structural point: Kirby and Schechner, 1965.

All twelve tones were present: *S*, p.26.

The sounds of the piece: for a description of the charts used, see *S*, pp. 57–9.

p.134   The sounds enter the time-space continuum: *S*, p.59.

p.135   the *Music of Changes* was composed: *S*, p.34.

Cage was charged by Henry Cowell: Gagne and Caras, 1976.

It was a very difficult process: Kirby and Schechner, 1965.

Tudor applied himself completely to that music: *FB*, p.178.

Judith Malina . . . and Julian Beck had . . . been leasing the Cherry Lane Theater: Norse, 1990, p.223.

p.136   The structure of *For MC and DT*: Dunn, 1962, p.7.

My thinking . . . that I didn't like the radio: Fleming and Duckworth, 1989, p.278; see *S*, p.30.

p.137   I wrote the music for radios feeling sure: Gagne and Caras, 1976.

a piece for radios as instruments: in *S*, p.62.

Cage conducted with great seriousness: Norse, 1990, p.207.

p.138   Picking up snatches of music and speech: ibid.

Henry Cowell suggested: Cowell, 1952, p.126.

In fact, there were all sorts of broadcasts: *FB*, p.169.

I knew that the piece was essentially quiet: Fleming and Duckworth, 1989, p.279.

stiff, soft-spoken, rather humorless: *Art and Architecture*, May 1962.

Everything he said was permeated: Jasper Johns, conversation.

John, I dearly love you, but I can't bear another: *S*, p.ix.

I didn't believe my ears: transcript of Hazel Johnson in the Columbia University Oral History archive.

On the road in 1950: suggested by *Dance Magazine*, May 1956, pp.40–1; there is a chance it was 1951.

p.139   Carolyn Brown: see ibid.

Cage was chatting . . . when a rather gaunt young man . . . Earle Brown: this section from this point is based on conversations with Brown, except where otherwise credited. On his music, see the relevant essay in Revill, 1992.

p.140   The closeness that I had had with Morty: Fleming and Duckworth, 1989.

Cage was involved with this because he was the only person: 'The Artist Speaks: Robert Rauschenberg', *Art in America*, 1966, 54/3, p.84.

p.141   I couldn't abide Pollock's work: Naifeh and Smith, 1992, pp.663, 890.

generally so drunk, and he was actually an unpleasant person: Kostelanetz, 1988, p.177.

p.142   maybe there is a connection: *FB*, p.74.

He sold the paintings by Mark Tobey: *M*, p.192.

meeting a man who had a desire: *I–VI*, p.361.

earn money in extraneous employment: *FB*, p.217.

I could go a long time: Shapiro, 1985.

So I decided not to look anymore: *FB*, p.218.

to limit my work to my composition: Shapiro, 1985.

and, if necessary, to die: *FB*, p.218.

he gave instructions to Tudor: Earle Brown, interview.

Would you like to be rich when you're dead?: *FB*, p.218.

not nearly enough: Jasper Johns, conversation.

not paying any attention to not having: *I–VI*, p.361.

You have to decide whether you want: Turner, 1990.

It is in living dangerously economically: *YM*, p.40.

p.143   We were all in the same boat: Earle Brown, interview.

Earle Brown bought one of the black paintings: Tomkins, 1968a.

Studie I: see Maconie, 1976, pp. 40–1, 70–4.

treated as sound-sources: Fleming and Duckworth, 1989, p.284.

p.144   the dance had a character that suggested: Fleming and Duckworth, 1989, p.283.

circumvent his aversion to jazz: see *S*, p.31.

at the fourth large structural division: instruction to score.

left his son a substantial inheritance: *FB*, pp. 187, 62.

p.145   roll of toilet paper: see *S*, p.31.

measured out the serialized durations: Maconie, 1976, p.41.

p.146   The quantity of the work: *FB*, p.124.

This was my first year of teaching: Gagne and Caras, 1976, p.252.

p.147   when preparing music for the Calder film: *FB* p.194.

the editing . . . caused serious difficulties: see *S*, p.85; Tomkins, 1968a.

After hearing a few . . . We're going to save you for Robinson Crusoe: *S*, p.272.

p.148   Cage and Brown . . . went up to Columbia: Earle Brown, interview.

carried out preliminary work on projected television: ibid.

and Morty would embrace Carolyn: ibid.

p.149   harmony could be taught in half an hour: Dufallo, 1989.

p.150   Bach wrote a random piece: see Helm, 1965.

p.151   identification: *S*, p.36.

p.152   here we are at the beginning: *S*, p.123.

fourteen repetitions of the same section: *S*, pp.119–23, and see p.ix.

Chance is a leap: *S*, p.162.

I write by using chance operations: *FB*, p.202.

By flipping coins to determine facets: *UCLA Daily Bruin*, November 11, 1955.

Chance operations . . . are a means of locating: *EW*, p.5.

p.153   What you need is not inspiration: *I–VI*, pp.412–13.

The principle underlying all the solutions acts: Cage, interview.

It was in fact his question: Dufallo, 1989.

p.154   Tastes, memory and emotions have to be: *FB*, p.56.

we can like chocolate sundaes: *Chicago Sun-Times*, May 11, 1969.

I am willing to have emotions: *FB*, p.56.

The question is not *not to want*: *FB*, p.90.

I'm losing my ability to make connections: *S*, pp. 249–50.

seeing the second of two like objects: *FB*, p.26.

p.155   as when one successfully performs a piece of music: see Green and Galweh, 1987.

It's a good question: Cope, 1980.

I only keep that amount of organization: *FB*, p.47.

a balance to my interest ... Games are very serious: Burch et al, 1986.

If Cage is going to hunt and eat: see *FB*, p.46.

p.156   Free the mind from its desire: Montague, 1985.

When I first tossed coins: *S*, p.163.

p.157   If we want to use chance operations: *FB*, p.94.

I begin to hear the old sounds: *S*, p.152.

to object-works ... to Beethoven: *FB*, p.136.

I managed in the case of Mozart: *YM*, p.22.

One can change one's way of hearing: see *Music Magazine*, July 1962.

Our lives are not ruined: *YM*, p.32.

What is irritating keeps us: *S*, p.44; *YM*, p.101.

studying being interrupted: for instance, *S*, p.218.

Distractions? Interruptions?: *YM*, p.11.

Responsibility is to oneself: *S*, p.139.

p.158   No "should" and no blame: *S*, p.140.

If I notice that I'm disturbed: Slivka, 1978–79.

if only out of respect: *Music Magazine*, July 1962.

each person, as well as each sound: *FB*, p.100.

Love = leaving space: *Themes and Variations*, also *I–VI*, p.444.

p.159   The ability to connect two things: *YM*, p.28.

I think that I have the right: *FB*, p.233.

This concept has grown: *Music Magazine*, July 1962.

I think the Golden Rule: Gillmor, 1976.

He's extremely opinionated: Margaret Leng Tan, interview.

He says he likes my music: Earle Brown, interview.

I don't think it makes much difference how I see it: *I–VI*, p.97.

When we remove the world: *S*, p.139.

p.160   the charts: the charts to *Water Music* are in the Special Collections Archive of the Lincoln Center, New York.

it did not really splash: *Medical Opinion and Review*, May 1966, p.41.

Each forty seconds determines: Lincoln Center notebook, op. cit.

Twelve

p.162   anybody who knows me knows this story: *YM*, p.134.

p.163   a physics laboratory: "the physics laboratory at Harvard" (Tomkins, 1968a); "Harvard physics lab" (Bruce Leibig, *Musical Happening*, September 1969); "Harvard University's anechoic (no echoes) chamber, which is used to test electronic equipment" *Montreal Star*, August 3, 1961.

when Cage sat down: This story is recounted in *S*, pp. 8, 13, 23, 51, 168; *YM*, p.134; *FB*, p.115; *I–VI*, p.1; Furman, 1979. The earliest traced published mention is in *The Dartmouth*, NH, March 23, 1955, p.1.

I had honestly and naively thought: *FB*, p.115.

Try as we may to make a silence: *YM*, p.98.

The situation one is clearly in: *S*, pp.13–14.

p.164   gave direction to what was: Cage, interview; word order changed for clarity.

incomprehensible in the European context: Fleming and Duckworth, 1989, p.48.

I didn't wish it to appear: Gillmor, 1976.

a canvas is never empty: quoted *S*, p.103.

mirrors of the air: *I–VI*, p.26.

hypersensitive: Tomkins, 1968a.

courage: *I–VI*, p.25.

gave me the permission: Gillmor, 1976.

p.165   Few composers leave behind: Henck in Charles, 1987–88.

I may have made a mistake: and see *I–VI*, p.21.

p.166   This score ... was published in *Source*: *Source*, vol. 1, no. 2 pp.46ff.

the pivotal composition: in *AAWW Journal*, January 1969.

find four places in Manhattan: *M*, p.140.

Demonstration of the Sounds of the Environment: *M*, p.xiii.

our definition of music: see Giles.

whether many people understand: Fleming and Duckworth, 1989, p.21.

4'55": *New York Post*, May 6, 1958.

The most important piece: Montague, 1985.

p.167   No day goes by: Fleming and Duckworth, 1989, p.21.

I always think of it: Montague, 1985.

I could be likened to a fundamentalist Protestant: Reynolds, 1962.

when I was growing up: Cage, 1972.

p.168   a mock-biblical description of his visit: *S*, p.52.

it's as stupid as believing in God: Fleming and Duckworth, 1989, p.30.

no one, not even God: Gillmor, 1976.

saint: Montague, 1985.

chaos: *S*, p.195.

following, of course, the general outlines: *S*, p.187.

I might alter it slightly now: Gillmor, 1976.

p.169   The early Zen gardens: see Hoover, 1978, p.102.

p.170   You could associate them: Low, 1985.

the means will exist for group improvisations: *S*, p.5.

p.171   Zen archery: Herrigel, 1953; Hoover, 1978, p.67.

How can I get a B♭ to come to me: *S*, p.48.

in an utter emptiness: *S*, p.160.

To see, one must go beyond: *S*, p.170.

appropriate in the sense of being: program note for Royal Albert Hall, London, May 22, 1972.

I wouldn't even dream: *EW*, p.118.

sobriety and quietness . . . Not disruptive: Fleming and Duckworth, 1989, pp. 108, 105.

Apollonian means the urge: Fleming and Duckworth, 1989, p. 108.

p.172   the god of boundaries: ibid., and see p.112.

emotions into someone else: *S*, p.250; see Fleming and Duckworth, 1989, p.112.

I had just heard *The Messiah*: Gagne and Caras, 1976.

Chance operations are an Apollonian procedure . . . univocal and unambiguous: Fleming and Duckworth, 1989, pp. 110, 111.

they are always impeccable: ibid.

p.173   John Cage . . . an extreme case of the artist: Fleming and Duckworth, 1989, p.114.

sparrowsitA gROsbeak betrays *itself*: *M*, p.35.

p.174   composers are continually mixing up music: *S*, p.276.

Stockhausen brought Boulez to the hotel: Peyser, 1976, pp. 9–10, on Cage's authority.

A phenomenon that seems so completely beyond the pale: quoted Worner, 1973, p.236.

p.175 Stockhausen ... is insistent that these came out of his own: see Worner, 1973, p.237.

p.176 the compositional equivalent of water color: see *FB*, p.44.
at points in time-space: *S*, p.163.
I looked at my paper: *FB*, p.44.
he relocated the paragraphs on publication: *S*, p.96.

p.177 The limited nature of this universe of possibilities: *S*, p.27.
events that are related to one another: *YM*, p.31.

p.178 It just happened that the series of numbers: *S*, pp.182–3.
a tape piece ... a vocal work: these two projected works were described to me by James Pritchett.

p.179 a jovial but essentially sympathetic ... notice: Nancy Seely, "You could have heard a piano drop," *New York Post*, April 15, 1954, p.3.
what a long and intense prayer: Tomkins, 1968a.
an average old ... Merce danced: *San Diego and Point Magazine*, December 1955, p.32.

p.180 a system was established: see *FB*, pp.61–2, 187.
most people interested in the idea: *FB*, p.186.
it was an experiment in substituting: *FB*, p.62.

p.181 he rang Guy G. Nearing: *S*, p.262.
he gathered skunk cabbage ...: *S*, p.262.
When she started to cook the mushrooms: *S*, p.95.
Graves sent Cage a letter-painting: held in the John Cage Mycology Collection at the University of California, Santa Cruz. The envelope is stamped October 19, 1956.

p.182 Cage once took Cunningham: Jasper Johns, interview.
Music Lovers' Field Companion: it ends *S*, pp.274–6.

p.183 the *Tofevo*, collided with the *Maasdam: New York Times*, October 4, 1954, 1:2 and 49; 2; October 5, 29:4.
time ... is the title of this piece: *S*, p.151.

p.184 it was Cage who would make the most judgments and decisions: Jasper Johns, interview.
a wider circle of gay artists: see Bockris, 1990, p.47.
Music for Piano, numbers 21 to ... 52: see *S*, pp.60–1.
It was even worse outside than in: Tomkins, 1968a.

p.185 Unfortunately, Ampex has not answered my letter: Cage to Barzun, May 11, 1956.

p.186 generally began with my trying to bring the students: Kirby and Schechner, 1965.
Practicality has always seemed to me: ibid.

Thirteen

p.187   an example used by Cage: *S*, p.35.

One drum is quite different: Turner, 1990

p.188   Cage discussed the work in a lecture: *S*, pp.35–6; *Klavierstuck XI* is also discussed in Maconie, 1976, pp.100–5.

Record collections . . . that is not music: *S*, p.215.

p.189   Concentration on the Now: quoted Harvey, 1975, p.85.

Absence of structure blurs: *M*, p.171.

The only thing I was being consistent: Tomkins, 1968a.

p.190   What has been composed?: *S*, p.61.

By the time you've worked out all this: Margaret Leng Tan, interview.

This is nice. What is it?: *FB*, p.22.

Finally we talked ourselves into it: Jasper Johns, interview.

p.191   The transparencies developed out: see *S*, p.28.

p.192   Merce conducted and it was beautiful: Jasper Johns, interview.

Cage gave the three lectures: *S*, pp.18–56.

My intention in putting the stories: *S*, p.260.

Earle Brown's *Indices*: *S*, p.266, and Earle Brown, interview.

p.193   the sensation of the day: *Rheinische Post*, October 17, 1958.

Nam June Paik suddenly approached me: *FB*, p.167.

p.194   *Lascia o radoppia*: I owe the details of this section to translations made by Maria Sansalone from contemporary newspapers, and also to the account in Tomkins, 1968a.

p.195   Spent the last four days in Venice: Cage to Crete and John senior, n.d.

p.196   a letter had arrived from Gianfranco Mingozzi: dated March 4, 1959.

it was not the sort of piece that should be performed: *YM*, p.51.

We had difficulty after that: Tomkins, 1968a.

there was no way in this case: *FB*, p.85.

I tried to explain changes: *New York Times*, September 3, 1972.

I found this objectionable and completely contrary: *FB*, p.86.

p.197   This last argument has really hurt: *New York Times*, September 3, 1972.

mushroom administration: Adam, 1989, p.149.

He subsequently received a postcard from Europe: *YM*, p.35.

Toshi Ichiyanagi: see the relevant entry in Revill, 1992.

I am not you: *I–VI*, pp.59–61.

p.198   It was really very valuable: Gagne and Caras, 1976.

p.199   these . . . became the topics: *S*, p.194.
        Do they know you're a Zen Buddhist: *YM*, p.69.
        Lecture on Commitment: which appears in *YM*, pp.112–19.
        We are as free as birds: *YM*, p.119.
        live in Zen but not by Zen: see Suzuki, 1991, p.12.
        Artists talk a lot about freedom: *S*, p.265.

p.200   Cage told of his studies: *YM*, pp.113–14.
        his alarming habit of suddenly singing: *S*, p.xi.
        I'd rather be drunk than sober: N.O. Brown, conversation.
        interested but often puzzled reviews: for example, Hollander, 1963;
        Morris, 1967.

p.201   he found a publisher: Gagne and Caras, 1976.

p.202   Richard Lippold was commissioned: on this episode see *New York
        Times*, August 12, 1962.

p.203   all decisions were made cooperatively: see *I–VI*, pp.179ff.
        there is a renowned archer: *YM*, p.137; *FB*, p.231.
        a trilogy corresponding to the lines: see *FB*, p.211.

p.204   As early as 1950 he had mooted the possibility: letter by Cage to
        Musical America, December 15, 1950.
        It's not a question of Satie's relevance: *S*, p.82.
        there are a lot more than eight hundred forty: *New York Herald
        Tribune*, September 11, 1963.

p.205   something had been set in motion: Tomkins, 1968a.
        find a cracked Mischa Elman recording: *New York Times*, August
        25, 1963.

p.206   Your son's music is magnificent: *YM*, p.69.
        Bernstein seemed unable to control: Jasper Johns, interview.

p.207   no musical training is necessary for this: *Los Angeles Times*, January
        30, 1977.
        Now instead of music we had a graph: transcript of Saul Goodman
        in the Columbia University Oral History Archives.
        the chance mixing . . . left the players baffled: Jasper Johns,
        interview.

p.208   Even if you were making your choices: Earle Brown, interview.
        I think he expects people all to be enlightened: ibid.
        the work and thought of Buckminster Fuller: *YM*, p.ix.

p.209   We are, as Fuller has pointed out: Burch et al, 1986.
        Cage wrote a dozen more until 1973: see *X*, p.155.
        John! How *dare* you?: *YM*, p.145.
        in 1964 I wrote letters: Gordon Mumma, conversation.

p.210   non-pop version someday: Lucier, 1988, p.3.

how much he disliked air-conditioning: ibid., p.6.

p.211   Lucier had begun making . . .: see the relevant entry of Revill, 1992.

p.212   Mosaic: which appears in *YM*, pp.43–9.

is to implement an environment in which the active: program note.

Adapt to physical circumstances: *Variations V*, score.

p.213   Non-focused: ibid. On *Variations V*, see Gena and Brent, 1982, pp. 114–15.

Changed function of composer: *Variations V*, score.

He made a gesture: *YM*, p.71.

Duchamp opined that dope: Jouffroy and Cordier, 1974.

Edward Lasker . . . ranked him one: Tomkins, 1968a.

Chess Piece: reproduced in Kostelanetz, 1971, figure 17.

I didn't wish to bother him: Jouffroy and Cordier, 1974.

p.214   I must have been fifty years ahead: *I–VI*, pp.110–11.

I saw him every night: Jouffroy and Cordier, 1974.

His complexion looked more like that: Dufallo, 1989.

I realized suddenly that it was foolish: Jouffroy and Cordier, 1974.

We got to know Marcel: Roth and Roth, 1973.

I was so delighted to be: ibid.

doubting everything, I had to find: Tomkins, 1968a.

it was easier to comply with other: ibid., for instance.

p.215   You could say I was saying the opposite: Roth and Roth, 1973.

Diary: Audience 1966: which appears in *YM*, pp.50–1.

Sitting downstage to one side: *YM*, p.133.

p.216   Cage met . . . Gavin Bryars: see Griffiths, 1985.

Everyone thought I was well cast: Goldberg, 1974.

John Cage as a perfect devil: *Village Voice*, July 21, 1966.

He devoured his part: *New York Times*, July 16, 1966.

The reason I've never liked Schoenberg: Goldberg, 1974.

was quite right: Cage, interview.

p.217   A scribbled note survives: in the John Cage Mycology Archive, University of California at Santa Cruz.

The evenings had no particular agenda: *Whole Earth* no. 55, Summer 1987, p.3, edited; brought to my attention by T.J. Pinch.

Fourteen

p.220   Cage is pretty good at putting on: Gagne and Caras, 1976, p.299.

Wendell Berry introduced Cage: and see *EW*, p.11.

is currently reading the complete: *Focus*, November 17, 1967.

I am enjoying and sharing: Cage to Walter Harding, April 8, 1968.

he had read *On the duty*: *EW*, p.4.

p.221   he had invited W. Stephen Thomas: on April 30, 1964.

Thoreau: see the biographies by Walter Harding and by Richard Lebeaux.

I went to the woods: Thoreau, 1947, pp.343–5.

keeping his ears and eyes open: Slivka, 1978–79.

Thoreau sought in nature: Mumford, 1973, p.40.

That government is best: Thoreau, 1947, p.109.

p.222   What ... attracted Cage ... to Thoreau: on Cage and Thoreau, see Gigliola Nocera, "Henry David Thoreau et le neo-transcendentalisme de John Cage," in Charles, 1987–88, pp.351–69.

the electronics age is extending: *Hartford Times*, April 23, 1966.

Sound is vibration, everything is vibrating: *Newsweek*, May 22, 1967.

If we push beyond the limits: *Chicago Sun-Times*, May 11, 1969.

mushrooms are making sounds: *New York Times*, October 2, 1966.

When I went into the anechoic chamber: *FB*, pp.220–1, and cf p.228.

p.223   Imagine people bringing objects: *Chicago Sun-Times*, May 11, 1969.

involved one or several musicians: *FB*, p.210.

Lejaren Hiller, Jr.: on Hiller, see the appropriate entry in Revill, 1992.

p.224   I'd like to do some computer music: Gagne and Caras, 1976, p.235.

and said he could arrange for me: *Source*, IV, p.11.

a long, narrow room level: *I–VI*, p.107.

When I got to Illinois: Gagne and Caras, 1976, p.74.

Ten Thunderclaps: see *M*, p.103; cf *FB*, p.211, where a passage is quoted.

the transformation of a live orchestra: *FB*, p.141.

will be composed in the same way as: *FB*, pp.211–12.

p.225   Voices singing Joyce's: *M*, p.117.

The last thunderclap will represent: *FB*, p.212.

I've always hated the harpsichord: *Chicago Sun-Times*, May 11, 1969.

p.226   He and Hiller sat in a trailer: Gagne and Caras, 1976, p.236.
the collaboration on *Double Music* ... had been by mail: ibid., p.257.
We worked very easily together: ibid., p.75.
Every single note was: *Minneapolis Star*, June 16, 1969.
Kobrin wrote a program: see Gena and Brent, 1982; the program is printed with commentary in *Source*, VIII.
if you have a question for which you want: Helms in Metzger and Riehm, 1978.
so I have a great supply: ibid.

p.227   Cage developed, or returned to: I first formulated these reflections in conversation with Jasper Johns.
Matthew's Music IVB: see Manning, 1985, p.243.
We could only integrate: *FB*, p.143.
Seventeen tapes mixed together ... can result from the accumulation of organizations: *M*, p.65; *FB*, p.195.
The harpsichord solos: see *FB*, p.143; *Source*, VIII, pp.11–12, 14–15.

p.228   he held a wake for her: see Gena and Brent, 1982, pp.163–4.
I had always admired that: *FB*, p.194.
they thanked Cage: 3M to Cage, June 24, 1969.

p.229   When Thoreau went to Walden: *Chicago Sun-Times*, May 11, 1969.
I've always been more interested: ibid.

p.230   It was a loss: *I–VI*, pp.107–9, *M*, p.70.
Not Wanting to Say Anything: plexigram four is reproduced, with its chance generation explained, in *Source*, VII; see also Kostelanetz, 1971.

p.231   Profanity is forbidden: *M*, p.70.
Me sure get some moose: Thoreau, 1947, p.83.

p.232   a great deal of elegance and precision: Jerome Rosen, interview.
attempted very subtle variations: *Source*, VII, p.23; for an account of the Mewantemooseicday, see the remainder of this article.
Cage called Cunningham from Davis: see Gena and Brent, 1982, p.116.
it distracted him from the continuous: see *FB*, p.177.
the most musical thing he has: *The Plain Dealer*, January 24, 1970.

p.233   it was becoming a shanty-town: *FB*, p.62 n.2.
I feel a little like: *FB*, p.187.
immoral ... absentee landlord ... transgression: ibid.

Ono and Lennon occasionally visited: see, for example, Gena and Brent, 1982, p.159.

p.234 Cage once wrote a birthday note: printed in *M*, p.94.

to Become/fRee: *EW*, p.131. Mesostics on Tobey's name and on that of Syvilla Fort were quoted above, in Chapter Six, II and Chapter Seven, I.

p.235 The poem would then have a spine: *M*, p.ix.

Who the fuck is this guy: Frank Lane, interview.

Lois Long is making a series: Cage to Smith, October 28, 1971.

p.236 I wish to emphasize: Cage to Bottoms, December 8, 1971.

From my own experience as a mushroom: Cage to Bottoms, December 26, 1972.

There was a very fine: *San Francisco Chronicle*, January 14, 1986, p.18.

made me happy ... I wanted you to know: Cage to Bottoms, January 17, 1973.

p.237 We've got the automobile: *M*, p.83.

an environment which works so well: *YM*, p.166.

contraceptive substances be added: *M*, p.16.

A global voltage: *YM*, pp.54–5.

Utility must ... be substituted: *FB*, p.62, *YM*, p.3.

Dymaxion Airocean World Map: *YM*, p.165.

Nothing is artificial: *M*, p.59.

Advertisements are all: *YM*, p.8.

Traffic lights could be installed: *M*, p.21.

The Soviets had been: *YM*, pp.65–6.

Even pollution will make us: *M*, p.98, and cf p.116.

Education could then teach us: see Burch et al, 1986, p.26.

p.238 The Renaissance was characterized: *Buffalo Courier-Express*, March 2, 1965.

false utility: *M*, pp.117, 210.

We're glad to hear unemployment's increasing: *YM*, p.8.

so you really have to put: Burch et al, 1986, p.25.

p.239 Dad ... was given a job irrigating: *YM*, p.58, line spacing removed.

Our proper work now ... is revolution: *YM*, p.ix.

We have only one mind: *YM*, p.158.

The revolution will be simple: *M*, p.107.

The revolution that we want: *Cinema Now*, pp.68–9.

They're doing more or less what: White, 1978.

p.240 Zen and chance and everything else: Richard Kostelanetz, speech at Wesleyan University, 1988.

I'm an anarchist: *YM*, p.53.

a point which he would often make: see, for instance, Montague, 1985.

I do it in order to be free: ibid.

to the time when no one votes: White, 1978.

the presidential business ... to have Greta Garbo as president: Burch et al, 1986, p.21.

Anarchism is fully practical: *FB*, p.19.

We don't need a president ... a little intelligence: White, 1978.

We should remove social controls: *YM*, p.64.

If the object is to reach a society: *FB*, p.53.

Men Against the State: see *YM*, p.59; Fleming and Duckworth, 1989, p.123.

p.241   I've made lots of statements: White, 1978.

I was recently asked to sign: ibid.

I don't think critical action: ibid.

Protestors just fan the flames: *The Daily Illinois*, November 11, 1967.

the ethical approach one can draw from Zen: discussed above, in Chapter Eleven, VII.

What Cornelius was doing didn't help music: Turner, 1990.

alter the nature of whatever: Burch et al, 1986, p.26.

discourage it through your lack: Montague, 1985.

When you see all those detergents and things: ibid.

p.242   My activity is anti-institutional ... I work best as an individual: White, 1978.

Spaceship Earth ... who's steering it?: I owe this gag to Thomas W. Simon.

Schoenberg's method is analogous: *S*, p.5.

Some composers today are writing music: note in the John Cage Archive, Northwestern University.

p.243   But if we wait until that time: Smalley, 1968.

Imagine that the music you're writing: Cage in Huddersfield, England, November 22, 1989.

not so much interested in experimental music: Earle Brown, interview.

what was urgent was not art: *YM*, p.158.

useful works: *YM*, p.34.

Music (not composition): *M*, p.8.

the composer ... simply facilitates: *YM*, p.68.

p.244 include action on the part of others: *YM*, pp.58–9.
a music by everyone: *M*, p.xiii.
The sooner I get on unemployment: Gillmor, 1976.
The reason I am less and less interested: *YM*, p.ix.
Personally, one of my life's greatest pleasures: Smalley, 1968.
Cage's music is as unlikely to make: ibid.
valor and courage: Norman O. Brown, conversation.

p.245 He felt less interested in electronic work: see his comments in *Middletown Press*, April 10, 1970; see *FB*, p.141 & n.
stands in complete contrast to my ... great love of Satie: *FB*, p.177.
he asked the *I Ching*: *FB*, p.179, 144.
The work returns to itself: *FB*, p.177n.
You're not *really* going to leave: Gordon Mumma, conversation.
Birdcage: see Appleton and Perera, 1975, p.173.

p.246 I think this work has three movements: *M*, p.xiv.
I added that I was withdrawing: *FB*, p.184n.
It obliges musicians: *M*, p.xiv.
I had offered them something: *FB*, p. 184n.
I am convinced that they play ... for revolution: *M*, p.xv; see *FB*, p.184n.
To play your music: *M*, p.xvi.
a minimum rehearsal requirement: *M*, p.xv.

p.247 The way Sultan played ... could be interpreted: *X*, pp.147–8.

p.248 a prophet of Utopia to Jeremiah: *EW*, p.ix.
I had become interested in writing: sleeve note to *Etudes Boreales*.
Communication without language!: *YM*, p.52.
it was by means of words: *S*, p.176.
syntax is the arrangement: *M*, p.x; *EW*, pp.11, 183.

p.249 Since at least 1965: *YM*, p.144.
haiku by Basho: see *M*, pp.70, 77. A transliteration from the Japanese with alternative translations exists in typescript at the John Cage Mycology Archive at the University of California at Santa Cruz. See also Kostelanetz, 1980.
to suggest the emptiness: ibid.
notAt evening: *EW*, p.12.
ean byo odo: *EW*, p.76.
high percentage of consonants: *S*, p.224.
music should be played at night: *YM*, p.49.

p.250 the doors and windows of the place: see *EW*, p.51; Slivka, 1978–79.

opening doors so that anything can go: *EW*, p.11.
began to distill water at home: Bronzell and Suchomski, 1986.
he's obliged, for instance, to drive: White, 1978.
I was born early in September: *EW*, p.136.

p.251   The thing I don't like about ... improvisation: *I–VI*, p.373.
I have thought of a variety of ways: *I–VI*, p.379.
If you divide the time of an improvisation: *I–VI*, pp.379–80.

p.252   You're discovering them: Gagne and Caras, 1976, p.76.
You have no control whatsoever over the conch: ibid., p.77.

p.253   these American tunes: *YM*, p.42.
Many people became annoyed simply because I superimposed: Gagne and Caras, 1976, p.75.
Jeers accompanied the first: *Los Angeles Times*, January 23, 1977.
I thought it would be a cheerful ... person to the next: Gagne and Caras, 1976, p.75.
to the USA, that it may become: *M*, dedication; *EW*, p.5.

p.254   Music is simply trying things out: *S*, p.189.
Finnegans Wake as it had appeared ... in *transition*: Ellmann, 1983 pp.588–9.
I was "too busy": *EW*, p.133.
"HCE" is mentioned variously: for instance *S*, pp.129, 134; *YM*, p.109.
I was caught in *Finnegans*: O'Driscoll, 1982, p.76.
I found myself from time to time: *EW*, p.136.
I am native to detailed attention: *EW*, p.136.

p.255   wrote because I decided to: O'Driscoll, 1982, p.76.

Fifteen

p.256   I am for the birds: *FB*, p.11.
a form that explodes in the stomach: *I–VI*, p.384.

p.257   Alan Watts' meat and truffle pie: *YM*, p.72.
Lois Long's fried chicken: *EW*, p.91.
for two days I lived in shock: *EW*, p.79.

p.258   Your energy asserts itself: Furman, 1979.
At the same time, I'm much more equable: ibid.
Communication: *S*, p.41.
a smoking story in *Where*: *S*, pp.208ff.
Every time the one who did not know: *X*, p.166; Montague, 1985.
These are the problems that should be addressed: Bronzell and Suchomski, 1986.

p.259 In other words, I accepted the diet: *I–VI*, pp.392–3.

Don't take the diet: see *I–VI*, pp.388ff. On Cage and macrobiotics see *EW*, p.79; *FB*, p.233n.; *I–VI*, pp.387–94; Furman, 1979.

Two birds with one stone: *FB*, p.179.

p.260 Cheap Imitation: on the solo violin version, see Gena and Brent, 1982, pp.101–3.

Freeman Etudes: see Gena and Brent, 1982, pp.103–6; Charles, 1987–88, pp.349–50.

Some of it will be absolutely impossible: *Horizon*, December 1980, p.7.

p.261 The *Etudes* are both fascinating: Gena and Brent, 1982, p.105.

they become ... superficially closer: I first formulated this consideration in conversation with Jasper Johns.

To trek with Gita: interview; see also Montague, 1985.

p.262 something connected with the knowing aspect: White, 1978.

p.263 *Who's Who in American Art* featured him: p.144.

a set of nine melodies: program to the 1987 Los Angeles Festival, p.F–21.

Il treno: see Charles, 1987–88, pp.116–17.

I love living on Sixth Avenue: Zwerlin, 1982.

The traffic never stops: Montague, 1985.

p.264 Now I don't need a piano: Sears, 1981.

so that they entered into my dreams: Montague, 1985.

I translate the sounds into images: Sears, 1981.

asking us to climb mountains: Lilah Toland, interview. See also her article in Gena and Brent, 1982, pp.121–2.

p.266 It was natural to add recordings: O'Driscoll, 1982, p.78.

If you don't have time to accomplish something: Montague, 1985; O'Driscoll, 1982, p.79.

two negatives make a positive ... I needed: ibid.

We went to Ireland and enjoyed every minute: ibid.

p.267 Somehow we were able to put up with it: ibid., p.80.

p.268 the imaginary dialogue with Satie ... in 1958: *S*, pp.76–82.

the piece is not an alphabet: *X*, p.55.

to remove the punctuation: *X*, p.55.

p.269 all those imaginary situations of buildings: Burch et al, 1986, p.25.

that's the – electronic immediacy: ibid.

to visit ... a small aquarium: *I–VI*, pp.67ff.

p.271 The air delicious, thus we are baptized: *M*, p.91.

Bridging of the river in the night: *X*, p.107.

Those seem to me to be the most important: Fleming and Duckworth, 1989, p.32.

p.272   the past must be Invented: *X*, p.145.

Thirty Pieces for Five Orchestras: see *I–VI*, pp.71–3; Timar et al, 1981; Montague, 1985.

I enjoyed that work so much: *I–VI*, p.71.

p.273   About three-quarters of the way through: Montague, 1985.

p.274   The Ryoanji garden: see Hoover, 1978, pp.105–11, and the comments above about the garden (Chapter Twelve, III).

the emptiness of the sand would allow: *YM*, p.137, *FB*, p.137.

I collect them for my garden ... There are so many faces: Low, 1985.

p.275   writing through Allen Ginsberg's ... *Howl*: see *I–VI*, p.341.

p.276   I wanted the feeling of "Here Comes Everybody": Schöning, 1984–85.

p.279   What I wanted to do ...: *I–VI*, p.444.

p.280   *Etcetera 2/4 Orchestras* ... further explores the stretched metrical time: *I–VI*, p.444.

p.282   Once in Amsterdam, a Dutch musician said: *S*, p.73.

Mila Repa: Chapter Nine, IV.

p.284   *Vision of the Inner Eye*: Kass, 1983.

forays with Orson K. Millar: Burch et al, 1986, p.28.

p.285   when everyone in the Appalachians: Ray Kass, telephone conversation.

p.287   aViary without birds: *M*, p.95.

There can be ... a purposeless writing: *FB*, p.60.

the *I Ching* provides a language: *M*, p.215.

p.288   *The First Meeting of the Satie Society*: excerpts appear in Charles, 1987–88, pp.281–6.

brings new ideas: *I–VI*, pp.338, 2; Burch et al, 1986, p.28.

In the nature of the use of chance: *I–VI*, p.6.

the question would be asked fifteen times: *I–VI*, pp.4–5.

Thoreau is into being played: *I–VI*, p.316.

p.289   a single mesostic would be constructed: *I–VI*, p.6. The repetitions mentioned occur on pp.224–5, 291–3, 393–4.

If a lecture is informative: Reynolds, 1962.

you have the opportunity with these lectures: *I–VI*, pp.316–17.

like flashes of light: Wayman Chin, telephone conversation, November 1990.

I was struck by its innumerable: Suzanne Stumpf, telephone conversation, November 1990.

a most temperate, peaceful: Wayman Chin, op. cit.

very expressive and very lovely: *I–VI*, p.99.

p.294   It is difficult to know: Crown Point Press press release, March 1991.

Sixteen

p.295   when I die, I'll be in perfect condition: Montague, 1985; *X*, p.168.

I'm on my last legs: *Panorama*, 10 May, 1969; see *M*, p.xv.

I am not as well physically: Cage to Hans Otte, February 11, 1971.

age is a special thing: *New York Post*, January 20, 1973.

even though I'm sixty years old: *FB*, p.182 n.2.

I'm getting old: *FB*, p.62 n.2.

anecdotes about old age: see *X*, pp.167, 169.

senior citizen concessions: see *X*, p.156; Chapter Fifteen, VII above.

I have nothing to complain about: Slivka, 1978–79.

p.296   That's a mystery the solution: Bossard, 1970.

I have no control over that: Cage's words at the Almeida Festival, London.

that I might die in an accident: Goldberg, 1976.

he described them as collecting: *Art News*, January 1981.

I'm becoming interested in more: *Horizon*, December 1980.

The older I get the more ... no fooling around possible: Montague, 1985.

the electronic techniques ... for Russian cosmonauts: *YM*, pp.65–6.

now he wished they were available to him: Robert Worby, reporting an exchange with Cage.

p.297   he had planned to compose a lecture: *Art and Architecture*, May 1962.

Every birthday that ends in a 5 or a 0: Sumrall, 1986.

I give as few concerts and accept as few engagements: Cage to Hans Otte, early 1971; see *FB*, p.218.

p.298   I think, for instance, that I need to be at home: Bodin and Johnson, 1965.

We have changed from one culture to another: ibid.

p.301   We are under the control of precisely those things: Gagne and Caras, 1982, p.80.

what is needed ... is a little intelligence: Burch et al, 1986.

Perhaps it will change, but . . . music has little effect: Gagne and Caras, 1982, p.80.

I'm afraid they will: White, 1978.

I've now done so much work: ibid.

p.302   My own concern now is to live: ibid.

an increase in the amount: *YM*, p.33.

the main stream has gone into delta: Turner, 1990.

p.303   The situation of being constantly on the brink: Slivka, 1978–79.

having shown the practicality: Murphy, 1985.

People can be plumbers or street cleaners: Slivka, 1978–79.

p.304   I think that each day we . . . we wake up: Burch et al, 1986, p. 20, ellipses original.

It's not futile to do what we do: Gillmor, 1976.

BIBLIOGRAPHY

ADAM, Judy (ed.). *Dancers on a Plane: Cage-Cunningham-Johns*. London: Anthony d'Offay Gallery, 1989.

ALCATRAZ, Jose Antonio. "John Cage: El Sonido como centro del universo." *Excelsior* (February 29, 1976).

— "Interview with John Cage." *Excelsior/Plural* (May 1976): 56.

ANON. "Percussion Concert." *Life* xiv/11 (1943): 42, 44.

— "Sound Stuff." *Newsweek* (January 11, 1954).

— "It's electronic ballet – or 48 hours of bad plumbing." *Daily Mail* (November 22, 1966).

— "Quiet composer voices loud ideas." *Scottsdale (AZ) Daily Progress* (April 4, 1975).

— "Arts." *Reporter* (Buffalo) (October 19, 1978).

— "John Cage on his 70th Birthday: West Coast Background." *Inter-American Music Review* (1982): 3–17.

APPLETON, John H., and PERERA, Ronald C., *The Development and Practice of Electronic Music*. Englewood Cliffs, New Jersey: Prentice-Hall, 1975.

ASHBERY, John. "Cheering Up Our Knowing." *New York* (April 10, 1978).

AVAKIAN, G. "About the Concert." *The 25-year Retrospective Concert of the Music of John Cage* (disc notes) (1958).

BACHMANN, Dieter (ed.). "Composer John Cage." Special issue of *Du* (Zurich), Heft 5 (May 1991).

BAKEWELL, Joan. "Music and Mushrooms – John Cage Talks About His Recipes." *The Listener* (June 15, 1972): 87.

BARNARD, Geoffrey. *Conversation Without Feldman*. Darlinghurst, NSW, Australia: Black Ram Books, 1980.

BARTSCH, W. et al. *Die unvermeidliche Musik des John Cage*. Kolb, 1969.

BATTCOCK, Gregory (ed.). *Breaking the Sound Barrier: A Critical Anthology of the New Music*. New York: Dutton Publishing, 1981.

BECKER-CARSTENS, W. "John Cage zieht im Den Haag." *Melos* 39.Jg.

Heft 4 (1972).

BINHEIM, Max (ed.). *Women of the West*. Los Angeles: Publishers' Press, 1928.

BITHER, David. "A Grand Old Radical." *Horizon* 23, no.12 (December 1980).

BOCKRIS, Victor. *Warhol*. London: Penguin, 1990.

BODIN, Lars Gunnar, and JOHNSON, Bengt Emil. "Bandintervju med Cage." *Ord och Bild* (1965): 74.

— "Semikolon: Musical Pleasure." (interview with Cage) *Dansk musiktidskrift* xli (1966): 36.

BOENDERS, Frans. "Gesprek met John Cage. De cultuur als delta." in *Sprekend gedacht*, Bussum, 1980.

BOSSARD, Jacqueline. "Pose a John Cage le questionnaire de Marcel Proust." *Musique de tous les Temps* (December 1970).

BOSSEUR, Jean-Yves. "John Cage: 'Il faut forger un nouveau mode de communication orale'." *La Quinzaine littéraire* (December 15, 1973).

BOULEZ, Pierre, and CAGE, John *Correspondance et documents*. Winterthur: Amadeus Verlag, 1990.

BRENT, Jonathan "Letters." *Tri-Quarterly* 52 (Fall 1981).

BROGAN, Hugh. *The Pelican History of United States of America*. London: Penguin, 1986.

BRONZELL, Sean, and SUCHOMSKI, Ann. "Interview with John Cage." in *Catch*, Galesburg, IL; Knox College; reprinted in SUMNER et al, 1986.

BROWN, Anthony. interview in **asterisk: A Journal of New Music* 1, no. 1 (1975).

BUNGER, R. *The Well-Prepared Piano*. Colorado Springs: Colorado College Music Press, 1973.

BURCH, Kathleen, SUMNER, Michael, and SUMNER, Melody. "Interview with John Cage." in SUMNER et al, 1986.

CAGE, John (ed.). *Possibilities*. New York: Wittenborn, 1948.

— *Silence*. Middletown, CT: Wesleyan University Press, 1961.

— "John Cage in Los Angeles." *Artforum* (February 1965); reprinted in Amy Baker SANDBACK (ed.). *Looking Critically*. Ann Arbor, MI: UMI Research, 1984.

— *A Year From Monday*. Middletown, CT: Wesleyan University Press, 1967.

— *Diary: Part III*. New York: Something Else Press, 1967.

— "Questions." *Perspecta* (Yale School of Architecture) (1967).

— *Silence*. English edition London: Marion Boyars, 1968.

— *A Year From Monday*. English edition London: Marion Boyars, 1968.

— *Diary: Part IV*. New York: Something Else Press, 1968.

BIBLIOGRAPHY

— *To Describe the Process of Composition Used in "Not Wanting to Say Anything About Marcel"*. Cincinatti: EYE Editions, 1969.

— "Response to Questionnaire." *Source* 6:3, no. 2 (1969).

— "The University and the Arts: Are They Compatible?" *Works and Days* 1, no. 1 (Spring 1969).

— contribution to C. H. WADDINGTON (ed.). *Biology and the History of the Future*. Edinburgh: Edinburgh University Press, 1972.

— *M*. Middletown, CT: Wesleyan University Press; London: Marion Boyars, 1973.

— *Writings Through "Finnegans Wake"*. New York: Printed Editions, 1978.

— *Empty Words*. Middletown, CT: Wesleyan Univerity Press, 1979.

— "Art in the Culture." *Performing Arts Journal* (1979): 10–11; German translation in *Theater heute* (January 1980).

— *Empty Words*. English edition London: Marion Boyars, 1980.

— "10 Questions: 270 Answers." *The Composer* X–XI (1980).

— *Another Song* (accompanying photographs by Susan Barron). New York: Callaway Editions, 1981.

— *Mud Book* (with illustrations by Lois Long). New York: Callaway Editions, 1982.

— *Themes and Variations*. Barrytown, NY: Station Hill Press, 1982.

— "About Roaratorio." in Robert O'DRISCOLL (ed.). 1982.

— *X*. first edition (withdrawn on Cage's authority due to faulty graphics) Middletown, CT: Wesleyan University Press, 1983.

— *X*. second edition, corrected Middletown, CT: Wesleyan University Press, 1986.

— *X*. second edition, corrected, English paperback original London: Marion Boyars, 1987.

— *I–VI*. Cambridge, MA. and London: Harvard University Press, 1990.

— and Kathleen O'Donnell HOOVER. *Virgil Thomson*. New York: Yoseloff, 1959.

— and Morton FELDMAN. "A Radio Conversation." *Circuit* (Spring–Summer 1967).

— et al. *Cinema Now*. Cincinnati: University of Cincinnati, 1968.

— and Alison KNOWLES. *Notations*. New York: Something Else Press, 1969.

— with Louis LONG and Alexander H. SMITH. *Mushroom Book*. New York: Hollanders Workshop, 1972.

— in conversation with Daniel CHARLES. *Pour les oiseaux*. Paris: Editions Pierre Belfond, 1976.

— in conversation with Daniel CHARLES. *For The Birds*. (translation of Cage and Charles, 1976) Salem, NH and London: Marion Boyars, 1981.

— and Merce CUNNINGHAM. "Questions Answered and Unanswered." *Middlebury* (Winter 1981).

— and Pierre BOULEZ. – see BOULEZ.

CHARLES, D. "Entr'acte 'Formal' or 'Informal' Music?" *MO*, li (1965): 144.

— "Soixante réponses à trente questions." *Revue d'esthétique* nos 2–4 (1968): 9.

— (ed.). *Gloses sur John Cage*. Paris: Union Generale d'Editions, 1978.

— (ed.). "John Cage." special issue of *Revue d'esthétique* Nouvelle Serie 13–14–15 (1987–88).

CHATENEVER, Rick. "Cage's 'Found Sound'." *Santa Cruz Sentinel* (August 20, 1982).

CLINE, Dorothy I. *Training For Recreation Under the WPA*. Chicago: University of Chicago Press, 1939.

CLOSE, Roy M. "Music creator Cage finds his ideas in nature." *Minneapolis Star* (April 18, 1975).

COMMANDAY, Robert. "Composing with the Camera." *San Francisco Chronicle/This World* (November 10, 1968).

COPE, David. "An Interview with John Cage." *Composer Magazine* (1980): 10–11.

CORDIER, Robert. "Etcetera pour un Jour ou Deux." *Had* (Paris) (1973).

COWELL, H. "Current Chronicle" *MQ*, xxxviii (1952): 123.

CUMMINGS, Paul. "Interview: John Cage May 2, 1974." in manuscript at the Archives of American Art (1974).

CURGEL, H. "Cage oder das wohlpraparierte Klavier." *Melos* 22.Jg Heft 4 (1955).

DANEY, S., and FARGIER, J.P. Interview with Cage in *Cahiers du cinema* (April 1982): 334–5.

DANNENBERG, P. "Wege zu Cage." *Stuttgarter Zeitung* (June 23, 1975).

DARTER, Tom. "John Cage." *Keyboard* (September 1982).

DIBELIUS, U. "John Cage oder gibt es kritische Musik?" *Melos*, xxxv (1968): 377.

DUBERMAN, Martin. *Black Mountain: An Exploration in Community*. New York: Dutton, 1972.

DUCKWORTH, William. "Anything I Say Will Be Misunderstood." [1985] in FLEMING and DUCKWORTH (eds).

DUFALLO, Richard. *Trackings*. New York: Oxford University Press, 1989.

DUNN, R. (ed.). *John Cage*. (an annotated catalog) New York, 1962.

DUNNETT, James, and STAMP, Gavin. *Ernö Goldfinger: Works 1*. London: Architectural Association, 1983.

ELLMANN, Richard. *James Joyce*. Oxford: Oxford University Press, 1983.

BIBLIOGRAPHY

ERNST, David. *The Evolution of Electronic Music.* New York: Schirmer, 1977.

FELDMAN, Morton (Bunita MARCUS and Francesco PELIZZI). "John Cage." *Res* 6 (Autumn 1983).

FILLIEU, Robert. "John Cage." in *Teaching and Learning as Performing Arts/Lebren und Lernen als Auffubrungskunste.* New York/Cologne: Verlag Gebr. Koenig, 1970.

FINEGAN, Don, et al. "Choosing Abundance/Things to Do." *North American Review* 6, nos 3 & 4 (Fall and Winter 1969).

FLEMING, R. and DUCKWORTH, William (eds). "John Cage at Seventy-Five." special issue of *Bucknell Review*, vol. XXXII, no. 2 (1989), Lewisberg: Bucknell, University Press.

FLETCHER, Laura, and MOORE, Thomas. "An Interview (with John Cage.)." *Sonus: A Journal of Investigations into Global Musical Possibilities* 3, no. 2 (1983).

FRANKENSTEIN, A. "In Retrospect – the Music of John Cage." *High Fidelity* x/4 (1960): 63.

FREEDMAN, Guy. "An Hour & 4'33" with John Cage." *Music Journal* (December 1976).

FURMAN, Maureen. "Zen Composition: An Interview with John Cage." *East West Journal* (May 1979).

FURST-HEIDTMANN, Monika. "John Cage's Werke für preparierte Klavier." *Musik und Bildung* 67.Jg.Heft 2 (1976).

— *Das preparirtre Klavier des John Cage.* Regensburg: Gustav Bosse Verlag, 1979.

GAGNE, Cole, and CARAS, Tracy. "An Interview with John Cage [1975]." *New York Arts Journal* 1, no.1 (May 1976).

— *Soundpieces: Interviews with American Composers.* Metuchen, NJ: Scarecrow Press, Inc, 1982.

GENA, Peter, and BRENT, Jonathan (eds) (assisted by Don Gillespie). *A John Cage Reader: In Celebration of His 70th Birthday.* New York/London/Frankfurt: C. F. Peters Corporation, 1982.

GILES, Gordon J. "Is 4'33" a piece of music?" manuscript (n.d.).

GILLMOR, Alan. "Interview with John Cage (1973)" *Contact* 14 (Autumn 1976); in Swedish, "Intervju med John Cage." *Nutida Musik* 21, no.1 (1977/78).

GILLMOR, Alan, and SHATTUCK, Roger. "Erik Satie: A Conversation (1973)" *Contact* 25 (Autumn 1982).

GLANVILLE-HICKS, P. "John Cage." *Musical America*, lxviii/10 (1948): 5.

GLIGO, Niksa. "Ich traf John Cage in Bremen." *Melos, Zeitschrift für Neue Musik* 1 (January–February 1973).

GOLDBERG, Jeff. "John Cage Interview." *Soho Weekly News* (September 12, 1974).

— "John Cage Interviewed." *Transatlantic Review* 55/56 (May 1976).

GOLDSTEIN, S. "John Cage." *Music Business* (April 1946).

GREEN, Barry, and GALLWEY, W. Timothy. *The Inner Game of Music*. London: Pan, 1987.

GREEN, Blake. "John Cage: Old Guard of Music's Avant-Garde." *San Francisco Chronicle* (1985).

GREGSON, David. "John Cage makes his music at random." *San Diego Union* (April 29, 1986).

GRIFFITHS, Paul. *Cage, Oxford Studies of Composers #18*. London/New York/Melbourne: Oxford University Press, 1981.

— *New Sounds, New Personalities*. London: Faber, 1985.

— —, — *Circus on* —. in *Prom Guide 1987*. London: BBC, 1967.

GWATHMEY, J. H. *Historical Register of Virginians in the Revolution*. Richmond, Virginia: Dietz Press, n.d.

HAHN, Otto. "Merce Cunningham." *L'Express* (June 11, 1964).

HARRISON, L. "The Rich and Varied New York Scene." *MM* xxi (1945): 181.

HARVEY, Jonathan. *The Music of Stockhausen*. London: Faber, 1975.

HELM, E. Eugene. "Six Random Measures of C.P.E. Bach." *Journal of Music Theory* X (1965): 139–50.

HELMS, H.G. "John Cage's Lecture 'Indeterminacy'." *Die Reihe* v (1959): 83–121.

— "John Cage zum 50 Geburtstag" (sendung für Radio Bremen) (October 25, 1962).

— "Gedanken Eines Progressiven Musikers uber die Beschadigte Gesellschaft." *Protokolle* (March 30, 1974); reprinted in METZER and RIEHM (eds).

HERING, D.M. "John Cage and the 'Prepared Piano'." *Dance Magazine* xx/3 196 (1946): 21, 52.

HERRIGEL, Eugen. *Zen in the Art of Archery*. London: Routledge and Kegan Paul, 1953.

HERSH, Paul. "John Cage" *Santa Cruz Express* (August 19, 1982).

HERTELENDY, Paul. "John Cage Sprouting at UC." *San Jose Mercury News* (January 24, 1980)

— "John Cage Rolls Dice at Cabrillo Music Festival." *San Jose Mercury News* (August 19, 1982)

HESCHEL, Abraham Joshua. *Man is Not Alone*. New York: Farrar, Strauss and Giroux, 1951.

HILLER, Lejaren, jr., and ISAACSON, L.M. *Experimental Music*. New York,

1959.

HILMES, Michele. *Hollywood and Broadcasting*. Urbana: University of Illinois Press, 1990.

HOCKMAN, D. "The Sounds and Silences of John Cage." *Downbeat* xxxi (May 7, 1964): 20.

HOLLANDER, J. "Review of 'Silence'." *PNM* i/2 (1963): 137.

HOLMES, Thomas B. "The Cage Interview." *Recordings* 3, no.3 (1981).

— *Electronic and Experimental Music*. New York: Charles Scribners, 1985.

HOOVER, Thomas. *Zen Culture*. London: Routledge and Kegan Paul, 1978.

I Ching or Book of Changes. translated into German by Richard WILHELM, rendered into English by Cary F. BAYNES with a foreword by C.G. Jung; London: Routledge and Kegan Paul, 1951.

ICHIYANAGI, Toshi. "John Cage." *Ongaku geijutso* xix/2 (1961).

JOHNSTON, J. "There is No Silence Now." *Village Voice* (November 8, 1962).

JOUFFROY, Alain, and CORDIER, Robert. "Entendre John Cage, entendre Duchamp." *Opus international* 49 (March 1974).

KASS, Ray, *Morris Graves: Vision of the Inner Eye*. New York: Braziller, 1983.

KAUFFMANN, Stanley (ed.). "The Changing Audience for the Changing Arts/Panel." in *The Arts: Planning for Change*. New York: Associated Councils of the Arts, 1966.

KELLER, Hans. "Caged." *The Spectator* (June 24, 1978).

— "Late Cage." *Spectator* (June 28, 1980).

KIRBY, Michael, and SCHECHNER, Richard, "An Interview." *Tulane Drama Review* 10, no.2 (Winter 1965).

KOBLER, John. "Everything We Do Is Music." *The Saturday Evening Post* (October 19, 1968).

KOCH, G. "Musik als Gegendenken." *Musica* 26.Jg. Heft 5 (1972).

KOSTELANETZ, Richard. "John Cage." in *The Theatre of Mixed Means*. New York: Dial Press, 1980. Reprinted London: Pitman, 1970; New York: RK Editions, 1980.

— "The American Avant-garde, Part 2: John Cage." *Stereo Review* xxii/5 (1969): 61. Reprinted in *Master Minds*. New York, 1969.

— (ed.). *John Cage*. New York: Praeger Publishers, Inc., 1970.

— (ed.). *John Cage*. London: Allen Lane/The Penguin Press (English edition of Kostelanetz, 1970), 1971.

— "John Cage in Conversation, Mostly About Writing." *New York Arts Journal* 19 (1980); reprinted as "John Cage (1979)." in *The Old Poetries and the New*. Ann Arbor: University of Michigan Press, 1981.

— (ed.). *Conversing with Cage*. New York: Limelight Editions, 1988.

— (ed.). *John Cage*. New York: Da Capo Press (updated reissue of KOSTELANETZ, ed., 1970), 1991.

LANGE, Art. "Interview with John Cage 10/4/77." *Brilliant Corners* 8 (Winter 1978).

LANZA, Alcides. "... We Need a Good Deal of Silence ..." *Revista de Letras* 3, no. 2 (September 1971).

LEBEL, Jean-Jacques. "John Cage entoure de nus, vite" *La Quinzaine litteraire* (December 15, 1966).

LEWINSKI, W.E. "Where do We Go from Here? a European View." *MO* lv (1969): 193.

LIST, K. "Rhythm, Sound and Sane." *New Republic* cxiii (1945): 870.

LITTLER, William. "Roratorio, an Irish circus of words blended with sound." *Toronto Star* (January 1982).

LOW, Lisa. "Free Association." *Boston Review* (July 1985).

LUCIER, Alvin. *Notes in the Marquis*. Middletown, CT: self-published, 1988.

MACDONALD, Malcolm. *Schoenberg*. London: Dent, 1987

MCGARY, K. "I have Nothing." *Antioch Review* xxii (1962): 248.

MACONIE, Robin. *The Works of Stockhausen*. London: Marion Boyars, 1976.

MANNING, Peter. *Electronic and Computer Music*. Oxford: Clarendon, 1985.

MARCUS, Geneviere. "John Cage: Dean of the Musical Avant-Garde." *Coast FM & Fine Arts* 11, no.3 (March 1970).

MAREN, R. "The Musical Numbers Game." *Reporter* xviii (March 6, 1958): 37.

MARKGRAF, B. "John Cage: Ideas and Practices of a Contemporary Speaker." *Quarterly Journal of Speech* xlviii (1962): 128.

MAZO, Joseph H. "John Cage Quietly Speaks His Piece." *Bergen Sunday Record* (March 13, 1983).

MEASHAM, Terry. *The Moderns*. Oxford: Phaidon, 1976.

MELLERS, W. "The Avant-Garde in America." *PRMA*, xc (1963–64): 1.

METZER, Heinz-Klaus. "John Cage oder Die freigelassene Musik." *Musik auf der Fluelt vor sich selbst* (Hrsg. v. Dibelius) 2 (1970) (Auflag Munchen).

— and RIEHM, Reiner. "Musik – Konzepte." *Sonderband*. Munchen: Text + Kritik, 1978.

MEYER, L.B. "The End of the Renaissance." in *Music, the Arts and Ideas*. Chicago, 1967.

MILES, Barry. *Ginsberg*. London: Viking, 1990.

MIMAROGLU Ilhan. "Interview with John Cage." *Discotea* (November 1965).

MONTAGUE, Stephen. "Significant Silences of a Musical Anarchist." *Classical Music* (May 22, 1982).

— "John Cage at Seventy: An Interview." *American Music*, vol. 3 no. 2 (Summer 1985).

MORERA, Daniela. "John Cage: i suoni della vita." *L'Uomo vogue* (March 1976).

MORRIS, E. "Three Thousand Seven Hundred Forty-seven Words about John Cage." *Notes: Quarterly Journal of the Music Library Association* xxiii (March 3, 1967): 468.

MUMFORD, Lewis. *Interpretations and Forecasts*. New York: Harcourt Brace Jovanovich, 1973.

MURPHY, Jay. "Interview with John Cage." *Red Bass* nos 8–9 (1985).

NAIFEH, Steven, and SMITH, Gregory White. *Jackson Pollock: An American Saga*. London: Pimlico, 1992.

NELLHAUS, Arlynn. "'New' Music a Wirey Maze." *Denver Post* (July 5, 1968).

NESTYEV, Israil. "Antimuzyka pod Glogom 'anarkhil'." *Sovetskaya Muzyka* 37 (September 1973).

NIEMINEN, Risto. "John Cage marraskuussa 1982. Taide on itsensa zyollistamista." *Synkoppi* (June 13, 1983).

NOCERA, Gigliola. "Alla Ricerca del silenzio perduto." *Scena* 2, no. 2 (April 1978).

NORSE, Harold. *Memoirs of a Bastard Angel*. London: Bloomsbury, 1990.

NYFFELER, Max. "Interview mit John Cage." *Dissonanz* (Zurich) 6 (September 1970).

NYMAN, Michael. "Cage and Satie." *Musical Times* 114 (December 1973): 1227–9.

— *Experimental Music: Cage and Beyond*. New York: Schirmer, 1974.

O'DRISCOLL, Robert (ed.). *Dream Chamber/About Roaratorio*. Dublin: Dolmen Press; Toronto: Black Brick Press, 1982.

PAGE, Tim. "A Conversation with John Cage." *Boulevard* 1, no. 3 (Fall 1986).

PATTERSON, Suzy. "Original Approach to Ballet." *Journal Herald* (Dayton) (December 31, 1966).

PAULI, Hj. "Kulturrevolutionare Musik." *Frankfurt Allgemeine Zeitung* (9 October 1973).

PENCE, J. "People call it Noise – but He calls it Music." *Chicago Daily News* (March 19, 1942): 4.

PEYSER, Joan. *Boulez: Composer, Conductor, Enigma*. New York: Schirmer Books; London: Cassell, 1976.

POLACZER, D. "Etuden vom anderen Stern." *Suddeutsche Zeitung* (June

23, 1975).

PRITCHETT, James. "From Choice to Chance: John Cage's Concerto for Prepared Piano." *Perspectives of New Music* 26/1 (Winter 1988).

RANTA, M.W. "The Avant-garde Scene: John Cage's 27' 10.554' for a Percussionist." *Percussionist* vii/1 (1969): 8.

RASMUSSEN, Karl Aage. "En samtale med John Cage – maj 1984." *Dansk Musikidsskrift* (1984–5): 49.

RAUSCHENBERG, Robert. "The Artist Speaks: Robert Rauschenberg." *Art in America* 54/3 (1966).

REIMER, Susan. "Music & dance: directing traffic." *The Post* (Ohio University) (April 10, 1973).

REPS, Paul. *Zen Flesh, Zen Bones.* Harmondsworth: Penguin, 1971.

REVILL, David. "Earle Brown," "Lejarer Hiller, Jr.," "Toshi Ichiyanagi," "Alvin Lucier," "Gordon Mumma," "Christian Wolff." in Pamela COLLINS and Brian MORTON (eds). *Contemporary Composers.* London and Chicago: St James' Press, 1992.

REYNOLDS, Roger. "Interview." *Generation* (January 1962). Reprinted in R. DUNN (ed.), and Elliott SCHWARTZ and Barney CHILDS. *Contemporary Composers on Contemporary Music.* New York: Holt, 1967.

ROBERTS, John, with RAYMOND, Silvy Panet. "Some Empty Words with Mr. Cage and Mr. Cunningham." *The Performance Magazine* 7 (1980).

ROCKWELL, John. *All American Music: Composers in the Late 20th Century.* New York: Alfred A. Knopf, 1983.

ROLLAND, Alain. "Entretien avec John Cage." *Tel Quel* 90 (Winter 1981).

ROTH, Moira and William. "John Cage on Marcel Duchamp." *Art in America* (November–December 1973).

ROY, K.G. "The Strange and Wonderful Sonic World of John Cage." *Hi-Fi/Stereo Review* v/5 (1960): 62.

SALZMAN, E. "In and out the piano with Cage." *New York Times* Section ii (February 14, 1960).

— "Milton Babbit and John Cage, Parallels and Paradoxes." *Stereo Review* xxii/4 (1969): 60.

— *Twentieth Century Music: An Introduction.* New York: Prentice-Hall, 1967, new editions 1974 & 1987.

SARGEANT, Winthrop. "Great Simplicity." (a profile of Suzuki) *New Yorker* (August 31, 1957).

SARRAUTE, Claude. "Cage et Cunningham à l'Opéra." *Le Monde* (November 2, 1973).

SCHAEFER, John. *New Sounds: A Listener's Guide to New Music.* New York: Harper and Row, 1987.

SCHNEBEL, D. *Die Kochende Materie Der Musik.* Cologne: Denklare Musik,

BIBLIOGRAPHY

1972.

— "Disziplinierte Anarchie." *Herausfoderung Schonberg*. Munchen: Edition U. Dibelius, 1974.

SCHOENBERG, Arnold, ed. Erwin STEIN. *Letters*. London: Faber, 1964.

SCHONBERGER, Elmer. " 'Ik componeer arme muziek voor arme mensen.' De toevalsmanipulaties van John Cage." *Vrij Nederland* (June 3, 1978).

SCHÖNING, Klaus. "Silence Sometimes Can Be Very Loud." in *Horspielmacher*. Konigstein/Taunus: Athenaum, 1978.

— "Gesprach uber James Joyce, Marcel Duchamp, Eric Satie: Ein Alphabet." *Neuland* 6 (1984–85).

SEARS, David. "Talking with John Cage: The Other Side." *Dance News* (March 1981).

SHAPIRO, David. "On Collaboration in Art." *Res* 10 (Autumn 1985).

SHOEMAKER, Bill "The Age of Cage." *down beat* (December 1984).

SLIVKA, Rose. "Lifecraft." *Craft Horizons* (December 1978 & January 1979).

SLONIMSKY, N. "If Anyone is Sleepy, Let Him Go to Sleep." *Christian Science Monitor* (December 14, 1961): 11.

SMALLEY, Roger. *The Listener* (September 19, 1968): 377.

— and SYLVESTER, David. "John Cage Talks." London: BBC.; reprinted in concert programme, Royal Albert Hall (May 22, 1972).

SMITH, Arnold Jay. "Reaching for the Cosmos: A Composers' Colloquium." *down beat* (October 20, 1977).

SMITH, Stuart. "Inteview with John Cage." *Percussive Notes 21*, no. 3 (March 1983).

SNYDER, E. "John Cage and Music Since World War II." dissertation, University of Wisconsin, 1970.

SONTAG, S. "The Esthetics of Silence." in *Styles of Radical Will*. New York, 1969, pp. 3–34.

STANTON, David. "John Cage: A Composer of Personal Vision." *Daily Trojan – Southern California Magazine* 61 (April 19, 1985).

STEINEM, G. "Music, Music, Music, Music." *Show* (January 1964): 59.

STERRITT, David. "Composer John Cage, Master of Notes – and Sounds." *Christian Science Monitor* (May 4, 1982).

SUMNER, Melody, BURCH, Kathleen, and SUMNER Michael (eds), *The Guests go in to Supper*. Oakland, California: Burning Books, 1986.

SUMRALL, Harry. "Cage in Ferment" *San Jose Mercury News* (May 2, 1986).

SUZUKI, Daisetz Teitaro. *Essays in Buddhism, Third Series*. London: Luzac, 1934.

— *Living By Zen*. London: Rider, 1991.

SYKES, Jill. "Breaking out of art's cage." *Sydney Morning Herald* (March

19, 1976).

TANNENBAUM, Rob. "A Meeting of Sound Minds: John Cage + Brian Eno." *Musician* 83 (September 1985).

TARTING, C. and JAUME, Andre. "Entretiens avec John Cage." *Jazz Magazine* 282 (January 1981).

THOMSON, V. "Expressive Percussion." in *The Art of Judging Music*. New York, 1948, p. 164.

— "John Cage Late and Early." *Saturday Review*, xliii (January 30, 1960): 38.

THOREAU, Henry David. *The Portable Thoreau*. New York: Viking, 1947.

TIERSTEIN, Alice. "Dance and Music: Interviews at the Keyboard." *Dance Scope* 8, no.2 (Spring/Summer 1974).

TIMAR, Andrew. et al. "A Conversation with John Cage." *Musicworks* 17 (Fall 1981).

TOMKINS, Calvin. "Figure in an Imaginary Landscape." *New Yorker* (November 29, 1964): 64, 68.

— *The Bride and the Bachelors*. New York: Viking, 1968a.

— *Ahead of the Game: Four Versions of the Avant-garde*, Harmondsworth: Penguin, 1968.

— "Social Concern." *New York Times Book Review* (January 21, 1968): 6.

— *Off the Wall*. Garden City: Doubleday, Penguin, 1980.

TURNER, S.S. "John Cage's Practical Utopias." *The Musical Times* (September 1990): 469–72.

ULMER, Gregory "The Object Of Post-Criticism." in Hal FOSTER (ed.). *The Anti-Aesthetic*, 1983, pp. 101–7.

VARGAS LLOSA, Mario. *The Perpetual Orgy*. London: Faber, 1987.

WEISS, Adolph. "Autoiographical Notes." *Bulletin of the American Composers' Alliance* vii (1958): 2–6.

WHITE, Robin. Interview with Cage. *View* 1 no. 1 (April 1978).

WILSON, M. "John Cage." *Canadian Musical Journal* iv/4 (1980): 54.

WOLFF, C. "John Cage." in John WINTON (ed.). *Dictionary of Contemporary Music*. New York, 1974, pp. 115–19.

WOMACK, Bill. "The Music of Contingency: An Interview." *Zero* (1979): 3.

WORNER, Karl. *Stockhausen: Life and Work*. London: Faber, 1973.

WUFFEN, Thomas. "An Interview with John Cage." *New York Berlin* 1, no. 1 (1984). German translation in *Zitty* (March 1985).

YATES, P. "Music for Prepared Piano." *Arts and Architecture* lxvi 4 (1949): 21.

ZIMMERMAN, Walter. "Desert Plants: John Cage." *Inselmusik*. Cologne: Beginner Press, 1981.

ZWERIN, Michael. "Silence, Please, for John Cage." *International Herald Tribune* (September 42, 1982).

— *Close Enough for Jazz*. London: Quartet Books, 1983.

CHRONOLOGY OF WORKS

1931
Allemande (lost)
Choruses from *The Persians*

1932
Songs from Ecclesiastes
Three Songs (Stein) voice and piano: Twenty Years After/It is as it Was/At East and Ingredients

1933
Solo with Obbligato Accompaniment and Six Short Inventions: any three or more instruments encompassing range g to g″ (15′ P 6752)
Sonata for Clarinet: clarinet solo (6′ P-6753; rec. Philip Rehfeldt, Advance FGR-4)
Sonata for Two Voices: two or more instruments with ranges as follows: 1. C′ to c″; 2. c to c′ (6′ P-6754)

1934
Composition for three voices: any three or more instruments (4′ P-6704)
Six Short Inventions: alto flute, Bb clarinet, Bb trumpet, violin, 2 violas, cello (7′ P. 6749); rec. ensemble cond. Cage, Avakian/New Music Distribution Service)
Music for Xenia: piano

1935
Quartet: percussion quartet (20′ P-6789)
Quest: piano (2′ P-66757)
Three Pieces for Flute Duet (Tossed as it is Untroubled) (6′ P-6761)
Two Pieces for Piano, revised 1974 (4′ P-6813; rec. Jeanne Kirstein, Columbia MS 7416 or M2S 819)

1936
Trio: suite for percussion (12′ P-6763)

353

1938

Five Songs for Contralto: voice and piano (cummings) (12' P-6710; rec. "Little Four Paws": Jan de Gaetani, Gilbert Kaliish, Nonesuch 9 79178-Z; rec. Meriel and Peter Dickson, Unicorn RHS 353 (England))

Metamorphosis: piano (15' P-6723; rec. Jeanne Kirstein, Columbia MS 7416 or M2S 819)

Music for Wind Instruments (8' P-6738b): I Trio (fl, Bb cl., bn); II Duo (ob, hn); III Quintet (fl, ob, Bb cl, hn. bn)

1939

First Construction (in metal): percussion sextet with assistant (9' P-6709; rec. Ensemble Percussione Ricerca, Ictus NOO 22; rec. Manhattan Percussion Ensemble, cond. Price, Avakian/New Music Distribution Service; rec. London Percussion Ensemble, cond. Farberman, MMG 105; rec. Percussions de Strasbourg, Philips 6526 017, CD, 420 233-2PH)

Imaginary Landscape No. 1: 2 variable-speed turntables, frequency recordings, muted piano and cymbal; to be performed as a recording or broadcast. (6' P-6716; rec. John and Xenia Cage, Doris Dennison, Margaret Jansen, Avakian/New Music Distribution Service; rec. Ensemble Musica Negativa, cond. Riehn, EMI 1 C 165-28954/57Y)

1940

Living Room Music: percussion quartet (6' P-6786; rec. Percussion Ensemble The Hague, Classical Records 180491 (Holland))

Second Construction: percussion quartet (6' P-6791; rec. Kroumata Percussion Ensemble, Conifer BIS LP 232, CD 232)

Bacchanale: prepared piano (6' P-6784; rec. Jeanne Kirstein, Columbia MS 7416, M2S 819; rec. Richard Bunger, Musical Heritage Society 4187)

1941

Third Construction: percussion quartet (15' P-6794; rec. Nexus, Nexus Records (Canada); rec. Ensemble Percussione Ricerca, Ictus N0022)

(with Lou Harrison) *Double Music*: percussion quartet (6' P-6296; rec. Manhattan Percussion Ensemble cond. Price, Time S8000, Mainstream MS/5011; rec. Percussion Ensemble The Hague, Classical Records 180491 (Holland))

1942

And the Earth Shall Bear Again: prepared piano (3' P-6811; rec. Joshua Pierce, Tomato 7016)

Credo in Us: percussion quartet (including radio or phonograph and piano) (12' P-6795; rec. Ensemble Musica Negativa, cond. Riehn, EMI 1 C 165-28954/57Y)

Forever and Sunsmell: (cummings) voice and percussion duo (5' P-6715; rec.

Carla Bley, Richard Bernas, Obscure OBS 5-A, Antilles AN 7031; rec. Joan LaBarbara, New Albion NA 035)

Imaginary Landscape No. 2 (March No. 1): percussion quintet (7' P-6721)

Imaginary Landscape No. 3: percussion sextet (3' P-6717)

In the Name of the Holocaust: prepared piano (3' 30" P-66755; rec. Margaret Leng Tan, mode 15 CD)

Primitive: string piano (4' 30" P-66756; rec. Margaret Leng Tan, mode 15 CD)

The City Wears a Slouch Hat: percussion quartet; written for the radio play by Kenneth Patchen

The Wonderful Widow of Eighteen Springs: (Joyce) (2' P-6297; rec. Arlene Carmen, John Cage, Avakian/New Music Distribution Service; rec. Rosalind Rees, David Starobin, Turnabout TV 34727; rec. Robert Wyatt, Richard Bernas, Obscure OBS-5A, Antilles AN 7031; rec. Cathy Berberian, Bruno Canino, Wergo 60054, 60054-50 (CD); rec. Matsumi Masuda, Hiroshi Wakasugi, Victor SJV 1513; rec. Joan LaBarbara, New Albion NA 035)

1942–3

Four Dances: piano, percussion and voice

1943

Amores: 2 solos for prepared piano and 2 trios for 3 percussionists (9' P-6264; rec. Maro Ajemian (I and IV only), Disc 875; rec. John Cage, Manhattan Percussion Ensemble, cond. Price, Time S8000, Mainstream MS/5011; rec. Avakian/New Music Distribution Service; rec. Blackearth Percussion Group, Opus One 22; rec. Reinbert de Leeuw with Ensemble, Philips 9500 920; rec. M. Wiesler, P. Pilat, Kroumata Percussion Ensemble, Conifer BIS-CD 272; rec. Ensemble Percussion Ricerca, Ictus N0022)

Our Spring Will Come: piano music for the dance by Pearl Primus (P-66763)

A Room: piano or prepared piano (2' P-6790; rec. Joshua Pierce, Tomato 7016)

She is Asleep: duet for voice and prepared piano and quartet for 12 tomtoms (P-6747 and 6746; rec. Carmen, Cage, Manhattan Percussion Ensemble cond. Price, Avakian/New Music Distribution Service; rec. Siegfried Fink Percussion Ensemble, THO MTH 149 (Germany); rec. Jay Clayton, Joshua Pierce, Paul Price Percussion Ensemble, Tomato 7016)

Tossed as it is Untroubled (Meditation): prepared piano (3' P-6722; rec. Jeanne Kirstein, Columbia MS 7417, M2S 819)

Totem Ancestor: prepared piano (2' P-6762; version for dance with Laban Notation P-6762A; rec. Joshua Pierce, Tomato 7016)

1944

A Book of Music: 2 prepared pianos (30' P-6702; rec. Joshua Pierce, Maro Ajemian, Tomato 2-1001)

Four Walls: piano solo with vocal interlude (c.40' P-66910; rec. Margaret Leng Tan, New Albion NA 037)

The Perilous Night: prepared piano (12' P-6741; rec. Jeanne Kirstein, Columbia MS-7416, M2S 819; rec. Ricard Bunger, Avant Records AR 1008; rec. William Nabore, PAN 130.032; rec. Margaret Leng Tan, New Albion NA 037)

Prelude for Meditation: prepared piano (1' P-6742; rec. Jeanne Kirstein, Columbia MS-7416, M2S 819)

Root of An Unfocus: prepared piano (4' P-6743; rec. Jeanne Kirstein, Columbia MS-7417, M2S 819)

Spontaneous Earth: prepared piano (c.3' P-66753)

The Unavailable Memory Of: prepared piano music for the dance (P-66764)

A Valentine Out of Season: prepared piano (4' P-6766; rec. Jeanne Kirstein, Columbia MS-7417, M2S 819; rec. Reinbert de Leeuw, Philips 9500 920)

1945

Daughters of the Lonesome Isle: prepared piano (12' P-6785)

Experiences 1: (cummings) piano duet (3' P-6708a; rec. Richard Bernas, Robert Wyatt, OBS 5-A, Antilles AN 7031)

Mysterious Adventure: prepared piano (8' P-6787)

Three Dances: 2 amplified prepared pianos (20' P-6760; rec. Maro Ajemian, William Masselos, Disc 643; rec. Michael Tilson Thomas, Ralph Grierson, Angel S-36059; rec. (I only) Henry Jacobs, Folkways F-6160)

1946

Ophelia: piano solo (5' P-6788)

Two Pieces for Piano: piano solo (4' P-6814; rec. Jeanne Kirstein, Columbia MS-7417, M2S 819)

1947

Music for Marcel Duchamp: prepared piano (5' P-6728; rec. Jeanne Kirstein, Columbia MS-7417, M2S 819; rec. Juan Hidalgo, Cramps CRSLP 6101 N.1; rec. Peter Roggenkamp, Wergo 60074; rec. Reinbert de Leeuw, Philips 9500 920)

Nocturne for Violin and Piano: (4' P-6740); rec. Paul Zukofsky, Gilbert Kalsih, Desto DC 6435/37; rec. Vera Beths, Reinbert de Leeuw, Philips 9500 920)

The Seasons: ballet for orchestra (15' P-6744; piano version P-6744a; rec. American Composers' Orchestra, cond. Davies, CRI SD-410)

1946–8

Sonatas and Interludes: prepared piano (10' P-6755; rec. Maro Ajemian, Dial 19, 20, reissued CRI 199; (excerpt) Avakian/New Music Distribution Service; rec. Yuji Takahashi, Fylkingen FYLPX 101–2, Denon OX 7059-ND, C37-7673 (CD); rec. Joshua Pierce, Tomato 2-1001; rec. Roger Miller, New World 203 (excerpts); rec. Peter Roggenkamp, Wergo 60074 (No. 13 only); rec. John Tilbury, Decca Headline 9; rec. Gerard Fremy, Etcetera ETC 2001; rec. K. Kormendi, Hung HCD 12569 (nos V, XI, Xiii-XV)

1948

Dream: piano solo (5' P-6707; arranged for viola solo with viola ensemble P-6707a; rec. Jeanne Kirstein, piano, Columbia MS-7417, M2S 819; rec. Karen Phillips, viola, Finnadar SR-9007)

In a Landscape: harp or piano solo (8' P-6720; rec. Richard Bernas, piano, Obscure OBS 5-A, Antilles AN 7031; rec. Susan Allen, harp, Arch Records S-1787)

Suite for Toy Piano: (or piano) (8' P-6758; rec. Jeanne Kirstein, Columbia MS-7417, M2S 819)

Experiences 2: (cummings) vocal solo (P-6708b; rec. Richard Bernas, Robert Wyatt, OBS 5-A, Antilles AN 7031)

Dreams that Money Can Buy: music for the film

1949–50

String Quartet in Four Parts: (20' P-6757; rec. New Music String Quartet, Columbia MS-4495; rec. La Salle Quartet, Deutsche Gramophon 2530735, 423 245 2GC (CD); rec. Concord String Quartet, Turnabout 34610, 3-Vox SVBX 5306; rec. mode 17)

(with Cowell, Harrison, Thomson) *Party Pieces* (rec. Gramavision CR7006)

1950

A Flower: voice and closed piano (4' P-6711; rec. Cathy Berberian, Bruno Canino, Wergo 60054, WER 60054-50 (CD); rec. Joan LaBarbara, New Albion NA 035)

Six Melodies for Violin and Keyboard: (15' P-6748; rec. Paul Zukofsky, Gilbert Kalish, Mainstream MS/5016; rec. Vera Beths, Reinbert de Leeuw, Philips 9500 920; rec. Eugene Gratowich, George Flynn, Finnadar 90023-1)

1951

Concerto for Prepared Piano and Chamber Orchestra: (22' P-6706; rec. Avakian JCS-1; rec. Yuji Takahashi, Buffalo Philharmonic Orchestra, cond. Foss, Nonesuch H-71202; rec. Toshi Ichiyanagi, Japan Philharmonic Symphony Orchestra, Victor SJX 1003 (Japanese))

Imaginary Landscape No. 4: for 12 radios, 24 players and conductor (4' P-6718)

Music of Changes: piano solo (43' vols 1–4, P-6256, 6257, 6258, 6259; rec. H. Henck, Wergo 60 099, WER 60099-50 (CD); rec. David Tudor, New World 214 (III and IV only)

Sixteen Dances: fl, trp, 4 perc, vn, vc, pfte (53' P-6792; rec. Paul Zukofsky, cond., with ensemble, CP2/15)

Two Pastorales: prepared piano (14' P-6765; rec. Joshua Pierce, Tomato 7016; rec. Carlos Santos, Edigsa AZ 70/11)

1952

For MC and DT: piano solo (2' P-6713)

Imaginary Landscape No. 5: any 42 recordings; score to be realized as a magnetic tape (4' P-6719)

Music for Carillon No. 1: graph score. 2 or 3 octave versions (4' P-6725 a/b; rec. David Tudor, 2-octave electronic carillon, Avakian/New Music Distribution Service; rec. Hearn-EM 1 C 065 02 469)

Music for Piano 1: (4' P-6729)

Seven Haiku: solo piano (3' P-6745; rec. Joshua Pierce, Tomato 7016)

Waiting: solo piano (1' P-6769)

Water Music: for a pianist, using radio, whistles, water containers, deck of cards; score to be mounted as a large poster (6' P-6770)

Williams Mix: 8 single-track or 4 double-track tapes (4' P-6774; rec. Avakian/ New Music Distribution Service)

4'33": tacet, any instrument or combination of instruments (4'33" P-6777; rec. Gianni-Emilio Simonetti, Cramps CRSLP 6101; rec. Wayne Marshall, Floating Earth FCD 004)

1953

Music for Piano 2: (4' P-6730)

Music for Piano 3: (P-6731)

Music for Piano 4–19: piano solo or ensemble (P-6732)

Music for Piano 20: (P-6733)

Music for Carillon Nos 2 and 3: (2' P-62761/b; rec. Hearn-EM 1 C 065 02 469)

59 1/2" for a string player: any 4-stringed instrument (P-6776)

1954

34'46.776" for a pianist: prepared piano (P-6781)

31'57.9864" for a pianist: prepared piano (P-6780)

1955

Music for Piano 21–36; 37–52: piano solo or ensemble (P-6734)

Speech: 5 radios with news-reader (42' P-6793)

26'1.1499" for a string player: any 4-stringed instrument (P-6779; rec. Bertram Turetsky, contrabass, Nonesuch H 71237)

1956

Music for Piano 53–68: piano solo or ensemble (P-6735)

Music or Piano 69–84: piano solo or ensemble (P-6736)

Radio Music: 1 to 8 performers each at one radio (6' P-6783); rec. Juan Hidalgo, Walter Marchetti, Gianni-Emilio Simonetti, Cramps CRSLP 6101 N.1)

27'10.554" for a percussionist: (P-6778; rec. Donald Knaack, Finnadar SR 9017)

1957

For Paul Taylor and Anita Dencks: solo piano (3' P-6714)

Winter Music: 1–20 pianists (P-6775; rec. George Flynn, Finnadar QD 9006; rec. Aki Takahashi, CP2 EAA-85013-15; rec. DGG 137 009; rec. mode 3/6)

1957–58

Concert for Piano and Orchestra: 63 pages, to be played, in whole or in part, in any sequence; 84 "types" of composition are involved (P-6705; rec. David Tudor, ensemble dir. Merce Cunningham, Avakian/New Music Distribution Service; rec. Mats Persson, Caprice CAP 1071 (piano solo only); rec. Hermann Danuser, Ensemble Musica Negativa con. Riehn, EMI 1C 165-28954/57Y)

1958

Aria: voice (any range) (P-6701; rec. Cathy Berberian, Time 58003, MS 5005 (with *Fontana Mix*); rec. Linda Hirst, Virgin VC7 90704, VC7 90704-2 (CD)

Fontana Mix: tape or any instrument(s) (P-6712; rec. Turnabout 34046 S, TV 4046 (tape version); rec. Folkways FT 3704; rec. Time 58003, MS 5005 (with *Aria*); rec. Max Neuhaus, Columbia MS-7139 (*Fontana Mix-Feed*); rec. do. Aspen 5-6 (1968); rec. do. Massart M-133)

Indeterminacy: reader (rec. John Cage, Folkways FT 3704)

Music Walk: 1 or more pianists, at a single piano, using radio and/or recordings (P-6739)

Solo for Voice 1: any range, to be played alone or with any part of *Concert* (P-6750; rec. EMI 1C 165-28954/57Y (with *Concert*)

TV Köln: solo piano (P-6764; rec. Richard Bunger, Avant Records AR 1008)

Variations I: any number of players, any sound-producing means (P-6767;

rec. Gerd Zacher, organ, Heliodor 2549009, Wergo 60033, 0310; rec. Zsignmond Szathmary, organ, Da Camera Magna 93237)

1959

Water Walk: tape (3' P-6771)
Sounds of Venice: TV piece

1960

Cartridge Music: for amplified "small sounds"; also amplified piano or cymbal; any number of players and loudspeakers (rec. John Cage and David Tudor, Time 58009, 8009, MS/5015, ICA 02 (England); rec. DGG 137 009)

Music for Amplified Toy Pianos: any number (P-6724; rec. Juan Hidalgo, Walter Marchetti, Gianni-Emilio Simonetti, Cramps CRSLP 6101 N.1; rec. Gentle Fire Ensemble, EMI 1 C 065 02 469)

Solo for Voice 2: any range, to be used alone or with *Concert*, *Fontana Mix* or *Cartridge Music* (P-6751; rec. Brandeis University Chamber Choir cond. Lucier, Odyssey 32160156 (0155); rec. EMI 1 C 165-28954/57 Y (with *Concert*)

Music for "The Marrying Maiden": magnetic tape for the play by Jackson MacLow (9' P-6737)

Theater Piece: 1 to 8 performers (musicians, dancers, singers etc.), parts to be used in whole or part, in any combination (P-6759a/h)

WBAI: auxiliary score for performance with lecture (*Where are we going? and what are we doing?*) or instrumental performance involving magnetic tape, recordings, radios etc. (P-6772; rec. David Tudor, Folkways FT 3704 with respect to *Concert* and *Fontana Mix*)

Where are we going? and what are we doing?: 4 single-track tapes to be used, in whole or part, to provide a single lecture, or used in any combination up to 4 to provide simultaneous lectures. Variations in amplitude may be made, following *WBAI* (P-6773)

1961

Atlas Eclipticalis: 86 instrumental parts to be played in whole or part, any duration, in any ensemble, chamber or orchestral, with or without *Winter Music*; an electronic version is possible by use of contact microphones with associated amplifiers and loudspeakers operated by an assistant to the conductor (P-6782; rec. Ensemble Musica Negativa, dir. Riehn, Deutsche Gramophon 137009, 2536 018, 643 543, 643 541-46 (with *Winter Music*, *Cartridge Music*)

Music for Carillon No. 4 #1: 3 or 2 octave version (10' P-6727)

Variations II: parts to be prepared from the score, any number of players, any sound-producing means (P-6768; rec. David Tudor, piano, Columbia MS-7051; rec. Antonio Taurello, Gerardo Gandini, two pianos, also

Horatio Vaggione, Pedro Echarte, tape and unusual instruments, ME-ME2 (Argentina); rec. Jourandos de Musica Experimental JME ME 1-2; rec. CBS France S 3461064)

1962
0'00" (4'33" no. 2): solo to be performed in any way by anyone (P-6796)

1963
Variations III: for any number of people performing any actions (P-6797); rec. Gerd Zacher, Juan Allende-Blin, organ, percussion and wind instruments, Deutsche Gramophon 139 442; rec. San Francisco Conservatory New Music Ensemble, Wergo 60057)

Variations IV: any number of players, any sounds or combinations of sounds produced by any means, with or without other activities (P-6798; rec. John Cage, David Tudor, Everest 6132, 3132, 3230)

1965
Electronic Music for Piano: solo piano with electronics (P-6801)

Rozart Mix: notes re preparation of a magnetic tape (P-6800; rec. Ensemble Musica Negativa, EMI 1C 165-28 954-57)

Variations V: 37 remarks re an audiovisual performance (P-6799)

1966
Variations VI: for a plurality of sound-systems (P-6802)

Variations VII: for various means

Music for Carillon No. 4 #2

1967
Music for Carillon No. 5: 4 octaves (P-6803)

Musicircus: for diverse performers

Newport Mix

1968
Reunion: for diverse performers, a plurality of electronic musics gated by a game of chess played on an electronically prepared board

1969
Cheap Imitation: piano solo (35' P-6805; rec. John Cage, piano, Cramps CRSLP 6117 N. 17)

Sound Anonymously Received: for an unsolicited instrument

33¹/₃: for records, gramophones and audience participation

1967–69
(with Lejaren Hiller, Jr.) *HPSCHD*: rec. Antoinette Vischer, Neely Bruce, David Tudor, harpsichords, Nonesuch H-71224)

1970

Song Books: (some may be used with *Atlas Eclipticalis*), solos for voice 3-58 (P-6806a), solos for voice 59-92 (P-6806b), instructions (P-6806); rec. John Cage, Schola Cantorum Stuttgart, cond. Clytus Gottwald, Wergo 60074 (with *Empty Words III*); rec. Joan LaBarbara, voice and tape realization, Chiaroscuro CR 196 (Tapesongs 1977) (no.45 only); rec. do., New Albion NA 035 (nos 49, 52, 67)

Mureau: voice

1971

Les chants de maldoror pulverises par l'assistance meme: 200 pages pour un public francophone de pas plus de 200 personnes

Sixty-two mesostics re Merce Cunningham: unaccompanied voice using microphone (P-6807; rec. Demetrios Stratos, Cramps CRSLP 6101 N.1; rec. Jack Brierce, Arch Records S-1752 (excerpt))

WGBH-TV: for composer and technicians (P-6808)

1972

Bird Cage: 12 tapes to be distributed by a single performer in a space in which people are free to move and birds to fly (P-6810)

Cheap Imitation: orchestra, 24, 59 or 95 players (P-6805 a/b/c)

1973

Etcetera: 1111 1101 P(6) 2Pf Str (5 single players) tape (P-6812)

1974

Score (40 drawings by Thoreau) and 23 parts: any instruments and/or voices. Twelve haiku followed by a recording of the dawn at Stony Point (P-6815)

Two pieces for piano (revision)

1974–75

Etudes Australes: solo piano books I–IV (P-6816a/b/c/d; rec. Grete Sultan, Tomato 2-1101 (I-XVI)

Empty Words: reader (rec. John Cage, Wergo WER 60074 (pt. III); rec. Edition Michael F. Bauer MFB 003–004)

1975

Child of Tree (Improvisation I): percussion solo using amplified plant materials (P-66685)

Lecture on the Weather: 12-speaker-vocalists, preferably American men who have become Canadian citizens, with tape and film (P-6817)

1976

Apartment House 1776: materials for a musicircus for any number of musicians, in observance of the bicentennial of the U.S.A. to which are to be added, live or recorded, Protestant, Sephardic and American Indian songs, and Negro calls and hollers, to be played with or without *Renga* (P-6819)

Branches: percussion solo, duet, trio or orchestra (of any number of players) using amplified plant materials (P-66684)

Quartets I–VIII: orchestra of 24, 41 or 93 instruments (P-66686/7/8)

Renga: 78 parts to be played alone or with *Apartment House 1776* or some other musicircus appropriate to another occasion than the Bicentennial of the U.S.A., an occasion, for example, such as the birth or death of another musically productive nation or person, or the birthday of a society concerned with some aspect of creation productive of sound e.g. birds, marine animals etc. (30–40′ P-6818)

1977

Cheap Imitation: violin solo (c.35′ P-66752; rec. Paul Zukofsky, CP2 no. 7)

Freeman Etudes: violin solo (P-66813a/b; rec. Paul Zukofsky, CP2; rec. Janos Negyesy, Lovely VR 2051–2)

Inlets (Improvisation II): indeterminate; for 3 players of water-filled conch shells and 1 conch player using circular breathing and the sound of fire (P-66787)

Telephones and Birds: 3 performers; telephone announcements and recordings of bird songs (or recordings of some other category (30′ P-66689)

49 Waltzes for the Five Boroughs: for performer(s) or listener(s) or record maker(s) (P-66735d; rec. Alan Feinberg, Yvar Mikhashoff, Robert Moran, Nonesuch D-79011)

1976–78

Quartet: concert band and 12 amplified voices (P-6820)

1978

Chorals: violin solo (P-66762; rec. Paul Zukofsky, CP2 no. 7)

A Dip in the Lake: Ten Quicksteps, Sixty-One Waltzes, and Fifty-Six Marches for Chicago and Vicinity: for performer(s) or listener(s) or record maker(s). Transcriptions may be made for other cities, or places, by assembling through chance operations a list of 427 addresses and then, also through chance operations, arranging these in 10 groups of 2, 61 groups of 3, and 56 groups of 4 (P-66761)

Some of "The Harmony of Maine" (Supply Belcher): organist and 3 assistants (c.45′ P-66840)

Variations VIII: no music or recordings. Indeterminate (P-66766)

Letters to Erik Satie: voice and tape

Pools: conch shells and tape

Il treno: 3 happenings for prepared trains
Sounday: 10-hour radio event

1978–9

Etudes Boreales: (15–20' for piano, P-66327 for violin, P-66328; rec. Frances-Marie Uitti, 'cello, Michael Pugliese, mode 1/2)

1979

——, —— *Circus on* ——: a means for translating a book into a performance without actors, a performance which is both literary and musical or one or the other (P-66816)

Hymns and Variations: 12 amplified voices (c. 20' P-66812; rec. Electric Phoenix EMI EL270452)

1980

Litany for the Whale: vocalize for two voices (c.12' P-66880)
Improvisation III (Duets)

1981

Thirty pieces for five orchestras: (c. 30' P-66879)

1982

Instances of Silence: installation using cassette recordings
A House Full of Music
Dance/4 Orchestras: (c. 18' P-66911)

1983

ear for EAR (Antiphonies): wordless text, for widely separated single voices, one visible, the other(s) not (P-66957)

Improvisation IV (Fielding Sixes): for 3 cassette players using machines equipped with a device designed by John Fullemann which allows one to change the playback speed from slow to fast (P-66954)

Postcard from Heaven: 1–20 harps (P-66923)

1984

Souvenir: organ (6' P-66988)
Thirty Pieces for String Quartet: (P-66987; rec. mode 17)
Eight Whiskus: voice (rec. Joan LaBarbara, New Albion NA 035)
Perpetual Tango

1983–85

Ryoanji: (P-66986 a–g; rec. Isabelle Ganz, Michael Pugliese, mode 1/2)

1985

A Collection of Rocks: orchestra with voices (20' P-67041)
ASLSP: solo piano (c.20' P-67070)

Mirakus²: text derived from Duchamp, *Notes*. Solo voice (c.8' P-67067; rec. Joan LaBarbara, New Albion NA 035)

Music for: title to be completed by adding the number of players performing (c.30' P-67040)

Nowth Upon Nacht: (Joyce) voice and piano (P-67039; rec. Joan LaBarbara, New Albion NA 035)

Selkus²: solo voice (c.9' P-67068)

Sonnekus²: solo voice (c.6' P-67069; rec. Joan LaBarbara, New Albion NA 035)

1986

But what about the noise of crumpling paper . . .: percussion ensemble (c.20' P-67074)

Etcetera 2/4 Orchestras: materials for orchestral performance with or without 4 conductors and a tape recording of the environment in which the materials were created (c.30' P-67119)

Haikai: gamelan (20' P-67145)

Hymnkus: 14 parts for alto flute, clar, alto sax, tenor sax, bn, tbe, 2 perc, accordion, 2 pfte, vn, cello and voice (P-67158)

Thirteen Harmonies: violin and keyboard instrument (38' P-67117)

1987

Europera I/II: scenario and libretto by Cage (P-67100a); an opera for 19 soloists and orchestra (P-67100)

Organ²/ASLSP: organ (P-67185)

Three cComposed Improvisations: 1) Steinberger Bass Guitar, 2) Snare Drum Alone, 3) One-sided Drums (8' to 16' each, P-67318a/b/c)

1988

Essay: writings through the *Essay: on the duty of civil disobedience* by Thoreau. Computer-generated tape (P-67180)

Five: 5 voices or instruments (5' P-67214)

Four Solos for Voices 93–96: sop, mezzo, ten, bass (c. 15' P-67226)

One: piano solo (10' P-67208)

Two: parts for flute and piano (c'15' P-67176)

Seven: fl, cl in Bb, perc, piano, vn, va, cello (20' P-67227)

1989

101: 4 (picc. alto) 4(EH) 4(Bcl) 4(Cbn) 6431 T, Perc (4) pfte hp str (18-16-11- 11-8) (P-67265)

Two²: 2 pianos, 4 hands (P-67302)

Four: 2 vn, va, cello (10-30' P-67304)

Swinging: piano solo (c.2' P-67301)

Three: 3 recorder players (sopranino, s, a, t, bassett, b, great bass) (P-67303)

Twenty-Three: 15vn 5va 5 celli (23' P-67228)

Europera III: 6 singers, 2 pianos, 6 gramophone operators, lighting, tape (70' P-67350)

Europera IV: 2 singers, 1 record player, 1 pianist, lighting (30' P-67350)

Sculptures Musicales: 4 performers using electronics (30' P-67348)

1990

Four²: SATB (7' P-67368)

One⁴: solo drummer (6'55" P-67349)

One⁵: piano solo (20'40" P-67356)

One⁶: violin solo (46'50" P-67357)

Seven²: bass fl, cl, trb, 2 perc, vc, cb (52' P-67351)

Scottish Circus: Scots folk band

1991

Eight: fl, ob, cl, bsn, hn, trp, tba (60' P-67409)

Europera V: pianist, 2 singers, lighting and tape (60' P-67405)

Four³: 4 performers (1 or 2 pianos, 12 rainsticks, violin or oscillator and silence) (c.30' P-67407)

One⁸: violoncello solo, to be played with or without *108* (for orchesra) (43'30" P-67408)

CHRONOLOGY OF
VISUAL WORKS

1969
(with Calvin Sumsion) *Not Wanting to Say Anything About Marcel*

1978
Score Without Parts (40 Drawings by Thoreau): Twelve Haiku
Seven Day Diary (Not Knowing), 7 etchings
17 Drawings by Thoreau, photo-etching
Signals, 36 related etchings

1979–82
Changes and Disappearances, 35 prints

1980–82
On the Surface, 36 related etchings

1981–82
Déreau, 38 related images

1983
Weather-ed, photographs realized by Paul Barton
(R3), R3, 2 drypoints
Where R=Ryoanji, 4 drypoints
HV, 36 monotypes

1985
Fire, series of 16 monotypes
Ryoku, series of 13 drypoints
Mesostics 12 collage monotypes

1986
Eninka, series of 50 monoprints

1987
Where there is where there, series of 38 related images

Deka, series of 35 related images
Variations, series of 35 monotypes

1988
New River Watercolors, 30 untitled paintings in 4 series

1989
Nine Stones, Nines Stones 2
Ten Stones, Ten Stones 2
Eleven Stones, Eleven Stones 2
Empty Fire
Urban Landscape (alteration of *Where there is where there*)
Global Village 1–36 and *37–48*

1991
Smoke Weather Stone Weather, 37 prints

1992
Variations III
Without Horizon

INDEX

369

INDEX

371

INDEX

INDEX

375